Datenbanksysteme

Internationales Symposium 1977

Herausgegeben
von
I. Nagler-Breitenbach und H. Schauer

Springer-Verlag Berlin Heidelberg GmbH

1978

ISBN 978-3-7908-0193-4

CIP-Kurztitelaufnahme der Deutschen Bibliothek

Datenbanksysteme: internat. Symposium / hrgs.
von Il. Nagler-Breitenbach; H. Schauer. –
Wien: Physica-Verlag, 1978.

NE: Nagler-Breitenbach, Ilse [Hrsg.]

© Springer-Verlag Berlin Heidelberg 1978
Ursprünglich erschienen bei Physica-Verlag, Rudolf Liebing KG, Wien 1978.
ISBN 978-3-7908-0193-4   ISBN 978-3-662-41567-2 (eBook)
DOI 10.1007/978-3-662-41567-2

<u>VORWORT</u>

Das vom 3. - 7. Oktober 1977 in Wien abgehaltene Symposium
"Datenbanksysteme" hat sich folgende Ziele gesetzt:

- Ausgehend von Erfahrungsberichten soll der aktuelle Stand
  des Einsatzes verschiedener Datenbanksysteme dargestellt
  und kritisch diskutiert werden

- Darüber hinaus sollen auch die neuesten Ansätze und
  Möglichkeiten für weitere Entwicklungen der Theorie
  der Datenbanksysteme vorgestellt und erörtert werden.

- Schließlich soll aus der kritischen Bestandsaufnahme und
  der Darstellung möglicher Entwicklungen versucht werden,
  Theorie und Praxis der Datenbanksysteme einander näherzu-
  bringen.

Die Veranstalter des Symposiums, das Institut für Höhere Studien
gemeinsam mit dem Wirtschafts- und Sozialwissenschaftlichen
Rechenzentrum und der Österreichischen Computergesellschaft
glauben, daß diese Ziele mit dem Symposium und dem vorliegenden
Tagungsband weitgehend erreicht wurden.

Die Beiträge der Herstellerfirmen, Softwarehäuser und Anwender
wurden ausgesucht, um einen umfassenden Überblick über die
unterschiedlichen Datenbanksysteme zu geben, nicht um spezielle
Systeme anzupreisen. Außerdem konnten einige renommierte aus-
ländische Gäste zu diesem Thema gewonnen werden.

Der Tagungsband enthält die beiden Überblicksvorträge von
Prof.Wedekind und Prof.Nijssen sowie die schriftlichen Fassungen
nahezu aller Beiträge. Die Ergebnisse der abschließenden
Podiumsdiskussion sind in einem kurzen Bericht zusammengefaßt.
Nicht enthalten ist das Eröffnungsreferat des Präsidenten der
Österreichischen Computergesellschaft, Sektionschef Dr.Frank.
Zur Erleichterung der Kontaktaufnahme sind am Ende dieses Bandes
die Adressen der Autoren zusammengestellt.

Herzlichen Dank an alle, die an der Vorbereitung und Durchführung der Tagung mitgewirkt haben. Insbesondere sei Herrn
Wang vom Wirtschafts- und Sozialwissenschaftlichen Rechenzentrum für seine tätige Mithilfe gedankt.

Unser besonderer Dank gebührt den Sitzungsleitern Prof.
Brockhaus, Prof.Mühlbacher, Prof.Vinek, Prof.Kraus und
Prof.Albrecht, die auch an der Podiumsdiskussion teilge-
nommen haben.

Dem Physica-Verlag ist für das Entgegenkommen bei der Heraus-
gabe dieses Tagungsbandes zu danken.

Für ihre intensive Mitarbeit bei der Zusammenstellung dieses
Bandes sind wir Frau Irene Hafner zu großem Dank verpflichtet.

Wien, im November 1977   Ilse Nagler-Breitenbach
                                          Helmut Schauer

Inhaltsverzeichnis

Stand der Entwicklung von Datenbanken

Prof. Dr. H. Wedekind
Technische Hochschule Darmstadt

Zusammenfassung:

Es werden die wesentlichen Entwicklungsziele für Datenbanksysteme herausgesetllt und eine Abgrenzung zu konventionellen
Datenverarbeitungssystemen vorgenommen. Die Entwicklungsziele
sind:

1. Trennung von Datenmanipulations- und Trägersprache,

2. Zentrale Integritätskontrolle,

3. Integrierte Auswertbarkeit der Dateien für den Bedarf in
   einem Informationssystem (inkl.Sekundärschlüsselzugriff),

4. Zeitgerechter Änderungsdienst,

5. Erweiterung der Berufsklassen "Programmierer" und "Betriebspersonal" um die Klassen der "Parametrischen Berufe" (angelerntes Schalterpersonal) und die Klasse der anspruchsvollen
   Laien,

6. Gewährleistung eines hohen Maßes an Datenunabhängigkeit.

Die wichtigsten Datenmodelle, das hierarchische Modell und das
relationale Modell werden dargestellt. Der Stand der Entwicklung von Datenbanksystemen wird mit den Entwicklungszielen
verglichen.

1. Entwicklungsziele

Die Unzulänglichkeiten in konventionellen Datenverarbeitungssystemen führten in den 6oer Jahren zu dem Gedanken, Dateien
zu zentralisieren und den Zugriff zu ihnen über ein Datenverwaltungssystem vorzunehmen. Es wurde der Begriff Datenbanksystem als begriffliche Zusammenfassung von Datenbank und Daten-

verwaltungssystem eingeführt. Eine Datenbank beinhaltet
zentral gespeicherte Daten, ein Datenverwaltungssystem alle
Prozeduren zu ihrer Handhabung. Das Datenverwaltungssystem
ist ein spezielles Betriebssystem, das unter dem allgemeinen Betriebssystem der Anlage läuft.

Folgende Funktionen sollten von diesem "Sonderbetriebssystem"
u.a. wahrgenommen werden: Auswahl von Zugriffspfaden, Übersetzung der Anweisungen in einer Datenmanipulationssprache,
Zugriffsoptimierung, Sperren und Entsperren von Datenobjekten,
Behandlung von Verklemmungen, Überwachung der Integritäts-
und Autorisierungsbedingungen. Struktur und Funktionen von
Datenverwaltungssystemen werden in diesem Aufsatz nicht im
einzelnen behandelt. Er bleibt im wesentlichen auf die Beschreibung der Datenbank beschränkt. Anhand der Entwicklungsziele für Datenbanksysteme soll in den weiteren Abschnitten
der tatsächliche Stand der relationalen und hierarchischen
Systeme bewertet werden.

Der Literatur über Datenbanksysteme ist zu entnehmen, daß sich
ein Datenbanksystem von einem konventionellen System mit
individuellen Dateien durch sechs Entwicklungsziele abhebt:

1. Trennung von Datenmanipulationssprache (DML) und Trägersprache (host language).

2. Zentrale Integritätskontrolle (system enforced integrity).

3. Integrierte Auswertung der Dateien für den Bedarf in einem
   Informationssystem.

4. Zeitgerechter Änderungsdienst.

5. Erweiterung der Benutzerklassen "Programmierer" und Betriebspersonal um die Klassen der parametrischen Benutzer
   (angelerntes Schalterpersonal) und die Klasse der anspruchsvollen Laien (Ingenieure, Mediziner, Kaufleute etc.).

6. Gewährleistung eines hohen Maßes an Datenunabhängigkeit.

Zu 1.
Eine Datenmanipulationssprache für das Auffinden und für den
Änderungsdienst der Daten in einer Datenbank kann in eine
universelle Programmiersprache (Trägersprache, host language)
eingebaut werden, oder aber sie kann als selbständige Sprache
(self-contained language) gehalten sein. Im zweiten Fall
spricht man auch von einer Query-Sprache. In Datenbanksystemen
wird die Unterscheidung zwischen den beiden Sprachen ganz
exakt getroffen. Es ist ein großes Verdinest der Codasyl-
Gruppe (4), auf diesem Gebiet richtungsweisend gewesen zu
sein.

Zu 2.
Es ist unbestritten, daß in kommerziellen Programmen der konventionellen Art ein enorm hoher Teil der Programmcodes ausschließlich für die Zwecke der Fehlersuche entworfen werden
muß. Es werden in den Codes Sortierfolgen geprüft, mit Prüf-
ziffern wird die Gültigkeit einer Nummer festgestellt oder
z.B. der Inhalt der Felder eines Satzes in einem Plausibili-
tätstest verglichen, um die Richtigkeit der Wertbeziehungen
zu testen. Jackson (11, Seite 95) nennt kommerzielle Programme
scherzhaft "data vetting programs" (to vet = tierärztliches
Untersuchen, veterinarian = Tierarzt), um darzutun, daß die
Komplexität der Programme durch Fehleraufdeckung und Fehlerbehandlung so groß geworden ist, daß ein tiermedizinisches
Studium eigentlich vonnöten ist. Die Garantie der Datenqualität oder Datenintegrität bestimmt die Struktur der
Programme und nicht das gestellte Problem. Integrititätsver-
letzungen sind einer der Kerne des Softwaredilemmas.

Wie bei anderen Waren hat in Datenbanksystemen nicht der Benutzer oder Verbraucher für die Korrektheit der Daten zu
sorgen, sondern das Datenverwaltungssystem bzw. der Produzent.
Es gibt drei Möglichkeiten, Integritităts- oder Qualitätsbe-
dingungen in das Datenverwaltungssystem einzubringen:

a) Durch Systemproduzenten, die im Bedarfsfall aufgerufen werden.
Der Codasyl-Vorschlag sieht diese Variante vor.

b) Durch ein Datenmodell. Im Codasyl-Vorschlag wird für bestimmte
Integrititätsbedingungen, die sich auf mehrere Dateien beziehen, ebenfalls dieser Weg beschritten. Das hierarchische
Datenkonstrukt "SET" impliziert diese Integrititätsbedingung
insofern, als eine Ausprägung der member-Satzes (Kindsatz)
immer einer Ausprägung des owner-Satzes (Vatersatz) zugeordnet sein muß. "Vaterlose Kinder" bedeuten eine Verletzung
der Datenintegrität. Auf die SET-Struktur wird im folgenden
noch genauer im Rahmen der hierarchischen Datenmodelle eingegangen werden.

c) Durch die Formulierung in einer nicht-prozedualen Sprache,
z.B. SEQUEL. In vollständigen relationalen Systemen wird eine
Integrititätsbedingung wie eine mathematische Gleichung
formuliert und in ein Subsystem eingebracht. Das **relationale**
Datenmodell und die Integrititätsbedingungen bleiben im
Gegensatz zum hierarchischen Modell strikt voneinander getrennt.

Zu 3.
Die integrierte Auswertung von Dateien bedeutet, daß eine Datei
nicht nur nach dem Primärschlüssel oder einem anderen Sortierbegriff verarbeitet werden kann. Die Verarbeitung im Hinblick
auf alle Felder und Feldkombinationen muß über mehrere Dateien
hinweg gewährleistet sein. Der Informationsbedarf und nicht die
Abspeicherung sollte die Auswertbarkeit bestimmen.

Zu 4.
Durch die Zentralisierung der Dateien wird eine Einmalspeicherung angestrebt. Wenn die Daten nicht in mehreren Dateien aufgeführt werden, so wird der Änderungsdienst wesentlich erleichtert.
Das Verstreuen gleicher Daten über mehrere Dateien hat in konventionellen Systemen häufig zu unlösbaren Aufgaben geführt.

Zu 5.

In konventionellen Systemen gibt es im wesentlichen nur zwei
Benutzerklassen, das System- und Betriebspersonal sowie die
Anwendungsprogrammierer. Durch Datenbanksysteme soll ermöglicht werden, daß anspruchsvolle Laien, die mit der Datenverarbeitung nur wenig Kontakt haben, aber Fachleute auf
ihrem Gebiet sind, Anfragen (queries) formulieren und eingeben können. Ferner soll z.B. das Schalterpersonal in den
Banken, auf den Flughäfen und in Ankunftsbüros mit Information
direkt aus der Datenbank zu versorgen sein. Die Feature
Analysis der Codasyl-Gruppe (5) nennt diese Benutzer zutreffend "parametric user". Es wird keine Formalisierung in
einer Datenmanipulationssprache verlangt, sondern es müssen
nur offene Parameter für ansonsten fertige Programme zur Verfügung gestellt werden. Eine Anlernzeit von wenigen Wochen genügt in der Regel, um die Funktionen eines parametrischen
Benutzers wahrnehmen zu können.

Zu 6.

Datenunabhängigkeit ist die Isolierung der Daten von den Pro-
grammem. Je höher der Grad an Datenunabhängigkeit ist, desto
geringer ist der Aufeand für Programmieränderungen im Falle
einer Änderung der Daten. Es gibt mehrere Arten von Datenunabhängigkeit. Besonders hervorzuheben sind die Speicherungs-
abhängigkeit (physische Unabhängigkeit) und die Zugriffspfad-
Unabhängigkeit (logische Unabhängigkeit). Eine physische
Datenunabhängigkeit, die auch schon in konventionellen Systemen
gewährleistet wird, bewirkt, daß eine Veränderung der tatsächlichen Abspeicherung auf den Geräten keinen Einfluß auf
die Programme hat. Zugriffspfad-Unabhängigkeit, die als eine
höhere Form der Datenunabhängigkeit anzusehen ist, bedeutet,
daß der Benutzer keine Kenntnisse darüber benötigt, wie der
Aufsuchprozeß beim Wiederauffinden, beim Modifizieren, beim
Einfügen oder beim Löschen im einzelnen vonstatten geht. Zugriffspfad-Unabhängigkeit ist nur dann möglich, wenn der Be-

nutzer in einer Datenmanipulationssprache Mengen von Sätzen
spezifizieren kann, ohne eine Satz-für-Satz-Prüfung vornehmen
zu müssen. Fragen des Typs "Finde alle Sätze, welche ...",
die also auf Grund bestimmter inhaltlicher Kriterien Datensätze qualifizieren, können pfadunabhängig in einer Datenmanipulationssprache formuliert werden. Die Zugriffspfade-
Unabhängigkeit öffnet dem anspruchsvollen Laien den Weg zum
System. Das Denken in Zugriffspfaden und den damit verbundenen Kontrollogiken bleibt dem Programmierer vorbehalten.

Die Entwicklungsziele müssen als Primärziele aufgefaßt werden.
Der Leser könnte die Position "Schutz vor unberechtigtem Zugriff" vermissen, über die im Rahmen des Datenschutzes in der
politischen Welt heftig debattiert wird. Aus der nüchternen
Entwicklungspraxis heraus kann als ein Nachteil der zentrali-
sierten Dateien angesehen werden, daß die Abwehr des unberechtigten Zugriffs zu einem besonderen Problem geworden ist.
Forderungen des Datenschutzes, wie die Forderungen des Umwelt-
und Denkmalschutzes, können nicht zu Entwicklungszielen erklärt werden; sie sind als Nebenbedingungen den Sytsmen auf-
zuerlegen. Es hat z.B. keinen Sinn, den Datenschutz eines
Systems zu maximieren, was Vertreter der Jurisprudenz-Daten-
verarbeitung gerne möchten. In einem solchen Fall würden wir
uns fast ausschließlich mit dem unberechtigten Zugriff beschäftigen. Zu produktiven Zugriffen käme es dann nicht mehr.
Der Unterschied zwischen Entwicklungsziel und Entwicklungs-
nebenbedingung, der von mir in der Literatur ausgiebig behandelt wird (16), sollte nicht aufgehoben werden.

Wenn im folgenden der Entwicklungsstand der Datenbanksysteme
in dem knappen Rahmen dieses Aufsatzes beschrieben wird, dann
sind die aufgeführten Entwicklungsziele als Meßlatten aufzufassen, mit deren Hilfe der tatsächliche Stand zu beurteilen
ist. Aus dem Defizit zwischen Stand und Ziel sollte man dann
erkennen können, wohin die Reise gehen kann.

2. Hierarchische Datenbanksysteme

Hierarchische Datenbanksysteme, denen auch die Systeme mit
einem Netzwerk als Datenmodell zuzurechnen sind, beherrschen
heute ohne Zweifel den Markt. Von Bedeutung sind auf der
einen Seite das

- IMS (Information Management System) von IBM

und auf der anderen Seite die Implementierungen nach dem
Codasyl-Vorschlag, der auf die alte COBOL-Erweiterung IDS
(Integrated Data Store) von Honeywell zurückzuführen ist.
Hier sind u.a. zu erwähnen:

- IDMS (Integrated Database Management System) von der Be-
  ratungsfirma Cullinane Corporation in Zusammenarbeit mit
  der B.F. Goodrich Company entwickelt.

- UDS (Universelles Datenbanksystem) von Siemens.

- EDMS (Extended Data Management System) von Xerox.

- DMS 1100 (Data Management System) von Univac.

Die Liste ist nicht vollständig. Einen guten Überblick über
die amerikanischen Implementierungen ist im EDP-Analyser
(9) zu finden. Es würde viel zu weit führen, hier anhand
der Firmenpublikationen Implementierungsdetails gegenüber-
zustellen und zu bewerten. Obwohl in Deutschland in der
Literatur seit meiner scherzhaft gemeinten Bemerkung zum
ersten Band "Datenbanksysteme" (13) häufig von scharfen
Auseinandersetzungen oder gar Religionskriegen zwischen den
Anhängern eines Relationalen Datenbanksystems (sogen.
Relationalisten) und den Anhängern eines hierarchischen
Systems (sogen.Hierarchisten) die Rede ist, findet der
eigentliche Wettbewerb zwischen dem IMS und den Codasyl-
Implementierungen statt. Der Wettbewerb wird durch das
System (ADABAS Software AG, Darmstadt)noch besonders
lebendig. ADABAS ist wegen der multiplen Felder kein
relationales System; es kommt diesen Systemen aber sehr

nahe. Hier wird nur die Datenstruktur SET als Grundtyp des Datenmodells im Codasyl-Vorschlag dargestellt, um dann den Stand der hierarchischen Systeme im Hinblick auf die Entwicklungsziele zu erläutern. Das Datenmodell des IMS kann als ein Sonderfall des Codasyl-Vorschlags aufgefaßt werden und wird deshalb hier nicht behandelt.

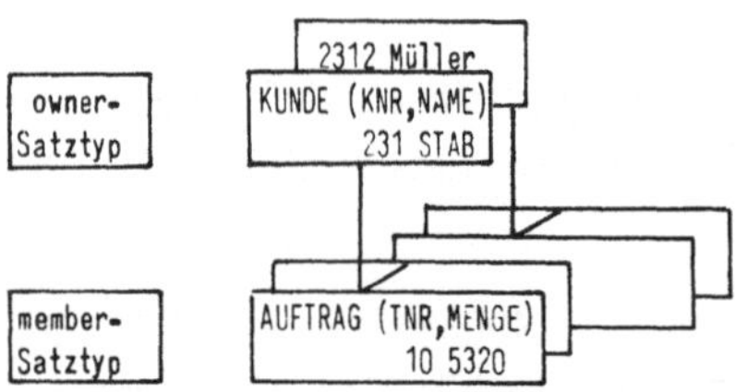

Bild 1: Darstellung eines SET nach CODASYL

Owner-Satztypen (hier KUNDE) und member-Satztypen (hier AUFTRAG) bestehen aus mehreren Sätzen. Im Sinne der Datenintegrität ist ein SET nur dann gültig, wenn ein member-Satz (Kindsatz) einem owner-Satz (Vatersatz) zugeordnet werden kann. Ist dies nicht der Fall, so gäbe es zum Beispiel Aufträge ohne Kunden, was durch das Datenmodell ausgeschlossen wird. Die Linie, die owner-Satztyp und member-Satztyp verbindet, hat drei Funktionen:

1. Sie stellt einen Zugriffspfad dar. Man gelangt von einem "Vater" ausgehend zu einem "Sohn" und nicht umgekehrt.

2. Sie ist eine Integrititätsbedingung in dem oben erwähnten Sinne.

3. Sie trägt Information (information bearing SET). Es wird der Linie die Bedeutung zugemessen, daß die Kunden-Nr. in KUNDE gleich der Kunden-Nr. ist, auf die sich die Aufträge beziehen. Würde die Linie entfernt, so weiß man nichts mehr über diese Zuordnung, da Information verloren geht.

Wie verhalten sich nun die hierarchischen Systeme im Hinblick
auf die Entwicklungsziele?

Zu 1.
Die Trennung der DML von einer Trägersprache wird voll durchgeführt.

Zu 2.
Die Datenintegrität wird zum größten Teil vom System durch
Systemprozeduren erzwungen. Es gibt spezielle Klauseln im
Codasyl-Entwurf, um Integrititätsroutinen einzubringen. Statt
über Routinen, die bei der Installation angefertigt werden
müssen, wird die Integrititätskontrolle auch über das Datenmodell bewirkt. Hier ist Kritik anzumelden, weil Gesichtspunkte der Anwendung und der Integrität miteinander vermengt
werden. Eine strikte Trennung beider Gesichtspunkte wird
in Relationalen Systemen vorgenommen. Von besonderem Nachteil
ist auch, daß die Verbindungslinien Informationen beinhalten.
Informationen sollten explizit und nicht implizit dargestellt
werden. Dies kann durch Normalisierung im Sinne der Relationalen
Systeme erreicht werden, indem der Schlüssel des owner-Satztyps
als Fremdschlüssel in den member-Satztyp eingebracht wird. Im
Beispiel würde das bedeuten, das KNR im AUFTRAG eingefügt
wird. Gerade im Hinblick auf neue Systeme ist allen potentiellen
Anwendern von hierarchischen Systemen zu empfehlen, normalisierte
SET-Strukturen einzuführen. Man hat nämlich dann de facto eine
relationale Datenstruktur erreicht, die man später nur mühselig
herstellen kann, wenn man sich für informationstragende Verbindungslinien entschieden hat.

Zu 3.
Durch die SET-Struktur gibt es feste Verknüpfungen zwischen
Satztypen (Dateien). Das Ziel "beliebig variable Verknüpfungen"
wie es allgemeine Informationssysteme verlangen, wird nicht
erreicht. Die Frage z.B. "Wie heißen die Kunden, die mehr als
5 000 Mengeneinheiten in Auftrag gegeben haben", kann nicht so

ohne weiteres beantwortet werden.

Zu 4.
Die Einmalspeicherung, die für einen Änderungsdienst günstig
ist, wird nicht erreicht, wenn zwischen owner-Satztyp und
member-Satztyp eine viele-zu-viele-Beziehung besteht. Wenn
hingegen die Anwendung mehrere member-Sätze genau einem
owner-Satz zuordnen will, ist das Ziel der Einmalspeicherung
erreicht.

Zu 5.
Das Ziel, die Benutzerklassen um die Klasse der Laien zu
vermehren, wird eindeutig nicht erreicht. Nur der Programmierer
kann Codasyl-Systeme handhaben. Es wird berichtet, daß Codasyl-
Programmierer sogar in zwei Wochen die Spracherweiterungen
in den Griff bekommen können (9, Seite 2). Es gibt Tendenzen
in der Codasyl-Gruppe, die von Bachman (11) geschildert werden,
denen zufolge man sich bemüht, durch ein Drei-Schemata-Modell
dem gesteckten Ziel näherzukommen, anspruchsvolle Laien an den
Rechner zu bringen.

Zu 6.
IMS-Systeme und der Codasyl-Vorschlag realisieren nur die physische Datenunabhängigkeit aber nicht die Zugriffspfad-Unabhängigkeit.

3. Relationale Systeme

Relationale Systeme, die auf Codd (6) zurückzuführen sind,
sind in ihrem Aufbau durch die strikte Trennung von mindestens
drei Ebenen gekennzeichnet. Man unterscheidet die logische
Ebene der Benutzer, die Zugriffspfadebene und die Ebene der
physischen Abspeicherung. Gegenstand des Datenmodells ist
die einfache Datei, Relation genannt. Der Ausdruck "flat file"
ist ebenfalls gebräuchlich, um eine Abgrenzung zu den
"Pyramiden" der hierarchischen Systeme anzudeuten.

KUNDE (KNR, NAME) und AUFTRAG(TNR,KNR,MENGE) sind zwei "flat files", die beliebig durch mengenorientierte Datenmanipulationssprachen,z.B. SEQUEL, ausgewertet und verändert werden können. Man kann sich auch zwei Tabellen vorstellen, deren Spalten benannt sind. Die Frage "Finde die Namen aller Kunden, die mehr als 5 ooo Mengeneinheiten bestellt haben", wird beantwortet, indem in der Spalte Menge alle Zeilen mit mehr als 5 ooo ME gesucht werden. Die dazugehörigen KNR werden mit den KNR in KUNDE verglichen. Bei Gleichheit wird der Kunden-Namen ausgeworfen.

Wichtig für beliebige Auswertungen in Relationalen Systemen ist die Vergleichoperation, um von einer Datei in eine andere zu "hüpfen". Integrititätsbedingungen (und auch die Sicherheitsbedingungen des Datenschutzes) werden in einer nicht-prozenduralen Sprache formuliert und von einem Subsystem verwaltet, das immer dann angesprochen wird, wenn Daten geändert werden.

In der Forschung und in der Entwicklung haben Relationale Systeme in den letzten sechs Jahren einen enormen Aufschwung erfahren. Es gibt ganze Bibliographien über Relationale Systeme (siehe auch (13)).

Das Zentrum der Forschung und Entwicklung sind die IBM Laboratorien in San José, Kalifornien. Hier ist das Relationale System "SYSTEM R" als Prototyp fertiggestellt worden, das bereits einige Vorgänger gehabt hat. Es gibt mittlerweilse in der Welt viele Implementierungen, jedoch keine, die von einem Hersteller in größerem Umfang unterstützt wird. Die Frage, warum das so ist, ist nur schwer zu beantworten. Der Autor wird u.U. einmal eine mehrsemestrige Vorlesung über "Datenbankpolitik" halten. Diese Bemerkung ist scherzhaft aufzufassen. Relationale Implementierungen werden in der Broschüre (7) zu einer Übersicht behandelt.

So wie das IDS der Ahne der Codasyl-Systeme ist, so kann der
BOMP (BILL of Material Processor), der zuerst von IBM in den
6oer Jahren auf den Markt gebracht wurde, bei einigem Wohl-
wollen als Urvater der Relationalen Systeme aufgefaßt werden.
Im folgenden seien Relationale Systeme mit den aufgeführten
Entwicklungszielen verglichen. Dabei muß aber der Mangel be-
achtet werden, daß kein Relationales System im großen Stil
vertrieben wird:

Zu 1:
Die Trennung zwischen DML und Trägersprache wird strikt
eingehalten. Durch die Bereitstellung eines Cursors in der
DML kann darüber hinaus sauber zwischen dem Zugriff zu Mengen
von Datensätzen und der Einzelsatzverarbeitung unterschieden
werden. Die Vorgehensweise der Strukturierten Programmierung
wird hierdruch erheblich unterstützt (15).

Zu 2.
Die zentrale Integrititätskontrolle wird gewährleistet. Große
Schwierigkeiten in Forschung und Entwicklung bereitet aber
noch der allgemeine, gleichzeitige Zugriff (shared access)
mehrerer Benutzer zu einem Datenobjekt. Diese Problemstellung
wird der Ablaufintegrität zugeordnet, die von der semantischen
Integrität und der Zugriffspfadintegrität entsprechend den drei
Ebenen zu unterscheiden ist. Hier liegt ein großes Feld für
eine sinnvolle Betätigung. Wie der gleichzeitige Zugriff in
netzverteilten Datenbanken auch nur annähernd vor sich gehen
soll, ist völlig unbekannt.

Zu 3.
Die integrierte Auswertbarkeit im Sinne der Aufgabenstellungen
durch Informationssysteme ist gewährleistet. Es zeigt sich,
daß eine Implementierung durch invertierte Listen gegenüber
den Adreßverkettungen deutliche Vorteile hat (13, Band II).

Zu 4.
Im Schlüsselbereich kann eine Einmalspeicherung nicht erreicht
werden. Der Änderungsdienst ist jedoch bei der Verwendung von
komprimierten Bitlisten zur Speicherung von Sekundärindizes
befriedigend (1o).

Zu 5.
Durch die Trennung der Benutzerebene von der Zugriffspfadebene
ist es in Relationalen Systemen sehr leicht, nicht-prozedurale
Sprachen wie SEQUEL einzuführen, die auch von Nicht-Programm-
ierern benutzt werden können.

Zu 6.
Die Drei-Ebenen-Philosophie hat zur Folge, daß Zugriffspfad-
Unabhängigkeit und physische Datenunabhängigkeit gewähr-
leistet werden können.

Bei der Beurteilung von angebotenen Datenbanksystemen sollte
auf weitere bereitzustellende Funktionen geachtet werden, ohne
die eine Betriebsfähigkeit nicht sichergestellt werden kann.
Diese Funktionen werden oft zu unrecht das "Grünzeug drum-herum"
genannt. Es handelt sich um die Funktionen, die von Datenfern-
verarbeitungs-Monitoren (TP-Monitore, Datenkommunikationsteile
etc.) wahrgenommen werden. Ferner müssen Prüfpunkt- und Wieder-
anlaufprogramme vorhanden sein. Die Revision der Datenbank und
die Wiederherstellung zerstörter Dateien muß ebenfalls unterstützt werden.

Die Entscheidung bei der Auswahl eines Datenbanksystems ist
zum heutigen Zeitpunkt inmitten einer schnellen Entwicklung
nur sehr schwer möglich. Wichtig ist die Beachtung des Grund-
satzes, daß der "point of no return" möglichst weit in die
Zukunft gelegt wird, damit der Entscheidende auch möglichst
wenig zu bereuen hat. Die Entwicklung der Datenbanksysteme
zeigt jedoch, daß Lerninvestitionen unvermeidbar sind. Auf

der anderen Seite wird eine Planung verlangt, da dieser gegenüber "flexiblen", lediglich reagierenden Entscheidungspraktiken deutlich der Vorrang zu geben ist. Bei den Unsicherheiten der Zukunft, über die, wenn es konkret wird, mehr spekuliert als prognostiziert werden kann, ist zu fragen, welche ersten Schritte zu tun sind.

Die empfehlenswerten Schritte beziehen sich auf Strukturen, auf Datenstrukturen sowie auf Programmstrukturen. Im Hinblick auf Datenstrukturen ist es die richtige Entscheidung, keine informationstragenden Verbindungslinien einzuführen. Für Programmstrukturen ist zu empfehlen, daß im Sinne der datenunabhängigen Strukturierten Programmierung die Zugriffslogik nicht in die Programme eingebettet wird (15). Herausgehobene Programmteile, die leicht ausgetauscht werden können, sollten den Zugriff bewerkstelligen. Der Form der Integritätsprüfung muß besondere Beachtung geschenkt werden. Es wird Zeit, daß die Produktion von langweiligen Cobol-Lehrbüchern aufhört und daß den Anwendern gezeigt wird, wie man strukturierte Cobol-Programme anfertigt, wobei ein Wechsel im Datenbanksystem mit in die Strukturierung einbezogen wird.

Literatur

(1) Bachman, C.W.: Trends in database management - 1975, in AFIPS National Computer Conference 1975, S.569-576.

(2) British Computer Society: Implementation of CODASYL Data Base Management Proposals, Proceedings of a two-day-Seminar. October 1974.

(3) Chamberlin, D.D. and Boyce, R.F.: SEQUEL: A Structured English Query Language, in Proc. ACM SIGFIDET Workshop on Data Description, Access and Control, May 1-3, 1974.

(4) Codasyl Data Base Task Group (DBTG) Report 1971 and Report 1973 (erhältlich bei IFIP Administrative Data Processing Group, 4o Paulus Potterstraat, Amsterdam).

(5) Codasyl Systems Committee: Feature Analysis of Generalized Data Base Management Systems, May 1971 (erhältlich bei IFIP Administrative Data Processing Group, 4o Paulus Potterstraat, Amsterdam).

(6) Codd, E.F.: A relational model for large shared data banks, in: Comm. of the ACM.Vol.13 (1970), No.6, S.377-387.

(7) Codd, E.F. (Hrsg.): Implementations of Relational Data Base Management Systems, Panel Discussion, National Computer Conference, Anaheim, Cal., May 21, 1975.

(8) Der Bundesminister für Forschung und Technologie: Drittes DV-Programm 1976-1979, Bonner Universitäts-Buchdruckerei, Bonn 1976.

(9) EDP Analyser: What's happening with CODASYL-Type DBMS, October 1974, Vol. 12, No.1o.

(1o) Härder, Th.: Selcting an optimal set of secondary indices, in: Proc. ECI-Conference 1976, Amsterdam, 9-12. May 1976, Springer-Verlag, Berlin-Heidelberg-New York, 1976, S.146-16o.

(11) Jackson, M.: Principles of program design, Academic Press, London, 1975.

(12) Steel, T.B.: Data Base Standardization. A Status Report, in: ACM-SIGMOD, May 14-16, 1975, San José, Cal., 1975.

(13) Wedckind, H.: Datenbanksysteme I, Bibliographisches Institut, Mannheim, 1974. Wedekind, H. und Härder, T.: Datenbanksysteme II, Bibliographisches Inszitut, Mannheim, 1976.

(14) Wedekind, H.: Die Überprüfung von semantischen Inte-
     gritität sbedingungen in Relationalen Datenbanksystemen,
     in: Tagungsband der 6. GI-Jahrestagung, Stuttgart 19.9.-
     1.1o.1976, Springer-Verlag, Berlin. Heidelberg, New York,
     1976, S.282-3oo.

(15) Wedekind, H.: Structured Database Programming, Carl-
     Hanser-Verlag, München, 1976.

(16) Wedekind, H.: Systemanalyse - Die Entwicklung von Anwendungs-
     systeme für Datenverarbeitungsanlagen, 2.Auflage, Carl-
     Hanser-Verlag, München, 1976.

On the gross architecture for the next generation
Database Management Systems

Dr. G.M. Nijssen
Control Data Europe

After analyzing the major problems with current information
systems, a description is given of how some of these problems
may be solved. An essential tool in narrowing the understanding gap between computer specialists on the one side
and managers and end-users on the other, is the conceptual
schema. The requirements for the concepts in the conceptual
schema are discussed and the major candidates for the
conceptual schema are briefly evaluated. A gross architecture
for the next generation database management systems is
presented; essential in this architecture is the conceptual
schema, the coextistence of various user mental models and
the coexistent use of various manipulation languages as well
as the coexistent use of various physical databases on one or
more computers. Hence we have given it the name:COEXISTENCE
model.

1. INTRODUCTION

The program for the IFIP Congress 77 will focus on the theme
"The maturing profession - perspectives and prospects."

Taking into account the enormous difficulties which users experience
in understanding and operating current database management
systems, one may conclude that these systems are rather immature.

A review of the mainstream of current literature on research
in database management, (21,29,38,42,43) indicates that there
is a low degree of maturity in database management; one is still

too busy with the CODASYL, hierarchical and normalized
relational approach. Kent (24) recently said it as follows:
"The popular models of today are driven by computer technology;"
furthermore he says, "Record technology is such an ingrained
habit of thought that most of us fail to see the limitations
it forces on us. It didn't matter much in the past, because
our real business was record processing almost by definition."
A generally accepted all encompassing framework is still
missing.

There are, on the other hand, some publications which bring
the perspective of a more mature and lasting approach to database management. It is reasonable to expect that the next
generation of database management systems will be based upon
a much better conceptual framework than current systems.

How mature will the next generation of database management
systems be? Taking into perspective the current research and
development efforts in database management, one may come to
the question: what are the prospects of having the next generation
database management systems available before 1980? What will be
the most salient characteristics of the next generation database
management systems? Is the conceptual schema an essential aspect
of a next generation database management system?

Answering all these questions would require a whole; however,
in this paper we have to try to do it whithin the limit of
8ooo words.

2. PROBLEMS WITH CURRENT INFORMATION SYSTEMS

The problems with current (formatted) information systems can be
classified into two categories; one is the too low degree of
understanding between managers and end-users on the one side;
the other one is due to the state of the art of database

management software.

Badly lacking today is a language in which it is possible
to describe:

- formally
- completely
- easy to formulate
- easy to understand
- easy to change

the Universe of Discourse covered by a set of information
systems. It is possible to design a language to be used by
managers, end-users and data processing experts which has
a reasonable chance of being accepted? This question will
be dealt with in section 3.

A database management system is not an aim in itself; it is
a tool to be used in the design, implementation, operation
and modification of information systems. Although the over-
whelming majority of current information systems do not use
this tool, it is the opinion of this author that this will be
reversed during the next decade.

Current database management systems result in the following
drawbacks:

a) facilities to build models are too computer oriented, and
   sometimes incomplete and unnecessary complicated

b) update and retrieval languages are too computer oriented,
   and often incomplete

c) productivity of data processing experts is too low

d) insufficient facilities to optimize computer resources

e) implementation cycle is too low

f) documentation not enough formal, nor complete

g) program maintenance costs too high.

Will these drawbacks be eliminated in the next generation
database management systems? To which degree and how this will
be done is indicated in section 4.

3. COMCEPTUAL SCHEMA: A MAJOR STEP FORWARD

Probably one of the major steps forward since the previous
IFIP Congress in 1974 is the increasing acceptance of a concept
called conceptual schema. In this section we will present an
intuitive description of this concept. Thereafter, we will
describe the requirement to be met by concepts to be used in
the conceptual schema. Various sets of concepts including the
network (CODASYL) and normalized relational approach will be
briefly evaluated using the just mentioned requirements.

3.1. Conceptual schema

During the last three to four years, one can observe an
increasing awareness of a need to have a description of the
structure of the information of interest for a set of information systems. Moreover this description must be precise,
complete, free of electronic data processing concepts and
readable by all involved. To be more specific, let us assume
that one may conceive an information base as a model which
consists of:

- a set of (atomic) elements
- a set of (atomic) sentences in which
  the atomic elements play a certain role.

An atomic sentence may be considered as a semantically irreducible relation in which are used, as domains, the sets of
atomic elements. Falkenburg (18,19) and other authors have
decribed this model in much more detail, although certain
variations exist among all these descriptions. (A semantically irreducible relation should not be confused with the
normalized relations introduced by Codd. (15). The normalized
relations of Codd are the result of normalization procedures
applied to complicated data processing concepts, called records;
the work of Codd has been very useful in making computer
experts aware of the somewhat unnecessary complextity of the
concepts in use.

A semantically irreducible relation (or elementary sentence
or atomic fact) is based upon the semantic deep structure of
sentences, an important concept in linguistics. The soucre
for Codd is the complicated record concept, while the soucre
for a semantically irreducible sentence is the semantic deep
structure of atomic sentences. A semantically irreducible
sentence has always the property of being in third normal form,
however a third normal form relation is very often not a
semantically irreducible sentence.

Let us return to our assumption that one may conceive the
informationbase as a set of atomic elements (objects) and
atomic sentences. If one wants to describe the informationbase
of a set of information systems, then one should describe the
types of elements and the types of sentences together with
constraints on elements and sentences. Such a description may
be considered as a set of decision rules which determine whether
certain sentences may or may not enter and reside on the
informationbase. This kind of description is needed for any
formal information system, computerised or not. This kind of
description can be considered as an agreement, or contract,
among all users of the set of information systems, where the
agreement defines explicitly which sentences are permitted within

the scope of the selected Universe of Discourse. A description
which defines the types of elements and types of atomic
sentences permitted within the Universe of Discourse, could
be called Universe of Discourse Schema. In the ANSI DBMS
report of 1975 (3) it is called conceptual schema. It is of
interest to see the analogy between grammar and conceptual
schema.

In this context a database, or better informationbase, may be
defined as the set of sentences available at a certain moment,
or period, and satisfying the Universe of Discourse Schema,
or conceptual schema.

3.2. Enterprise schema and gdms central schema

It is sometimes asserted that are two kinds of conceptual
schema. One of these, call it enterprise schema, is used by
management, end-users and computer experts as an explicit
description of the types of elements and sentences selected
to be within the Universe of Discourse. The other one, call
it gdms (generalised database management system) central
schema is used by the GDMS as the central description of the
permissible sentences. It is clear that the gdms central
schema is derived from the enterprise schema (see fig.1).
The quetsion is: is the mapping a 1:1?

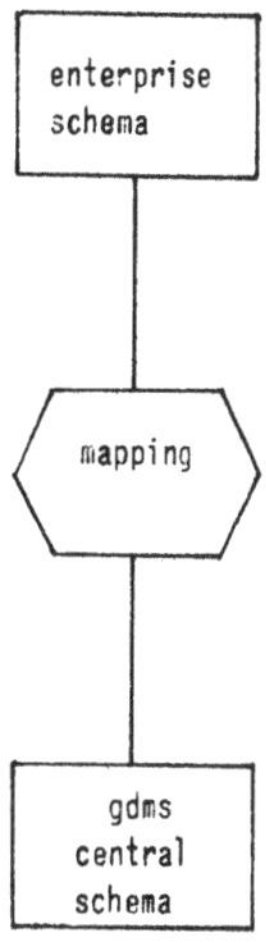

Fig.1

It seems to us that there are only minor variations between
the enterprise schema and the gdms central schema. Both
describe the type of atomic elements, the types of atomic
sentences and other constraints on these elements and
sentences.

However, it could be argued that the enterprise schema should
contain, on top of the types of elements, sentences and
constraints, a description which informs the people involved
about the relation between the elements and sentences in the
enterprise schema and the objects in reality to which these
refer. Such an additional description, call it a semantic
bridge, needs to be in terms of a conceptual framework, common
to or shared by the people involved.

For the Generalized Database Management System, such a semantic
bridge can be considered as comment to the gdms central schema,
where comment is used in the sense that no compiler or processor
will operate on such comment.

3.3. Requirements for the concepts in the conceptual schema

A conceptual schema, contains rules which are used to determine for each instance of a sentence whether it may or may not enter and reside in the information base.

(i) Powerful

The concepts of the conceptual schema should impose no restrictions on the mental model which is selected by the users as a "grid" covering a certain part of the perceivable reality (as long as we restrict ourselves to discrete structures). Said otherwise, the concepts of the conceptual schema should be powerful enough to describe any discrete structure.

(ii) Easy to formulate and read

The conceptual schema is the basis for discussions about the information systems ranging over the selected Universe of Discourse.This means that managers and end-users need to be able to acquire the capability to forumulate a conceptual schema with an average educational effort of about five days.

Furthermore, managers and end-users need to be able to acquire the capability to read a conceptual schema with an average educational effort of about two or three days.

If these aims could be met, it means that managers and end-users can easily check whether the Universe of Discours Schema describes that part of the perceivable reality in which they are interested.

The requirement of easy in formulating and reading can only be met if the distance of understanding between concepts in the

conceptual schema and concepts in the minds of the collective
users is minimal. Said otherwise, the semantic distance
between the concepts in the conceptual schema and concepts
in the mental model of the average users, should be minimal.

(iii) Formal

To describe the formal component of the requirements, we quote
a description given by Steel (40).

"The language must be a 'system' in the sense of logic; that it
must consist of a formally definable set of allowable expressions,
each of which is assigned a 'meaning' by a semantic 'mapping' to
concepts (concrete or abstract) in the real world."

"'Formal' (formally definable) is to be interpreted as the
notion that whether an expression is 'allowable' is recognizable
from its syntactic structure alone. This concept is equivalent
to the assertion that all meaningful expressions can be
identified by a machine on the basis of its form alone. Thus,
the system must be unambiguous."

(iv) Easy to change

It is fairly common practice that users of information systems
change their interests. Very often the new interests area is
covered by the previous Universe of Discourse Schema augmented
with the rules which describe the new permissible sentences.
The concepts in the conceptual schema should be such that change
may conveniently be implemented.

(v) Ease to transformation

It may be expected that some users want, for some special
applications, a specific mental model, while the majority of

users want to see the database via their preferred "natural"
model. It is necessary to permit different and coexistent
views on the same information base. If more than one set of
requirements equally satisfy the four previous requirements,
then that set should be selected which provides the easiest
transformation to the various mental models.

To summarize, the concepts in the conceptual schema need to
satisfy the following requirements:

- complete
- easy to formulate and read
- formal
- easy to change
- easy to transform

Remark: In several sets of concepts discussed today, one observes
that the concepts are not atomic mainly because they are based
upon one or the other machine efficiency criterion of grouping.
This emans that the degree of orthogonality of concepts in the
conceptual schema is to be taken as an additional requirement.
One could say that this is a special facet of minimizing the
semantic distance. This is true, but for teaching purpose we
have found it useful to mention orthogonality explicitly.

3.4. Alternative sets of concepts for the conceptual schema

In this section, we will very briefly discuss five sets of
concepts which are considered as possible candidate for the
set of concepts in the conceptual schema. We will start with
the description of a set of concepts based on the deep structure
of sentences, an important concept in linguistics (Chomsky,
(1o) and Falkenberg (18)). This set will be used as formalism
to describe the other alternative sets.

(i) <u>ENALIM approach</u>

Information systems deal with sentence of natural language, with
the restriction that sentences in formatted information systems
have to satisfy several additional constraints such as con-
forming to prior made agreement, no ambiguity etc.

From this it may be concluded that concepts based on the
structure of sentences in natural language are primary candidates
for the conceptual schema.

In the sequel, we will describe four primitive concepts and
some derived concepts. The four primitive concepts are directly
borrowed from linguistics and the derived concepts are borrowed
from set theory and programming. It has been shown (34) that
this set of concepts can be used to easily explain current data
models such as the network (CODASYL) and the normalized relation
approach. Because of the fact that this set of concepts for
the conceptual schema is considered by the author as a starting
point of an intersting development process in database technology,
we have given this set of concepts for the conceptual schemathe
name ENALIM, Evolving NAtural Language Information Model.

During the years to come, we hope that this set will evolve,
as various research efforts come to fruition. It is furthermore
of interest to note that we use the words Information Model and
not Data Model, because of the emphasis on semantic aspects as
opposed to emphasis on notational aspects. (The term data model
will be described in section 4, after we have introduced the
necessary framework to discuss this concept).

In the ENALIM approach there are the following four primitive
concepts:

In the ENALIM approach there are the following four primitive
concepts:

- atomic object
- role
- name
- classification

and the following derived concepts:

- atomic object type
- atomic object population
- atomic sentence
- atomic sentence type
- atomic sentence population
- name type
- constraint declarations

    . identifier
    . subset
    . database procedure (db proc)

The following informal definitions apply to the primitive
concepts. (We apologize that in a short paper we cannot be
as precise as we would like to be.)

An atomic object is an object that is considered as an un-
dividable entity of a selected Universe of Discourse.

A role is a function which an atomic object plays in an atomic
sentence.

A name is a unique reference for an element in a given context.

Classification is an intellectual process which divides a set
of elements into a set of disjoint subsets; all and only the
elements.

in a subset share a certain common characteristic.

The following definitions apply to the derived concepts:

An atomic sentence is a set of one or more pairs, where each pair consists of an atomic object name and a role name, and removal of one or more pairs makes the atomic sentence meaningless in the given context.

Remark: Sentences which consist of one place predicates could be considered as a special case of two place predicates. This, however, is a subject of research which will be covered in a separate paper.

A few examples may illustrate the forgoing definitions:

1. John Kennedy was born in Massachusetts
2. John Kennedy died in Texas
3. John Kennedy lived in California
4. John Kennedy lived in Massachusetts

We have here four **atomic sentences**. In sentence 1, John Kennedy is the name which is (assumed to be) a unique reference for an atomic object in this context; Massachusetts is a unique reference to another atomic object. In sentence 1, John Kennedy plays the role of native son, in sentence 2 of deceased person, in sentence 3 and 4 the role of resident. In sentence 1, Massachusetts plays the role of birth-state, in sentence 2 Texas plays the role of state-of-death, while in sentence 4 Massachusetts plays the role of state-of-residence, the same as California plays in sentence 3.

An atomic object type is the set of all possible objects which have a certain characteristic in common.

An atomic object population is the set of all atomic objects at a given moment in time, which belong to the same atomic object type.

An atomic sentence type is the set of all possible sentences which consists of object-role pairs belonging to the same object type and having the same role.

An atomic sentence population is the set of all atomic sentences at a given moment in time, which belong to the same atomic sentence type.

A name type is the set of all possible names which have a certain characteristic in common.

Contraints can be specified in various linguistic ways, such as procedural or declarative. It is our opinion that one should try to describe constraints in a declarative way such that a DBMS can "understand" the constraints. We are currently investigating the use and possible extentions of TAMALAN; (Vandijck (44)) as a declarative constraints language for the conceptual schema.

When discussing the transformability of one view (data model?) into another (or discussing the transformability among currently existing data models), it is very useful to give emphasis to two kinds of constraints, namely the "identifier" and the "functional subset".

An identifier of an atomic sentence type is a declaration of a set of object-role pairs whose value (concatenation of names is unique within any atomic sentence population of that atomic sentence type, and any object-role pair of the atomic sentence which is not included in the identifier, is determined by the identifier.

In the traditional literature one often calls an identifier
a "key" or a declaration to keep some elements "unique"
within a population; no two sentences in a sentence population
have the same value for a set of object-role pairs which consti-
tutes an identifier. For example, in sentence 1, native-son
is an identifier, just as deceased person is in sentence 2.
This is clear because a person can only be born in one state
and only die in one state. In sentence 3 and 4, the combination
of resident and state-of-residence is the identifier, because
a president can have been resident of many states.

A functional subset is a declaration which describes that the
set of some object-role pairs must be a subset of another set
of object-role pairs; the latter must constitute an identifier.

A database procedure (dbproc) is a program which describes
the actions which have to be taken when one or more atomic
sentences are added to or deleted from the database (or
Universe of Discourse).

During the design of a conceptual schema one can easily
determine whether a sentence is semantically irreducible
(atomic, elementary) or not, using the decision table of fig.
1.b.

	Rule 1	Rule 2	Rule 3	Rule 4	Rule else
number of roles in sentence is n	n-1	n 1	n 1	n 1	
number of identifiers in sentence	1	1	1	1	
number of roles in each identifier	1	n	n-1	n-1	
semantically irreducable sentence	X	X	X	X	
semantically reducable or otherwise incorrect sentence					X

Fig. 1.b. Decision table for determining semantical irreducibility
of sentences.

Remark: In this short paper, we have skipped over three aspects
of the ENALIM model which are essential in a full treatment.
In our opinion, it is necessary to permit:

1. sentences in which one or more of the arguments are
   sentences (objectified sentences, or nested sentences)

2. descriptive constraints understandable to the GDMS to
   replace as much as possible the database procedures.

3. the treatment of time.

These extensions are necessary in order to satisfy the
requirements of completeness, minimal semantic distance,
graceful evolution and coexistent different mental models
(to be discussed in section 4). All those three aspects will
be discussed in a separate paper.

(ii) <u>Information structure diagrams</u>

Communication among human beings as well as communication
between a human being and a machine can often be improved
by using graphical symbols or diagrams.

For the ENALIM information model, we have tested, since mid
1975, some alternatice sets of graphical symbols in seminars
on conceptual schema design; as a result of these experiences,
we propose to use the following symbols for the ENALIM
information model.

Atomic object type

Fig.2. A circle, or ellipsis, containing a name, or having
       a name close to it, represents an atomic object type
       with that name.

Atomic sentence type

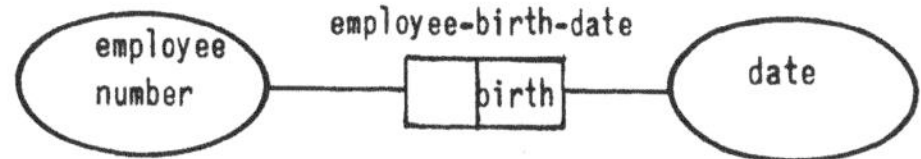

Fig.3. One or more rectangles, each rectangle connected via
       a straight line with exactly one atomic object type,
       and optionally containing the role which the atomic
       object type plays in this sentence, represent an
       atomic sentence type; each two rectangles have to
       share one common side. The sentence type name may
       be placed above the rectangles.

Identifier

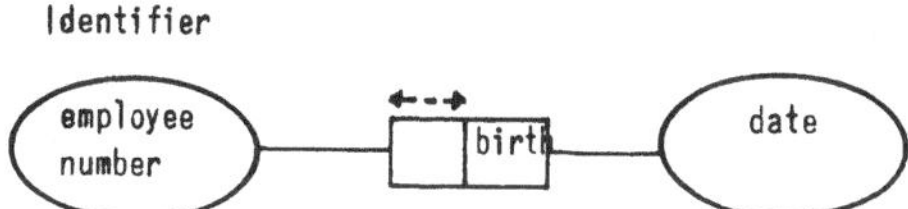

Fig.4. A dotted line, at each end having an arrow, ranging
       over some roles in an atomic sentence type, represents
       an identifier.

With atomic sentences of two object role pairs, one has
one of the following four possibilities:

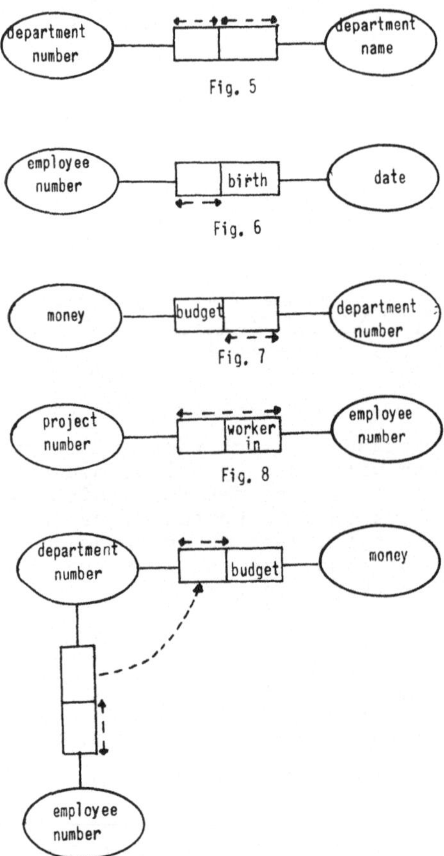

Fig.9. A dotted line between two object-role pairs (or two
       concatenations of object-role pairs) with at one end
       of the dotted line an arrow, represents a subset, where
       the object-role pairs to which the arrow points is the
       range of the total function and the other object-role
       pairs, the domain of the total function. There is a
       syntax rule specifying that the arrow can only point
       to an identifier.

In fig.9 the following is represented: the sentence describing
that a specific employee referred to by an employee number
works for a specific department, referred to by a department
number, is only permitted to enter the Universe of Discourse,
or database, if for this department the sentence is in the
database which describes the budget of this department.

The symbols described so far refer to type declarations; one
therefore could call these diagrams information structure
type diagram.

When teaching database concepts, using various diagrammatic
techniques, it became clear to us that type diagrams need
to be complemented with population diagrams. The concurrent
use of both type and population diagrams can help to increase
the understanding.

For the information structure population diagrams, we propose
to use the following symbols:

Population of atomic objects
all belonging to the same
atomic object type.

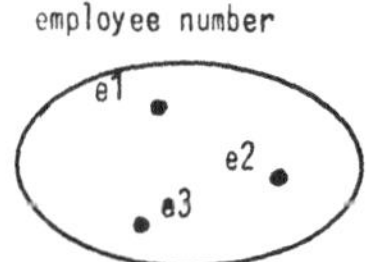

Fig. 1o

We propose to use, in analogy with the symbol commonly used
in set theory, to represent a population of atomic objects
as an ellipsis, containing a named dot to stand for each
atomic object of the population;the name of the atomic
object type is put outside the ellipsis.

Population of atomic sentences all belonging to the same
atomic sentence type.

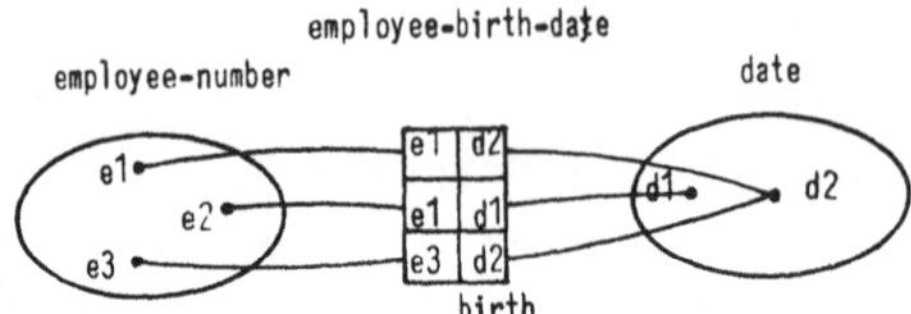

Fig.11. One or more rectangles, each rectangle connceted
with exactly one atomic object via a straight line,
and each rectangle containing the name of the atomic
object playing a role in this rectangle represents
an atomic sentence instance; each two rectangles have
to share one common side. If an atomic sentence population contains more than one atomic sentence instance
the instances are piled up. Optionally one can place
the name of the atomic sentence at the top of the
pile, and the roles at the bottom.

Identifier and subset

The symbols for identifier and subset used in the type diagrams
can be used in the same way in the population diagrams.

Remark: One argument sentence may be represented as in fig.12.

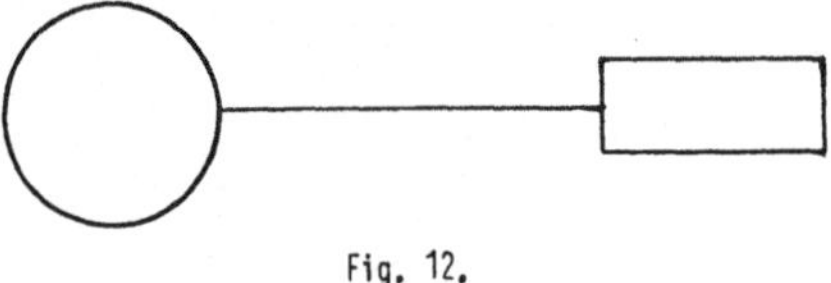

Fig. 12.

Overlapping types can be respresented as illustrated in fig.13.

Objectified sentences can be represented as illustrated with
an example in fig. 14.

(iii) <u>Binary model</u>

In the binary model, the two main constructs seem to be the
atomic objects, and atomic sentences all consisting of two
object-role pairs, or two cases. For more .details on the
binary models, one is referred to some excellent papers by

Abrial, (1), Bracchi, (7) and Senko (37).

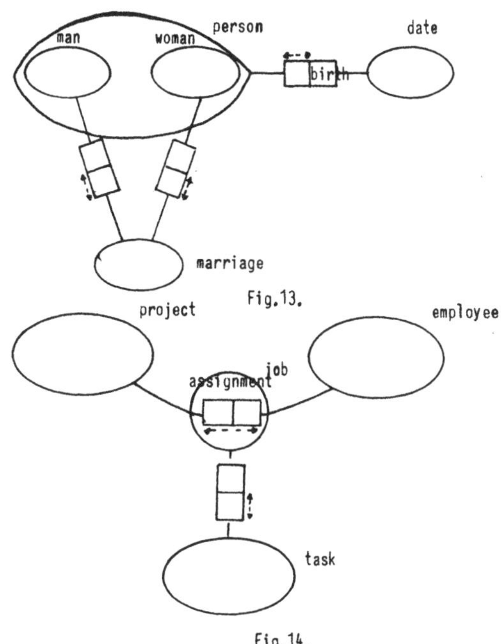

Fig.13.

Fig.14.

It is a pity that additional integrity constraints such as the
concept of identifier, subset and database procedure, get so
little attention in some papers on the binary model.

It seems to us that the binary model is worth a detailed
investigation as a candidate for the conceptual schema concepts.

(iv) <u>Normalized relational approach</u>

In the normalized relational approach, the concepts of domain,
normalized relation and functional dependency play a central
role. In terms of the ENALIM model, one may say that the
normalized relational approach groups together into one

relation type all those atomic sentence types in which the
same atomic object type is an identifier, thereby suppressing
all identifiers expect one.

The advantage of the normalized relational approach has
been that it has created an awareness of the unnecessary
complexity of some database constructs in which both
conceptual and physical aspects were incorporated into
one concept. It is therefore understandable why this has
so many supporters among computer scientists. One of
the important aims of normalization is "to reduce the
incidence of undersirable insertion, update and deletion
anomalies" (Codd, 15), page 1o18)).

Additional integrity constraints have only received
margininal attention in most papers on the normalized
relational approach.

(v) <u>Conceptual schema concepts in the CODASYL database approach</u>

In the CODASYL database approach the concepts of data item,
data aggregate, record, coset (COdasyl SET) and database
procedure seem to be the main concepts. In terms of the
ENALIM model, an atomic fact can be represented in the
CODASYL database approach in three entirely different ways:

- as a data item in a record
- as an element in a data aggregate
- as a coset between two records

In (32) and (33), we have evaluated various aspects of this
approach.

Most constructs in the CODASYL database approach are the
same as the major constructs of IDS. (4) In 1964, IDS was
an interesting step forward in the sense that one could make

more use of random access memory; considerations of physical
efficiency ("the single most important of the older concepts
is that of storing data records on a direct access device
in such a way that it would not be necessary to scan the
records sequentially to access a specific record" (Olle,(35),
page 998) were the main reasons for introducing the IDS and
CODASYL concepts.

(vi) The ANSI conceptual schema concepts

The ANSI conceptual schema concepts (chapter 4 of (3) are
the:

- conceptual field
- conceptual group
- conceptual record
- conceptual plex

The complexity of these concepts cannot be explained in
such a short paper as this one.

We confine ourselves to remark that these concepts are
unnecessarily complex because both conceptual, physical
and user mental view are mixed together.

(vii) Tabular evaluation

It is often dangerous to present in one table an evaluation
of such complex matters as current database approaches. In
such a table one can hardly bring in all the nuances which
are necessary for a scientific evaluation. It is with this
disclaimer in mind that one has to interpret the tabular
evaluation. We have included the conceptual schema concepts of five database approaches and taken seven evaluation
criteria. One may conclude that the binary approach and
ENALIM model are the better candidates for the conceptual
schema concepts; both the current CODASYL and current ANSI

conceptual schema concepts are no serious candidates for the concepts in the conceptual schema; the normalized relational concepts is a major improvement with respect to the ANSI AND CODASYL concepts for the conceptual schema.

requirement for the conceptual schema schema / approach	complete-ness	case of formulation	case of under-standing	degree of formalization	case of change	case of transfor-mation	orthogonality of concepts
EMALIM model	Very High	Very High	Very High	Very High	Very High	Very High	High
Sinary model	High	Very High	High	Very High	Very High	High	Very High
Normalized relations	High	Medium	Medium	Very High	High	High	High
CODASYL database approach (1973,1975)	High	Very Low	Very Low	Medium	Low	Very Low	Low
ANSI DSMS approach (1975)	Medium	Very Low	Very Low	Very Low	Low	Low	Low

Fig. 15.

4. A GROSS ARCHITECTURE FOR THE NEXT GENERATION DATABASE MANAGEMENT SYSTEM

There is a growing awareness that the conceptual schema, describing the "deepest structure" of the sentences considered to be of interest for a set of information systems, is the key element in the gross architecture for the next generation generalized database management (gdms) systems, (see fig.16)

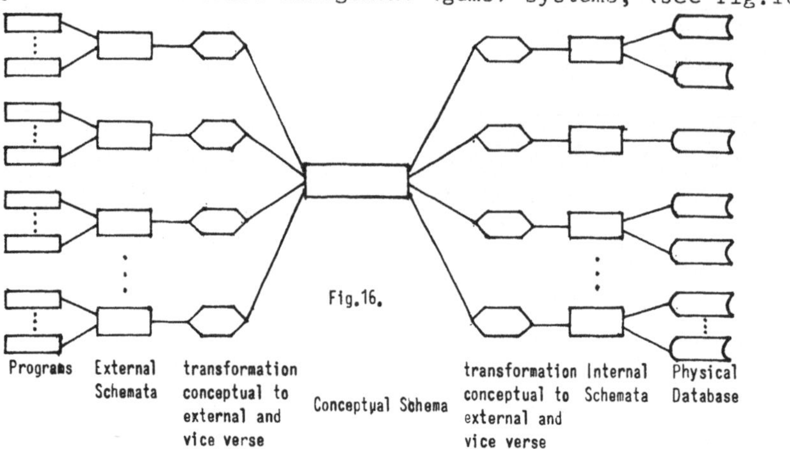

Fig.16.

Another key element of the gross architecture of the next
generation gdms is the coexstistence of various user
mental models, and various user manipulation languages to
operate on a user mental model. Such a user mental model,
often referred to as external schema, is derived from the
conceptual schema. For methodological reasons, we prefer
to show this mapping explicitly in the diagram although
in practical applications such a mapping is often included
in the external schema. Various external schemata is a
necessity if we want to get to creation and innovation
because a user who is forced to "think" in only one mental
model can hardly be expected to find creative solutions for
a problem. One could say that coexistent external schematy
are necessary for human efficiency.

The same reasoning can be applied to manipulation languages.

The sentences which make up the Universe of Discourse, have to
be physically recorded in mass storage; and inserting and
retrieving sentences require certain computer resources.
There is a separate description, which can be used as
decision rules as to how to store physically the sentences.
Concepts like grouping, physical nearness, access paths,
pointers, controlled redundancy etc. are relevant in this
physical schema, storage schema or internal schema. There
need to be a mapping between the conceptual and internal
schema; if this mapping is powerful enough, there is no
insurmountable problem in having the sentences of the Universe
of Discourse physically distributed in mass storage associated
with computers in a network.

Because coexistence of various external schemata, manipulation
languages and internal schemata is a major aspect of this
gdms architecture, we have given it the name COEXISTENCE model.
(Nijssen, (34)).

The practical aspects of such a gross architecture of a
gdms have been tested by a group of people at Control
Data Europe in Brussels. In this system, two user mental
models or views are provided, namely a network (corrected
and extended CODASYL) and a normalized relational view;
there is a DML for COBOL, FORTRAN and SYMPL to operate on
the network view, while TAMALAN (Vandijck, (44)) is used
as normalized relational retrieval language. The results
obtained since late 1974 indicate that different users
prefer to use different views and different languages. Re-
garding computer efficiency, it has been measured that the
efficiency of a gdms based on the coexistence architecture
is at least the same as the computer efficiency of most
of the commercially available database management systems.
The major improvements however are the increased productivity
in information systems analysis and design, and increased
programmer productivity.

Remark: The term "data model" is very often used in the
database management literature. One may say that a data model
covers some aspects of the conceptual schema, some of the
internal, some of the external schema, and some aspects of
database manipulation languages. Because of this impreciseness,
it seems to me better to drop the concept "data model".

5. SUMMARY AND CONCLUSIONS

There is a growing recognition to introduce generalized
database management systems as a major tool in building,
running and modifying information systems using a common
informationbase.

In the current generation of database management systems,
there is a too low degree of insulation of application
programs from physical aspects of the data, and there is not

enough guarantee that the database (informationbase) cannot
be polluted by some application programs, mainly because
there is no conceptual schema enforcing sufficient correct-
ness; computer efficiency is too low with current database
management systems; programming is unnecessarily complex
and programmer productivity too low. For non-computer
professionals, it is very difficult to have a useful
communication on database (informationbase) problems because
of the lack of a commonly understandable framework.

In this paper, we have outlined an approach for improvement
in these areas. It is good to observe that there is an
increasing acceptance of the conceptual schema. Reviewing
the results of recent IFIP Conferences on Database Management,
one may say that there are two likely candidates for the set
of concepts in the conceptual schema; one is based on the
deep structure of sentences and the other is an extension of
the binary model. Further investigations are underway in this
area.

A result of the approach outlined in this paper is the posibility
of direct involvement of non-computer experts in the design,
operation and modification of information systems. We regard this
as a step toward maturity in information systems.

It is not to be excluded that some database management systems
of the next generation will enter the field before 1983.

<u>AKNOWLEDGMENT</u>

I would like to express my appreciation to Robert Endert, one
of my previous managers, who some ten years ago encouraged
me to spezialize on databases.

I aknowledge many intersting discussions with the members of
the group which has successfully implemented the first version
of a coexistence GDMS at Control Data Europe.

It is a pleasure to mention the author's indebtedness
to R.Durchholz, GMD, Bonn (nature of the concept of schema),
to E.Falkenberg, Siemens, München (the object-role model),
to M.Senko, IBM, New York (the binary model) and to T.Steel,
Equitable Life Assurance Society, New York (formalization).

Discussions within IFIP WG 2.6. (Databases) have helped to
correct and clarify a number of aspects of the COEXISTENCE
model.

G.M.Nijssen, "On the Gross Architecture for the next generation
    Data base Management Systems", from G.Gilchrist (ed.),
    "Information Processing 77", pp.327-335, IFIP, North-
    Holland Publishing Company (1977).

REFERENCES

(1)   J.R.Abrial, Data semantics, in Data Base Management,
       Proceedings of the IFIP-Working Conference on
       Data Base Management, held in Cardese, Corsica,
       April 1-5, 1974, edited by J,W.Klimbie and K.L.
       Koffeman, North-Holland Publishing Company,
       Amsterdam 1974.

(2)   M.Adiba, C.Delobel and M.Leonard, A unified approach
       for modelling data in logical data base design,
       see reference 31.

(3)   ANSI, Interim report study group on data base management
       systems, American National Standards Institute,
       ANSI/X3/SPARC DBMS Study Group, February 1975.

(4)   C.W.Bachman and S.B. Williams, A general purpose
       programming system for random access memories,
       Proceedings of Fall Joint Computer Conference,
       October 1964, vol.26, pp.411-422.

(5)   E.Benci, F.Bodart, H.Bogaert and A.Canabes, Concepts
       for the design of a conceptual schema, see reference
       31.

(6)   H.Biller, W.Glatthaar and E.J.Neuhold, On the semantics
       of data bases: The semantics of data manipulation
       languages, see references 31.

(7)   G.Bracchi, A. Fedeli and P.Paolini, A multilevel relational
       model for data base management systems, in Data Base
       Management, Proceedings of the IFIP-Working Conference
       on Data Base Management, held in Cargese, Corsica,
       April 1-5, edited by J.W.Klimbie and K.L.Koffeman,
       North-Holland Publishing Company, Amsterdam 1974.

(8)   G.Bracchi, P.Paolini and G.Pelagatti, Binary logical
       assiciations in data modelling, see reference 31.

(9)   D.D.Chamberlin, Relational data-base management sytsems,
       ACM Computing Surveys, vol. 8, no.1, March 1976.

(1o)   N.Chomsky, Aspects of a theory of syntax, Cambridge,
       Massachusetts, 1965.

(11)   CODASYL, Data Base Task Group Report 1969, ACM, New York.

(12)   CODASYL, Data Base Task Group Report 1971, ACM, New York,

(13)   CODASYL, DDL journal of development, June 1973, report.

52

(14) CODASYL, Cobol journal of development, published by the
        Technical Services Branch, Department of Supply and
        Services, Ottawa, Ontario, Canada, 1975.

(15) E.F.Codd, Recent investigations in relational data
        base systems, in Information Processing 1974,
        Proceedings of IFIP Congress, August 5-1o, 1974,
        Sweden, North-Holland Publishing Company,
        Amsterdam 1874.

(16) R.Durcholz. Relation representation by tables and by
        functions, Information Systems, vol. 1, no.3,
        October 1975.

(17) R.Durcholz and G.Richter, Information management concepts
        (ICM) for use with DBMS interfaces, see references 31.

(18) E.Falkenberg, Significations: The key to unify data base
        management, Information Systems, vol.2, no.1, 1976,
        pp.19-28.

(19) E.Falkenberg, Concepts for modelling information,
        see references 31.

(2o) Fillmore, The case for case, in Universale in Linguistic
        Theory, Bach and Harms (eds.), pp.1-9o.

(21) J.P.Fry and E.H.Sibley, Evolution of data base management
        systems, ACM Computing Surveys, vol.8, no.1, March 1976.

(22) G.Grotenhuis and J.Van den Broek, A conceptual model for
        information processing, see reference 31.

(23) P.Hall, J.Owlett and S.Todd, Relations and entities,
        see references 31.

(24) W.Kent, New criteria for the conceptual model, in Systems
        for Large Data Bases, edited by P.C.Lockeman and
        E.J.Neuhold, North-Holland Publishing Company,
        Amsterdam 1976.

(25) S.C.Kleene, Introduction to metamathematics,Van Nostrand,
        Princeton, New Jersey 1952.

(26) B.Langefors and B.Sundgren, Information systems architecture,
        Petrocelli/Charter, New York, 1975.

(27) G.Leech, Semantics, Penguin Books, 1974.

(28) C.Machgeels, A procedual language for expressing integrity
        constraints in the coexistence model, see reference
        31.

(29) A.S.Michaels, B.Mittman and C.R.Carlson, A comparison
      of the relational and Codasyl approaches to data
      base management, ACM Computing Surveys, vol.8,
      no.1, March 1976.

(3o) P.Moulin, M.Teboul, S.Savoysky, S.Spaccapietra and
      H.Terdieu, Conceptual model as a data base design
      tool, see references 31.

(31) G.M.Nijssen, (editor), Modelling in data base management
      systems, Proceedings of the IFIP Working Conference
      on Modelling in Data Base Management Systems, held
      in Freudenstadt, Germany, January 5-8, 1976, North-
      Holland Publihsing Company, Amsterdam, 1976.

(32) G.M.Nijssen, Set and Codasyl set or coset, in Data
      Base Management Description, Proceedings of the
      IFIP Special Working Conference on Data Base
      Description Languages, an in-depth technical
      evaluation of the CODASYL DDL, held in Wepion,
      Belgium, January 13-17, 1975, edited by B.C.M.
      Douque and G.M.Nijssen, North-Holland Publishing
      Company, Amsterdam 1975.

(33) G.M.Nijssen, Two major flows in the Codasyl DDL 1973
      and proposed corrections, in Information Systems,
      vol. 1, Pergamon Press, 1975, pp.115-132.

(34) G.M.Nijssen, A gross architecture for the next generation
      database management systems, see reference 31.

(35) T.W.Olle, Current and future trends in data base management
      systems, in Information Processing 74, Proceedings
      of IFIP Congress, August 5-1o, 1974, Sweden,
      North-Holland Publishing Company, Amsterdam 1974.

(36) J.Ruchti, Data descriptions embedded in context, see
      reference 31.

(37) M.E.Senko, DIAM as a detailes example of the ANSI SPARC
      architecture, see references 31.

(38) E.H.Sibley, The development of data base technology,
      ACM Computing Surveys, vol. 8, no.1, March 1976.

(39) T.B.Steel Jr., Data base standardization: A status report,
      in Data Base Description, Proceedings of the IFIP
      Special Working Conferences on Data Description
      Languages, an in-depth technical evaluation of the
      CODASYL DDL, held in Wepion, Belgium, January 13-17,
      1975, edited by B.C.M.Douque and G.M.Nijssen,
      North-Holland Publishing Company, Amsterdam 1975.

(40) T.B.Steel Jr., Discussion at the IFIP WG 2.6 (Databases)
        meeting, September 1976.

(41) B.Sundgren, Theory of data bases, Petrocelli/Charter,
        New York, 1975.

(42) R.W.Taylor and R.L.Frank, CODASYL data base management
        systems, ACM Computing Surveys, vol.8, no.1,
        March 1976.

(43) D.C.Tsichritzis and F.H.Lochovsky, Hierarchical data
        base management, ACM Computing Surveys, vol.8,
        no.1, March 1976.

(44) L.Vandijk, Towards a more familiar relational retrieval
        language, accepted for publication in Information
        Systems.

DMS – 170

Heinz Ringlhofer
Control Data Wien

Das Datenbanksystem DMS-170 wurde für die Rechnerfamilien Control Data
CYBER 70/170 entwickelt. DMS-170 besteht aus einer Anzahl von Software-
Moduln , die in einzelnen, getrennten Blöcken eingesetzt werden können.
Dieser blockweise Aufbau erlaubt die Erzeugung eines maßgeschneiderten
Datenbanksystems für jede Problemstellung. DMS-170 kann daher ebenso
(unter Zuhilfenahme von nur einigen Moduln des Systems) für einfache
Dateiverwaltungssysteme wie auch für komplexe Datenbanken im Echtzeit-
betrieb eingesetzt werden.

Die Größe und Komplexität dieser Moduln ist verschieden und variiert
zwischen einem ANS-74 Cobol-compiler und einem Booleschen Listenpro-
zessor.

Der Anwender kann entscheiden, welche der Möglichkeiten, die DMS-170
beinhaltet, er für sein reales Problem einsetzen will. Zusätzlich kann
die Komplexität seiner Applikation zwischen Cobol-Dateistrukturen bis
hin zu einer kompletten Datenbank im CODASYL-Sinne oder Relationen-
modell variieren. Auf diese Weise kann eine abrupte Umstellung von
Applikationen, und die damit verbundenen Risikofaktoren,durch den
Einsatz von DMS-170 als Datenbanksystem vermieden werden.

DMS-170 kann in folgende Baugruppen gegliedert werden:

- Datenzugriffsmethoden   Cyber Record Manager
- Daten Definition und   Data Description Language
  Speicherabbildung
- Datenmanipulation über   Cobol, Assembler, Fortran
  "Host Languages"
- Datenmanipulation über   Query/Update

- Querverbindungen zwischen   Cyber Data Control
  Daten, Wiederanlaufpunkte,   System (CDCS)
  Hilfsprogramme, Daten-
  kontrolle

DMS - 17o GENERAL OVERVIEW

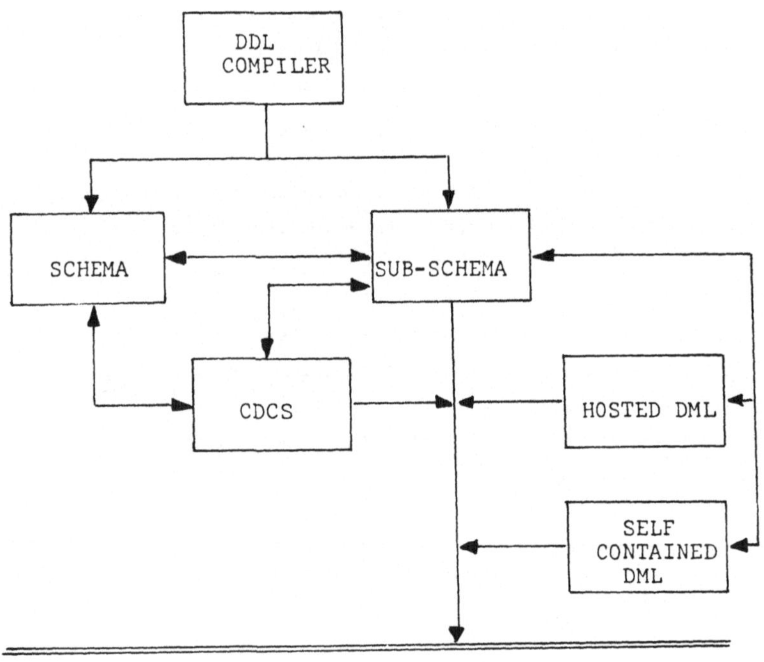

CYBER   RECORD MANAGER

CYBER RECORD MANAGER

Der Kern von DMS-170 ist der Cyber Record Manager. Dieser Baustein besteht aus den Standardzugriffsmethoden innerhalb des
Systems. Zusätzlich enthält der Cyber Record Manager die gemeinsamen Zugriffsmethoden auf externe Medien für die Sprach-
prozessoren, verwaltet das Blocken und Entblocken von logischen
Sätzen, verarbeitet Dateikennsätze und nimmt die Fehlerbehandlung
bei Schreib- oder Lesefehlern auf externen Geräten vor.

Der Cyber Record Manager verwaltet (auf Speichereinheiten, die
direkten Zugriff unterstützen) folgende fünf Zugriffsmethoden:

- Sequentiell
- Index-Sequentiell
- Direktzugriff (Random Access)
- Adresslistenzugriff (Actual Key)
- Relative Adressierung (Word addressable)
- Multiple-Index-Processor

CYBER RECORD MANAGER FILE ORGANIZATIONS

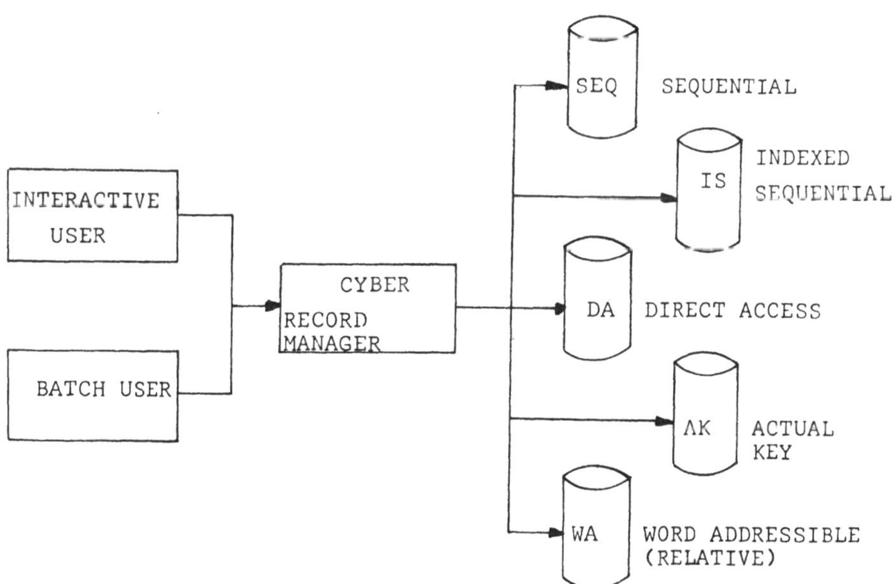

Cyber Record Manager - Zugriffsmethoden

Sequentiell

Sequentieller Zugriff kann sowohl auf Speichermedien, die Direktzugriff unterstützen, als auch auf Magnetbändern und ähnlichen
Geräten verwendet werden. Die Verarbeitung wird von einer Anzahl
von,je nach Blockungsfaktor und Satzart (fixer oder variabler
Länge etc.) unterschiedlichen, Routinen gesteuert. Diese Routinen
können vom Anwender sowohl zur Kompilationszeit als auch bei Ausführung ausgewählt, beziehungsweise geändert werden.

Index-Sequentiell

Index-sequentieller Zugriff erlaubt sowohl sequentielles als auch
direktes (über Schlüssel) Absuchen von Daten.

In der innerhalb des Cyber Record Manager's implementierten index-
sequentiellen Zugriffsmethode werden folgende Systemeigenschaften
verwirklicht:

- Es ist ein nahezu unbegrenztes Wachstum der
  Daten,ohne Überlaufbereiche angeben zu müssen,
  möglich. Dies wird durch eine automatische Aufteilung von Datenblöcken ("block-splitting")
  im Falle von Blocksaturation bewirkt. Ebenso
  werden neue Indexebenen automatisch generiert.

- Die Anzahl der benötigten Zugriffe zu einem
  bestimmten Datenbereich ist genau berechenbar.

- Es können sowohl Sätze fixer als auch variabler
  Länge im System gespeichert werden.

- Der Benützer kann Faktoren wie Blockgröße oder
  Indexgröße selbst festsetzen.

Direktzugriff

Direktzugriff verwendet einen Verschlüsselungsalgorithmus
("hashing") des Suchbegriffes, um Daten abzuspeichern,
beziehungsweise abzufragen. Die wichtigsten Systemeigenschaften sind:

- Falls die vom System gelieferte Verschlüsselungs-
  routine nicht den Bedürfnissen des Anwenders entspricht, kann dieser eine eigene Routine verwenden,
  um eine optimale Datenverteilung zu erreichen.

- Es kann bei der Datenerstellung zwischen drei
  verschienen Überlauforganisationen gewählt werden.

- Es sind Hilfsprogramme zur Analyse des Verteilungs-
  effektes für Verschlüsselungsalgorithmen vorhanden.

Adresslistenzugriff (Actual Key)

Diese Methode bietet sehr effizienten Zugriff zu Sätzen über einen
vom System zugeordneten Schlüssel. Diese Methode wird dann günstig
eingesetzt, wenn der Anwender selbst diese Schlüsseltabellen verwalten kann, indem er Hilfsdateien für diese anlegt. Der Zugriff
zu Sätzen, die mittels dieser Methode verwaltet werden, ist dann
fast mit einem echten Zugriff auf Plattenspeicher gleichzusetzen.

Relative Adressierung

Relativer oder Wort-adressierbarer Zugriff erlaubt einen Zugriff
über einen Schlüssel, der eine Adresse, relativ zum Beginn der Datei,
enthält. Diese Methode wird als Basis für die COBOL "ORGANIZATION
IS RELATIVE" sowie "ORGANIZATION IS STANDARD" Klauseln verwendet
und kann auch direkt von FORTRAN durch Anwendung der Routinen
READMS / WRITEMS eingesetzt werden.

Multiple-Index-Processor

Der Multiple-Index-Processor (MIP) kann zusammen mit Daten, die
index-sequentiell, direkt oder Actual Key organisiert sind, angewendet werden. Der Multiple-Index-Processor erlaubt, außer der
Definition des Hauptzugriffes über den sogenannten Primärschlüssel,
der der jeweiligen Datenorganisation unterworfen ist, die Definition
von weiteren Schlüsselfeldern (Sekundärschlüsseln), die vom Haupt-
zugriff unterschiedlichen direkten Zugriffsfelder innerhalb des
Datenbestandes zu definieren. Die Definition, sowie der Zugriff zu
solchen Feldern, erfolgt über die standardisierten Cyber Record
Manager Schnittpunkte. Der Multiple-Index-Processor bietet, unter
anderem, die für Mehrfachindizierung definierten ANSI-Cobol 74
Spezifikationen. Zusätzlich zum ANSI 74 Standard, der nur die Unterstützung von index-sequentiellen Dateien definiert, unterstützt der
Multiple-Index-Processor auch Direktzugriff und Adresslistendateien.
Der Zugriff über Sekundärschlüssel kann sowohl sequentiell als auch
direkt erfolgen.

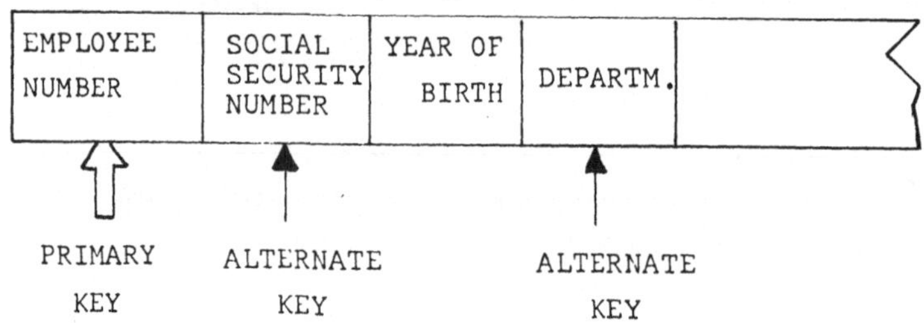

Wie das vorhergehende Beispiel zeigt, kann auf einen in dieser
Art verschlüsselten Satz über drei verschiedene Wege direkt
zugegriffen werden. Das nächste Diagramm zeigt das Konzept
zwischen Sekundärschlüssel und der bestehenden Datenstruktur.

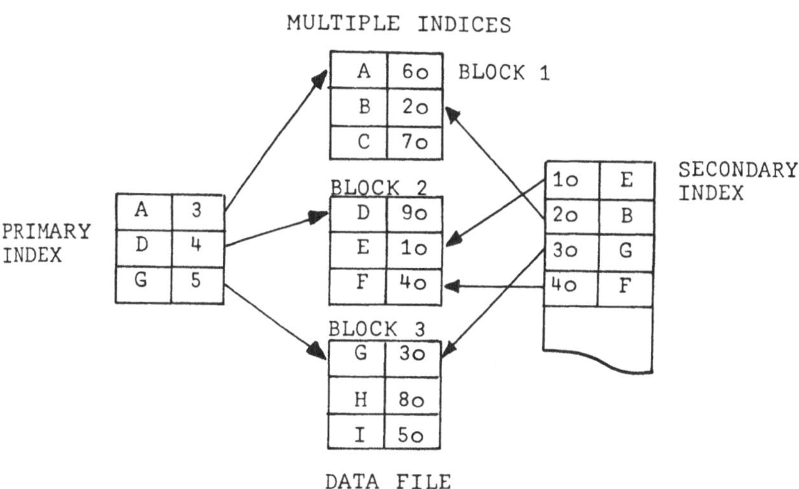

Die drei Blöcke in der Mitte des Bildes veranschaulichen drei
Datenblöcke in einer index-sequentiellen Datei. Die Eintragungen
(Schlüssel) im Primärindex der index-sequentiellen Datei adressieren
jeweils den ersten Satz in jedem der drei Datenblöcke. Dies ist
die normale Adressierungsmethode, die innerhalb des Cyber

Record Manager's für index-sequentielle Dateien verwendet wird.
Der Sekundärindex auf der rechten Seite des Bildes erlaubt nun
direkten Zugriff zu denselben Datenbeständen über ein anderes
Feld, das in diesem Fall numerische Werte (zum Unterschied vom
Primärschlüssel) enthält.

Um nun einen Satz über einen Sekundärschlüssel im System aufzu-
finden, wird der zu diesem Sekundärschlüssel gehörende Sekundär-
index abgesucht und danach mit dem dort aufgefundenen Wert des
Primärschlüssels auf den Datenbestand zugeriffen. Es kann sowohl
direkt als auch sequentiell auf die beiden Schlüsselfelder zugegriffen werden. Es besteht keine Begrenzung für die Anzahl
der Sekundärschlüssel im System, die dann, jeder für sich, einen
anderen Weg des direkten Zugriffs definieren.

Das folgende Bild zeigt eine schematische Übersicht der Interaktion
des Systems mit den Benutzern.

MULTIPLE INDEX PROCESSOR

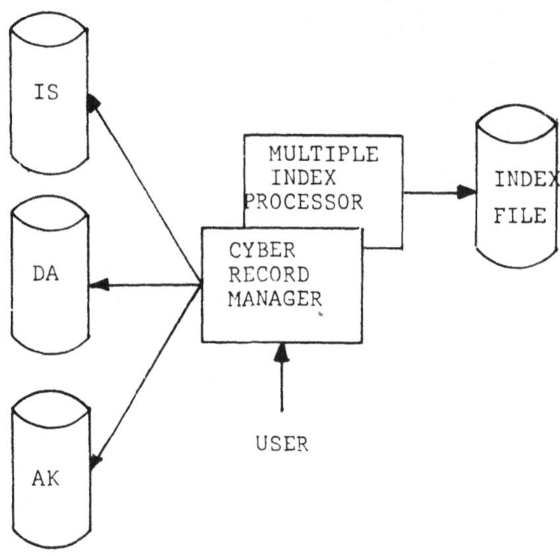

Der Benutzer kann nun entweder einfache Absuchkriterien für
Primär- oder Sekundärschlüssel spezifizieren oder auch über
Sekundärschlüssel eine Liste von Primärschlüsseln erhalten,
die seinen Suchkriterien entsprechen. Diese zweite Art der
Abfrage wird für logische Operationen innerhalb von Schlüsselfeldern verwendet und besonders bei Abfragen von Datenbeständen
durch Query/Update eingesetzt. Wenn Datenbestände geändert werden,
werden vom System aus automatisch alle Sekundärindices mitver-
ändert.

Einem Datenbestand ist immer eine Indexdatei, die alle zugehörigen
Sekundärindices enthält, zugeordnet. Diese Indexdatei kann sowohl
auf der gleichen Massenspeichereinheit wie der zugehörige Datenbestand gespeichert sein als auch, um schnelleren Zugriff zu
erreichen, auf anderen Einheiten, wie zum Beispiel Zusatzkernspeicher
(Extended Core Storage).

DATEN DEFINITION (Data Definition Language)

Die Datendefinitionssprache dient dazu, dem Datenbankverwalter die
Möglichkeit zu geben, eine Datenbank sowohl dem Inhalt nach als
auch die Attribute dieser Datenbank zu beschreiben. Weiters können
damit alle Kontrollfunktionen, die bei Verwendung der Datenbank ausgeführt werden sollen, beschrieben werden.

Durch die Verwendung der Datendefinitionssprache, werden Datenbe-
schreibungen von Programmen, die auf eine Datenbank zugreifen,
logisch getrennt. Dadurch entsteht eine zentrale Kontrolle für Zu
griffe auf Datenbanken und es wird die Unabhängigkeit von Datenbeständen in Beziehung zu Anwenderprogrammen gewährleistet. Es können
damit Datenbestände ihre logische sowie physische Struktur ändern,
ohne daß es zu Änderungen in Anwenderprogrammen, die diese Bestände
verwenden, kommen muß. Die in DMS-170 enthaltene Datendefinitionssprache verwendet als Basis die CODASYL Spezifikationen und ist damit
ähnlich der Cobol "DATA DIVISION".

DATA DESCRIPTION LANGUAGE

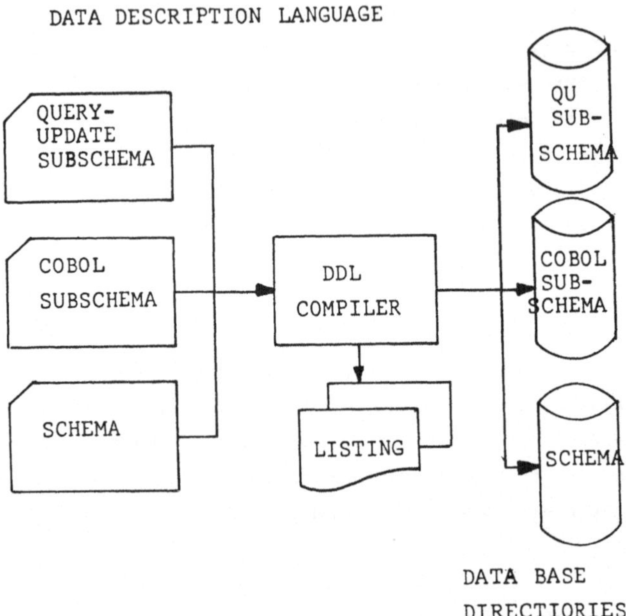

Die Datenbeschreibung wird durch die Exekution von Datenbe-
schreibungsprogrammen erreicht. Der Definitions-Compiler erzeugt
daraus Beschreibungsdateien, die im System permanent abgespeichert
werden. Drei Arten von Datendefinitionen sind innerhalb von DMS-17o
unterstützt:

- Die Gesamtbeschreibung einer Datenbank (Schema)
- Teilbeschreibungen (Subschema) für Cobol
- Teilbeschreibungen (Subschema) für Query/Update

Die in diesem Prozess generierten Beschreibungen werden vom Datenbankkontrollsystem (CDCS) bei Programmausführung in das jeweilige
Programm integriert und dienen zur Kontrolle der dem Benutzer zu
übergebenden Datenuntermengen. Auf diese Weise werden Daten vor unbefugtem Zugriff auf Feldebene abgesichert.

CYBER DATA BASE CONTROL SYSTEM

Das Datenbankkontrollsystem (CDCS) überwacht den Datenfluß
zwischen Anwendern und Datenbank im System. Es verarbeitet
Benutzerbefehle, bereitet die Daten in die vom Subschema vorgegebenen Strukturen auf und führt den Zugriff zu den abgespeicherten
Daten über den Cyber Record Manager aus.

Die in diesem Modul vorhandenen Anwendungsmöglichkeiten können
generell in zwei Klassen getrennt werden:

>   Anwenderbezogene Merkmale   sowie
>   Datenverwaltungsbezogene Merkmale.

Merkmale, die die Anwendung unterstützen, erlauben Programme für
eine effektive Problemlösung unter Zuhilfenahme einer Datenbank
zu generieren.

Merkmale, die der Datenverwaltung dienen, werden vom Datenbank-
Administrator angewendet und dienen der Kontrolle und Überwachung
des Datenflusses im System.

Anwenderbezogene Merkmale

Datenunabhängigkeit wird durch eine separate Datenbeschreibungssprache und durch die Verknüpfung von Schema/Subschema erreicht. Dies
beinhaltet auch die automatische Konversion von Daten, die im Subschema abweichend vom Schema beschrieben sind.

Verknüpfungen von Dateien (im Unterschied zu hierarchischen Strukturen)
werden durch die Verwendung des Multiple-Index-Processors und Normalisierung von Daten im Sinne des Relationenmodells erreicht.

Die Datenbank selbst wird in konventionellen Cyber Record Manager
Dateien abgespeichert und ermöglicht damit den Benutzern eine Auswahl der Zugriffsmethoden, sowie die Vereinfachung der Umstellung für
vorhandene Programme.

Der Zugriff zur Datenbank erfolgt über normale Cobol Ein-/Aus-
gabenbefehle anstelle von komplizierten Datenmanipulationen über
CALL- oder ENTER-Befehle. Einige zusätzliche Erweiterungen wurden
speziell zum READ-Befehl implementiert, der nun sowohl auf normale
Sätze als auch auf Relationen zugreifen kann ("Relational Read").

Merkmale der Datenverwaltung

Datensicherheit wird von einer Anzahl von Mechanismen unterstützt.
Auf niedrigster Stufe unterstützt das Betriebssystem die Sicherung
vor unbefugten Zugriffen auf Dateien durch das Passwort-Konzept.

Einschränkungen des Schemas sowie Unterteilungen des Datenbestandes
werden durch das Schema/Subschema-Konzept auf Feldebene erreicht. In
der letzten Stufe besteht die Möglichkeit, eigene Prüfroutinen, die
den unbefugten Zugriff auf Datenbestände absichern, einzusetzen.

Die Prüfung des Datenbestandes auf Richtigkeit ist einer der Wege,
der in der Verwaltung des Datenbestandes eingesetzt werden kann.
Dies wird durch spezielle Prüffunktionen, die im Schema definiert
werden, erreicht. Diese Prüffunktionen können sowohl das Format als
auch den Inhalt von Datenfeldern prüfen.

Es können von Anwendern definierte Funktionen in das Datenbanksystem
einbezogen werden. Diese Funktionen können Datenbestände auf Vollständigkeit prüfen, Daten verschlüsseln und entschlüsseln sowie
virtuelle Ergebnisse erzeugen. Auf diese Weise kann das System auf
die speziellen Erfordernisse der Anwender ausgerichtet werden.

Als letzten Punkt können Daten zur Wiederherstellung auf Trans-
aktionsdateien geschrieben werden. Es kann sowohl eine Kopie der
Daten vor der Änderung als auch nach der Änderung abgespeichert
werden. Spezielle Hilfsprogramme dienen der Wiedererstellung der
Datenbank.

Die zur Erstellung einer Datenbank unter DMS-170 nötigen
Schritte sind:

1. Beschreibung der Datenstruktur durch das Schema
   (Data Definition Language) sowie durch das Subschema für Applikationsprogramme.

2. Ausführung eines Programmes, das die Datenbank
   selbst erstellt. In diesem Programm wird ein
   Subschema eingesetzt, das den gesamten Datenbestand beschreibt und über CDCS die Datenbank
   generiert.

Relationen zwischen Datenbeständen

Es können komplexe Datenbestände innerhalb von DMS-170 definiert
werden. Diese Strukturen können von einfachen sequentiellen Strukturen
über Baumstrukturen bis zu Netzwerken reichen. Sie werden extern
vom Anwenderprogramm im Schema beschrieben. Zur Ausführungszeit
werden diese Strukturen dynamisch durch CDCS generiert.

Anwenderbezogene Sprachen

Da alle Daten in konventionellen Dateien gespeichert sind, kann
auf diese direkt von jedem Programm zugegriffen werden.

In einer echten Datenbank-Applikation, die durch das Schema/Subschema-
Konzept gesteuert wird, sind in DMS-170 zur Zeit zwei Sprachen unterstützt. Cobol greift direkt auf DMS-170 Subschema zu und ruft automatisch CDCS auf. Die Cobol Syntax wurde nur in wenigen Punkten geändert. In allen Fällen wurde bei den Ein-/Ausgabebefehlen dem ANSI 74
Standard gefolgt, obwohl dieser keine Schema/Subschema Verben enthält.
Die dazu in Cobol benötigten Erweiterungen sind:

- Die Spezifikation eines Subschemas im SPECIAL NAMES-
  Paragraph.

- Alle Definitionen (ausgenommen die SELECT
  Klausel) für durch Subschema gesteuerte Dateien
  wurden aus dem FILE CONTROL-Paragraph sowie
  der FILE SECTION entfernt.

- Die PROCEDURE DIVISION bleibt unverändert bis
  auf die zusätzliche Anwendung des relational
  READ Verbs.

- Fehlercodes werden in derselben Weise wie
  normale Cyber Record Manager Codes behandelt.

QUERY / UPDATE

Query/Update, als Teil des gesamten DMS-170 Paketes, ist eine sowohl
interaktiv als auch im Stapelbetrieb einfach anzuwendende Abfrage-
sprache. Query/Update wurde in Blickrichtung auf ad hoc Abfragen einer
Datenbank entwickelt. Neben den normalen logischen und arithmetischen
Befehlen, die in solch einer Sprache vorhanden sein müssen, enthält
Query/Update einen sehr anspruchsvollen, jedoch leicht einzusetzenden
Listengenerator.

Die Syntax von Query/Update basiert auf normalem Englisch.

Zusammenfassung

Aus den in dieser Beschreibung angeführten Punkten ergeben sich folgende
Vorteile des Einsatzes von DMS-170:

- Einfachheit der Konvertierung
  Da DMS-170 sowohl das klassische Dateiprinzip
  als auch komplexe Relationen in Datenbeständen
  verarbeiten kann, ist eine Umstellung der vorhandenen Applikationen mit nur geringen
  Schwierigkeiten möglich.

- Flexibilität in der Auswahl der Datenorganisation. Der Anwender selbst kann in
  DMS-170 entscheiden, welche der im System
  vorhandenen Datenorganisationen seine
  speziellen Anforderungen optimal unterstützt.

- Volle Datenunabhängigkeit
  Durch das Schema/Subschemaprinzip wurde
  volle Unabhängigkeit der gespeicherten
  Daten von ihren Beschreibungen erreicht.

- Kontrollfunktionen zur Datenbanküberwachung
  Es steht den Benutzern eine große Palette
  von Hilfsprogrammen zur Datenbanküberwachung
  zur Verfügung.

- Netzwerk und hierarchische Strukturen
  Es können Datenstrukturen von jeder gewünschten
  Komplexität gebildet werden.

- Mehrfachzugriff
  Durch die im Betriebssystem befindlichen
  Zugriffsmethoden ist das Problem des mehr-
  fachen gleichzeitigen Zugriffs auf dieselben
  Daten gelöst.

NIMS
Network Information Management System

Dipl. Math. Norbert Vorstädt
GEI Aachen

Zusammenfassung:

Nachdem lange Zeit die physischen Aspekte bei der Konzeption
von Datenbanksystemen im Vordergrund gestanden haben, tendiert
die Entwicklung der letzten Jahre auf diesem Gebiet dahin, der
logischen Struktur der Datenbank das ihr gebührende Interesse
zu schenken. Begriffe wie Redundanzfreiheit, Integrität, Datenschutz und Benutzerfreundlichkeit treten immer weiter in den
Vordergrund.

NIMS (Network Information Management System) ist ein Datenbanksystem, das in dieser zweiten Entwicklungsperiode entstanden
ist, und die Gesamtheit dieser Denkansätze in seinem Design
integriert.

Als eines der entscheidenden Entwurfskriterien bei NIMS ist
die völlige Trennung von logischer Datenstruktur und physischer
Implementationsart zu sehen.
Sie stellt einen wichtigen Schritt in Richtung des Relationen-
modells dar, ohne die Effizienz der Implementierung aus dem
Auge zu verlieren. Hierfür ein Beispiel:

- Unabhängiger Einstieg (Zugriff über den Wert eines Items)

  Die logische Struktur "unabhängiger Einstieg" kann physisch
  mit folgenden Methoden realisiert werden:

- DIRECT

  Bei dieser Methode wird die Datenbankadresse (DBA) unmittelbar aus dem Wert eines numerischen Items abgeleitet.

- RANDOM

  Hierbei wird die DBA durch Anwendung einer Transformationsroutine (Hash-Transformation) auf ein beliebiges Item gewonnen.

- INVERTED FILE

  Die Zuordnung Wert - DBA erfolgt über eine invertierte
  Datei.

Trotz dieser völlig verschiedenen physischen Realisationen
des unabhängigen Einstiegs sind die benutzerbezogenen Eigenschaften in allen drei Fällen im wesentlichen gleich.

Daraus resultiert, daß der Benutzer nicht mit der physischen
Implementationsart einer Datenbank konfrontiert wird. Das ist
jedoch nicht der einzige Vorzug dieses Konzeptes. Es übt auch
einen großen Einfluß auf die Klarheit und Übersichtlichkeit des
Datenbanksystems selbst aus. Dadruch konnten sowohl im logischen
wie auch im physischen Bereich Methoden und Hilfsmittel mit
überzeugenden Eigenschaften implementiert werden.
Zum Beispiel:

- Symmetrische Relationen

  Sie bilden ein grundlegendes Hilfsmittel zur "adäquaten"
  Darstellung von gemäß ihrer Natur symmetrischen Datenbeziehungen in einer Datenbank. Damit werden viele Nachteile
  von Datenbankmodellen, die lediglich hierarchische Strukturen
  zulassen, beseitigt und eine weitgehend redundanzfreie
  Speicherung ermöglicht.

- Unabhängigkeit von Einspeicherungs- und Zugriffsmethoden

Die Zielsetzung beim Einspeichern von Daten und dem Zugriff
auf solche sind grundsätzlich verschieden. Aus diesem Grunde
werden bei NIMS diese beiden Vorgänge völlig entkoppelt, so
daß z.B. die Datenbankadresse für die Einspeicherung durch
einen Zufallszahlengenerator ermittelt werden kann, während
ein oder mehrere "unabhängige Einstiege" die Methode DIRECT
oder RANDOM verwenden.

Durch diese Entkoppelung wird einerseits eine optimale Gleich-
verteilung der Daten über den Speicher - und damit eine optimale Nutzung des Speichers - erreicht, andererseits die
Anwendung des jeweils günstigsten Zugriffsverfahrens möglich.
Außerdem schafft sie die Möglichkeit, beliebig viele unabhängige Einstiege beliebigen Typs für ein Segment definieren
zu können.

- Datenkompression

Den verschiedenen Organisationen auf der physischen Ebene
stehen entsprechende Datenkompressionsmethoden zur Verfügung
z.B. Kompressionen von Zeichenwiederholungen über Itemgrenzen hinweg für Nutzdaten und "Vorgängerkompression"
bei invertierten Dateien. Die aufsteigende Schlüsselsortierung in invertierten Dateien wird also zu einer besonders effizienten Kompression genutzt.

Diese Beispiele sind repräsentativ für die ausgereifte
Konzeption aller Bestandteile von NIMS. Das gilt für den zentralen
Verwaltungsteil, die Datensicherung, den Datenschutz und die
Restrukturierung genauso wie für das Paket von Dienst- und
Analyseprogrammen.

Eine noch weitgehende Erfüllung von Forderungen, die für
relationale System gestellt werden, wird mit der Benutzer-
sprache GIRL (General Information Report Language) erzielt.
Durch die wird nicht nur zeitraubende Host-Language-

Programmierung vermieden (Einsparung von ca.80%). Der
Benutzer wird auch von der Kenntnis der logischen Struktur
der Datenbank fast völlig befreit. Während er seine Programme
datenbezogen beschreibt, werden die strukturbezogenen Eigenschaften der Datenbank vom GIRL-Compiler "beigesteuert". Dadurch bleibt ein Benutzerprogramm in GIRL von Änderungen des
physischen und logischen Aufbaus der Datenbank weitgehend
unberührt.

I. DAS DATENBANKSYSTEM NIMS

1. Programmtechnische Angaben

Das Datenbanksystem NIMS kann sowohl für Batch-Anwendungen
als auch im Dialog-Betrieb unter der Kontroll eines TP-
Monitors eingesetzt werden. Beiden Betriebsarten kommt der
vollständig modulare Aufbau von NIMS zugute. Jeder logischen
Datenbankoperation - wie z.B. Einspeichern oder Lesen über
eine Relation - entspricht genau ein Modul. Bei der Bear-
beitungseröffnung durch einen OPEN-Befehl werden nur diejenigen Module zugeladen, die für die vorliegende Anwendung
erforderlich sind. Eine weitere Senkung des Speicherbedarfs
und gleichzeitig Steigerung der Effizienz wurde erzielt, indem
alle Module in Assemblersprache und voll reentrant programmiert
wurden. Letzteres ist insbesondere im Multi-User-Betrieb von
außerordentlicher Bedeutung.

Das Benutzerinterface zu NIMS bietet folgende Möglichkeiten:

- Host-Language-Programmierung mit COBOL
- Host-Language-Programmierung mit PL/I
- "Self-Contrained System" mit GIRL
- Dialoginterpreter

Die Host-Language-Programmierung wird durch einen Satz von
Makros (bei COBOL: COPY-Blöcken) zur Beschreibung der

Kommunikationsbereiche erheblich erleichtert. Der Aufruf von
NIMS-Befehlen geschieht mittels des CALL-Statements. Der
GIRL-Compiler wird im Kapitel II vorgestellt.

Speicherbedarf:

- Nettobedarf   3o - 4o KByte
- Puffer   3o KByte

Die Puffergröße ist vom Benutzer frei wählbar. Der angegebene
Wert ist als Richtgröße anzusehen. Der Netto-Speicherbedarf
hängt wie oben dargestellt vom Anwendungsbefehl und somit von den
zugeladenen Moduln ab.

2. Logische Organisation

Jeder von uns wird bereits die Erfahrung gemacht haben, daß
sich sowohl abstrakte wie auch reale Dinge wesentlich schneller
und auch besser in unser Gedächtnis einprägen, je klarer und
übersichtlicher ihr Aufbau und ihre Struktur ist. Das ist nicht
anders bei der Handhabung von Datenbanksystemen. Daher wurde
bei der Entwicklung von NIMS besonders großer Wert auf ein klares
logisches Konzept gelegt.

Der erste Schritt war dabei die völlige Trennung von logischen
Strukturen und ihrer physischen Implementationsart.Wie wir
später sehen werden, erscheint eine NIMS-Datenbank dem Benutzer
gegenüber als ein strukturiertes Gebilde, das aus Segmenten,
unabhängigen Einstiegen und Relationen zusammengesetzt ist.
Die physische Organisation der Datenbank ist allein Sache des
Datenbankadministrators.

Das Gunrdkonzept der logischen Organisation einer NIMS-Datenbank basiert auf folgenden Forderungen:

- Es muß zwischen den Daten selbst und den zwischen ihnen
  bestehenden Beziehungen (Relationen) unterschieden werden.

- Das Auffinden von Daten sollte sowohl über ihren Wert, als
  auch über ihre Relation zu anderen Daten sowie über eine
  Kombination von beiden möglich sein.

- Das System sollte eine adäquate Implementierung aller
  in der Praxis vorkommenden Relationen ermöglichen.

- Die Struktur des Systems sollte eine möglichst redundanzfreie Speicherung der Nutz- und Hilfsdaten ermöglichen.

- Benutzerprogramme sollen unabhängig von der physischen
  Darstellung der Daten und der physischen Realisierung
  der Relationen und Zugriffsmethoden sein.

Bei NIMS ist es gelungen, alle diese Forderungen zu erfüllen.
Das daraus resultierende logische Grundkonzept wird im
folgenden dargestellt.

2.1 Daten

Zur Darstellung der Daten werden folgende Strukturbegriffe
verwendet:

- Segment
- Item
- Groupitem
- Arrayitem

Das **Item** ist die kleinste ansprechbare Struktur im System. Es
repräsentiert in der Modellwelt der Datenbank eine spezielle
Eigenschaft aus der realen Welt.

Ein **Segment** stellt die Zusammenfassung mehrerer logisch zusammengehöriger Items dar. "Logisch zusammengehörig" bedeutet
dabei in den meisten Fällen "zum selben Objekt gehörig". Ein

Segment entspricht etwa der bei CODASYL als "Record Type"
bezeichneten Struktur. Eine Ausprägung eines Segments -
vergleichbar mit einem Satz einer Datei - wird Segmentexemplar genannt.

Schematische Darstellung:

Segment   Segmentexemplar

Group- und Arrayitem sind beides Strukturen, die lediglich
der Vereinfachung der Schreibweise dienen. Gehören mehrere
Items in ganz elementarer Weise zusammen - wie z.B. TAG,
MONAT, JAHR - so kann es sinnvoll sein, sie auch formal zusammenzufassen, um sie gemeinsam unter einem Namen - hier
z.B.DATUM - ansprechen zu können. In ähnlicher Weise fungieren
die Arrayitems.Sie können als Wert Vektoren oder Matrizen
aufnehmen, deren Komponenten einfache Items sind. Sie können
und sollen auf keinen Fall als Ersatz einer hierarchischen
Relation dienen; die Anzahl ihrer Komponenten wird in der
Datenbankbeschreibung (DDT) festgelegt.

2.2. Zugriffsstrukturen

2.2.1. Unabhängige Einstiege

Um ein spezielles Segmentexemplar anhand eines vorliegenden
Itemwertes zu selektieren, wird die Struktur mit der Bezeichnung "unabhängiger Einstieg" verwendet.

Schematische Darstellung:

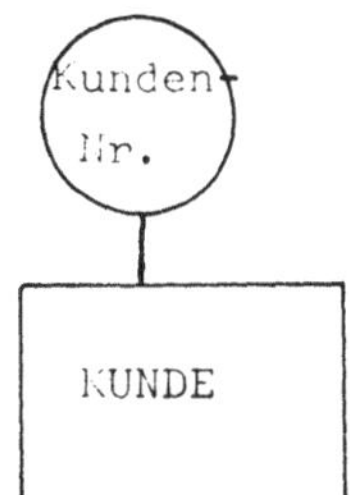

Eine Reihe von physischen Zugriffsmethoden, von denen im
nächsten Kapitel die Rede sein wird, stellt auch bestimmte
Forderungen an die Einspeicherung der Daten. Die daraus ent-
stehenden Verquickungen und Einschränkungen bei der Einrichtung von unabhängigen Einstiegen verlangen bei vielen
Datenbanksystemen den Anwendern eine erhebliche Aufmerk-
samkeit ab.
Durch die Einführung von speziellen Zugriffsdaten, die für
den Benutzer natürlich "unsichtbar" bleiben, werden bei
NIMS alle diese Nachteile aus dem Wege geräumt. Bei der
Definition und Handhabung ist keinerlei Rücksicht auf die
Art der Einspeicherung mehr erforderlich. Für jedes Segment
können beliebig viele unabhängige Einstiege mit beliebigen
physischen Methoden definiert werden. Dabei bleibt auch die
physische Zugriffsmethode für den Benutzer "unsichtbar".

Weitere Vorteile dieser Vorgehensweise:

- Die nachträgliche Definition von unabhängigen Einstiegen
  ist jederzeit ohne Umarrangieren schon gespeicherter
  Daten möglich.

- Für saisonale Auswertungen können temporäre Einstiege
  definiert werden.

- Der Zugriff über Groupitems ist möglich.

2.2.2. Relationen

Die Beziehungen zwischen Daten, die in unterschiedlichen
Segmenten gespeichert sind, werden in sogenannten <u>Relationen</u>
festgehalten. Obwohl diese eigentlich Informationsträger sind,
werden sie hier unter Zugriffsstrukturen beschrieben, da
die in ihnen gespeicherten Informationen häufig zur Selektion
von Segmentexemplaren benutzt werden.

NIMS kennt zwei Typen von Relationen. Die <u>symmetrischen
Relationen</u> stellen Relationen im mathematischen Sinne dar,
nämlich eine Teilmenge des kartesischen Produkts zweier
Mengen - in diesem Fall zweier Mengen von Segmentexemplaren.
Der Zusatz "symmetrisch" sollte betonen, daß beide einbe-
zogenen Segmente in gleicher Weise an der Relation parti-
zipieren (im Gegensatz zu hierarchischen Relationen).
Manchmal wird dafür auch der Begriff many-to-many-relation
verwendet, der hervorhebt, daß ein Segmentexemplar eines
Segments mit mehreren Exemplaren des jeweils anderen
Segments verknüpft werden kann.

Schematische Darstellung:

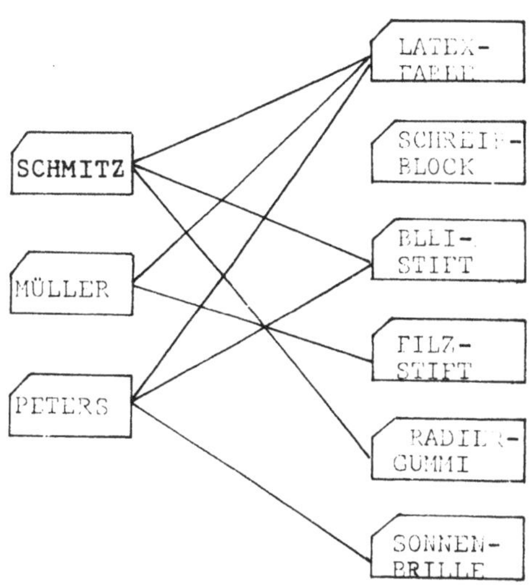

Ein Spezialfall dieses Relationentyps - und zwar ein so
wichtiger, daß man für ihn eine eigene Bezeichnung eingeführt hat - ist die <u>hierarchische Relation</u>, die nicht
zwei "gleichwertige" Segmente, sondern ein Parent - und
ein Childsegment miteinander verbindet. Ein Parentexemplar
kann zwar mit mehreren Childexemplaren verknüpft werden,
doch jedes Childexemplar darf nur einem Parentexemplar
zugeordnet sein. Daher auch der Name one-to-many-relation,
der manchmal verwendet wird. Im allgemeinen muß sogar
jedes Childexemplar genau einem Parentexemplar zugeordnet
werden, es sei denn die Relation erhält das Attribut
"optional".

Schematische Darstellung:

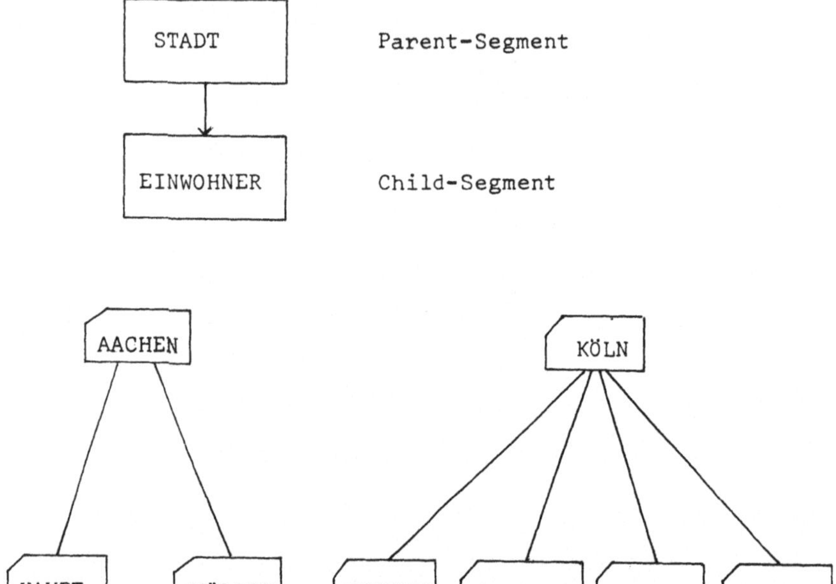

Um der genannten Forderung nach kombiniertem Zugriff über
eine Relation und dem Wert eines Items gerecht zu werden,
ist es bei NIMS möglich, für eine Relation (symmetrisch oder
hierarchisch) das Attribut "SORTED ON item" zu spezifizieren.
Die Werte des genannten Items werden dann dazu benutzt,
auf der Menge der Segmentexemplare, die mit einem Parent-
oder Partnerexemplar verknüpft sind, eine Ordnung zu
definieren. Wird die Verknüpfung zweier Segmentexemplare
in die Relation eingefügt, so geschieht dies unter Berücksichtigung der Sortierung nach den Werten dieses Items.
Dieses wird daher auch Insertitem genannt. Bei einem Zugriff
über eine solche Relation kann dann mit einem Befehl ein
Childexemplar gelesen werden, das gleichzeitig einen bestimmten Wert des Insertitems enthält.

2.3. Datenbankdesign

Jede NIMS Datenbank besteht aus logischer Sicht - und damit
gleichzeitig aus der Benutzersicht - aus den bisher beschriebenen Elementen. Der Aufbau eines Datenbankmodells
aus diesen Elementen gehört zu den Aufgaben des Datenbank-
administrators und soll hier nicht näher beschrieben werden.
Ein entscheidender Schritt bei diesem Prozeß ist es, das
Modell in die sogenannte dritte Normalform zu bringen. Sie
bildet die Voraussetzung für eine redundanzfreie Speicherung
und die Vermeidung der unter den Namen "Update-, Deletion-
und Insertion-Anomalien" bekannten Phänomene. Diese dritte
Normalform kann aber mit der ausschließlichen Verwendung
hierarchischer Relationen i.a. nicht - oder nur unter Verwendung von Hilfsstrukturen - erreicht werden. Daraus ist
die große Bedeutung der symmetrischen Relationen im Daten-
bankdesign zu verstehen. Erst sie ermöglichen eine weitgehend redundanzfreie Speicherung.

Daß symmetrische Datenbeziehungen in der Praxis nicht selten
vorkommen, mögen folgende Beispiele belegen:

Studenten	-	Vorlesung
Kunden	-	Artikel
Mitarbeiter	-	Projekte
Bücher	-	Stichworte
usw.		

DATENBANKBEISPIEL

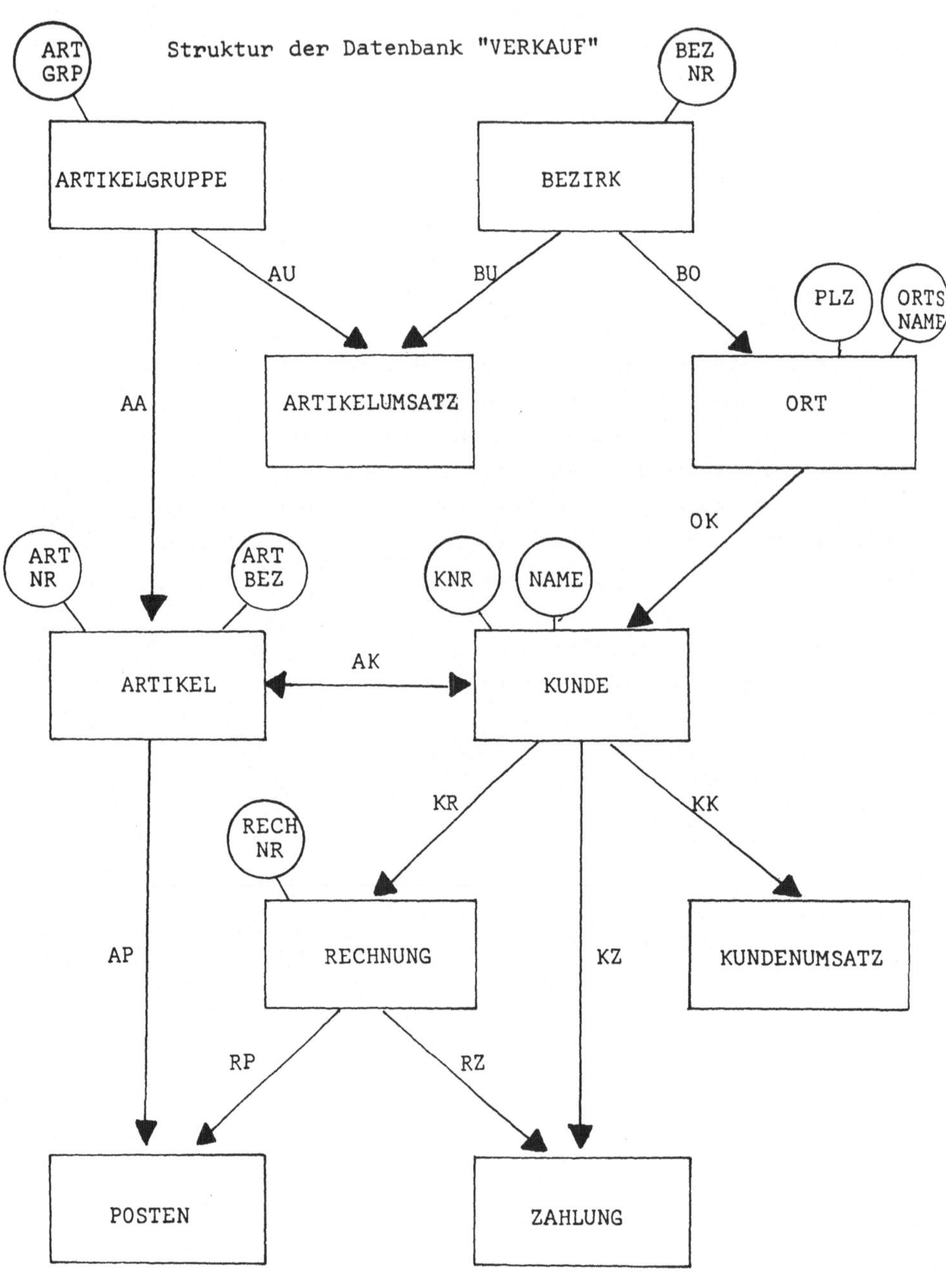

3. PHYSISCHE ORGANISATION

Nachdem der logische Aufbau einer NIMS-Datenbank festgelegt
ist, werden den einzelnen logischen Elementen, wie z.B.
Segment, Relation usw. vom Datenbankadministratir physische
Organisationsmethoden zugewiesen. Diese werden im folgenden
getrennt nach Einspeicherungsmethoden und Zugriffsmethoden
beschrieben.

3.1. Einspeicherungsmethoden

Für die physische Realisation eines Segmentes sind folgende
Punkte von Bedeutung:

- Welchem Speicherbereich soll das Segment zugeordnet
  werden?

- Wieviele Segmentexemplare werden erwartet?

- Wie sollen diese auf den zur Verfügung stehenden
  Platz verteilt werden?

- Soll eine Datenkompression durchgeführt werden?

Die Speicherbereiche für Nutzdaten werden bei NIMS als <u>Areas</u>
bezeichnet. Sie sind als Direktzugriffsdateien organisiert,
und der Datentransfer erfolgt blockweise. Jeder Area können
ein oder mehrere - im Extremfall alle - Segmente zugeordnet
werden. Dabei kann ein Area-Block mit Segmentexemplaren
mehrerer unterschiedlicher Segmente gefüllt werden.

Für die Ausnutzung des Speicherplatzes innerhalb einer Area
ist die Art der Datenverteilung von großer Bedeutung. Ge-
meinsames Ziel aller Einspeicherungsmethoden ist es, die
Daten möglichst gleichmäßig über die gesamte Area zu verteilen. Folgende Verfahren werden dazu von NIMS angeboten:

- DIRECT   Die Datenbankadresse (DBA) eines ein-
zuspeichernden Segmentexemplars wird
durch den Wert eines im Segment enthaltenen Items bestimmt.

- RANDOM   Die DBA wird durch eine (Hash-)Transfor-
mation eines im Segment enthaltenen Items
bestimmt. Dabei kann auch eine benutzereigene Transformationsroutine verwendet
werden.

- NEAR   Die DBA ist proportional zur DBA eines
Segmentexemplares eines anderen Segments.

- INPUT-
SEQUEN-
TIALLY   Die Segmentexemplare werden in äqui-
distanten Abständen in der Reihenfolge
ihrer Einspeicherung über die Area verteilt.

- ARBI -
TRARILY   Die DBA wird durch einen Zufallszahlengenerator ermittelt.

Wie schon erwähnt dienen alle Einspeicherungsmethoden nur zur
gleichmäßigen Verteilung der Segmentexemplare über eine Area.
Die Methoden DIRECT und RANDOM sind daher nicht mit den gleich-
namigen Zugriffsmethoden zu verwechseln.

Die physische Realisation eines Items geschieht durch die
Festlegung seines Datentyps. Die von NIMS unterstützten Daten-
typen nebst ihren COBOL-Entsprechungen sind in der umseitigen
Tabelle dargestellt.

Bei der Festlegung der Länge eines Items tritt häufig die
Problematik auf, daß die maximal zu erwartende Länge nicht bekannt ist oder die mittlere Länge erheblich übersteigt. In
beiden Fällen ist man zu einer Art "Überdimensionierung" ge-

NIMS-Datentypen

Type	COBOL	
Cnnn	PIC X (nnn)	Alphanumerisches Feld
Np [.q]	PIC S9(p) [V9(q)]	Dezimalzahl mit Vorzeichen in Charakterform
Up [.q]	PIC 9(p) [V9(q)]	vorzeichenfreie Dezimalzahl in Charakterform
Dp [.q]	PIC S9(p) [V9(q)]	Dezimalzahl mit Vorzeichen, gepackte Form
Bp [.q]	PIC S9(p) [V9(q)] COMP	Dezimalzahl mit Vorzeichen, binäre Form
FS	COMP-1	Gleitkommazahl einfach lang
FL	COMP-2	Gleitkommazahl doppelt lang

Datenkompression

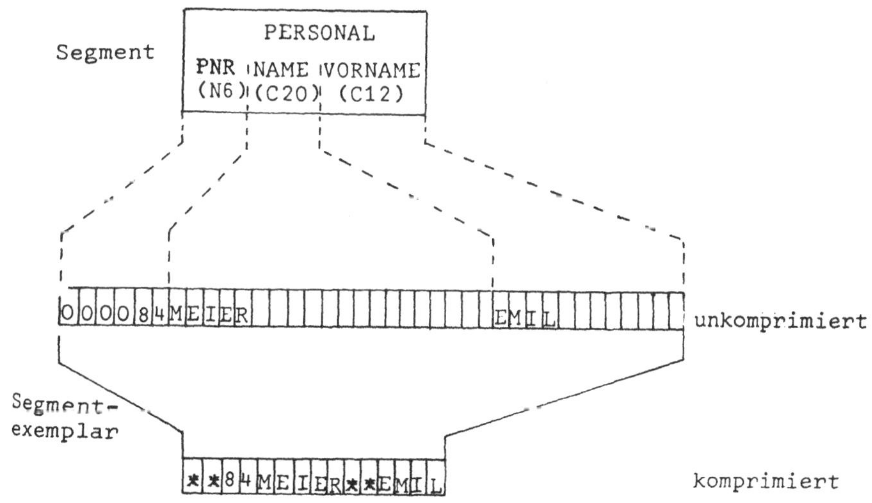

zwungen. Das geeigneste Mittel, diesem Dilemma zu entrinnen,
ist die Anwendung einer Datenkompression.

Die NIMS-Datenkompression ersetzt jeden String von drei oder
mehr gleichen Zeichen durch ein oder zwei "Steuerzeichen".
Dies geschieht ohne Rücksicht auf Itemgrenzen. Mehrere aufein-
anderfolgende unbesetzte Items werden dabei verschmolzen.

Für ein Segment können folgende Kompressionsmodi spezifiziert werden:

- Keine Kompression
- Unbedingte Kompression
- Bedingte Kompression (hierbei wird nur bei
        einer vorgegebenen Mindesteinsparung
        komprimiert)

Bei der Anwendung dieser Datenkompression können Items be-
denkenlos "überdimensioniert" werden, ohne damit Speicherplatz zu verschwenden.

In Verbindung mit der Typspezifikation der einzelnen Items
kann außerdem eine Plausibilitätskontrolle vereinbart werden.
NIMS sieht dafür zwei Möglichkeiten vor:

- Value-Check   Dabei wird ein Wertintervall für
                 das betreffende Item spezifiziert.

-Routine-Check   Die Wertprüfung erfolgt über eine
                 benutzereigene Routine.

Bei jedem Einspeicherungs- und Modifikationsvorgang werden vom
System die notwendigen Prüfungen durchgeführt bzw. veranlaßt.

3.2. Zugriffsmethoden

3.2.1. Unabhängiger Einstieg

Die physische Realisation eines unabhängigen Einstieg kann
bei NIMS auf drei Arten geschehen:

- DIRECT   Die Datenbankadresse wird aus dem Wert
  eines (numerischen) Items bestimmt.

- RANDOM   Die Datenbankadresse wird aus dem trans-
  formierten Wert eines Items gewonnen
  (Hash-Transformatio).

- INVERTED-FILE   Die Zuordnung Itemwert - DBA wird in
  einer invertierten Datei gespeichert.

Wie schon erwähnt, werden auch bei den Methoden DIRECT und
RANDOM eigene Zugriffsdaten verwendet. um diese unabhängig
von der Einspeicherung zu machen. Daher stellt bei DIRECT
der Wert des Key-Items noch nicht unmittelbar die DBA, sondern
den Platz in einer Tabelle von Datenbankadressen dar. Analoges
gilt für die Zugriffsart RANDOM. Dadurch wird der Zugriff nur
unwesentlich verlangsamt, da der Speicherbedarf für die ge-
nannte Tabelle gering ist und somit große Teile im NIMS-
Bufferpool resident sein können.

Physische Realisation eines Direct-Access

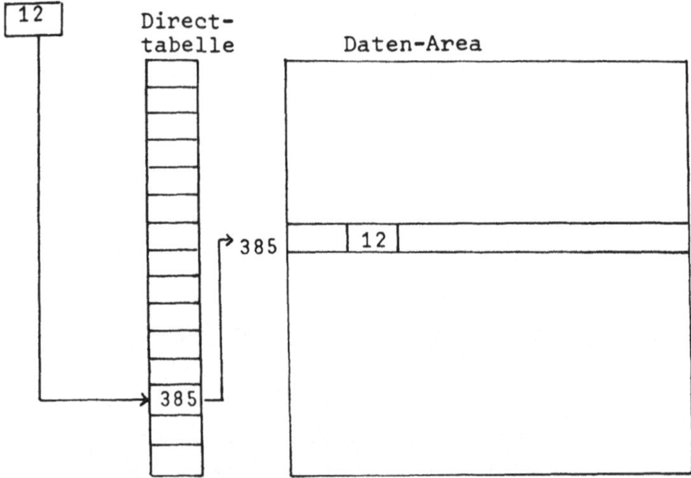

Besondere Erwähnung verdient in diesem Zusammenhang die besonders effiziente Schlüsselkompression bei invertierten Dateien.
Sie wirkt auf zwei Arten:

- Unterdrückung nachfolgender Blanks

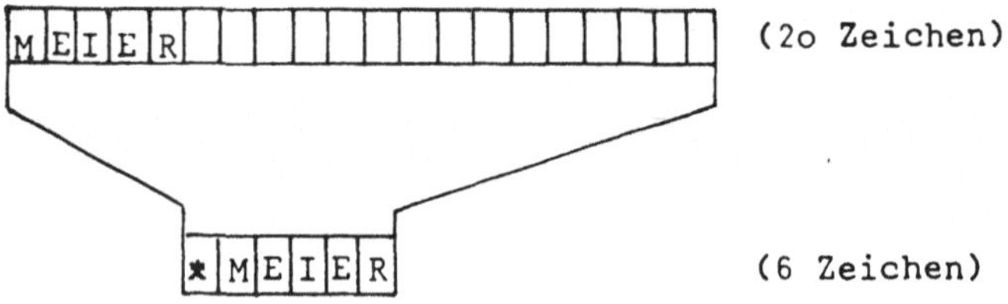

- Zusätzliche Vorgängerkompression

Dabei werden alle Zeichen am Beginn eines Schlüssels, die
mit dem Vorgängerschlüssel übereinstimmen, durch ein entsprechendes Steuerzeichen ersetzt. Beispiel:

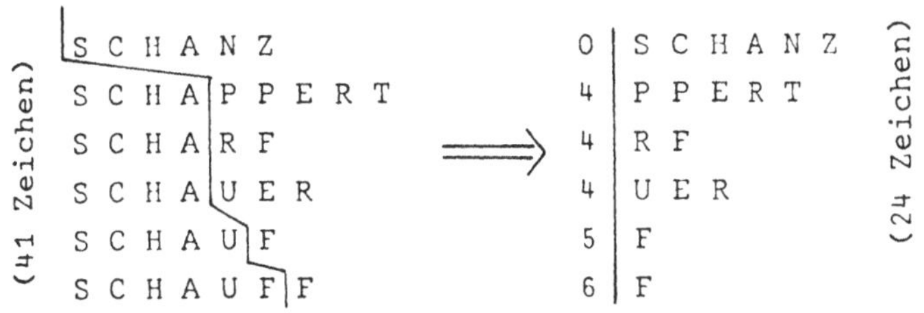

```
                S C H A N Z              0 | S C H A N Z
  (41 Zeichen)  S C H A P P E R T        4 | P P E R T      (24 Zeichen)
                S C H A R F     ======>  4 | R F
                S C H A U E R            4 | U E R
                S C H A U F              5 | F
                S C H A U F F            6 | F
```

Bei dieser Technik wird also die Eigenschaft der aufsteigenden Schlüsselsortierung zu einer wirksamen Kompression genutzt.

Die Einsparung an Speicherplatz beträgt bei dieser Methode
meist über 6o%.

3.2.2. Relation

Für die physische Realisation von Relationen stellt NIMS zwei
Implementationsarten zur Verfügung.

- INVERTED-FILE

  Eine invertierte Datei kann nicht nur dazu verwendet
  werden, eine Zuordnung der Form Itemwert - DBA herzustellen. Beim Einsatz zur Speicherung einer Relation
  tritt an die Stelle des Itemwertes die Datenbankadresse
  des Parentexemplars.

Mit dieser Methode können sowohl hierarchische als auch symmetrische Relationen verwirklicht werden.

- CHAIN

Segmentexemplare können über sechs verschiedene Kettenarten miteinander verbunden werden:

F	Forward	
FL	Forward mit Last-Child-Pointer	
FB	Forward/Backward	
FP	Forward	+ Parent-Pointer
FLP	Forward mit Last-Child-Pointer	+ Parent-Pointer
FBP	Forward/Backward	+ Parent-Pointer

4. DATENSCHUTZ

Der Datenschutz gewinnt in der heutigen Zeit zunehmend an Bedeutung. Für die Wirksamkeit der getroffenen Vorkehrungen sind dabei zwei Punkte von besonderer Bedeutung:

- Flexibilität und Bequemlichkeit bei der Anwendung
- Sicherheit gegen die Umgehung der Schutzmaßnahmen

Die Sicherheit der Maßnahmen spielt eine entscheidende Rolle, da Schutzvorkehrungen, die leicht zu umgehen sind, nicht die angestrebte Wirkung erzielen. Dies allein reicht jedoch noch nicht für einen wirksamen Schutz aus. Datenschutzeinrichtungen die schwer oder umständlich zu handhaben sind oder den praktischen Betrieb des Systems behindern, kommen erfahrungsgemäß selten zum Einsatz.

Der NIMS-Datenschutz erfüllt beide oben genannten Forderungen in hohem Maße. Durch folgende Einrichtungen wird das System gegen unbefugte Benutzung geschützt:

- Beim Eintritt in das System

  Der Eintritt in das System wird nur bei Angabe einer
  zulässigen Kombination von Benutzername und Paßwort gestattet. Diese sind im System wie alle Benutzerdaten in
  verschlüsselter Form gespeichert.

  Da die Möglichkeit besteht, daß einmal ein Paßwort bei
  der Eingabe (über Terminal oder Lochkarten) einem Fremden
  bekannt wird, kann jeder Benutzer sein Paßwort selbst
  ändern oder auch durch das System verändern lassen.
  Dazu spezifiziert er einen (benutzerspezifischen) Ver-
  änderungsalgorithmus, der bei jedem Systemeintritt
  ausgeführt wird.

- Inhaltsunabhängiger Datenschutz

  Der Zugriff auf alle Datenbankobjekte wird über sogenannte "Permissions" geregelt, die als natürliche Zahlen
  von 1 bis 999 dargestellt werden. Jeder Benutzer erhält
  eine oder mehrere Permissions, die in seinen Benutzerdaten festgehalten werden.

  In der Datenbankbeschreibung wird außerdem für jedes
  Objekt festgelegt, welche Permissions für welche Opera-
  tionen erforderlich sind. Geschützt werden können Areas,
  Segmente, Items, Relationen, wobei für jede der folgenden
  Operationen jeweils eine Permission festgelegt werden
  kann: Retrieve, Store, Modify, Delete, Insert, Remove.

  Zum OPEN-Zeitpunkt wird für alle angesprochenen Datenbankobjekte geprüft, ob der Benutzer über entsprechende
  Permissions verfügt (siehe umseitige Skizze).

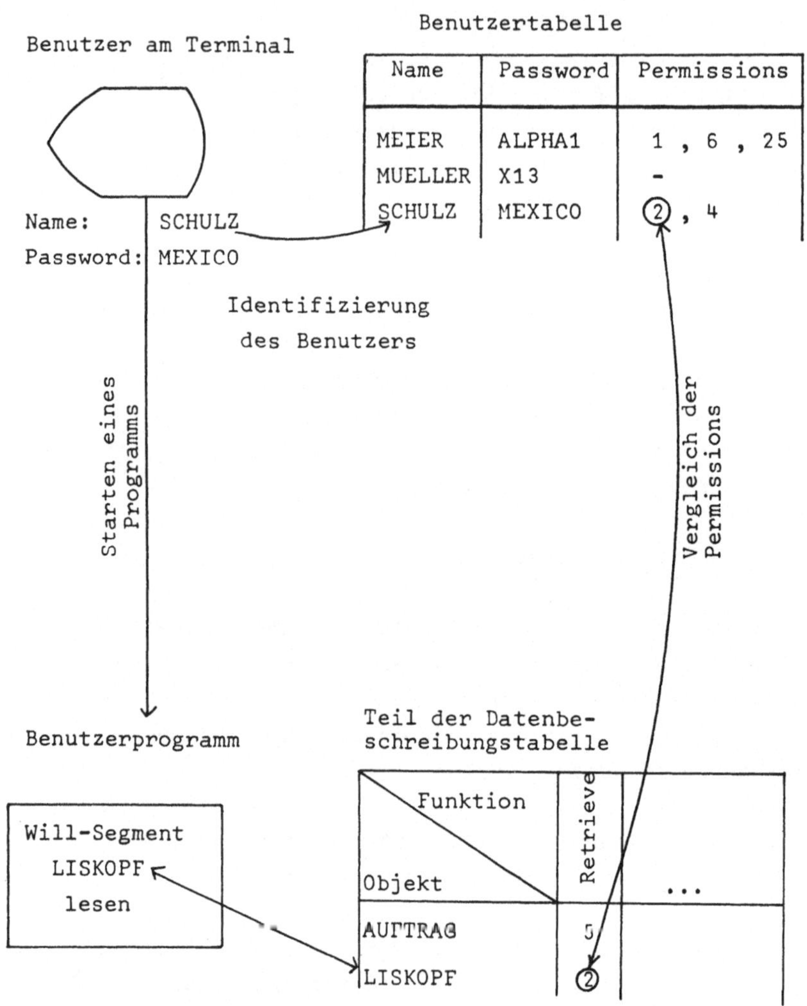
Benutzer am Terminal
Benutzertabelle
Name
Password
Permissions
MEIER   ALPHA1   1 , 6 , 25
MUELLER   X13   -
SCHULZ   MEXICO   2 , 4
Name: SCHULZ
Password: MEXICO
Identifizierung
des Benutzers
Starten eines
Programms
Vergleich der
Permissions
Benutzerprogramm
Teil der Datenbe-
schreibungstabelle
Will-Segment
LISKOPF
lesen
Funktion
Retrieve
Objekt
AUFTRAG   5
LISKOPF   2
Permission
erforderlich

- Inhaltsabhängiger Datenschutz

  Beim inhaltsabhängigen Datenschutz (nur für Items) wird
  bei jedem Zugriff auf das geschützte Item eine in der DDT
  spezifizierte Routine aktiviert. Dieser wird der Itemwert
  übergeben. Die Schutzroutine ermittelt daraus die zum
  Zugriff erforderliche Permission.

- Verschlüsselung

  Wird für eine Area das Attribut ENCODE vereinbart, so
  werden alle Daten beim Einspeichern in die Area verschlüsselt.

Dieses Gesamtkonzept bietet gleichzeitig starke Flexibilität,
hohen Benutzerkomfort und große Sicherheit.

5. DATENSICHERUNG

Unter Datensicherung sollen hier alle Mechanismen verstanden
werden, die zum Schutz einer Datenbank vor logischer und
physischer Zerstörung dienen. Dazu gehören zunächst die

- regelmäßige Back-up-copy (Dump) der Datenbank durch den
  Datenbankadministrator

- Führung eines Logtapes

Ersteres wird mit Hilfe einer NIMS-Utility durchgeführt,
während letzteres von NIMS auf Wunsch automatisch vorgenommen
wird. Dabei sind folgende Betriebsarten einstellbar:

- Bei einer Veränderung wird nur der alte Stand auf dem
  Logtape festgehalten.

- Bei einer Veränderung wird nur der neue Stand auf dem

Logtape festgehalten.

- Bei einer Veränderung werden der alte und neue Stand auf
  dem Logtape festgehalten.

Als Synchronisationspunkte auf dem Logtape dienen sogenannte
Checkpoints, die vom Benutzer gesetzt werden können. Nach einer
Zerstörung der Datenbank können dann entsprechend der Aufzeich-
nungsart des Logtapes folgende Regenerierungsläufe durchgeführt werden:

- Vorwärtsauswertung des Logtapes ausgehend von einer Back-
  up-copy bis zu einem Checkpoint

- Rückwärtsauswertung des Logtapes ausgehend vom aktuellen
  Stand bis zu einem Checkpoint

Beide Regenerierungsarten sind selektiv für bestimmte Teile
der Datenbank anwendbar. Einhergehend mit dem Regenerierungs-
vorgang oder auch separat kann eine Analyse des Logtapeinhalts
mit wählbarem Ausführlichkeitsgrad erstellt werden.

An dieser Stelle sei ein Optimierungsalgorithmus erwähnt, der
die Regenerierung wesentlich beschleunigt (ca. 7o% Zeitein-
sparung). Er sei an einem Beispiel beschrieben.

Logtape:

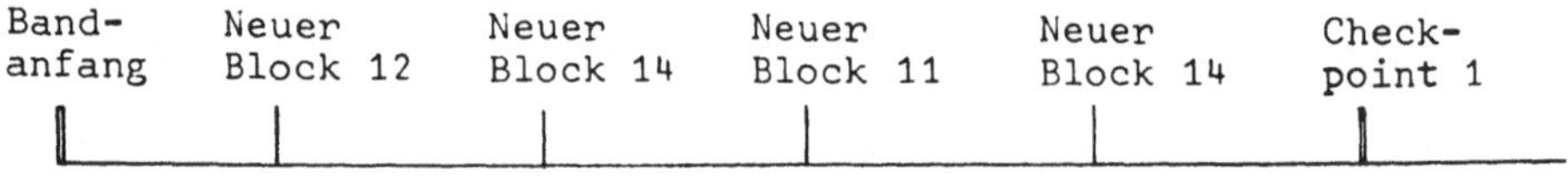

Bei einer Vorwärtsauswertung dieses Logtapes bis zum Checkpoint 1
würde Block 14 zweimal in die Datenbank zurückgeladen, dabei
das erste Mal vergeblich, da er beim zweiten Mal überschrieben
wird. Um dies zu vermeiden, wird das Logtape vom Checkpoint 1

angefangen rückwärts gelesen und bereits zurückgeschriebene
Blöcke auf dem Logtape übergangen. Analoges gilt natürlich für
die Rückwärtsauswertung.

Neben der Regenerierung nach erfolgter Zerstörung kommt dem
Schutz der Integrität einer Datenbank eine hohe Bedeutung zu.
Damit werden insbesondere die Probleme beim concurrent update
mehrerer Benutzer angesprochen.

Um Gruppen von NIMS-Befehlen geschlossen ausführen zu können,
verwendet NIMS das Transaktionenkonzept. Mehrere Befehle, die
zu einer Transaktion zusammengefaßt werden, werden entweder
alle oder gar nicht ausgeführt. Die während einer Transaktion
notwendige Sperrung von Daten für andere Benutzer erfolgt auf
Blockebene. Dadurch entstehende Deadlocks werden von NIMS
selbst erkannt und aufgelöst.

6. DATENUNABHÄNGIGKEIT

Eines der Hauptziele bei der Anwendung von Datenbanksystemen
ist es, alle Bearbeitungsprogramme unabhängig von der logischen
und physischen Struktur der Daten zu halten. Dieses Ziel wird
bei NIMS zum einen durch die Trennung der logischen Datenstrukturen von ihrer physischen Implementation erreicht, zum
anderen durch ein entsprechendes Benutzer-Interface. Zu dieser
Unabhängigkeit tragen im wesentlichen folgende beiden Punkte bei:

  - der dynamische Aufbau von Parameterblöcken aus der DDT

  - selektive Itemübertragung

Bei letzterer findet die Übertragung der Itemwerte eines
Segmentexemplars in den Benutzerbereich unter der Kontrolle
eines SITCB (selective item transmission control block) statt.
Dieser gibt an:

- auf welche Items der Benutzer zurückgreifen möchte

- in welche Reihenfolge die Items in seinen Bereich
  übertragen werden sollen

- welche Operationen er mit welchem Item durchführen möchte
  (Retrieve, Store, Modify).

Selbst Host-Language Programme sind dadurch unabhängig von der
Reihenfolge, Verschiebung oder Neuhinzunahme von Items in einem
Segment.

7. RESTRUKTURIERUNG

Nachträgliche Strukturänderungen sowohl physischer als auch
logischer Art können jederzeit mit Hilfe der NIMS-Restruktur-
ierungssoftware problemlos durchgeführt werden. Als Struktur-
änderung gelten beispielsweise:

- das Hinzufügen oder Entfernen von Items, Segementen,
  Areas, Relationen, unabhängigen Einstiegen, usw.

- Die Änderung der Attribute von Items, Segmenten, Areas,
  Relationen, unabhängigen Einstiegen, usw.

Jede Änderung des Datenbankaufbaus hat eine Änderung der DDT
zur Folge. In vielen Fällen ist das auch die einzige erforderliche Korrektur, wie z.B. bei der Hinzufügung eines Items.
In den restlichen Fällen, wo Änderungen an der Datenbank
selbst vorzunehmen sind, werden zur Durchführung dieser
Änderungen von der Restrukturierungssoftware automatisch
Programme generiert.

Wie bereits im vorigen Kapitel dargestellt wurde, brauchen
Anwenderprogramme bei einer Restrukturierung in der Regel nicht
geändert zu werden.

II. GIRL

1. ALLGEMEINE BESCHREIBUNG

GIRL (General Information Report Language) ist eine höhere
Programmiersprache, die u.a. die Handhabung von NIMS-Datenbanken gestattet und mit NIMS ein "self-contained system"
bildet. Sie ist speziell für den Batch-Betrieb geeignet und
enthält neben dem NIMS-Interface auch Sprachelemente zur
Weiterverarbeitung der Daten, die aus einer NIMS-Datenbank
gelesen werden:

- Integrierter Report-Writer
- Automatische Gruppenwechselsteuerung
- Tabellenverarbeitung
- Arithmetik, Schleifensteuerung, Prozeduren
- String handling
- Tabellensuchoperationen
- Graphische Ausgabe
- Macro facilities

Diese vielfältigen Möglichkeiten machen GIRL zu einer eigen-
ständigen Programmiersprache und heben es weit über den Rahmen
eines reinen Datenbank-Interfaces hinaus. Im folgenden werden
jedoch lediglich die Sprachelemente von GIRL beschrieben, die
zur Bearbeitung von NIMS-Datenbanken erforderlich sind.

2. RETRIEVAL-STATEMENTS

Zur Extraktion von Daten aus einer NIMS-Datenbank stehen die
Statements SELECT und LOCATE zur Verfügung. Anders als bei
der Host-Language-Programmierung können durch diese Statements
mehrere Segmente gleichzeitig angesprochen werden (bei Host-

Language-Programmierung maximal 2). Dabei braucht   dem
Benutzer die logische Struktur der Datenbank nicht bekannt
zu sein; sie wird vom GIRL-Compiler der DDT entnommen. In
GIRL-Programmen erscheinen von allen Datenbankobjekten fast
ausschließlich die Items. Dies ermöglicht auch Nicht-Daten-
bankspezialisten einen einfachen Umgang mit dem System.

Das SELECT-Statement dient zur Bearbeitung einer Menge von
"Datenbanksätzen", die alle einer vorgegebenen Bedingung
genügen. Mit "Datenbanksätzen" ist hier die Konkatenation
von Exemplaren mehrerer Segmente zu verstehen, die durch
Relationen miteinander verknüpft sind. Zur Bearbeitung werden
diese Sätze (auf Wunsch sortiert) in einer Programmschleife
zur Verfügung gestellt, deren Steuerung ebenfalls das SELECT-
Statement übernimmt.

SELECT-Syntax:

$$\text{SELECT} \quad \left[\text{condition}\right] \quad \begin{bmatrix} \text{ACCESS VIA dbitem} \\ \\ \text{SORT sortstring} \end{bmatrix}$$

$$\left[\text{DEACTIVATE relation} \quad \left[\text{relation2}\right] \quad \ldots \right] \quad ;$$

Beispiel:

```
PROGRAM A,  DATABASE  VK;
SELECT  ORTSNAME = 'KOELN' AND NAME = 'SCHMITZ',
        SORT  NAME  VORNAME

        PRINT  VORNAME  NAME  ANSCHRIFT;
NEXT;
END PROGRAM;
```

Dieses Programm z.B. würde die Anschriften aller Kölner Kunden
mit Namen Schmitz ausdrucken, und zwar sortiert nach Name und
Vorname. Dabei wird vom GIRL-Compiler geprüft, ob die
Sortierung durch die Ausnutzung der Eigenschaften von unabhängigen Einstiegen und Relationen der Datenbank geschehen
kann, oder ob eine echte Zwischensortierung erfolgen muß.

Das LOCATE-Statement dient zur Ermittlung <u>eines</u> Segmentexemplars (des LOCATE-Segments), das einer vorgegebenen Bedingung genügt. Diese Bedingung kann jedoch Items aus mehreren
Segmenten enthalten.

<u>LOCATE-Syntax:</u>

```
LOCATE SEGMENT segment1 WITH condition

      ⌈ACCESS VIA dbitem                      ⌉
      ⌊USING CURRENT SEGMENT segment2⌋

      ⌈DEACTIVATE relation1 ⌈relation2⌉ ... ⌉ ;
```

<u>Beispiel:</u>

```
LOCATE KUNDE WITH NAME " 'SCHMITZ' AND ORTSNAME = 'KOELN';
```

Existieren mehrere Segmentexemplare, die der angegebenen Bedingung genügen, so wird das zuerst gefundene zurückgeliefert.

Die in der Syntax dargestellte CURRENT-Klausel ermöglicht die
Bezugnahme auf bereits gefundene Segmentexemplare. Obiges
Beispiel könnte man damit auch so formulieren:

<u>Beispiel:</u>

```
LOCATE ORT WITH ORTSNAME = 'KOELN';

LOCATE KUNDE WITH NAME " 'SCHMITZ' USING CURRENT ORT;
```

3. UPDATE-STATEMENTS

Zum Update von NIMS-Datenbanken dienen die Statements STORE,
MODIFY, DELETE, INSERT und REMOVE. Die Anwendung von STORE
und MODIFY ist leicht den folgenden Beispielen zu entnehmen:

<u>Beispiel:</u>

```
    STORE   KUNDE;
            MOVE  'SCHMITZ'  TO NAME;
            MOVE  'ALFRED'   TO VORNAME;
    END STORE;
```

<u>Beispiel:</u>

```
    LOCATE   KUNDE  WITH   ORTSNAME  = 'KOELN'
                    AND   NAME       = 'SCHMITZ'
                    AND VORNAME      = 'GERTRUD';
    MODIFY KUNDE;
            MOVE 'MUELLER' TO NAME;
    END MODIFY;
```

Im letzten Beispiel wurde der Name von Fräulein Gertrud Schmitz
aus Köln in 'Gertrud Müller' geändert. Der eigentlichen Modi-
fizierung muß natürlich das Auffinden des zu modifizierenden
Segmentexemplars vorausgehen, hier in Form eines LOCATE-
Statements.

Das DELETE-Statement kann zu folgenden Zwecken eingesetzt werden:

- Löschen eines Segmentexemplars
- Löschen eines Segmentexemplars und aller davon über
  hierarchische Relationen unmittelbar und mittelbar abhängigen Segmentexemplare

- Löschen eines Segmentexemplars und aller davon über
  vollständige hierarchische Relationen unmittelbar und
  mittelbar abhängigen Segmentexemplaren.

<u>Beispiel</u>:

```
LOCATE  ORT  WITH  ORTSNAME = 'KOELN';
DELETE  ORT  ALL;
```

Diese beiden Statements bewirken die Löschung des Segmentexemplars 'KOELN' und aller damit verknüpften Kundenexemplare
usw. aus der Datenbank.

Die Statements INSERT und REMOVE dienen dem Update der
Relationen, soweit dies nicht schon bei anderen Statements,
wie z.B. STORE, automatisch geschieht.

<u>Beispiel</u>:

Es soll die Information, daß der Kunde mit der Kundennummer K den Artikel mit der Artikelnummer A gekauft hat,
in der Datenbank gespeichert werden.

```
LOCATE  KUNDE  WITH  KNR  = K;
LOCATE ARTIKEL WITH ARTNR = A;
INSERT INTO KAUFT-ARTIKEL;
```

Dies geschieht, indem das Paar von Segmentexemplaren der
Segmente KUNDE und Artikel in die (symmetrische) Relation
KAUFT-ARTIKEL eingesetzt wird.

4. UNTERSTÜTZUNG DURCH DEN GIRL-COMPILER

Neben den zum Teil sehr mächtigen Statements zur Bearbeitung
von NIMS-Datenbanken bietet der GIRL-Compiler dem Datenbank-

benutzer noch andere Erleichterungen:

Die Deklaration von Latenbankobjekten ist überflüssig. Im
PROGRAM-Statement wird lediglich der Kurzname der verwendeten
Datenbank spezifiziert. Daraufhin sind dem GIRL-Compiler die
Namen aller Datenbankobjekte, ihre Attribute, und die Daten-
bankstruktur "bekannt".

In vielen Anwendungsfällen besteht die Aufgabe, den Inhalt
eines Datenbankitems in einer Variablen zwischenzuspeichern.
Zur Deklaration einer "passenden" Variablen braucht der
Programmierer den Datentyp des Datenbankitems nicht zu kennen.
Die Klausel TYPE LIKE dbitem veranlaßt den GIRL-Compiler, den
Datentyp des Datenbankitems zu verwenden. Dies erhöht die
Unabhängigkeit des GIRL-Benutzers gegenüber Datenstruktur-
änderungen in der Datenbank.

Konzept der integrierten Datenbank IDS II

Dr. Paul Gara
Honeywell Bull Wien

1. Geschichte von IDS

1961   Entwicklung von IDS durch Charles W. Bachmann.

1963   Erste Fertigstellung von IDS im Assembler G 200.

1965/66 Fertigstellung von COBOL-IDS auf einer G 400/600.

1966   Im Rahmen von CODASYL Einrichtung der Arbeitsgruppe Data
         Base Task Group (DBTG). Ziel dieser Gruppe ist die Unter-
         suchung, welche neuen Funktionsmerkmale bei künftigen Er-
         weiterungen der COBOL-Sprache zu berücksichtigen sind.

1969   Die Arbeitsgruppe DBTG untersucht die sich aus der Unab-
         hängigkeit der Programme und Daten ergebenden Probleme.
         Es erfolgt eine zweite Veröffentlichung von Arbeitsergeb-
         nissen, in denen die Grundlagen der getrennten Sprache
         DDL, einer Sprache zurBeschreibung der Daten, und DML,
         einer Sprache für die Verarbeitung dieser Daten, dargestellt
         worden.

1975   Ankündigung der Integrierten Datenbank IDS II.

2. Integration der Daten

Über adressierbare Speicher können direkte Verbindungen zwischen
verschiedenen Informationen hergestellt werden, unabhängig davon,
wo sich diese Informationen innerhalb des Speichers befinden.

104

Die Gesamtheit der Informationen ist so organisiert, dass bei jeder Abfrage
oder Verarbeitung ein Direktzugriff auf die benötigten Bereiche erfolgen kann.

Am Beispiel eines Wörterbuchs kann dies dargestellt werden. Ist das Wörter-
buch in einer integrierten Datei enthalten, so können folgende Begriffe
direkt gefunden werden:

. Alle Wörter, die mit der Buchstabenkombination "Konst" beginnen (dies ist
  nicht weiter schwierig, da die Wörter wahrscheinlich in alphabetischer
  Reihenfolge geordnet sind.

. Alle Wörter mit einer bestimmten Wurzel oder alle Wörter mit derselben
  Wurzel wie ein gegebenes Wort.

. Alle Synonyme eines Worts usw.

Alle Informationen sind in Form von Sätzen gespeichert. Jeder Satz enthält
alle benötigten Informationen z.B. über einen Kunden, einen Mitarbeiter, ein
Konto, eine Rechnung, eine Bestellung oder einen Lagerartikel, usw.

Ansprechen der Informationen
Um Verbindungen zwischen den einzelnen Sätzen einer integrierten Datei her-
stellen zu können, wird jedem Satz bei seiner Aufnahme in die betreffende
Datei eine eindeutige, unverwechselbare Adresse zugeordnet. Auf jeder Seite
der Datei (= Page), die die Transporteinheit zwischen dem anzusprechenden
Medium und dem Hauptspeicher darstellt, können mehrere Sätze enthalten sein.
Um also einen Satz anzusprechen, ist die Nummer der Seite nicht ausreichend.

Der Seitennummer wird eine Zeilennummer angefügt, die sich von den auf dieser
Seite bereits zugeordneten Zeilennummern anderer Sätze unterscheiden muss.

Die Zeilennummer ist also ein einfacher Code zur Unterscheidung der einzelnen
auf einer Seite gespeicherten Sätze.

Seitennr. (Page-Nr.)	Seitenkopf	
Zeile 1		Zeile 2
Zeile 7		
Zeile 5	Zeile 3	
Zeile 8		Zeile 12

Wenn die Adresse (Seiten- und Zeilennummer) eines Satzes dem System bekannt ist, so kann ein Direktzugriff erfolgen. Wird der Satz aus der Datei gelöscht, steht die Adresse wieder für einen neuen Satz zur Verfügung, und der von dem gelöschten Satz belegte physische Bereich wird durch Verschieben der auf der Seite nachfolgenden Sätze wieder neu gewonnen.

Verknüpfen der Sätze untereinander

Um eine Verbindung zwischen den Sätzen A und B herzustellen, genügt es, wenn einer der beiden Sätze die Adresse des anderen enthält. A enthält beispielsweise die Adresse von B.

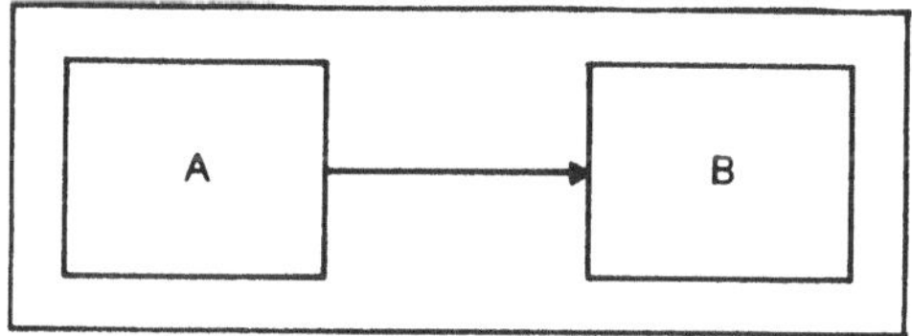

In gleicher Weise kann eine Verbindung von C und B, D und C, E und B hergestellt werden, ebenso eine Verbindung der nachstehend gezeigten Art:

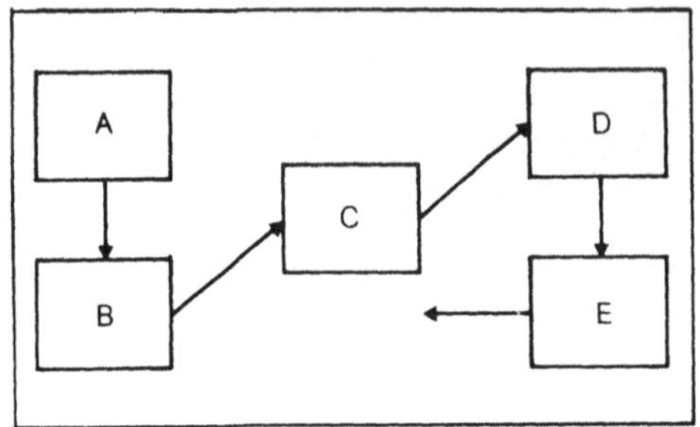

Dazu ist zu bemerken, dass diese Verbindungen, die dadurch möglich werden,
dass jeder Satz eine eigene, unverwechselbare Adresse besitzt, nichts über
die physische Gruppierung der Sätze A, B, C, D und E aussagt. Jeder dieser
Sätze kann sich an einem beliebigen Platz innerhalb der Datenbank befinden.

In dem oben gezeigten Beispiel kann man, wenn man den Satz B direkt angesprochen hat (da dessen Adresse bekannt war), daran anschliessend sukzessive
die Sätze C, D und E aufgreifen, nicht aber A, da B nicht die Adresse von A
enthält.

Um diesen Fall zu vermeiden, wird diese Satzfolge als Kette aufgebaut; dabei
enthält der letzte Satz wieder die Adresse des ersten.

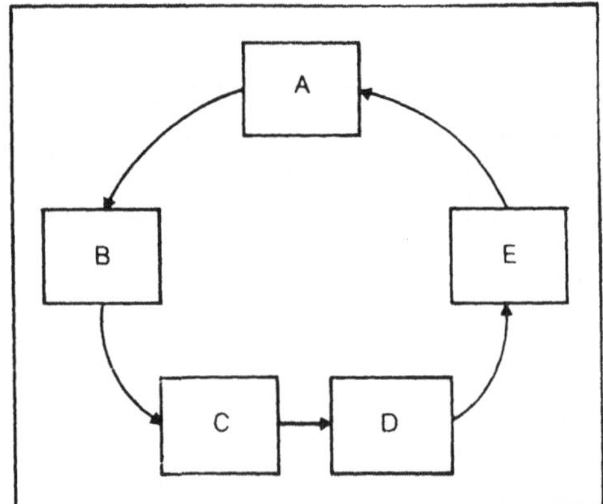

Enthält jeder Satz in der Kette nicht nur die Adresse des nachfolgenden
Satzes, sondern die des vorangegangenen und die des ersten Satzes, so erhält
man eine Gruppierung, die bei IDS II als "Set" bezeichnet wird.

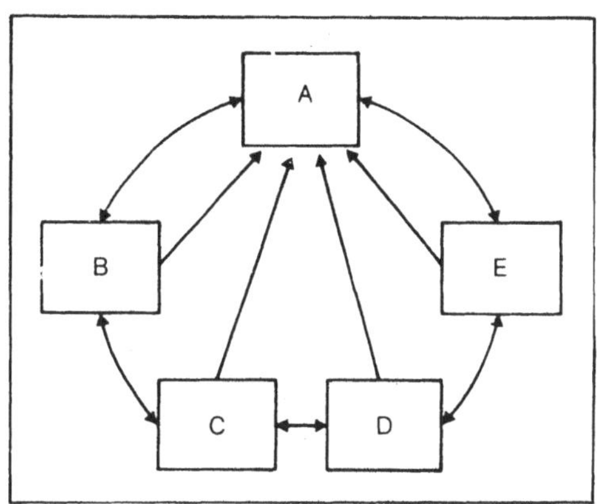

Durch diese Struktur des "Set" ist es möglich, alle mit dem betreffenden Satz
in Verbindung stehenden Sätze anzusprechen, gleichgültig, wo sich diese Sätze
im Speicher befinden.

Ein Satz kann Bestandteil mehrerer "Sets" sein, d.h. dass ein Satz in verschiedenen Gruppierungen vorkommen kann.

Beispiel:

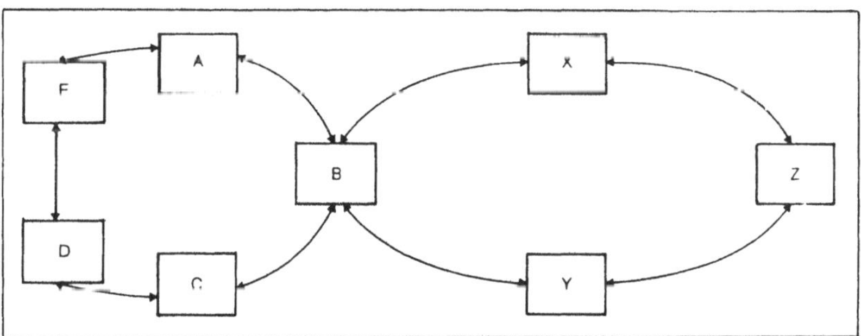

3. "Owner"- und "Member"-Sätze

Ein "Set" setzt sich aus zwei Arten von Sätzen zusammen:
. Einem für das betreffende Set spezifischen Satz, dem sog. Owner-Satz
  (Stammsatz);
. einer beliebigen Anzahl von Sätzen, die als Member-Sätze (Teil-Sätze
  bezeichnet werden.

Beispiele:

- Ein Kunde und seine Bankkonten
- Ein Bankkonto und seine Bewegungen
- Ein Artikel und seine Besteller
- Ein Kunde und seine Bestellartikel
- Eine Baugruppe und ihre Teile

Grundsätzlich enthält der Owner-Satz alle Informationen, die den Member-
Sätzen gemeinsam sind. Es ist also nicht erforderlich, diese Informationen
in den Member-Sätzen zu wiederholen. Ist beispielsweise ein Owner-Satz
mit der Kontonummer vorhanden, so enthalten die Sätze mit den Kontobe-
wegungen diese Nummer nicht mehr, da sie zum gleichen Set gehören.
Ein Satz kann sowohl Member in einem Set als auch Owner in einem anderen
Set sein.

Beispiel:

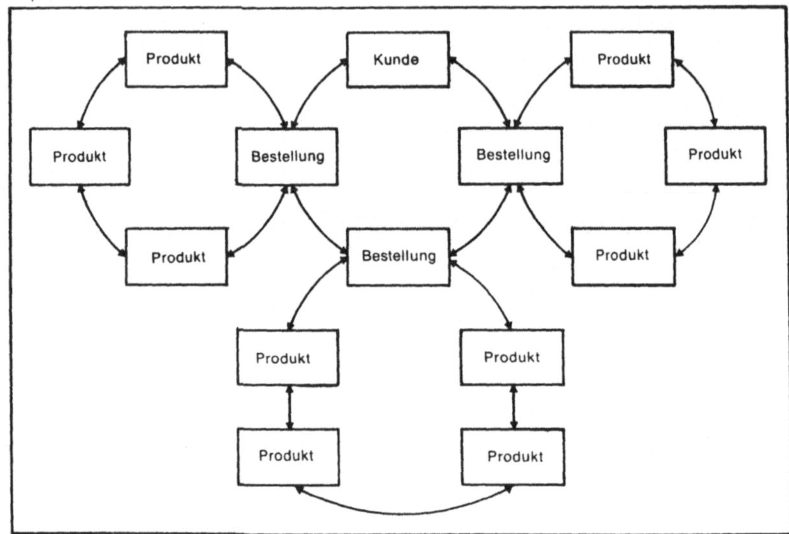

Anmerkung:

In diesem Schaubild sind die direkten Member-Owner-Beziehungen nicht dargestellt. Die Bestellsätze sind Member-Sätze in dem Set, dessen Owner die
Kundensätze darstellen.

Die Bestellsätze enthalten Informationen wie die Nummer der Bestellung, das
Lieferdatum, die Transportart, den Gesamtwert der Bestellung, usw.

Jede Bestellung enthält eine variable Anzahl von Bestellzeilen (Bestellungen
für verschiedene Produkte), die durch die Produktsätze dargestellt werden.

Jeder Produktsatz enthält den Code des Produkts wie die Bestellmenge, usw.

Jeder Bestellsatz ist Owner in einem Set, dessen Member-Sätze die Produktsätze darstellen.

Es ist möglich, ein leeres Set aufzubauen, d.h. ein Set ohne Member-Sätze.
Das könnte beispielsweise ein Kunde sein, der keine Bestellung aufgegeben
hat.

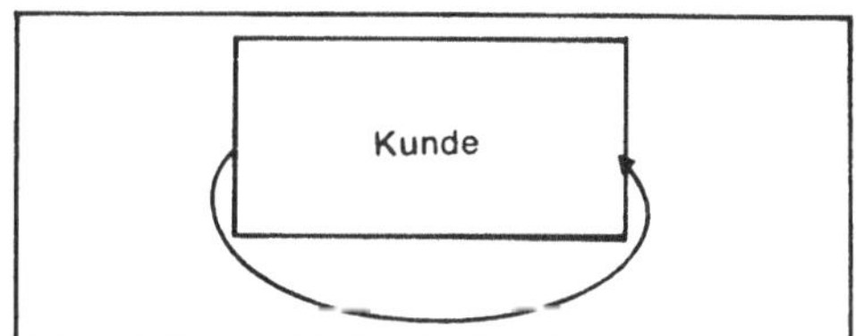

Es ist jedoch andererseits nicht möglich, ein Set ohne Owner-Satz aufzubauen.

II. INFORMATIONSSTRUKTUREN

1. Darstellung der Strukturen

Wenn die Darstellung der oben benutzten Sets mit zwei oder drei Satzarten, die innerhalb etwa gleich vieler Sets untereinander verbunden
sind, auch für einfache Dateien ausreichend ist, ist sie für komplexere
Informationsstrukturen jedoch absolut unzureichend.

Die im folgenden gezeigten Diagramme dienen dazu, in kompakter und ver-
einfachter Form solche komplexere Informationsstrukturen zu beschreiben.

Diese Art der Darstellung ist deshalb bedeutsam, weil sie Strukturen
darstellt, die bisher aufgrund der in Systemen mit sequentiellem
Zugriff vorgenommenen künstlichen Aufteilung von Informationen nicht
dargestellt werden konnten.

In dem folgenden Diagramm ist das Rechteck das Symbol für eine Satzart, und der Pfeil eine Art von Set, z.B.:

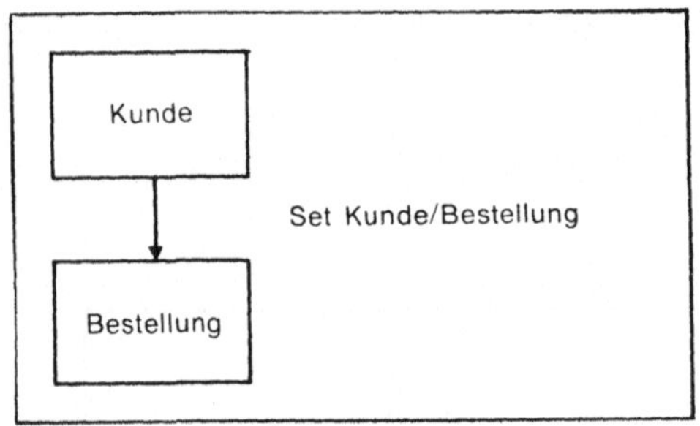

Dadurch wird folgendes Verhältnis dargestellt:

- Die Datei enthält eine gewisse Anzahl Kundensätze und Bestellsätze;
- Jeder Kundensatz ist Owner in einem Set "Kunde-Bestellung", dessen
  Members sich aus Bestellsätzen zusammensetzen.

Umgekehrt ist
    jeder Bestellsatz Member in einem Set "Kunde-Bestellung", bei dem
    ein Kundensatz den Owner darstellt.

Wir wollen nun die Sätze in der Datei betrachten, die die Rechnungen
darstellen. Dabei gibt es zwei Arten des Aufbaues:

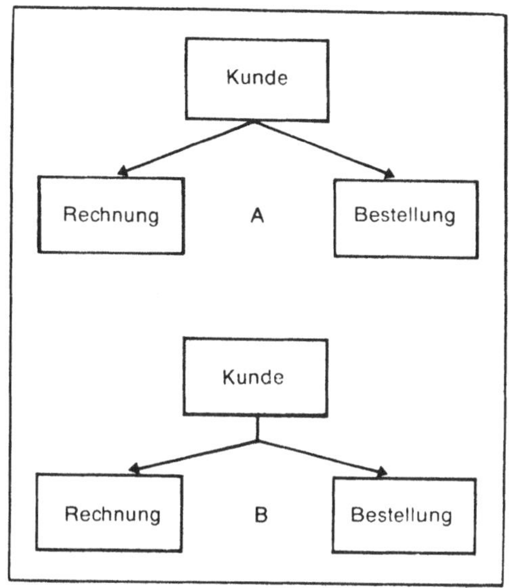

In A ist jeder Kundensatz Owner in zwei Sets. Ein Set enthält seine Rechnungen, das andere seine Bestellungen. Es wäre jedoch auch möglich, alle Bestellungen und Rechnungen eines Kunden in einem gemeinsamen Set aufzunehmen (B).

Es sollen nun die Produktsätze eines Auftrags (je einer pro Bestellzeile) hinzugefügt werden. Dadurch ergibt sich der folgende Aufbau:

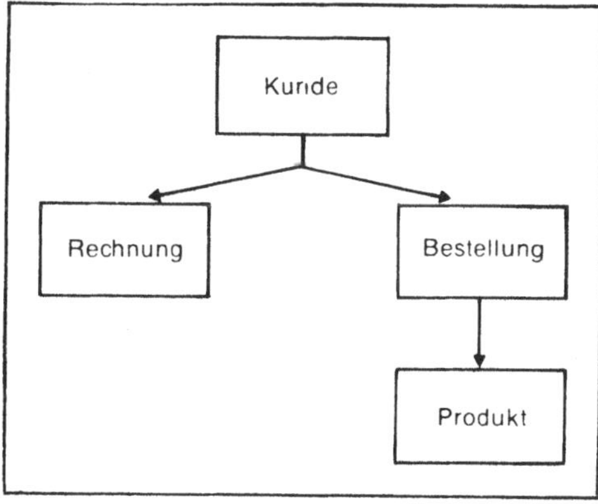

Wir erhalten somit vier Satzarten und zwei Arten von Sets.

Wird nun ein Satz "Lagerbestand" für jede Art von Verkaufsprodukt
hinzugefügt, kann die Verwaltung des Lagerbestandes dadurch erfolgen,
dass in einem Set alle Bestellungen für ein bestimmtes Produkt
zusammengefasst werden:

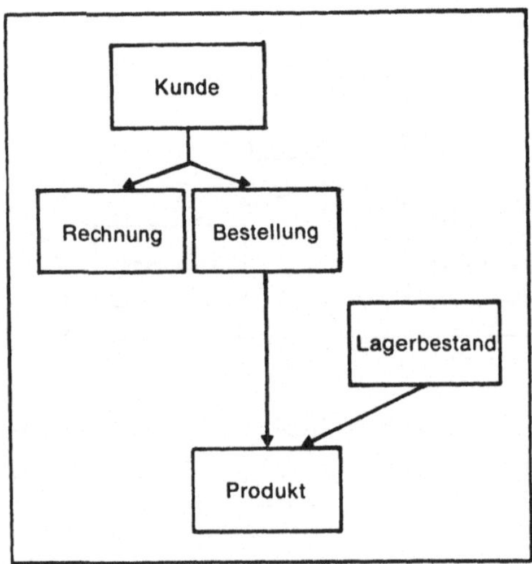

Das obige Schema zeigt eine Informationsstruktur, die in IDS-Anwendungen
von besonderer Bedeutung ist:

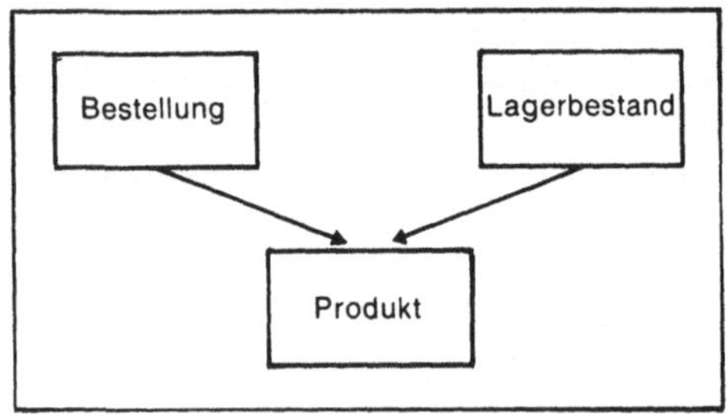

Der Produktsatz ist Member in zwei Sets. Diese Struktur ist sehr
verbreitet, wenn sie auch nicht immer erkannt wird. Wir müssten nun
zwei Dateien mit sequentiellem Zugriff erstellen. In diesem Fall muss
eine Datei "Bestellungen" und eine Datei "Lagerbestand" erstellt
werden, wobei sich gewisse Informationen in beiden Dateien überschneiden.

IDS gestattet uns nun die Organisation dieser Informationen in einer
gemeinsamen Datei, wodurch der Umfang der Datei gleichzeitig vermindert
wird.

Alle Informationen über eine Bestellung (Bestellnr., Datum, Lieferdatum, Gesamtbetrag, usw.) werden nur einmal in einem Satz "Bestellung"
gespeichert; alle Informationen zur Art eines Produkts (Codenummer,
Beschreibung, Einzelpreis, Mindestabnahmemenge, usw.) befinden sich in
einem Satz "Lagerbestand". Es ist nicht mehr erforderlich, diese
Informationen in den Produkt-Sätzen zu wiederholen, da jeder dieser
Sätze sowohl mit einem Bestellsatz als auch mit einem Lagerbestandssatz verknüpft ist. Die einzige Information, die im Produktsatz
erforderlich ist, ist die effektive Bestellmenge.

Diese integrierte Datei kann sowohl für die Lagerbestandsführung als
auch für die Lieferung bestellter Waren und für die Fakturierung
herangezogen werden.

2. Verknüpfungssätze

Jeder Produktsatz stellt eine Beziehung zwischen einem Bestellsatz
und einem Lagerbestandssatz her. Solche Sätze werden als Verknüpfungssätze bezeichnet.

In einigen Fällen enthalten die Verknüpfungssätze keine Informationen,
sondern dienen nur dazu, Beziehungen zu anderen Satzarten herzustellen.
In der folgenden Struktur können beispielsweise gefunden werden:

. Alle von einem bestimmten Lieferanten gelieferten Artikel
  (Produkte)

. Alle Lieferanten, die einen bestimmten Artikel liefern.

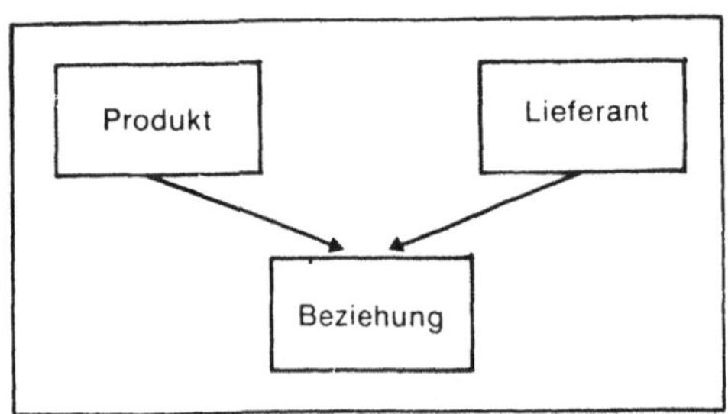

In diesem Fall dient der Verknüpfungssatz lediglich als Verbindungs-
glied zwischen einem Produkt und dem Lieferanten; man könnte statt
dessen in diesen Sätzen auch die Mindestliefermenge, die übliche
Lieferzeit, usw. speichern.

3. Doppelverknüpfung

Es ist auch möglich, mit einem Verknüpfungssatz zwei Sätze der gleichen
Art miteinander zu verbinden (im vorangegangenen Beispiel wurde eine
Verbindung zwischen zwei verschiedenen Arten von Sätzen hergestellt).

Nehmen wir beispielsweise an, dass es verschiedene Produkte gleicher
Art gibt, so dass bei ungenügendem Bestand des einen Produkts ersatz-
weise auf ein anderes zurückgegriffen werden kann. In einem solchen
Fall wird für jedes Paar gleichartiger Produkte ein Verknüpfungssatz
erstellt.

Die hier beschriebene Struktur wird im folgenden Beispiel unter A dargestellt. Die Darstellung B wird nicht benutzt, da hier dieselbe Satzart zweimal dargestellt werden muss, was nicht logisch ist.

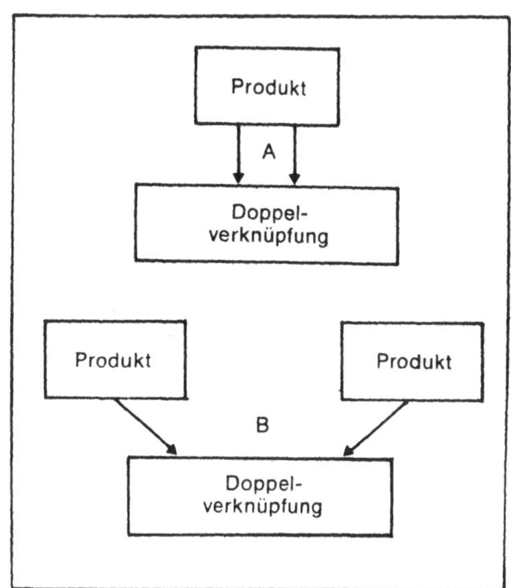

Die gezeigte Verknüpfungsart wird speziell in der Fertigung angewendet:
in Stücklistenverwaltung und ähnlichen Bereichen, wo aus Teilen und Baugruppen komplexe Fertigungserzeugnisse hergestellt werden.

Die Datei, in denen die Gesamtheit der Teile enthalten ist, muss unbedingt die folgenden beiden Informationen geben können:

. Eine Liste aller für die Herstellung eines anderen Teils benötigten
  Teile.
. Eine Liste aller Teile, in denen ein bestimmtes Teil Verwendung findet.

Die IDS-Lösung ist ebenso logisch wie einfach:

116

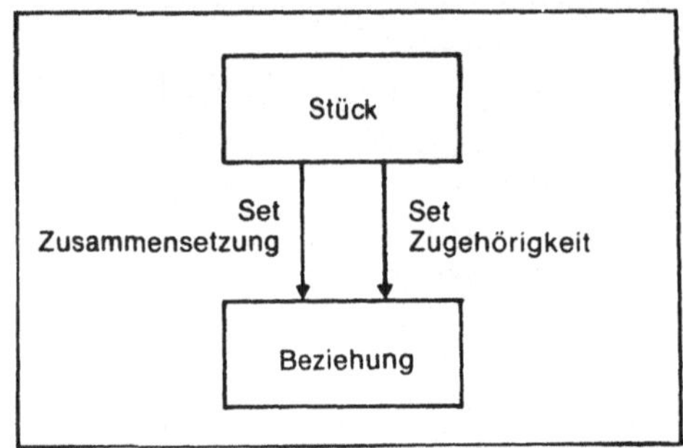

Betrachten wir bei einem Teil X das Set "Zugehörigkeit", so finden wir
dort alle Teile, die direkt oder indirekt dieses Teil benutzen. Dagegen
finden wir im Set "Zusammensetzung" alle Teile, die zur Herstellung von
X erforderlich sind.

Üblicherweise enthält eine solche Datei auch Informationen über den Lagerbestand und die Lieferanten jedes Teils.

Die Fortschreibung dieser Datei wird dadurch erleichtert, dass jedes Teil
durch einen eigenen Satz dargestellt wird.

Diese Art der Anwendung ist bei Speichern mit sequentiellem Zugriff sehr
schwierig durchzuführen, da sie mehrere Durchgänge beim Fortschreiben,
Sortieren und Neuordnen erfordert.

Wir zeigen hier die detaillierte Darstellung einer kleinen Datei, die nur
6 Teile umfasst, und zwar mit den folgenden Beziehungen:

A setzt sich aus B, C und F zusammen
B setzt sich aus D und E zusammen
C setzt sich aus E und F zusammen
E und F sind Teile, die gekauft werden müssen.

Die Sets "Zugehörigkeit" sind in dieser Darstellung gestrichelt gezeichnet, während die Sets "Zusammensetzung" durchgezogene Linien haben.

Die Verknüpfungssätze in diesem Beispiel enthalten die Mengen der Teile,
die nötig sind, um eine Einheit eines zusammengesetzten Teils herzustellen.

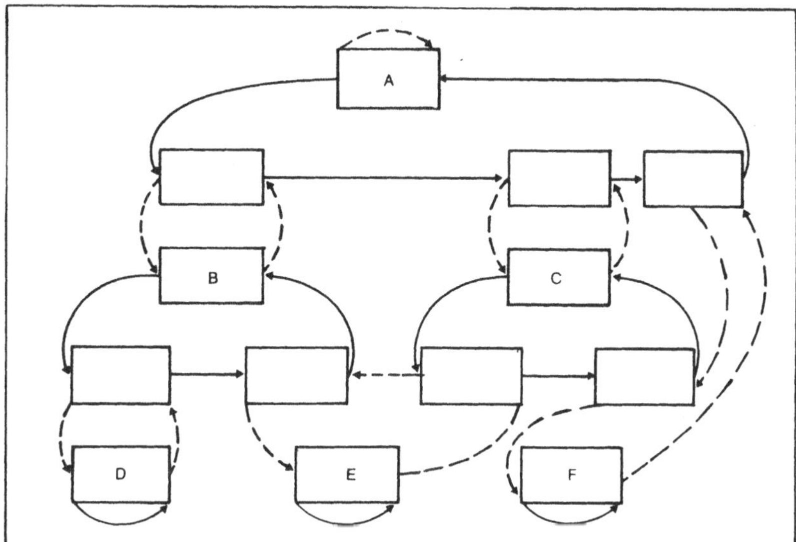

4. Physische Satzanordnung in IDS II

Aufbau der IDS II-Datei

Die logische IDS II-Datei setzt sich aus einer Anzahl physisch unabhängiger
Dateien zusammen, die als Areas bezeichnet werden. Diese wiederum sind
unterteilt in Pages.

Das Prinzip der Aufteilung der Datenbank in physisch unabhängige Dateien
bringt eine Reihe von Vorteilen:

118

. Die Zugriffssicherungen können von Datei zu Datei variieren,

. Bei Änderung oder Zerstörung einer Datei kann die Wiederherstellung
erfolgen, ohne dass die Bearbeitung anderer Dateien unterbrochen
werden muss.

. Die Grösse der Pages kann von Datei zu Datei variieren, je nach der
Art der Sätze, die in der betreffenden Datei gespeichert werden.

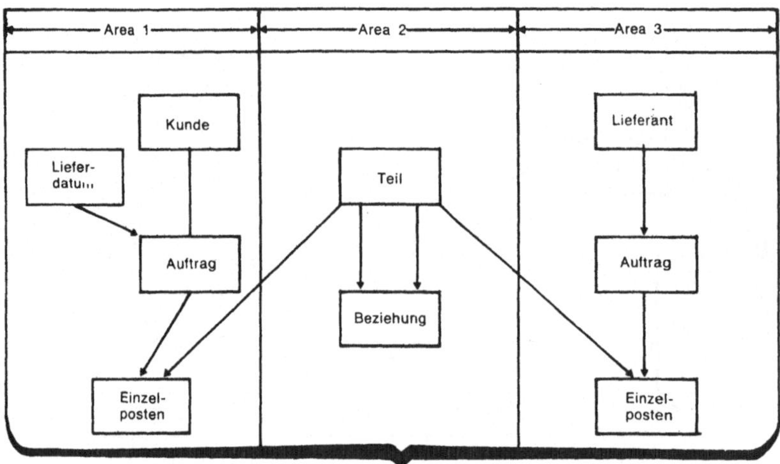

Die Page

Die Page stellt die Transporteinheit zwischen Massenspeicher und Zentralspeicher dar. Alle Pages einer bestimmten Area sind von gleicher Länge.

Die Pages sind nach dem UFAS-Prinzip (Unified File Access System) aufgebaut, d.h. ihr Aufbau entspricht dem der Standard-Dateien der Serie 60.
Jede Page setzt sich aus drei Teilen zusammen:

. Der Kopf der Page, der als Verwaltungszone hauptsächlich die Nummer der
Page, den zur Verfügung stehenden Platz und die Anzahl der nicht benutzten
Zeilen enthält.

. Der Hauptteil der Page, der als Benutzerzone dient und die einzelnen
Sätze aufnimmt.

. Am Page-Ende enthält ein Pointer pro Zeile die Adresse des Satzes relativ
zum Page-Beginn mit der betreffenden Zeilennummer in der Page.

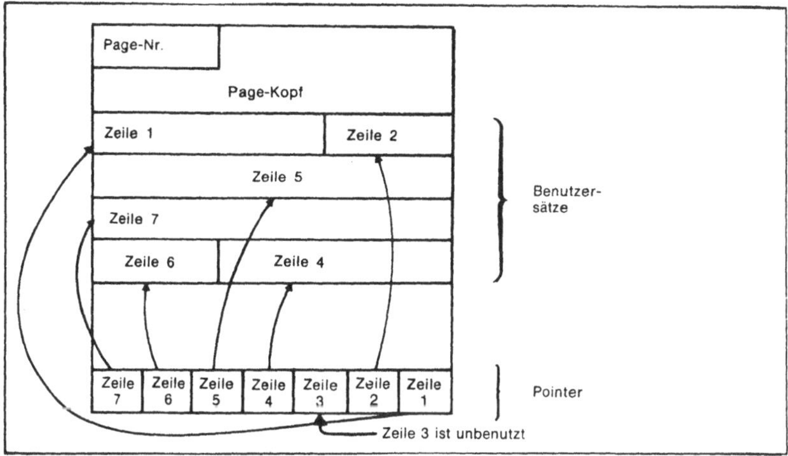

<u>Die IDS Adresse</u>

Diese setzt sich aus einer Verbindung von Pagenummer und Zeilennummer
zusammen.

Bei jeder Art von Satz hat diese Adresse eine durch die Software definierte
Länge von 2, 3 oder 4 Zeichen (Bytes), je nachdem wieviele Adressen zur
Aufnahme aller Sätze in diesem Bereich vorgesehen sind.

120

5. Verteilung der Sätze

Die Verteilung der Artikel auf die verschiedenen Areas der Datenbank kann
erfolgen nach:

. Satzart
   Beispiel: 1 bis n Areas enthalten die Sätze "Kunde"
             1 bis n Areas enthalten die Sätze "Produkt"
             1 bis n Areas enthalten die Sätze "Lieferant"

. Merkmal für einen bestimmten Typ.
   Beispiel: Ein Merkmal des Satzes "Kunde" ist die Nummer des Vertriebs-.
             bereiches, zu dem er gehört.
   Die Sätze "Kunde" können also je nach Vertriebsbereich auf verschiedene
   Areas aufgegliedert werden.

. Aktivitätsgrad eines bestimmten Typs.
   Sowohl bei den Kunden einer Bank als auch bei den Fabrikationserzeug-
   nissen eines Herstellers oder einem Lagerbestand kann zwischen aktiven
   und ruhenden Elementen unterschieden werden. Durch Aufgliederung auf verschiedene Areas nach dem Grad ihrer Aktivität kann bei der Bearbeitung
   von Sätzen ein Zugriffsvorrang auf die aktivsten Sätze eingeräumt werden.

   Position eines Satzes in Beziehung zu dessen Owner-Satz.

   Das System kann beispielsweise dazu veranlasst werden, den Auftrag eines
   Kunden möglichst nah bei diesem Kundensatz zu speichern.

   Die Aufträge gehören also derselben Area an wie der Kunde und, sofern dies
   möglich ist, sogar derselben Page.

   Die gleiche Technik kann angewendet werden, um die Bestellposten-Zeilen
   eines Auftrags zusammenzufassen.

   Es können somit Satzfamilien gebildet werden, die normalerweise in derselben Programmfolge verarbeitet werden und die mit einem einzigen
   physischen Zugriff auf die Datenbank in den Zentralspeicher übertragen

werden können.

6. Organisation der Sätze in den Areas

Bei jeder Satzart kann der Benutzer die Methode der gewünschten Speicherung,
die als "physische Speicherung" bezeichnet wird, und die Methode der Einfügung des Satzes in die Struktur des Informationssystem, die als "logische
Speicherung" bezeichnet wird, angeben.

. Physische Speicherung:
  Hier stehen dem Benutzer drei verschiedene Möglichkeiten zur Verfügung:

  - Kalkulierte Speicherung (vergleichbar Indexsequentiell).
    Ein Algorithmus des Systems konvertiert den Ordnungsbegriff (z.B.
    die Kundennummer) in eine Datenbankadresse, wobei die Synonyma vom
    System verwaltet werden. Diese Art der Speicherung gilt für Sätze,
    die punktuell verarbeitet werden sollen und als Einsprungspunkt in
    eine Satzfamilie dienen.

  - Sekundäre Speicherung.
    Jeder Member-Satz eines Sets kann in der Nähe des entsprechenden
    Owner-Satzes gespeichert werden. Die Gesamtheit der Member-Sätze,
    die ein Set darstellen, werden also innerhalb der Page, die den
    Owner-Satz enthält, physisch abgespeichert.

  - Primäre Speicherung (vergleichbar Random).
    Der Benutzer gibt dem System die Adresse an, wo der betreffende Satz
    eingefügt werden soll. Damit können zum Beispiel Tabellen erstellt
    werden. Hier bietet sich noch eine Reihe anderer interessanter
    Möglichkeiten, deren Beschreibung den Rahmen dieser Broschüre über-
    schreiten würde.

. Logische Speicherung:
  Ist ein Satz in der Datenbank physisch gespeichert, so müssen die Ketten-
  verbindungen hergestellt werden, die die Einfügung des Satzes in die
  Struktur des Informationssystems gestatten.

Für jedes Set, dem der Satz angehört, muss die Art der Einfügung definiert werden. In dem nachfolgenden Beispiel "Aufträge-Kunden" z.B. kann ein neuer Satz "Auftrag" eingefügt werden:

- Am Beginn des Sets (FIRST); das Set wird also nach Eingang der Aufträge in absteigender Reihenfolge geordnet.

- Am Ende des Sets (LAST); das Set wird also nach Eingang der Aufträge in aufsteigender Reihenfolge geordnet.

- Nach Auftragsnummer oder Lieferdatum (SORTED). Ein solches Set, das nach einem im Satz selbst enthaltenen Kennzeichen sortiert wird, wird als "sortiertes" Set bezeichnet.

- Vor (PRIOR) oder nach (NEXT) dem letzten Satz des Sets, auf das das Programm zugegriffen hat.

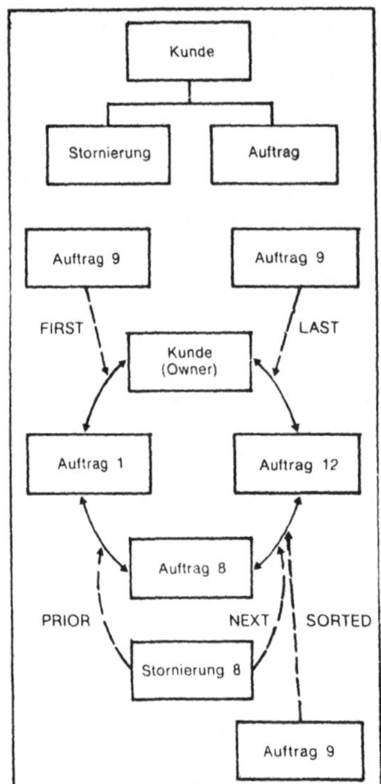

Diese beiden Modi sind dann interessant, wenn mit einem Set gearbeitet wird, das· verschiedene Arten von Members hat.

Beispielsweise könnte die Stornierung eines Auftrags vor oder
hinter den entsprechenden Auftrag gespeichert werden.

7. Zugriffsmethoden

Eine Anforderung des Benutzers an die Datenbank kann mehr oder weniger
komplexer Natur sein. Je nach der für die Anforderung gewählten Befehls-
struktur wird intern eine Reihe von Grundfunktionen des Zugriffsmoduls
ausgeführt. Dabei stehen folgende Grundfunktionen zur Verfügung:

a - Direkter Zugriff auf einen Satz

   . Satz mit kalkulierter Speicherung:
   Der Ordnungsbegriff (z.B. die Kundennummer des gesuchten Satzes
   wird dem IDS-Algorithmus zur Verfügung gestellt, der dann - wie bei
   der Speicherung - diesen Ordnungsbegriff in eine Datenbankadresse
   übersetzt.

   . Satz mit primärer Speicherung:
   Bei diesen Sätzen kennt der Benutzer die Datenbank-Adresse. Das
   Suchen eines Satzes ist daher problemlos.

b - Sequentieller Zugriff auf einen Satz

   . Logische Folge: Die Suchfolge wird durch die Pointer der Sets gesteuert.

Im nachfolgenden Beispiel sind alle Aufträge eines Kunden dadurch zu finden,
dass einfach das Set Kunde/Aufträge durchlaufen wird.

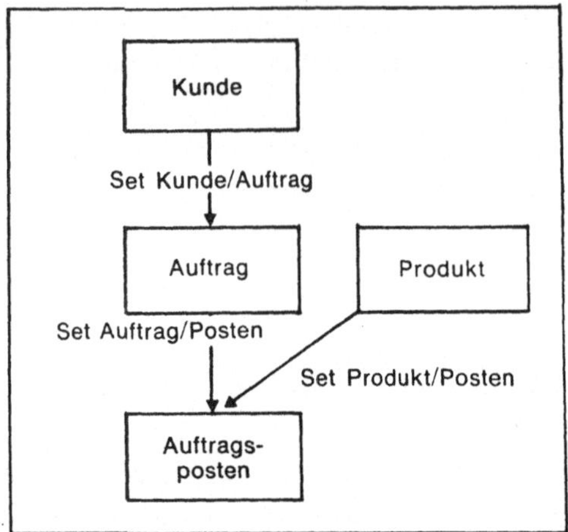

Die Auftragsposten können durch das Durchlaufen des Auftrags-/Posten-Sets
gefunden werden, ja es kann sogar über das Produkt-/Posten-Set das jeweilige
Produkt ermittelt werden.

Physische Folge. Das Absuchen erfolgt in der Reihenfolge, in der die
Sätze in der jeweiligen Area gespeichert wurden.

Das System kann beispielsweise auf Wunsch des Benutzers alle IDS-Sätze in
der Area Nr. 5 oder alle Kundensätze in der Area Nr. 5 aufsuchen. Dies
geschieht durch sequentielles Absuchen der betreffenden Area.

III. MÖGLICHKEITEN BEIM AUFBAU EINER IDS II-DATENBANK

1. Grundlagen und Einschränkungen

Eine Datenbank muss ebenso dem derzeitigen wie dem künftigen Bedarf
des Benutzers entsprechen. Es bedarf keiner weiteren Erläuterung,
dass der künftige Bedarf wesentlich schwieriger zu ermitteln ist.
Daher muss es möglich sein, Struktur und Inhalt einer Datenbank

weiterzuentwickeln, ohne sämtliche bestehenden Programme vollständig
erneuern zu müssen.

Die Entwicklung der Struktur und des Inhalts einer Datenbank stellt
keinerlei Problem dar wenn die richtigen Hilfsmittel zur Verfügung
stehen; wesentlich schwieriger ist es, die Programme zur Verarbeitung
des Datenbankinhalts so zu gestalten, dass sie von der weiteren Entwicklung der Datenbank nicht beeinträchtigt werden.

Im CODASYL-Bericht von September 1972, veröffentlicht unter dem Titel
"Data Base Task Group" wird die folgende Lösung empfohlen, um die
Unabhängigkeit zwischen Daten und Programmen zu gewährleisten:

. Die Struktur der Datenbank und die Beschreibung ihres Inhalts
  werden mit Hilfe einer speziellen Sprache, der Data Description
  Language DDL, in ein Schema gebracht.

  Jede Veränderung in der Datenbank muss ihren Niederschlag in diesem
  Schema finden.

. Der Teil der Struktur, der sich auf einen bestimmten Anwendungsbereich bezieht, wird in einem Subschema beschrieben.

  Dieses Subschema stellt somit eine Teilansicht der Datenbank her und
  wird in dem betreffenden Anwendungsbereich (d.h. in den einzelnen
  Programmen) angesprochen.

Eine Änderung an der Datenbank, die nicht dieses bestimmte Subschema
betrifft, hat auch keinerlei Einfluss auf die Programme, die auf dieses
Subschema zugreifen.

Diese Lösung ermöglicht die gewünschte Unabhängigkeit von Daten und
Programmen.

Wenn der Vorteil, bei einer Veränderung der Datenbank Programme nicht
neu kompilieren zu müssen, auch wichtig ist, so sind wir jedoch der

Ansicht, dass die Bedeutung der Unabhängigkeit zwischen Daten und
Programmen viel umfassender ist, als dass wir sie hier auch nur annähernd darstellen können.

2. Unabhängigkeit von Programmen und Daten bei IDS II

Folgende Definition kann gemacht werden:

Die Unabhängigkeit zwischen den Daten und den Programmen wird erreicht
durch die Trennung des Speicherabbilds, wie es vom Programm verarbeitet
wird (virtuelles Speicherabbild) und dem echten Zustand des Speichers,
wie er auf dem Datenträger existiert (reales Abbild), wodurch zwei Ziele
erreicht werden:

. Von einem realen Speicherabbild können verschiedene, voneinander
  unabhängige virtuelle Abbilder erzeugt werden.

. Es sind nur wenige oder gar keine Rekompilierungen erforderlich, wenn
  Änderungen des realen Abbilds vorgenommen werden.

Beide Punkte sind gleich wichtig. Nehmen wir nun ein Beispiel mit nur
einem Satz. Dabei könnten verschiedene Anwendungsprogramme auf die
unterschiedlichsten Abbilder ein und desselben realen Abbilds zugreifen.

Ein Programmierer könnte beispielsweise das mit einem ganz bestimmten
PICTURE ausgestatteten Element eines Satzes sehen. Ein anderer Blick-
winkel wäre ein Unterbereich des realen Abbilds.

Für einen anderen Programmierer könnte ein Element die Aneinanderfügung
zweier oder mehrerer Elemente dieses Satzes sein.

An diesen Beispielen wird die Bedeutung der oben erwähnten Möglichkeiten
sichtbar, besonders dann, wenn berücksichtigt wird, dass in einem echten
Programm verschiedene Arten von Sätzen vorhanden sind.

Beim Schema und den Subschemas hat der Benutzer der Datenbank IDS II folgende Variationsmöglichkeiten:

. Änderung der Beschreibung der Datenfelder (Art, Picture).

. Auslassen bestimmter Satzelemente.

. Kombinieren von Sätzen oder Satzelementen innerhalb eines Sets.

. Auslassen bestimmter Arten von Sätzen, Sets oder Areas.

. Änderung der Klassifizierungskriterien für Sätze innerhalb eines
  Sets.

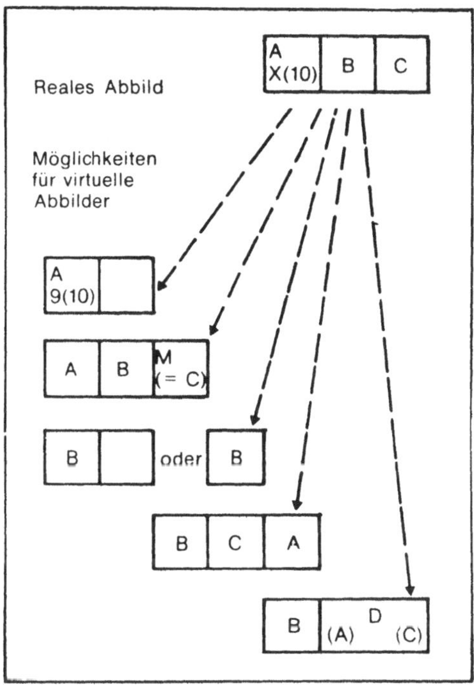

Am Schema können folgende Veränderungen vorgenommen werden, ohne dass
die vorhandenen Programme berührt werden:

. Änderung der Charakteristika eines Elements.

. Änderung der Zusammensetzung eines Satzes.

. Hinzufügen neuer Arten von Sätzen, Sets, Areas.

. Hinzufügen neuer Elemente in bestehende Sätze.

. Änderung der Charakteristika eines Sets oder einer Area.

3. Schema - Subschema

Schema:

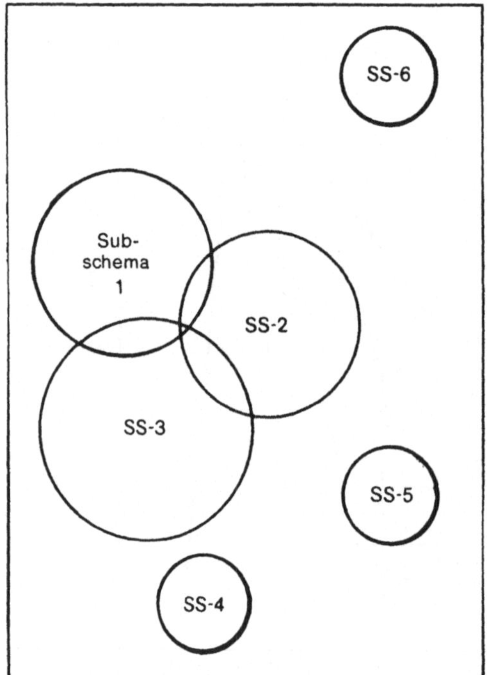

. Die Subschematas können einander überlagern.

. n Subschematas können zu einem Schema gebildet werden.

. 1 Subschema pro Programm

. 1 Schema pro Datenbank

. 1 Datenbank pro Schema

. n Programme pro Subschema

IV. SPRACHEN DER DATENBANK IDS II

1. Sprache zur Beschreibung des Schemas

Zur Beschreibung des Schemas sind zwei Sprachen erforderlich:

a - Die "Data Description Language" DDL, die nach den Empfehlungen von CODASYL entwickelt wurde und folgende Möglichkeiten bietet:

- Beschreibung der Struktur des Systems in Form von Areas, Sets, Sätzen, Satzelementen.
- Einsetzung der Steuer- und Kontrollprozeduren, die vom System automatisch abgerufen werden.

b - Die "Device Media Control Language" DMCL dient zur Angabe der physischen Charakteristika der Datenbank.

- Beschreibung der Areas.
- Spezielle Charakteristika der physischen Speicherung.

Durch die DMCL wird die totale Unabhängigkeit der Programme von der physischen Darstellung der Datenbank gewährleistet.

2. Sprache zur Beschreibung des Subschemas

Gemäss den von CODASYL veröffentlichten Empfehlungen wird das Subschema in der Sprache des Anwendungsprogramms beschrieben. Es steht demnach eine DDL in COBOL zur Verfügung.

Einige Elemente (Sets, Sätze, Satzelemente) können je nach Bedarf der betreffenden Anwendungen neu benannt oder neu beschrieben werden.

3. Sprache zur Bearbeitung der Datenbank

Die Sprache, mit der die Datenbank IDS II angesprochen wird, ist COBOL 74.

Die wichtigsten COBOL-Verben sind:

READY	(Zur Eröffnung der Areas)
STORE	(Speicherung eines Satzes)
FIND	(Lesen eines Satzes)
GET	(Zur Verfügungstellung des Satzinhaltes)
MODIFY	(Modifikation von Sätzen, Satzelementen oder logischen Verknüpfungen)
CONNECT	(Einfügen eines Satzes in ein Set)
DISCONNECT	(Löschen eines Satzes aus einem Set)
ERASE	(Physisches Löschen eines Satzes)
FINISH	(Abschliessen der Areas)

Neben diesen Bearbeitungsbefehlen stehen noch die Angaben zur Erstellung von Programm- und Dateicheckpoints zur Verfügung, mit denen die Wiederherstellung von Programmen oder Dateien bei einem anormalen Abbruch erleichtert wird.

Anmerkung: Alle notwendigen Steueroperationen bei Mehrfachzugriff sowie die Journalisierung für alle im System vorhandenen Dateien werden durch ein zentrales Verwaltungsmodul ausgeführt.

4. Verwaltungshilfen

Erstellung und Pflege des Verzeichnisses.

Diese Funktionen werden durch die Datenbank selbst ausgeführt. Dadurch können die für die Verwaltung der Datenbank Verantwortlichen folgende Informationen erhalten:

- Die aus einem Schema abgeleiteten Subschematas.
- Inhalt der Unterschematas.
- Sperrvermerke bzw. Sperroutinen für die einzelnen Subschematas.
- Unterschematas, in denen ein bestimmtes Set, ein Satz oder ein Satzelement erscheint.

Dienstprogramme
____

Mit der Datenbanksoftware IDS II werden alle vorhandenen Dienstprogramme geliefert, die dem Benutzer bei der Ausführung seiner
Arbeit helfen, wie:

. DB-PRINT: Durckprogramme zum logischen Ausdruck von

  - bestimmten oder allen Sätzen
  - bestimmten oder allen Sets
  - bestimmten oder allen Areas

. DB-ANALYS: Analyseprogramme zur

  - Darstellung der im Augenblick bestehenden Datenstruktur einer
    Datenbank.
  - Simulation der Einspeicherung von Benutzerdaten in eine Daten-
    bank zum Zweck der Optimierung einer Datenbankkonzeption.

Einsatz des Datenbanksystems SESAM
in der Österreichischen Elektrizitätswirtschaft-AG

Dkfm. Heinz Gindl
Verbundgesellschaft Wien

EINLEITUNG:

Die Österreichische Elektrizitätswirtschafts-AG (Verbundgesellschaft) verwendet zur Bewältigung für Teile ihrer
Aufgaben das Datenbanksystem SESAM, ein Programmprodukt
der Firma SIEMENS DATA.

Zu diesen Aufgaben gehören sowohl technische als auch kauf-
männische. Darüber hinaus hat die Verbundgesellschaft durch
die ihr vom Staat übertragene Versorgungsverpflichtung gegenüber der Allgemeinheit zusätzliche Aufgaben und Verantwortung
übernommen.

Zu diesen Pflichten gehört die Bereitstellung der Energie
in ausreichendem Maß in allen jenen Stellen, wo potentielle
Abnehmer dies fordern.

ÜBERBLICK ÜBER DAS DATENBANKSYSTEM SESAM

SESAM ist die Abkürzung für System elektronischer Speicherung
alphanumerischer Merkmale oder englisch: System for the
Electronic Storage of Alphanumeric Material.

Es ermöglicht die Speicherung unterschiedlich strukturierter
formatierter Eingabedateien - unabhängig von deren Block-,
Satz- oder Feldformaten - in der gleichen Datenbank. Die
Datenstruktur der Datenbank wird vom Anwender durch feld-
(aspekt)beschreibende Angaben festgelegt, die jederzeit änder-
bar sind. SESAM benutzt nicht Satzhierarchien, sondern Aspekte

Die Datenwiedergewinnung (Retrieval) kann in beliebigen, frei
bestimmbaren Teilmengen erfolgen. Die in der Datenbank gespeicherten Daten können sowohl direkt bzw. on-line geändert
oder ergänzt werden als auch durch das SESAM-Dienstprogramm
SEBE im Batch-Betrieb. Grundsätzlich erfolgt im SESAM-Daten-
banksystem die Datenwiedergewinnung und Direktänderung (Updating) über eine logische Schnittstelle der Programme SESAM1
bzw. SESAM2 mittels eigenen Benutzerprogrammen. Die entsprechenden SESAM-Module (SESMOD) werden in Form von Unterprogrammen im Benutzerprogramm aufgerufen. SESAM ist also ein
operierendes Datenbanksystem. Weiters besteht auch die Möglichkeit das Retrieval und Updating über SESAM-Standard-Be-
nutzerprogramme vorzunehmen.

Für den Einsatz von SESAM ist folgende Mindestkonfiguration
erforderlich:

- 1 Zentraleinheit ab 4oo4/35 mit 128 K.
  Der genaue Arbeitsspeicherbedarf ergibt sich auf Grund
  der vom Benutzer festgelegten Lade-Option.

- 1 Magnetplattenspeicher

- 2 Magnetbandgeräte

SESAM kann mit den Betriebssystemen BS1OOO und BS2OOO ab
SESAM-Version 11 betrieben werden.

Die Benutzerprogramme können in den Programmiersprachen ASSEMBLER,
COBOL und FORTRAN abgefaßt sein. Da in der Verbundgesellschaft
ein wesentlicher Teil der Programme in PL/1 geschrieben werden
und die Zugriffsmöglichkeit auf die Datenbank von in PL/1 pro-
grammierten Programmen erforderlich ist, wurde eine eigene
SESAM-Schnittstelle für PL/1-Programme erstellt.

Man kann das Datenbanksystem in vier Funktionsbereiche gliedern
(Abb. 1), wobei die SESAM-Dienstprogramme (SEDI) sowohl die
Datenverwaltung und den Datenbankaufbau als auch die Datenwieder-
gewinnung und Direktänderung unterstützen.

Funktionsbereich	Aufgaben	Programme
Datenverwaltung und Datenbankaufbau	Aufbau und Verwaltung des Aspektkataloges	SEFO
	Best. idsverwaltung	SEBE
	Aufname der Aspektwerte in die Aspektwertlisten	SEAL
	Aufbau und Wartung des Paßwortkataloges	SEPA
Datenwiedergewinnung und Direktänderung	Datenwiedergewinnung und Direktänderung Direktänderung	SESAM 1 bzw. SESAM 2
Dienstprogramme	Formatieren der Datenträger	SEDI 10
	Parametrieren der Datenbank	SEDI 12
	Ausgabe Aspektkatalog	SEDI 40
	Ausdrucken ZDR-Änderungsprotokolle	SEDI 50
	Umstellen der Zentraldaten auf geänderte Formate	SEDI 35
	Änderung der Speicherungsform	SEDI 36
	Ermittlung aufzunehmender Aspektwerte	SEDI 31
	Abzug des SVB und beliebiger DB-Blöcke	SEDI 19
	Korrespondenzabwicklung mit der Datenbank	SEDI 60 - SEDI 63
	Auswertung der Direktänderungs-Protokollbänder	SEDI 70
	Umsetzung der Protokollbänder auf SEBE-Format	SEDI 71
	Umsetzung der Protokollbänder auf SESAM-Schnittstellenformat	SEDI 72
	Datenbankrekonstruktion in Sonderfällen	SEDI 72 I
	Protokollierung des Korrespondenzablaufes	SEDI 90 - SEDI 91
Standardbenutzerprogramme	On-line-Abfrage und Änderung	SESAM F 1
	Verbale Abfragesprache	SEKOM
	Listengenerator	LIGE

Abb. 1

DATENVERWALTUNG UND DATENBANKAUFBAU:

Datenbankaufbau:

Das Datenbanksystem SESAM ist so konzipiert, daß für jede
Datenbank zwei getrennte Datenbestände aufgebaut werden:

- Die ZDR (Zentral-Daten-Random)-Datei enthält die
  Primärdaten.   Dies sind die eigentlichen Daten,
  mit denen der Benutzer weitere Verarbeitungen vornehmen kann.

- Die ORG (Organisationsdatei)-Datei enthält die
  Sekundärdaten. Sie dienen zur Beschreibung der in
  der ZDR befindlichen Primärdaten   und enthalten eine Reihe von Informationen, die für die
  Datenbankverwaltung und Datenwiedergewinnung notwendig sind.

Die ORG-Datei wird durch das Programm SEDI1Ø in Blöcke gleicher
Länge (3 424 Bytes) aufgeteilt, die fortlaufend numeriert sind.

Sie enthält folgende Teilbereiche (Abb. 2):

ORG-Datei:

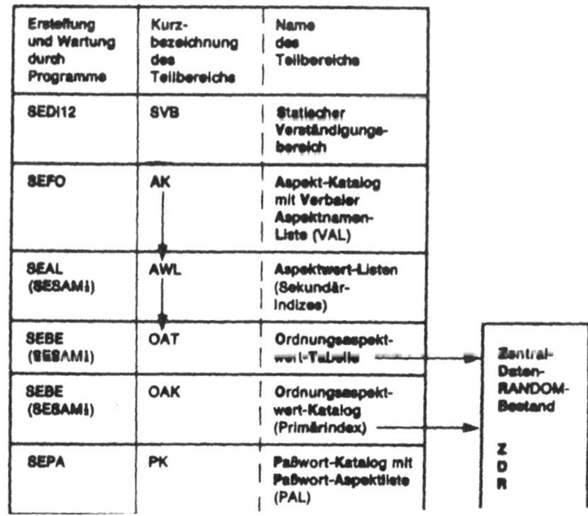

Erstellung und Wartung durch Programme	Kurzbezeichnung des Teilbereichs	Name des Teilbereichs
SEDI12	SVB	Statischer Verständigungsbereich
SEFO	AK	Aspekt-Katalog mit Verbaler Aspektnamen-Liste (VAL)
SEAL (SESAMi)	AWL	Aspektwert-Listen (Sekundär-Indizes)
SEBE (SESAMi)	OAT	Ordnungsaspekt-wert-Tabelle
SEBE (SESAMi)	OAK	Ordnungsaspekt-wert-Katalog (Primärindex)
SEPA	PK	Paßwort-Katalog mit Paßwort-Aspektliste (PAL)

Sie läßt sich in einen

- festen Bereich
- variablen Bereich und
- freien Bereich

unterteilen.

Der feste Bereich enthält die Informationen mit festem Volumen: SVB und AK mit VAL.

Der variable Bereich enthält diejenigen Informationen, deren Volumen im Verlauf der Datenbankwartung variieren kann: AWL, OAT, OAK und PK mit PAL. Außerdem gehören zu ihm Arbeitsbereiche, die das System intern benötigt.

Seine Größe legt der Benutzer beim Parametrieren der Datenbank mittels des Programms SEDI12 durch die Angabe der Blockzahl für den Paßwortkatalog (PK) und durch die Angabe der Parzellengröße fest. Eine Parzelle ist die logische Zusammenfassung einer Anzahl von ORG-Blöcken. Im Standardfall 8 Blöcke. Die Parzellengröße hat nur für OAK, OAT, AWL und Temporärdateien Auswirkungen. Für jeden der genannten Teile der ORG-Datei wird mindestens eine Parzelle angelegt und freigehalten, bei Bedarf werden weitere Parzellen zur Verfügung gestellt. Eine zu groß gewählte Parzelle führt besonders im Zusammenhang mit dem Anlegen von Temporärdateien bei multi-using leicht zu einer unnötigen Aufblähung des Platzbedarfes der ORG-Datei.

Der freie Bereich besteht aus Überlaufparzellen für die variablen Informationen. Außerdem werden in ihm die Temporärdateien aufgebaut, die bei speziellen Fragestellungen der Datenwiedergewinnung entstehen. Er schließt an den variablen Bereich an und kann innerhalb des Maximums von 16 ORG-Plattenstapeln eine beliebige Ausdehnung haben. Die Größe seiner Parzellen wird ebenfalls mit dem Programm SEDI12 festgelegt.

In der ZDR-Datei erfolgt die Speicherung der Primärdaten
sequentiell in aufsteigender Reihenfolge der Ordnungsaspektwerte (OAW) der Datenbanksätze. Der OAW ist der Ordnungsbegriff und darf nicht mehrfach vergeben werden. In den Datenbanksätzen werden nur signifikante Aspektwerte gespeichert,
d.h. Felder, die in den Eingabedaten belegt waren. Alle
Aspektwerte werden - es sei denn, daß es vom Benutzer anders
festgelegt ist - ohne redundante Daten (Füllzeichen: Zwischen-
raum oder Null) gespeichert, d.h. es wird je nach angegebenem
Speicherformat (zeichenweise, gepackt oder binär) komprimiert
gespeichert.

Neben der sich daraus ergebenden Ersparnis an Speicherplatz
auf der Magnetplatte liegt der große Vorteil des Nichtanlegens
leerer Datenfelder in der organisatorischen Flexibilität bei
der Datenbankdefinition.

Dadurch kann die Datenbankdefinition, d.h. die Festlegung der
Bedeutung und die Reihenfolge der Datenfelder (Aspekte) im
Datenbanksatz, auf maximale Erfordernisse ausgelegt werden.
Jeder aktuelle Datensatz enthält trotzdem nur die für ihn
relevanten Daten. Diese Speicherungsform zeigt ihre besonderen
Vorteile, wenn beim Datenbankaufbau Vorstellungen über den
Gesamtsatz vorhanden sind, aber ein Teil der Daten erst später
in die Datenbank übernommen wird.

Alle in der ZDR-Datei enthaltenen Daten sind zu Blöcken mit
der Standardlänge von 4 o96 Bytes zusammengefaßt. Die Daten-
belegung der Blöcke im Grundzustand kann der Benutzer mit
Hilfe eines Density-Faktors festlegen.

In engem Zusammenhang mit der ZDR-Datei stehen zwei Teilbereiche der ORG-Datei, nämlich der Ordnungsaspektwert-Katalog
(OAK) und die Ordnungsaspektwert-Tabelle (OAT).

Der OAK ist ein Blockindex. Er enthält den jeweils letzten
OAW eines ZDR-Blockes. Je nach Umfang der in der ZDR-Datei
gespeicherten Daten werden über dem OAK weitere Indexstufen
aufgebaut.

Der OAK ermöglicht beim Retrieval und Updating ein gezieltes
Aufsetzen auf bestimmte Sätze des Datenbestandes - vorausgesetzt, in der Fragestellung oder Änderungsanweisung wurden
OAW's oder OAW-Gruppenwerte angegeben. Der Indexzugriff erfolgt über den Primärindex.

Neben dem OAW wird bei Datenbanken mit Satznummern (SNR) noch
eine Ordnungsaspekt-Tabelle (OAT) erstellt. In ihr ist für
jede SNR ein Platz reserviert, an dem die Blocknummer des
ZDR-Blocks eingetragen wird, in dem der durch die SNR
charakterisierte ZDR-Satz beginnt.

Die OAT ist für den sog. Direktzugriff von Bedeutung. Die in
den Aspektwert-Listen (AWL) ermittelten Satznummern der möglichen Antworten führen über die OAT direkt zum gewünschten
ZDR-Satz, also algorithmischen Zugriff über invertierte Listen
(inverted files). Der Benutzer kann diese Zugriffsart auch an-
steuern, wenn er bei seinen Operationen eine Satznummer angibt.

Die Datensätze der ZDR-Datei sind durch den Ordnungsaspekt eindeutig charakterisiert, d.h. sein Wert, der OAW, kommt in der
Datenbank nur einmal vor. Über ihn ist jeder Datenbanksatz
adressierbar.

Das Datenbanksystem SESAM ermöglicht das Einspeichern von
Dateien unterschiedlicher gegenseitiger Abhängigkeit in die
ZDR-Datei. Um Sätze den Dateien zuordnen zu können, wird man
organisatorisch alle OAW's der gleichen Datei mit demselben
Anfangsbuchstaben beginnen lassen und dahinter die entsprechende
Nummer folgen lassen. Dabei ist zu beachten, daß alle OAW's
der Datenbank die gleiche Länge haben müssen.

<u>Aufbau und Verwaltung der Formate:</u>

Für jedes Datenfeld mit unterschiedlicher Bedeutung, dessen
Inhalt (Aspektwert) in der ZDR-Datei gespeichert werden soll,
muß der Benutzer einen Aspekt definieren, d.h. es müssen die
Eigenschaften - das Format -, die ein bestimmtes Datenfeld
haben soll, festgelegt werden.

Die Angaben werden im Aspektkatalog (AK) verwaltet, der pro
Datenbank 26 136 unterschiedliche Aspektbeschreibungen aufnehmen kann. Folglich könnte sich jeder Datenbanksatz aus
bis zu 26 136 Datenfeldern zusammensetzen.

Diese Zahl ergibt sich daraus, daß der SESAM-intern benötigte
symbolische Aspektnahme (SAN) aus drei Zeichen AAA bis Z99,
wobei I,O und Ø nicht vorkommen dürfen und das 1. Zeichen ein
Buchstabe sein muß, besteht. Für den OAW ist der SAN "AAA"
obligatorisch festgelegt.

Zu den Formatangaben zählen die Länge des Aspektwertes (max.
256 Bytes im AK und 248 Bytes in der AWL), die Dezimalstellen,
die Ausrichtung, die Systemfunktion, die System-Suchmethode,
das Speicherungsformat usw. Diese Formatfestlegung geschieht
mit dem Programm SEFO.

Bei der Vergabe von symbolischen Aspektnamen (SAN) sollte
darauf geachtet werden, daß Aspekte mit zusammenhängender
organisatorischer Bedeutung einer aufsteigenden symbolischen
Namensreihe zugeordnet werden. Dadurch wird bei der Daten-
wiedergewinnungs-Operation "Anfrage" die Bildung von Aspektgruppen unterstützt.

Der verbale Aspektname (VAN) ist die Bezeichnung des Aspektes.
Sie kann beispielsweise auch ein "sprechender" Schlüssel sein.
Der Zugriff auf die ZDR-Daten ist wahlweise über den SAN oder
VAN, deren Namen eindeutig vergeben sein müssen, möglich. Im

140

Hinblick auf das Retrieval und Updating kann es für Gruppen-
bildungen sinnvoll sein, für logisch zusammengehörige Aspekte,
VAN zu vergeben, die mit dem gleichen Wortstamm beginnen.

Obwohl SESAM die Aspektwerte nur in ihrer signifikanten Länge
speichert, werden sie dem Benutzerprogramm in der gemäß AK
definierten Länge zur Verfügung gestellt.

Aufbau und Wartung der Zentraldaten:

Aufbau und Wartung der ZDR-Datei, des OAK und OAT erfolgt im
BATCH-Betrieb mit dem Bestandsverwaltungsprogramm SEBE. Neben
den normalen Änderungsfunktionen enthält das Programm auch
Routinen für Reorganisation, Reparatur und Sicherung der
Zentraldaten.

Voraussetzung für einen SEBE-Lauf ist der AK in der ORG-Datei.

Der Benutzer kann mittels SEBE für jeden Aspekt vorhandene
Aspektwerte ändern, neue hinzufügen oder löschen.

SEBE prüft sowohl die Anweisungen und das Format der Eingabedaten als auch auf aufsteigende Sortierfolge.

Für die Ablaufsicherung benutzt SEBE den SVB, in dem system-
interne Informationen über den Datenbankzustand gespeichert
werden. In diesem "Gedächtnis" des Systems stehen auch jene
Informationen, die zur Datenbankrekonstruktion notwendig sind.

Da SEBE die Sätze in der Folge aufsteigender OAW's in der
Datenbank aufbaut, wird es auch für Aufgaben der Reorganisation
eingesetzt. Diese ist jedoch nur nötig, wenn ein hoher Anteil
der Arbeiten mit der Datenbank diese sequentielle Folge bevor-
zugt.

Während des Aufbaus des ZDR-Datenbestandes wird in der ORG-
Datei der OAK angelegt. Der OAK gestattet den direkten Zugriff
auf Sätze, deren OAW den Benutzern bekannt ist.

Bei SEBE-Läufen werden automatisch Sicherungsbänder angelegt.

Aufbau und Wartung der AWL:

Um auf Datensätze direkt zugreifen zu können, von denen kein
Ordnungsbegriff, sondern nur die Inhalte einzelner Felder bekannt sind, ist das Anlegen eines Verzeichnisses, das die Werte
bestimmter Felder und die Sätze, in denen diese vorkommen, erforderlich. Diese Verzeichnisse heißen Direktzugriffslisten,
Sekundärindizes, invertierte Listen oder inverted files. In der
SESAM-Terminologie heißen sie AWL.

Die Anlage von AWL's wird vom Benutzer durch den Eintrag
"Suchmethode = direkt" beim Programm SEFO gesteuert. Die Verwaltung der AWL's wird mit den Programmen SEDI31 und SEAL
durchgeführt.

Bei der Anlage von AWL's sollte der Benutzer darauf achten, daß
beim Updating von Direktzugriffsaspekten umfangreiche Pflege-
vorgänge in den AWL's durchgeführt werden. Die bei Suchvorgängen gewonnene Zeit muß gewissermaßen durch höhere Änderungs-
zeiten erkauft werden. Die Entscheidung über die Definition von
Direktzugriffsaspekten hängt vom Verhältnis Suchvorgänge zu
Änderungen ab.

Aufbau und Wartung des Paßwort-Kataloges:

Eine SESAM-Datenbank kann Daten von unterschiedlicher Herkunft
und für verschiedenartige Verarbeitungsprogramme enthalten.
Normalerweise kann jedes Programm oder jeder Benutzer alle in
der Datenbank enthaltenen Informationen bei Wiedergewinnung ab-
rufen oder sämtliche Informationen durch Direktänderung ver-

ändern. Um Mißbrauch zu verhindern, ist es jedoch häufig
notwendig, den Zugriff auf bestimmte Daten und das Recht
sie zu verändern, nur bestimmten Programmen oder Benutzern
zu gestatten.

Im System SESAM ist es möglich, den Datenschutz durch die
Vergabe von Paßwörtern zu realisieren. Jedem Paßwort kann
eine konkrete Berechtigung zugeordnet werden, die eine Wieder-
gewinnungs- und/oder Direktänderungsberechtigung sein kann.
Die jeweilige Berechtigung kann gezielt auf bestimmte
Ordnungsaspekt(gruppen)-Werte, d.h. Datenbanksätze beschränkt
werden, innerhalb der Sätze auf bestimmte Aspekte und/oder
Aspektgruppen. Für einen Aspekt gilt in allen mit dem gleichen
Paßwort angesprochenen Sätze die gleiche Berechtigung. Zur
Verdeutlichung soll das folgende Beispiel (Abb. 3) dienen.

Alle für eine Datenbank festgelegten Paßwörter werden im Paßwortkatalog (PK) - falls die einem Paßwort zugeordneten Berechtigungen differenzierter sind, in der Paßwort-Aspektliste
(PAL) mit ihren Berechtigungen eingetragen. Zur Erstellung
und Wartung des PK und der PAL dient das Programm SEPA.

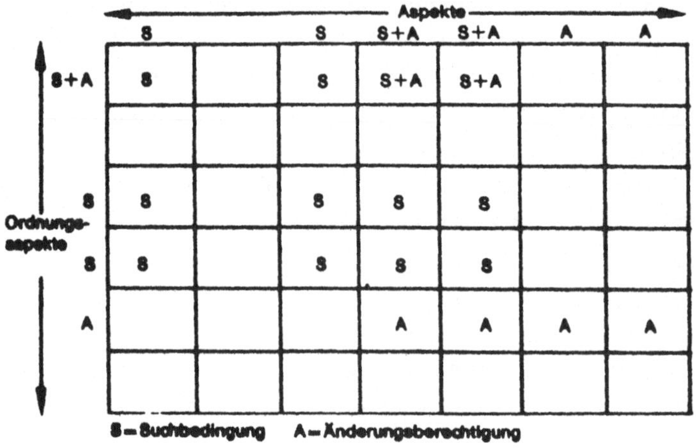

DATENWIEDERGEWINNUNG UND DIREKTÄNDERUNG

Die Datenwiedergewinnung und -direktänderung im Datenbanksystem SESAM wird bei Verwendung von Benutzerprogrammen über
die Programme SESAM1 und SESAM2 abgewickelt.

Diese unterscheiden sich dadurch, daß SESAM1 für Single-File-
Betrieb und SESAM2 für Multi-File-Betrieb geeignet ist. Mit
SESAM2 hat man die Möglichkeit, auf bis zu 256 verschiedene
Datenbanken zuzugreifen.

Sowohl bei SESAM1 als auch bei SESAM2 können bis zu 13 Benutzerprogramme (die unter einem eigenen Befehlszähler ablaufen)
gleichzeitig mit der (den) Datenbank(en) korrespondieren,
ohne aufeinander Rücksicht nehmen zu müssen. Diese Programme
können sich auch untereinander direkt verständigen.

Außerdem kann jedes Programm mehrere getrennte Aufträge enthalten.

SESAM_2^1 kann bis zu 99 Auftragsnummern unterscheiden, die beliebig
auf die einzelnen Programme verteilt sein dürfen.

Sobald ein Programm abgeschlossen ist, kann unter dem selben
Befehlszähler ein neues Programm nachgeladen werden. Auch die
Prioritätsfolge laufender Programme kann geändert werden.

Beim Laden von SESAM_2^1 werden durch den Ladeaufruf die Parameter
(teilweise Options), die Overlays, die speicherresidenten
Tabellen usw., die die Zugriffsgeschwindigkeit und den Kern-
speicherbedarf bestimmen, festgelegt.

In jedes benutzereigene Programm muß der Korrespondenzmodul SESMOD
eingebunden werden. Dieser Modul ruft SESAM_2^1 auf, baut die gewünschte Korrespondenz auf und führt den anfallenden Datentransfer
zwischen Benutzerprogramm und SESAM_2^1 durch.

Die gewünschten Operationen können im Benutzerprogramm über eine
sog. CALL-Schnittstelle an beliebiger Stelle aufgerufen werden.

SESAM-Operationen

Sie lassen sich in die Gruppen

- OPEN und CLOSE
- Datenwiedergewinnung
- Direktänderungen

einteilen.

Die Operationen setzen die Einrichtung und Versorgung von Parameterbereichen voraus. Dies sind der Anweisungs-, Quittungs-, Antwort- und Fragebereich.

Im Anweisungsbereich ist bei allen Aufrufen anzugeben, um welche Operationen es sich handelt. Außerdem muß die Operation durch Angaben in diesem Bereich näher spezifiziert werden.

Im Quittungsbereich wird die Auftragsnummer angegeben. SESAM teilt dem Benutzerprogramm dann durch eine sogenannte Status-meldung mit, ob die aufgerufene Operation ordnungsgemäß durchge-führt wurde und ob sich eine Antwort ergeben hat. Außerdem werden in diesem Bereich Fehlerhinweise abgeliefert. Die Antworten im Quittungsbereich sind vom Anwenderprogramm auszuwerten.

Im Antwortbereich liefert SESAM jeweils satzweise die Daten in der Reihenfolge ab, wie sie durch die Einträge im Anweisungsbereich angefordert wurden.

Im Fragebereich sind gegebenenfalls Vergleichswerte oder Änderungs-werte anzugeben, mit denen eine Operation über die Angaben im Anweisungsbereich hinaus spezifiziert werden soll.

Operationen OPEN und CLOSE:

Operationen mit Datentransfer setzen ein Datenbank-OPEN für
die entsprechende Datenbank und ein Auftrags-OPEN für das
Benutzerprogramm bzw. den jeweiligen Auftrag voraus.

Nach Beendigung des Datentransfers sollte der Auftrag gelöscht
werden, und nach dem letzten Zugriff auf eine bestimmte Datenbank sollte diese geschlossen werden, um den Befehlszähler für
ein neues Programm frei zu bekommen und um dadurch die Kapazität des Multi-Using bzw. Multi-File nicht unnötig zu belasten.
Das geschieht durch ein Auftrags- bzw. Datenbank-CLOSE.

OPEN

Mit dem OPEN veranlaßt der Benutzer die Eröffnung der Korrespondenz mit der Datenbank. Unter anderem ist der Datenbankname,
ein Paßwort und ein Funktionszeichen anzugeben. Über das Paßwort wird die Zugriffsberechtigung des Benutzers geprüft. Das
Funktionszeichen gibt den

Benutzerwunsch	erlaubt für andere
lesen	nur lesen
lesen	lesen und/oder ändern
lesen und/oder ändern	nur lesen
lesen und/oder ändern	lesen und/oder ändern

an.

CLOSE

Mit dem CLOSE wird die Korrespondenz mit der Datenbank abgeschlossen.

Operationen zur Datenwiedergewinnung:

Aspektauskunft

Um die Ergebnisse der Frage-Operationen auswerten zu können, muß
der Benutzer (bzw. das Programm) sehr oft neben den symbolischen
Aspektnamen auch die verbalen Aspektnamen sowie die Aspektformate kennen. Falls hier Bedarf besteht, liefert die Aspekt-
auskunft die entsprechenden Informationen aus dem AK. Sie ist
also dann zu benutzen, wenn die drei genannten Aspektkomponenten
nicht vollständig bekannt sind und/oder die Möglichkeit besteht,
daß zwischenzeitlich Aspektformate geändert wurden. Die Aspekt-
auskunft gewährleistet dem Benutzerprogramm Flexibilität hinsichtlich des Datenformates und somit den Einsatz formatunab-
hängiger Benutzerprogramme. Das Programm kann sich durch Benutzung dieser Operation den unterschiedlichen Datenstrukturen
anpassen.

Informationsfrage

Diese Operationen informiert über die signifikanten Aspektwerte frei auswählbarer Datenbanksätze. Der Benutzer bestimmt
einen gewünschten Satz durch Eingabe des Ordnungsaspektwertes
in den Fragebereich. Eine Satzfolge wird dementsprechend durch
einen Ordnungsaspekt-Gruppenwert oder zwei Ordnungsaspektwerte
festgelegt.

Pro Datenbanksatz darf sich der Benutzer die Werte und Formate
einer Aspektfolge ausgeben lassen, deren Anfang und Ende er frei
bestimmen kann. Analog zur Satzfolge-Bestimmung wird dieses
Satzsegment durch Angabe zweier Aspekte bestimmt.

Die Informationsfrage liefert im Regelfall eine variabel lange
Antwort ab. Denn die zwischen den angegebenen Grenzaspekten
liegenden "Aspekte ohne Wert" (nicht signifikant) werden bei
der Ausgabe unterdrückt.

Man kann sich eine SESAM-Datenbank als Matrix vorstellen, deren
Y-Achse durch die Ordnungsaspektwerte und deren X-Achse durch
die Aspekte gebildet werden. Bei Zugrundelegung dieser Matrix-
Vorstellung liefert die Informationsfrage demnach alle möglichen
rechteckigen Matrix-Ausschnitte von einem Aspektwert eines Satzes
bis hin zu allen Aspektwerten sämtlicher Sätze. Folglich ist
die Informationsfrage zweckmäßigerweise dann zu gebrauchen, wenn
der Benutzer den Satzaufbau nicht oder nur teilweise kennt. Das
bedeutet, daß der Benutzer Verarbeitungsstrukturen erst während
des Programmlaufs aufbauen kann.

Anfrage:

Die Anfrage ähnelt der Informationsfrage. Sie unterscheidet sich
von dieser dadurch, daß von den gewünschten Sätzen nicht nur
eine, sondern bis zu 256 Aspektfolgen erfragt werden können,
also Feldauswahl betrieben werden kann. Sie bietet damit gegenüber der Informationsfrage erweiterte Möglichkeiten.

Die Anfrage liefert stets Antworten fester Länge. Diese entspricht dem in der Anweisung festglegten Format. Aspekte ohne
Werte (nicht sifnifikant) werden als Leerstellen ausgegeben.
Demnach ist die Anfrage zweckmäßigerweise dann zu gebrauchen,
wenn

. der Benutzer ihm bekannte Aspekte ansprechen möchte, ohne
  die Antwort von deren Inhalt, d.h. von den Aspektwerten
  abhängig zu machen,

. aus der gegebenen Struktur der Datenbanksätze die für die
  jeweilige Verarbeitung benötigte Struktur auf Benutzerpro-
  gramm-Ebene erzeugt werden soll.

Suchfrage:

Diese Operation sucht aus dem Datenbestand diejenigen Sätze her-
aus, welche die vom Benutzer festgelegten Suchkriterien erfüllen.
Sie werden definiert durch die Angabe von logisch verknüpften
Aspekten, denen konkrete Vergleichsbedingungen zuzuordnen sind.

Die Suche kann vom Benutzer gezielt auf eine Teilmenge des
Satzbestandes beschränkt werden. Dies geschieht (analog zur
Informations- und Anfrage) durch Versorgung des Fragebereichs
mit einem oder zwei Ordnungsaspekt(gruppen)-werten. Die Teilmenge kann also im Extremfall aus 1 Datenbanksatz bestehen.
In diesem Fall nimmt die Suchfrage den Charakter einer Kontroll-
frage an.

Demnach ist die Suchfrage dann zu gebrauchen, wenn der Benutzer
wissen möchte, welche Sätze bestimmte Bedingungen erfüllen.

Antwortabruf:

Der Antwortabruf bildet eine logische Ergänzung der drei Frage-
Operationen. Bei diesen wird nur die 1. Antwort in den Antwortbereich des Benutzerprogramms übergeben, von wo aus sie vom
Programm weiterverarbeitet werden kann. Weitere Antworten werden
durch den sogenannten Antwortabruf bereitgestellt.

Der Antwortabruf kann auch in modifizierter Form gestartet werden.
In diesem Fall werden (analog zur Frage-Operation) im Fragebereich 1 oder 2 Ordnungsaspekt(gruppen)werte neu eingetragen.
Diese ersetzen den Fragebereichseintrag der vorausgegangenen
Frage. Durch den modifizierten Antwortabruf können also Erweiterungen oder Einschränkungen des abzuprüfenden Ordnungsaspekt-
wert-Spektrums bewirkt werden.

Operationen der Direktänderung:

Direktänderung

Mit der Direktänderung kann der Benutzer den Datenbestand während
des Programmablaufs verändern. Es ist möglich, pro Operation
einen beliebigen Satz in beliebigen Teilmengen zu ändern oder
zu löschen oder einen neuen Satz mit einer variablen Anzahl von
Aspektwerten in den Bestand aufzunehmen (Obergrenze sind 512
Aspekte in einer Anweisung).

Folge<u>änderung</u>:

Sollen in mehreren Sätzen die gleichen Aspekte verändert werden,
kann ab dem 2. Satz die Folgeänderung benutzt werden. Diese
Operation bildet eine vereinfachte Variante der Direktänderung.
Bei ihr fehlen die Angaben darüber, welche Satzteile, d.h.
welche Aspekte geändert, gelöscht oder neu aufgenommen werden
sollen.

<u>Zugriff über Satznummer (SNR)</u>:

Bei den Operationen Anfrage, Informationsfrage, Suchfrage und
Direktänderung kann statt des OAW's auch die SNR als Kennzeichen für den zu verarbeitenden Satz benutzt werden. Diese
interne SNR wird von SEBE vergeben. Bei Neuaufbau eines Satzes
durch Direktänderung vergibt SESAM$^{1}_{2}$ diese Satznummer. Der
Zugriff über Satznummer ist im allgemeinen wesentlich schneller
als der über den OAW, da sie unmittelbar die relative Blocknummer
innerhalb der ZDR-Datei liefert. Der Zugriff über den OAW erfordert hingegen meist eine Arbeit mit mehreren Indexstufen.

DER EINSATZ VON SESAM IN DER VERBUNDGESELLSCHAFT

<u>Ausgangssituation für den Einsatz einer Datenbank</u>:

Um eine den Anforderungen entsprechende Arbeitsabwicklung zu
erzielen, bestand in der Verbundgesellschaft der Wunsch verschiedener Fachabteilungen, auf ihre Daten im On-line-Betrieb
über Bildschirm zugreifen zu können. Nachdem die Wünsche an-
wenderseits, was die einzelnen Dateien und Verarbeitungsvor-
gänge anbelangt, heterogen waren, entstand das Problem, ob man
für jedes dieser Anwendungsgebiete eine eigene Datei bzw.
mehrere Dateien im herkömmlichen Sinne errichten solle. Mit
diesem Problem eng verbunden war die Frage nach dem Sicherungskonzept für den On-line-Betrieb. Weiters war mitzuüberlegen,
wie viele periphere Einheiten für den On-line-Betrieb zur Ver-

fügung gestellt werden können und inwiefern einzelne Fach-
gebiete sich überschneiden und daraus ein "Integrations-
effekt" zu nützen is.. Für die Lösung dieser Probleme bot
sich der Einsatz eines Datenbanksystems an, da man mit ihm
eine Zentralisation von Dateien erzielte. Sie hat den Vorteil der Einmalspeicherung sowie die Vorteile, die sich aus
dem Änderungsdienst ergeben. Ein weiterer Vorteil aus der
Zentralisation von Dateien ist, daß Auswertungen quer über
viele Bereiche integriert vorgenommen werden können und
daß der RZ-Maschinenbetrieb nur eine einzige Datei für den
On-line-Betrieb zur Verfügung zu stellen und zu verwalten
hat. Des weiteren ist bei einer Zentralisation der Dateien
das Sicherungskonzept nur auf diese eine Zentraldatei ab-
zustellen. D.h., man hat von der Peripherie her gesehen nur
eine Magnetbandstation belegt. Bei einer Führung von "Einzel-
dateien" für den On-line-Betrieb wären sicherlich mehrere Band-
stationen mit der Sicherung belegt, wenn man ein ordnungsge-
mäßes Sicherungskonzept anstrebt. Mit dem Vorhandensein mehrerer
Sicherungsbänder steigen auch die Möglichkeiten einer Fehlbe-
dienung.

Neben der Zentralisation von Dateien sprach auch die Datenunabhängigkeit für den Einsatz eines Datenbanksystems, da die
Realisierung der Programme für die einzelnen Anwendungsgebiete
sukzessive erfolgt. Weiters ist man nicht an einmal vorge-
nommene Dateiaufbauten, Ordnungsbegriffe und eine ausgewählte
Programmiersprache gebunden. Seitens des Programmierers ist
somit gewährleistet, daß den Wünschen der benutzenden Fachabteilungen rasch und problemlos nachgekommen werden kann.
Durch den Einsatz eines Datenbanksystems ist es also möglich,
eine hohe Flexibilität, was Benutzerwünsche anbelangt, zu erreichen.

Alle diese Überlegungen führten zum Entschluß, in der Verbundgesellschaft ein Datenbanksystem einzusetzen, wobei als Ideal-
vorstellung vorschwebte, die Daten aller On-line-Applikationen

in einer Datenbank zu verwalten. Durch die zentrale Speicherung
dieser Daten soll eine ständige Präsenz der Daten für alle On-
line-Anwender ermöglicht werden. Der Benutzer sollte zu Zeitpunkten, die er aus seiner Tätigkeit heraus für geeignet hält,
zu seinen Daten zugreifen und sie verarbeiten können. Er ist
auch für den Inhalt der Daten verantwortlich. Weiters besteht
die Möglichkeit, Auswertungen im Batch-Betrieb vornehmen zu
können.

Nachdem die Entscheidung eine Datenbank einzusetzen gefallen
war, war die Frage nach dem einzusetzenden System zu beantworten. Hier bot sich das im BS1000 nicht gebührenpflichtige
Standarddatenbanksystem SESAM der Firma Siemens Data an.
SESAM trägt sowohl der Datenanforderung als auch dem Sicherungskonzept genüge. Die Erstellung eines selbstprogrammierten
Systems wurde aus Gründen der Programmierkosten und der Flexibilität, die bei einem Datenbanksystem zu berücksichtigen
sind, nicht in Betracht gezogen.

<u>Anlagenkonfiguration:</u>
SESAM ist seit Herbst 1974 im BS1000 auf einer Anlage
SIEMENS 4004/151 mit derzeit 640 K Kernspeicher und folgender
Peripherie im Einsatz:

- 8 Plattenstationen mit je 55 Mio Bytes
- 2 Plattenstationen mit je 7 Mio Bytes
- 4 Magnetbandstationen
- 1 Lochkartenleser
- 1 Lochkartenstanzer
- 1 Schnelldrucker

Zur Zeit stehen für den On-line-Betrieb 9 Bildschirmgeräte
Olivetti TCV 270 mit teilweise angeschlossenen Terminal-
druckern zur Verfügung. Der Datenfernverarbeitungsbetrieb
wird über das Echtzeitprogramm ASMUS abgewickelt.

<u>Datenvolumen:</u>

Von den 26 136 maximal möglichen Aspekten in einer SESAM-
Datenbank sind bei der Verbundgesellschaft derzeit 45o belegt.

Der SESAM-Datenbestand umfaßt 99 Mio. Zeichen (Bytes) und geht
über zwei 55-Mio.-Platten. Die ZDR-Datei belegt davon 85 Mio.
Zeichen und die ORG-Datei 14 Mio. Zeichen. Die Aufteilung der
beiden Dateien auf die zwei Platten ist folgendermaßen:

- Platte 1:   35o Zylinder   ZDR-Datei
- Platte 2:   1oo Zylinder   ORG-Datei
               27o Zylinder   ZDR-Datei

An Kernspeicherplatz benötigt SESAM$^1_2$ auf Grund der zur Zeit
angegebenen Lade-Option 144 K.

<u>SESAM-Einsatzgebiete:</u>

In der Verbundgesellschaft werden für die Arbeitsgebiete

- Hauptlastverteiler
- Präliminareüberwachung
- Finanzabteilung und
- Energievertrags- und Tarifwesen

Daten in der SESAM-Datenbank verwaltet.

<u>Hauptlastverteiler:</u>

Die Daten des Hauptlastverteilers wurden als erste in die
Datenbank aufgenommen. Mit der Aufnahme dieser Daten wurde die
Länge des OAW's mit 15 Zeichen festgelegt, die auch für die Länge
der Ordnungsbegriffe der übrigen Arbeitsgebiete bindend ist.

Zur Vielfalt der Tätigkeiten des Hauptlastverteilers gehören die
Netzführung der Leitungen der Verbundgesellschaft, die Stromauf-
bringung durch den Kraftwerkseinsatz, die Stromabgabe Inland, wie
Großabnehmer, ÖBB und Landesgesellschaften, Stromexport und -import

sowie die Erstellung von Prognosen, die ein Teil des Fahrplanes sind. Die Registrierung all dieser Vorgänge in der
Datenbank geschieht teilweise zum Zwecke der eigentlichen
Betriebsführung, ein großer Teil der Informationen ist jedoch Grundlage statistischer Auswertungen im Hauptlastverteiler
selbst und in der Abteilung Energiewirtschaft.

Die Erfassung (Ein/Ausgabeprogramm) der Daten des Hauptlast-
verteilers erfolgt mit einem während des ganzen Tages resident
geladenen Programms über Bildschirm. Die wichtigsten Funktionen
dieses Programms sind: Datenerfassung, Überprüfen von Daten auf
Plausibilität (numerische Grenzen), Korrigieren von Daten,
Berechnen von Formeln (einfache arithmetische Operationen),
Speichern der Daten in die Datenbank, Lesen und Ausgeben von
Daten.

Da das Ein/Ausgabeprogramm die wichtigsten Aufgaben des Warten-
personals erfüllt, nimmt es eine Sonderstellung ein, und muß
permanent verfügbar sein.

Zu den Auswertungsprogrammen zählen Programme zur zusätzlichen
Formelberechnung, Darstellung der Energiesituation, Tagesaus-
wertung, Integration der Leistungswerte und viele andere.

Die Protokollierungsprogramme sind Listausdrucke und Plotter-
darstellungen nach eigenen variablen Entwürfen wie beispielsweise der Fahrplanausdruck für den Kraftwerkseinsatz des
nächsten Tages, die Auslandsabrechnung, der Speichereinsatz usw.

Eine weitere Gruppe von Hauptlastverteiler-Programmen sind die
Definitionsprogramme. Sie dienen zur Festlegung des Bildauf-
baus, der Formate, der Grenzen, der Formeln, der Kurzbezeichnungen,
Schlüsseln und Stationsnamen.

154

Datenbankaufbau der HLV-Daten:

Die in der Datenbank gespeicherten Hauptlastverteiler-Daten
gliedern sich in

- eigentliche Hauptlastverteiler-Daten und
- Organisationsdaten.

Die eigentlichen Hauptlastverteiler-Daten sind halbstündige
Leistungswerte, Arbeitswerte, Spannungen, Speicherinhalte usw.
Alle eingegebenen Daten und vom Rechner errechneten Werte und
Ergebnisse werden für den Zeitraum der letzten zwei Monate und
die nächste Woche vorausgespeichert. Dazu wird für jeden Tag ein
gleichbleibender zweidimensionaler Raster angelegt, in dem
sämtliche Daten eingetragen werden. Eine Dimension ist bestimmt
durch einen 8-stelligen Schlüssel, der eine Meßstelle, ein Kraft-
werk, einen Rechenwert oder ähnliches definiert, die zweite
Dimension ist bestimmt durch einen 3-stelligen SAN, der die Art
des Wertes angibt, wie z.B. Leistungswert um 22.3o, Leistungswert um 23.oo Uhr, Arbeitswert von o6.oo - 13.oo Uhr oder
ähnliches. Durch Angabe eines Datums und eines Schlüsses wird
von SESAM die entsprechende Zeile des Rasters übergeben. Das
Dateikennzeichen, das Datum und der Schlüssel bilden den
15-stelligen Ordnungsbegriff (OAW). Durch zusätzliche Angabe
von bestimmten Aspekten kann aus dieser Zeile jeder beliebige
Wert ausgewählt werden, wobei nicht für jeden Schlüssel jeder
Aspekt einen Wert hat. Auf diese Weise entstehen in der Daten-
matrix logische Lücken.

Die Organisationsdaten bestehen aus Tabellen, Grenzwerten,
Schlüsseln, Namen, Kurzbezeichnungen, Formeln usw. Alle
organisatorischen Daten, die zum Betrieb der Bildschirmprogramme
notwendig sind, werden in einheitlichen Tabellen in der Datenbank abgespeichert. In jedem Bild, das aufgerufen werden kann,
existiert täglich eine Tabelle. In ihr sind sämtliche Informationen, die zur Behandlung dieses Bildes für diesen Tag erforderlich sind, enthalten. Die Maximallänge dieser Tabelle beträgt
1oo6 Bytes, die Mindestlänge 6 Bytes. Sie ist in der Datenbank
unter folgender Kennzeichnung gespeichert:

- Datum

- 3-stellige Kurzbezeichnung des Bildes ("Zentralstation")

- Grundtypus (halbstündig, einstündig, Tarifzeiten)

Jede Tabelle besteht aus vier Teilen:

- Hinweisdatum (6 Bytes):
  Gilt die Tabelle eines vergangenen Tages, so muß sie unter
  dem Hinweisdatum gesucht werden.

- Formulartabelle (580 Bytes):
  In ihr sind die Zeilen des Bildes definiert. Sie enthält
  Zeilennummer, Schlüssel der Zeile, Grenzwerte für Plausibi-
  litätsüberprüfung und Formeln, falls ein Rechenwert vorliegt.

- Überschrift (2o Bytes)

- Schlüsseltabelle (4oo Bytes):
  Sie enthält die den Schlüsseln entsprechenden Namen der
  Zeilen.

Energievertrags- und Tarifwesen (ETW):

Ausgehend von den bereits errechneten Daten des Hauptlastverteilers, die in der Datenbank gespeichert sind, werden über
Bildschirm von der Abteilung Energievertrags- und Tarifwesen
die dazugehörigen Kosten eingegeben, in der Datenbank gespeichert
und eine Vor- und Nachkalkulation der Ertragslage der Verbundgesellschaft ermittelt. Die Resultate der Kalkulation werden in
der Datenbank gespeichert und sind über Bildschirm abrufbar.

Nach der täglichen Erstellung des Sollfahrplanes des Hauptlastverteilers kann die Abteilung Energievertrags- und Tarifwesen
eine genaue Kalkulation der Ertragslage auf Grund des Stromge-
schäfts durchführen. Damit ist eine bessere Disposition bezüglich
der Gewinn- und Verlustermittlung, die eine Rückwirkung auf eine
neuerliche Berechnung des Fahrplanes hat, möglich.

Für die Berechnung wird auf die 1/2-Stunden-Leistungswerte
und Arbeitswerte je Tag des Fahrplanes zugegriffen. Hinzu
kommen Kalkulationsdaten der Abteilung Energievertrags- und
Tarifwesen, wie:

- die Formel zur Berechnung der entsprechenden Zeile

- Arbeitswerte im Hoch- bzw. Niedertarif

- Fixkosten, spez. Kosten in Groschen/kWh und allgemeine
  Kosten

- Leistungswerte in MW-Leistung der spez. Kosten (Form
  MW $*$ g/kWh).

Als Resultate in der Datenbank werden die Vor- und Nachkalku-
lationswerte und die Bewertungen aus Kosten und Leistung/Arbeit,
der Tauschenergie, der spez. Kosten usw. gespeichert.

Als Ergebnis dieser Berechnung wird für den jeweiligen Tag
u.a. der tägliche Durchschnittserlös sowie der tägliche bzw.
fortlaufende Gewinn/Verlust über Bildschirm ausgegeben.

<u>Präliminareüberwachung:</u>

Alle in der Verbundgesellschaft zu tätigenden Investitionen
sind nach Projekten gegliedert zu präliminieren. Es handelt
sich dabei um Investitionen am baulichen, stark- und schwach-
stromtechnischen Sektor sowie um sonstige Investitionen.

Die Gesamtkosten der einzelnen Projekte werden vom Beginn bis
zum Ende der Arbeiten durch die Innenrevision kontinuierlich
überwacht.

Erfaßt werden die ursprünglich genehmigten Gesamtkosten des
Projekts und alle Nachgenehmigungen, die ursachengemäß nach
Umgliederungen, Einsparungen, Projektsänderungen, Erschwernisse,
Verschätzungen und Gleitungen gegliedert werden, sowie der Aufwand
unter Berücksichtigung der geleisteten Anzahlungen und offenen
Bestellungen.

Im Gegensatz zu den anderen Arbeitsgebieten, die bis jetzt
mit Hilfe der Datenbank abgewickelt werden, war beim Präli-
minare bereits ein Überwachungssystem auf Jahreskostenbasis
mit mehreren Dateien vorhanden. Es mußten daher bei der
Installation der Gesamtkostenüberwachung neben der Neuerfassung
von Daten mit Hilfe von sogenannten Überleitungsprogrammen viele
relevante Daten aus den bereits bestehenden Dateien in die
Datenbank gebracht werden.

Datenbankaufbau der Präliminare-Daten:

Für die Abwicklung der Präliminareüberwachung sind drei verschiedene Sätze erforderlich (siehe Abb. 4):

   - projektspezifische Daten (P-Sätze)
   - positionsspezifische Daten (Q-Sätze)
   - Bewegungsdaten (R-Sätze)

Die Sätze werden durch P, Q und R in der ersten Stelle des OAW's
voneinander unterschieden.

Der bereits vorgegebene 15-stellige OAW hat folgenden Aufbau (Abb.4):

   eine Stelle Satzkennzeichen
   drei Stellen Projektnummer
   zwei Stellen Abteilungsnummer
   zwei Stellen Positionsnummer
   drei Stellen Kostenstellennummer
   vier Stellen Zeitinformation

Projektspezifische Daten

Die projektspezifischen Datensätze enthalten den Text, eine
Kurzbezeichnung und ein Projektkennzeichen. Auf Grund des OAW's,
der in der Stelle ein P hat, lassen sich die Texte folgendermaßen zuordnen:

Beim Vorhandensein der 3-stelligen Projektnummer handelt es
sich um Projektstexte.

Zusammenhang der Sätze der Präliminareüberwachung:

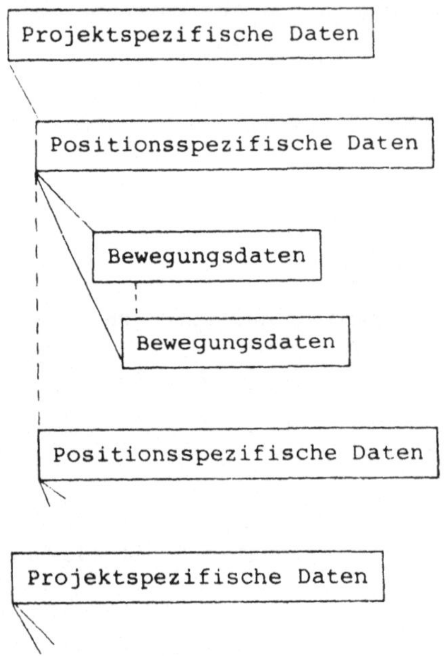

<u>OAW:</u>

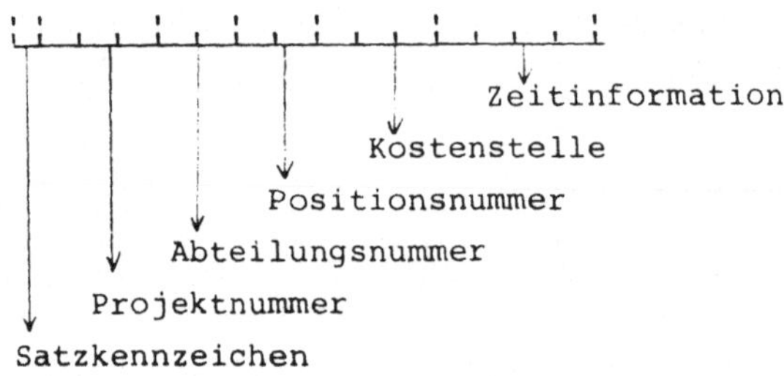

<u>Darstellung des OAW der P-Sätze:</u>

Projekttext:

Abteilungsbezeichnung:

Kostenstellenbezeichnung:

Ist nur die 2-stellige Abteilungsnummer besetzt, so enthält das Textfeld die Abteilungsbezeichnung.

Weiters handelt es sich um die Kostenstellenbezeichnung, wenn nur die 3-stellige Kostenstellennummer besetzt ist.

Bei sequentieller Durchsuche nach dem OAW erhält man bei diesen Daten zuerst alle Kostenstellentexte, dann die Abteilungsbezeichnungen und schließlich die Projekttexte. Diese Anordnung ist für die verschiedensten Auswertungen erforderlich.

Positionsspezifische Daten:

Sie enthalten im OAW die Kennzeichnung Q sowie die Projekt-, Abteilungs-, Positions- und Kostenstellennummer.

Die dazugehörigen Aspekte enthalten die Kontonummer und Positionstexte sowie Werte für Aufwand, Bestellung, Anzahlung, Gesamtkosten u.a.m, die Saldencharakter haben.

Bewegungsdaten:

Unter den Bewegungsdaten sind die einzelnen Transaktionen, die in der Datenbank abgespeichert werden, zu verstehen. Die Sätze bestehen aus der Konto-Nr., Betrag, Beleg, Datum, Text, Bestell-Nr., Satzart usw. Der OAW hat in der ersten Stelle das Kennzeichen R, dann die Kontierung wie die Positionssätze und anschließend ein 4 Byte großes Zeitfeld. Es ist binär verschlüsselt und enthält die Maschinenzeit, zu der dieser Bewegungssatz angelegt wurde. Da mehrere Bewegungsdatensätze mit dem gleichen Ordnungsbegriff vorkommen können und SESAM nur eindeutige OAW's zuläßt, mußte dieses Zeitfeld angelegt werden. Man sieht daraus, daß die Zulassung von eindeutigen OAW's, wie es bei SESAM geschieht, nicht immer von Vorteil ist.

<u>Präliminare-Programme</u>:

Die Programme der Präliminare-Überwachung lassen sich in

- Überwachungsprogramme
- Änderungsdienstprogramme
- Konzeptdatenprogramme
- Auskunfts- und Auslistungsprogramme

einteilen.

Überwachungsprogramm

Das laufende Investitionsgeschehen wird mit Hilfe eines Bild-
schirmprogramms sowie eines Batchprogramms laufend überwacht,
und zwar in der Form, daß anfallende Bestellungen, Anzahlungen
und Aufwendungen bzw. Gutschriften mit Hilfe des Überwachungs-
programms über Bildschirm eingegeben werden. Der Präliminare-
Sachbearbeiter sieht sofort, ob seine Transaktion gedeckt ist.
Wenn sie gedeckt ist, wird sie verarbeitet und in der Datenbank
abgespeichert. Ist dies nicht der Fall, bekommt er eine Mit-
teilung und die betreffende Transaktion wird nicht verarbeitet.
Aufwendungen und Gutschriften, die in Form von Lochkarten in der
Buchhaltung anfallen, werden mittels eines Überwachtungsprogramms
im Batch-Betrieb durchgeführt. Für jede Transaktion wird ein
Bewegungssatz angelegt und der Positionsdatensatz saldenmäßig
auf den letzten Stand gebracht.

Änderungsprogramm

Dieses On-line-Programm ist für das Anlegen und Ändern von
Projektssätzen vorgesehen. Für die Eröffnung von neuen Projekten
muß zuerst der Projektssatz angelegt werden.

Konzeptdatenprogramm

Für den Präliminierungszeitpunkt 1. Jänner eines jeden Jahres
werden im September des Vorjahres Konzeptvordrucke mit dem
momentanen Projektstatus pro Projekt und Abteilung im Batch-
Betrieb erstellt. Diese Vordrucke sind um etwaige Änderungen
bzw. Neuvorhaben von den Fachabteilungen zu ergänzen und dem

Vorstand zur Genehmigung vorzulegen. Nach der Genehmigung
werden die Konzeptdaten über Bildschirm erfaßt und in der
Datenbank gespeichert. Da dieser Vorgang einige Wochen Zeit
in Anspruch nimmt und die Überwachung der laufenden Vorhaben
während dieser Zeit weiter geschieht, werden die Daten aus der
Konzeptdatenerfassung auf sog. "Neu-Felder", die ein Äqui-
valent zu den laufenden Feldern im Positionsdatensatz sind,
gespeichert. Nach Abschluß des Erfassungsvorgangs und mit
Beginn des neuen Präliminarejahres werden die "Neufelder" in
die laufenden Felder übernommen.

Auskunfts- und Auslistungsprogramm
Der Sachbearbeiter in der Fachabteilung hat über Bildschirm
die Möglichkeit sich über den Stand des Präliminares zu in-
formieren. Er kann nach bestimmten Ordnungsbegriffen suchen
oder seine Frage in Form von logischen Verknüpfungen stellen.

Weiters werden für Berichte die diversesten Auswertungen nach verschiedensten Sortierkriterien gemacht. Um diese Auswertungen
möglichst rationell abzuwickeln, wollte man das SESAM-Standard-
Benutzerprogramm LIGE einsetzen. Einige Tests haben gezeigt,
das LIGE den Anforderungen, verschiedene Zeilenstrukturen zu
drucken, nicht gewachsen ist. An dieser Stelle sei vermerkt,
daß in der Verbundgesellschaft keine SESAM-Standard-Benutzer-
programme eingesetzt werden. Es wurde für die Auswertungen ein
eigenes Datenauswahl-Programm erstellt. Der Benutzer kann auf
Lochkarte seine Auswahl-Parameter angeben. Die gewünschten
Daten werden auf ein Band abgezogen, sortiert und mit dem gewünschten Druckaufbereitungsprogramm ausgelistet.

Zu den Auslistungsprogrammen zählt noch der Projektsabschluß-
bericht, der am Ende eines Projektes die gesamte Entwicklung
wiedergibt. Im Anschluß daran wird das Projekt aus Sicherheitsgründen auf ein Band abgezogen und aus der Datenbank gelöscht.

<u>Finanzabteilung:</u>

Der Finanzabteilung der Verbundgesellschaft obliegt mit wenigen
Ausnahmen die Beschaffung von Finanzmitteln für den Verbund-
konzern. Alle diese Daten werden als zentrale Kreditdatei in
der Datenbank gespeichert und stehen jederzeit für den Abruf
über Bildschirm bereit. Sie werden über Bildschirm erfaßt bzw.
Teile davon automatisch errechnet und abgespeichert.

Der 15-stellige Ordnungsbegriff, der in der ersten Stelle als
Kennzeichen ein K enthält, hat folgenden Aufbau:

- Stelle 2 - 3: Währung
- Stelle 4 - 5: Art des Kredits: z.B. Anleihe, Kredit,ERP usw
- Stelle 6 - 9: Konzerngesellschaft, für die der Kredit auf-
  genommen wurde
- Stelle 1o - 15: Begebungs- bzw. Aufnahmedatum

Durch diese Gliederung des OAW's ist es leicht möglich, Auswertungen nach den Kriterien Währung, Kreditart, Gesellschaft
und Laufzeit durchzuführen.

Für jeden Kredit werden u.a. folgende Aspekte wie Nominale,
Währung, Umrechnungskurs, Laufzeit, Provision, Kosten, Gebühren,
Bankverbindungen, Tilgungsplan, Zahlungsplan, Zinssätze usw.
erfaßt. Diese Daten werden mit dem Erfassungsprogramm über
Bildschirm erfaßt. Mit diesem Programm kann man weiters Felder
abfragen, Kredite löschen, Daten einfügen und Daten von einem
Kredit zum anderen kopieren.

Im Batch-Betrieb werden verschiedene Auswertungen wie Tilgungspläne, Tilgungsvorschau, Zahlungspläne und Zahlungsvorschau
nach den verschiedensten Kriterien, wie Auslands- und Inlands-
kredit, nach den einzelnen Fremdwährungen zusammengefaßt, nach
Konzerngesellschaften gegliedert usw., erstellt.

Für die Erfassung der Tilgungspläne, bei denen die Konditionen
mathematisch formulierbar sind, beispielsweise ERP-Kredit,
werden über Computer errechnet und in der Datenbank abgespeichert. Desgleichen werden die verschiedenen Renditen und
Zahlungspläne für Fremdwährungen mit Hilfe eines Programms errechnet und in der Datenbank abgespeichert.

Weitere Ausbaustufen:

Bei den bereits bestehenden Datenbank-Anwendungsgebieten werden
laufend Benutzerwünsche, wie weitere Auswertungen, berücksichtigt.

Für die nächste Zukunft ist die Übernahme von Buchhaltungs-
daten innerhalb eines On-line-Systems in die Datenbank geplant.

Weiters sind zur Zeit Überlegungen in Richtung des Einsatzes
von METHAPLAN (Methodenbank-Ablaufsystem für Planung und
Analyse) in Verbindung mit SESAM für Berechnungen am energie-
wirtschaftlichen Sektor im Gange.

Installation von SESAM:

Das Datenbanksystem SESAM konnte ohne Änderungen übernommen
werden. Anfänglich waren softwaretechnische Schwierigkeiten
vorhanden. Diese sind spätestens ab Einsatz der SESAM-Version 9.3
ausgemerzt.

Die Installation von SESAM sowie die ersten SESAM-Benutzer-
Programme wurden unter Unterstützung und Mithilfe der Firma
Siemens Data realisiert.

Für die SESAM-Benutzer-Programme sind die Programmiersprachen
Assembler, PL/1 und FORTRAN im Einsatz. Da die Programmier-
sprache PL/1 in SESAM nicht standardmäßig unterstützt wird und
PL/1 eine der häufigst verwendeten Programmiersprachen der
Verbundgesellschaft ist, wurde von der Verbundgesellschaft
eine eigene PL/1-Schnittstelle für SESAM erstellt.

Wartung der Datenbank:

Die Sicherung wird durch den RZ-Maschinenraum mindestens
zweimal täglich im Großvater-Vater-Sohn-Prinzip durchgeführt. Während des laufenden Betriebs werden Protokoll-
bänder mitgeführt, die nach Ausfällen ein schadloses Wieder-
aufsetzen ermöglichen.

Weiters wird die Datenbank zweimal wöchentlich reorganisiert.
Bei vielen Direktänderungen mit SESAM - bei der Verbundgesellschaft machen die Direktänderungen gemäß mitgeführten
Statistikband ein Drittel aller SESAM-Operationen aus -
kann das Zeitverhalten bei der Wiedergewinnung von Daten
negativ beeinflußt werden. Durch das Reorganisieren der
Zentraldaten werden die Zugriffszeiten wieder verbessert.

Neben der regelmäßigen Sicherung der Datenbank werden die
Daten für bestimmte Arbeitsgebiete zusätzlich auf Band gesichert.

Bisherige Erfahrungen:

Nach bisher im allgemeinen durchaus zufriedenstellenden Erfahrungen mit SESAM, ist festzuhalten, daß von Benutzerseite
im Dialog-Betrieb der berechtigte Wunsch nach beschleunigten
Zugriffszeiten besteht. Der Engpaß besteht also in der Zugriffsgeschwindigkeit (47,5 ms mittlere Zugriffsgeschwindigkeit) der Plattenstationen.

Um diesen Wunsch nachzukommen, wurden besonders vordringliche
Programme mit fixen Prioritäten versehen, hardwaremäßig ein
zusätzliches Paar von Selektorkanälen installiert und soft-
waremäßig werden im Bedarfsfall SESAM-Statistik-Bänder mitgeführt. Auf Grund der Auswertung dieser Statistikbänder
wird überlegt, ob in nächster Zukunft die Ladeoption für
$SESAM_2^1$ verändert werden soll. Dies würde eine Erhöhung des

Kernspeicherbedarfs von bisher 144 K auf 164 K bedeuten.
Es würden durch diese Maßnahme einige SESAM-Overlays und
Tabellen kernspeicherresident, wodurch weniger Plattenzu-
griffe erforderlich werden.

Als Resümee kann gesagt werden, daß sich der Einsatz von
SESAM für ein Arbeitsgebiet dann anbietet, wenn Daten im
direkten Zugriff verschieden strukturiert, verarbeitet
und verknüpft werden sollen bzw. wenn die formatierten
Datensätze nicht vollständig mit Werten belegt sind.

IMS
Information Management System

Hans Simon
IBM Wien

ENTWICKLUNG UND KOMPONENTEN VON IMS/VS

Das Information Management System IMS/VS ist ein Vertreter der universell verwendbaren Data Base/Data Communication (DB/DC) Systeme. IMS/VS entstand Mitte der sechziger Jahre als reines batch-orientiertes Datenbanksystem unter dem Namen Data Language 1 (DL/1). Damit war die Möglichkeit gegeben, hierarchische Datenstrukturen von COBOL-Programmen anzusprechen.

Später bekam DL/1 einen Datenfernverarbeitungsteil, wodurch Terminalbenutzer mit Hilfe von parallel ablaufenden Nachrichtenverarbeitungsprogrammen auf die DL/1-Datenbanken zugreifen konnten. Aus DL/1 entstand 1969 schließlich IMS/360, welches mehrere Implementierungsmethoden für Datenbanken enthielt und gleichzeitigen Online- und Batch-Zugriff auf die Datenbanken ermöglichte.

Aus IMS/360 entstand mit der Einführung des virtuellen Speicherkonzeptes schließlich IMS/VS. Das System wurde wesentlich weiterentwickelt und bietet heute eine Fülle von Funktionen, mit deren Hilfe komplexe Informationssysteme aufgebaut werden können. IMS/VS stellt IBMs einziges Datenbanksystem für formatierte Daten dar, was die Bedeutung dieses Produktes unterstreicht. IMS/VS kann unter den Betriebssystemen OS/VS1 und OS/VS2 (SVS und MVS) betrieben werden. Unter dem Betriebssystem DOS/VS steht ein Subset des Datenbankteils (DL/1) von IMS/VS zur Verfügung, wobei die damit erstellten Datenbanken mit IMS-Datenbanken verträglich sind.

IMS/VS besteht aus folgenden Teilen (siehe Abbildung 1):

1. Datenbankverwaltung (DB) unterstützt den Benutzer bei Definition, Aufbau und Betrieb von integrierten Datenbanken, welche nicht redundante, verknüpfte Datenelemente enthalten. Beliebige Benutzerprogramme verarbeiten die Datenbanken im Stapelbetrieb.

2. Datenfernverarbeitungsteil (DC) besteht aus einem Teleprocessing-Steuerprogramm, welches die Nachrichtenübertragung zwischen Terminals und IMS/VS steuert und dynamisch Benutzerprogramme aktiviert, welche Nachrichten verarbeiten und auf die Datenbanken zugreifen. Batch- und On-line-Programme können parallel auf die Datenbanken zugreifen und diese verändern.

3. Multiple Systems Coupling (MSC) ermöglicht die Verbindung von
   mehreren IMS/VS-On-line-Systemen, welche in gleichen oder in
   verschiedenen Processoren aktiv sind. Damit kann ein Netz von
   miteinander kommunizierenden IMS/VS-DB/DC-Systemen aufgebaut
   werden, wobei ein Terminalbenutzer die Möglichkeit hat, Daten
   und Anwendungen aller angeschlossenen Systeme bei Bedarf zu
   benutzen.

4. Fast Path (FP) ist ein Zusatz zum IMS/VS-DC-Teil, welcher für
   Benutzer interessant ist, die für bestimmte Anwendungsgebiete
   nicht die vollen Fähigkeiten von IMS/VS benötigen, sondern
   eine große Anzahl von einfachen Transaktionen möglichst schnell
   verarbeiten müssen. Als Beispiel möge eine Transaktion bei
   einem Bankschalter dienen, welche relativ einfach aufgebaut
   ist, keine komplexen Datenstrukturen benötigt, aber in großen
   Mengen anfällt und eine möglichst kurze Antwortzeit erfordert.

5. Interactive Query Facility (IQF) bietet dem Terminalbenutzer
   eine einfache Abfragesprache, mit deren Hilfe er auf die Datenbanken zugreifen kann, ohne daß Anwendungsprogramme vorhanden
   sein müssen. IQF eignet sich für ungeplante Anwendungen, bei
   denen sich eine Programmentwicklung aus zeitlichen oder ökono-
   mischen Gründen nicht lohnt. Ein weiterer Vertreter von Abfra-
   gesprachen ist das Generalized Information System GIS/VS, mit
   dem sowohl batch als auch on-line auf IMS/VS-Datenbanken zugegriffen werden kann.

Eine der wichtigsten Komponenten eines DB/DC-Systems sind Sicher-
eitseinrichtungen und Wiederanlauffunktionen. IMS/VS bietet hier für
alle Komponenten im System integrierte Funktionen, die für die Er-
haltung der Datenintegrität, den Datenschutz, die Rekonstruktion von
zerstörten Daten bei allen Arten von Fehlern und einen schnellen
Wiederanlauf verantwortlich sind.

IMS und CODASYL

IMS kann nicht als Implementierung von CODASYL-Empfehlungen betrachtet werden, wenngleich analoge Funktionen feststellbar sind. IMS
wurde und wird streng nach den praktischen Bedürfnissen unserer Benutzer entwickelt. Dabei waren z.B. Funktionen der Datensicherung
und der Datenwiederherstellung vom Anbeginn von ganz besonderer Bedeutung. Aufgrund dieser jahrelangen Erfahrungen hat IBM dann auch
zu der Entwicklung von CODASYL ihren Beitrag geleistet. Viele dieser
Beiträge führten zu der bevorstehenden, für 1978 zu erwartenden in
wesentlichen Belangen veränderten Neufassung des Journal of Development.

Aber auch dann sollte man nicht nach der Verträglichkeit eines Da-
enbanksystems mit CODASYL's DDL und DML fragen, sondern danach ob
ein COBOL-Compiler Datenbankfunktionen aufweist.

Wie immer man die Sache sieht, vorerst sollte das neue DDLC-Journal
of Development vorliegen, damit der tatsächlich erreichte Entwicklungsstand erkennbar wird.

DATENSTRUKTUREN

IMS/VS-Datenbanken besitzen hierarchisch segmentierte Datenstrukturen, welche untereinander wahlweise zu Netzwerken verbunden
werden können, um redundante Datenspeicherung zu vermeiden. Näheres zu den Möglichkeiten, Netzwerke aufzubauen, im Kapitel "Logische Datenbankverknüpfungen".

Die Zugriffseinheit einer hierarchischen Datenstruktur ist das
Segment, welches eine Gruppierung logisch zusammengehöriger Datenfelder, die meist gemeinsam verarbeitet werden, enthält (z.B.
könnte ein Segmenttyp "Adresse" die Felder: Postleitzahl, Ort,
Straße und Hausnummer enthalten). Wahlweise kann auch ein Schlüsselfeld definiert sein, welches die Sortierordnung von mehrfach
vorkommenden Segmenten unter ihrem übergeordneten Segment bestimmt.
Jede Datenstruktur von IMS/VS kann bis zu 255 Segmenttypen mit unterschiedlicher Länge und Aufbau auf 15 hierarchischen Stufen
(Levels) angeordnet enthalten. Beispiel siehe Abbildung 2. Basierend auf der natürlichen Struktur der Daten werden Segmentarten
in einer hierarchischen Baumstruktur dargestellt, wobei folgende
Regeln gelten:

- Ein Datenbanksatz (Record) besteht aus einem Segment auf der
  höchsten Stufe (Root-Segment) und allen davon abhängigen
  (dependent) Segmenten.

- Jedes vom Root-Segment abhängige Segment kann wieder eine beliebige Anzahl von abhängigen Segmentarten haben (bis maximal
  255 Segmentarten auf 15 Segmentebenen).

- Jedes vorkommende Segment einer bestimmten Art kann eine beliebige Anzahl (auch 0) von davon abhängigen Segmenten verschiedener Typen besitzen.

- Kein abhängiges Segment kann ohne sein unmittelbar übergeordnetes (parent) Segment existieren.

- Jedes abhängige Segment hat genau ein übergeordnetes Segment
  (Ausnahme: IMS/VS-Netzwerke).

Die Summe aller Datenbanksätze (beliebige Anzahl) bildet eine
IMS/VS-Datenbank. Man beachte, daß IMS/VS die Definition von beliebig vielen Datenbanken mit unterschiedlicher Struktur erlaubt.
Jedes Anwendungsprogramm kann auf beliebig viele Datenbanken
zugreifen.

Die hierarchischen Datenstrukturen bieten viele Vorteile, wie:

- Einfache Handhabung von variabel langen Datensätzen
- Verminderung der Redundanz
- Leichte, einfache Anwendungsprogrammierung
- Leichte Erweiterung der Strukturen

DATENBANKBESCHREIBUNGEN (DBD und PSB)

Jede physische Datenbankstruktur wird vom Datenbankadministrator
in einer Data Base Description (DBD) beschrieben. Ein Beispiel
finden Sie in Abbildung 3. Eine DBD beschreibt die hierarchische
Datenstruktur, die physische Implementierungsmethode der Datenbank und alle Attribute, die für die Speicherung dieser Datenbank am externen Speichermedium notwendig sind.

In Quellenform besteht eine DBD aus einem Satz von Assembler-
Makro-Anweisungen, die nach der Umwandlung in einer Ladebiblio-
thek für IMS zur Verfügung stehen und bei der Durchführung von
Anwendungsprogrammen durch IMS/VS dynamisch geladen und zur Interpretation von Datenbankanforderungen verwendet werden. Die
DBD beschreibt eine physisch existierende Datenbank aus der Sicht
des Systems, unabhängig von allen Anwendungsprogrammen.

Die aus der Sicht eines Benutzerprogrammes benötigten Datenstrukturen werden mit Hilfe von Program Communication Blocks (PCB) beschrieben. Jeder PCB bezieht sich auf eine in einem DBD beschriebene Datenbankstruktur. Alle für ein Programm benötigten PCB werden zu einem Program Specification Block (PSB) zusammengefaßt.
Beispiele siehe Abbildung 4. Program Specification Blocks bestehen
in Quellenform ebenso wie Data Base Descriptions aus Assembler-
Makro-Anweisungen, die nach der Umwandlung in einer Ladebiblio-
thek gespeichert werden und bei einer Programmausführung von IMS/VS
dynamisch geladen werden. Die in einem PCB beschriebene Datenstruktur ist meist eine Untermenge der im entsprechenden DBD
definierten Struktur, da verschiedene Programme in der Regel
nicht die gleichen Segmentarten verwenden oder aus Sicherheitsgründen bestimmte Segmentarten nicht ansprechen dürfen. Die für
ein Programm in einem PCB definierten Datenbanksegmente heißen
"sensitive" Segmente. Ein Beispiel hiezu finden Sie in Abbildung
5 und 6.

Eine in einem PCB definierte Datenstruktur existiert nicht für
sich am externen Speicher, sondern besteht aus einer Abbildung
von Strukturteilen einer in einem DBD beschriebenen physischen
Datenbank oder eines Netzwerkes verschiedener verknüpfter physischer Datenbanken (siehe Kapitel "Logische Datenbankverknüpfungen").

PCB-Datenstrukturen sind ebenso wie die zugrundeliegenden DBD-
Strukturen reine hierarchische Baumstrukturen. Sie haben die
gleichen Eigenschaften und es gelten die gleichen Bildungsre-
geln wie bei Data Base Descriptions.

Da ein PCB eine Datenstruktur vom Standpunkt eines einzelnen
Benutzers repräsentiert, ist es sinnvoll, darin auch gleich die
Zugriffsbefugnisse des Benutzers und die Verarbeitungsfolge zu
definieren.

Folgende Zugriffsarten können je Segmenttyp im PCB definiert
werden:

> - Kein Zugriff (Segment in PCB nicht sensitiv)
> - Nur Schlüssel darf gelesen werden
> - Lesen
> - Einfügen neuer Segmente
> - Verändern bestehender Segmente
> - Löschen bestehender Segmente

Die Verarbeitungsfolge legt die Reihenfolge fest, in der die
Datenbanksätze dem Anwendungsprogramm zur Verfügung gestellt
werden, weiters, welches Segment als Root-Segment verwendet wird
und welcher Begriff als Schlüssel des Root-Segments definiert
ist. Die Verarbeitungsfolge unterscheidet sich nur dann von der
im DBD definierten Folge, wenn zusätzliche Indexdatenbanken definiert wurden (siehe Kapitel "Sekundärindizes").

Mit Hilfe der von den Anwendungsprogrammen unabhängigen DBDs
und den PCBs, die das Benutzerdatenmodell beschreiben, kann ein
hohes Maß von Datenunabhängigkeit erreicht werden. Beispiel
siehe Abbildung 7. Anwendungsprogramme arbeiten nur mit den in
den PCBs definierten logischen Datenstrukturen, ohne von den
physischen Implementierungsmethoden, von den Speichermedien und
von Erweiterungen der Datenstruktur abhängig zu sein. Damit kann
der Wartungsaufwand für Programme beträchtlich gesenkt und die
Integration neuer Anwendungen in bestehende Applikationssysteme
wesentlich erleichtert werden. DL/1 ermöglicht den Einsatz von
neuen Entwicklungen im Hard- und Software-Bereich, ohne daß
zeit- und kostenaufwendige Umstellungsarbeiten bei bestehenden
Applikationen anfallen.

ZUGRIFFSSPRACHE UND SPRACHEN-INTERFACE

Datenbankanforderungen werden von IMS/VS-Anwendungsprogrammen
mittels Unterprogrammaufruf (CALL) durchgeführt. Um die Anforderungen für IMS/VS von der verwendeten Host-Language unabhängig
zu machen, existiert ein Sprachen-Interface, welches die Sprachen Assembler, COBOL und PL/1 unterstützt.

Die Verbindung zwischen Programmen und der Datenbank erfolgt zur
Ausführungszeit über den Program Specification Block (PSB), der
die PCB-Definitionen aller im Programm benötigten Datenstrukturen enthält. Ein Anwendungsprogramm bekommt von IMS/VS die Adressen
aller im PSB definierten PCBs als Entry Point Parameter zur Verfügung gestellt. Beispiel siehe Abbildung 8 a).

Bevor auf den Aufbau der Zugriffssprache eingegangen werden kann,
sind noch einige Begriffe zu klären:

a)   Die "hierarchische Reihenfolge" definiert die Reihenfolge,
     in der Segmente einer Datenbank von IMS/VS sequentiell durch-

laufen werden. Beim Aufbau von Datenbanken werden die Seg-
mente in dieser Reihenfolge geladen. Die Definition lautet:
Für jedes beliebige Segment sucht IMS/VS ein davon abhängiges
Segment. Falls keines existiert, wird das erste Segment lo-
kalisiert, welches sich auf der gleichen hierarchischen
Stufe rechts vom Ausgangssegment befindet.

Falls ein solches nicht existiert, wird auf der nächsthöheren
Ebene das erste Segment, welches noch nicht verarbeitet wurde
(rechts vom letzten verarbeiteten) aufgesucht.

Segmente der gleichen Art (Twins) unter dem gleichen Parent-
Segment werden gemäß ihrer Sortierfolge verarbeitet. Existieren mehrere abhängige Segmentarten unter einem Parent-Segment,
werden sie in der Reihenfolge von links nach rechts verarbeitet.

Ein Beispiel zeigt Abbildung 8 b).

b)   Der "hierarchische Path" besteht aus der Folge von Segmenten,
     die vom Root-Segment direkt zu einem Segment auf einer tieferen
     Ebene führt. Der hierarchische Path enthält je ein Segment je
     hierarchischer Ebene und spielt bei der Verarbeitung von ab-
     hängigen Segmenten eine Rolle.

Jeder DL/1-Call verarbeitet ein oder mehrere in einem hierarchischen Path liegende Segmente einer mittels PCB definierten Datenstruktur und besteht aus folgenden Teilen:

a) dem Namen des entsprechenden Entry Points des Sprachen-Interface
   und
b) den Argumenten:
   Adresse des PCBs, CALL-Funktion, Ein-/Ausgabebereich und wahlweise Segmentsuchargumente (SSAs). Beispiel siehe Abbildung 9.

Folgende CALL-Funktionen stehen zur Verfügung:

- GET UNIQUE (GU) liest das durch die Suchargumente definierte
  Segment direkt ein.

- GET NEXT (GN) liest ausgehend von der bestehenden Datenbank-
  position in der hierarchischen Reihenfolge das nächste Segment,
  welches die Qualifikation erfüllt. Die bestehende Datenbankpo-
  sition wird durch einen vorhergehenden Lese- oder Zugangsbe-
  fehl am verarbeiteten Segment gesetzt.

- GET NEXT WITHIN PARENT (GNP) arbeitet wie GET NEXT, aber nur
  innerhalb eines durch einen vorhergehenden GU oder GN Call
  festgelegten Parent-Segments.

- INSERT (ISRT) fügt ein neues Segment ein.

- DELETE (DLET) löscht ein Segment einschließlich aller abhängigen Segmente.

- REPLACE (REPL) verändert bestehende Segmente.

- GET HOLD (GHN, GHU, GHNP) hat die gleichen Funktionen wie die anderen Lesebefehle und wird vor DELETE und REPLACE Callss benötigt.

Segmentsuchargumente haben den in Abbildung 10 gezeigten allgemeinen Aufbau und können für alle im hierarchischen Path liegenden Segmente bis zum gewünschten Segment angegeben werden. Generell enthalten SSAs einen Segmentnamen (unqualifiziertes SSA) und wahlweise ein oder mehrere Bedingungen (qualifizierte SSAs). Werden die Bedingungen weggelassen, erfüllt jedes vorkommende Segment dieser Art die Qualifikation.

Bedingungen bestehen aus mathematischen Vergleichsausdrücken, welche ihrerseits mit den Boole'schen Operatoren "UND" bzw. "ODER" verknüpft sein können. Die Vergleichsausdrücke beziehen sich auf Felder, die in der DBD bei der entsprechenden Segmentart definiert sind.

Ein DL/1-Call wird dann erfolgreich beendet, wenn ein Segment gefunden wird, für das sämtliche Suchbedingungen erfüllt sind. Werden bei einem DL/1-Call nicht sämtliche SSAs für alle Segmente im hierarchischen Path angegeben, substituiert IMS von der Call-Type abhängige implizite SSAs (z.B. unqualifizierte SSAs bei GN und GNP). Ein GN-Call ohne SSAs liefert das nächste Segment in der hierarchischen Reihenfolge.

Für jeden PCB wird im Anwendungsprogramm eine Maske definiert, mit deren Hilfe die von IMS nach der Durchführung eines Calls zur Verfügung gestellten Informationen (Segmentname, verketteter Schlüssel aller Segmente im hierarchischen Path, Status-Code usw.) abgefragt werden können. Ein Beispiel für die Programmstruktur eines Batch-PL/1-Programmes finden Sie in Abbildung 11.

IMPLEMENTIERUNGSMETHODEN FÜR DATENBANKEN

Ein Datenbanksystem sollte in der Lage sein, sich unterschiedlichen und rasch ändernden Anforderungen möglichst optimal anpassen zu können, wobei Änderungen keinerlei Auswirkungen auf bestehende Benutzerprogramme haben dürfen.

IMS bietet vier verschiedene Implementierungsmethoden für Datenbanken, die aus der Sicht der Benutzerprogramme voll verträglich sind. Zusätzlich stehen zwei Implementierungsmethoden zur Verfügung, welche die Definition von Standard-Files (unstrukturiert) als Datenbanken zulassen. Übersicht siehe Abbildung 12.

Die Implementierungsmethoden lassen sich in drei Gruppen mit unterschiedlichen Charakteristika einteilen:

a) Kompatibilitätszugriffsmethoden:

- GSAM (Generalized Sequential Access Method) ermöglicht
  die Verarbeitung von sequentiellen Files aller Arten
  als nicht strukturierte Datenbanken (Root only).

- SHISAM (Simple Hierarchic Index Sequential Access Method)
  dient zur Verarbeitung von indexierten VSAM-Files als
  nicht strukturierte Datenbanken.

b) Hierarchisch sequentielle (HS) Implementierungsmethoden
    besitzen folgende Charakteristika:

- Alle zu einem Datenbanksatz gehörigen Segmente werden
  in der hierarchisch sequentiellen Reihenfolge nebeneinander in einem Logical Record des Hauptdatenbereiches
  gespeichert. Bei Überlauf des Logical Records wird ein
  neuer Logical Record im Überlaufbereich angelegt und
  mit den bestehenden Records mittels Physical Pointer
  (Relative Byte-Address = Abstand des logischen Satzes
  vom Bestandsbeginn in Bytes) gemäß der hierarchischen
  sequentiellen Reihenfolge verkettet (Abbildung 13).

- Bei gelöschten Segmenten wird ein Kennzeichen im Seg-
  ment gesetzt. Der Speicherplatz wird erst bei einer
  Reorganisation frei (Ausnahme: bei Löschung eines ganzen
  Datenbanksatzes wird der Platz sofort freigegeben).

- Einfügen von Segmenten zwischen bestehenden erfordert
  eine Verschiebung von Teilen des Datenbanksatzes am
  externen Speichermedium.

- Bei Zugriff auf ein beliebiges abhängiges Segment
  müssen intern alle Segmente, die innerhalb dieses Datenbanksatzes in der Hierarchie vor dem gewünschten
  Segment liegen, gelesen werden.

- HSAM (Hierarchic Sequential Access Method)
  ist eine rein sequentielle Implementierungsmethode (siehe
  Abbildung 14). Datenbanken können nur gelesen oder neu geladen werden. Es existieren keine Veränderungsmöglichkeiten,
  es gibt keine Überläufe. Datenbanken können mittels HSAM
  auch auf Magnetband gespeichert werden.

  Anwendungen: z.B. historische Daten, auf die hauptsächlich sequentiell zugegriffen wird.

- HISAM (Hierarchic Index Sequential Access Method)
  siehe Abbildung 15. Jeder Datenbanksatz ist über den Schlüssel des Root-Segmentes indexiert. Über den Index kann auf
  jeden Satz direkt zugegriffen werden. Bei sequentieller
  Verarbeitung werden die Datenbanksätze in der aufsteigenden Reihenfolge des Root-Segment-Schlüssels zur Verfügung

gestellt. Der Zugriff auf den Hauptdatenbereich erfolgt mit den OS-Zugriffsmethoden ISAM oder VSAM. Der Überlaufbereich wird mittels VSAM oder der IMS-eigenen internen Zugriffsmethode OSAM (Overflow Sequential Access Method) verarbeitet.

Anwendungen: für eher gering strukturierte Datenbanken mit nicht zu starker Veränderungshäufigkeit.

Vorteile:

- Schneller direkter Zugriff auf Datenbanksatz (Root-Segment) über Index
- Schnelle sequentielle Verarbeitung
- Geringer Speicherbedarf

c)   Hierarchisch direkte (HD) Implementierungsmethoden (Abbildung 16) besitzen folgende Charakteristika:

- Alle Segmente eines Datenbanksatzes sind mittels Direct Pointer (= Relative Byte-Address) gemäß der hierarchischen Datenstruktur verknüpft. Alle Pointer werden von IMS aufgebaut und verwaltet und sind für die Anwendungsprogramme transparent.

  Mit Hilfe von Pointers (RBA eines Segmentes) können Segmente sehr schnell direkt verarbeitet werden. Es gibt eine große Anzahl von Pointer-Arten, deren Beschreibung den Rahmen dieses Artikels sprengen würde. Die am häufigsten verwendeten Pointer-Arten sind "Physical Child" und "Physical Twin" Pointer. Physical Child Poiter verbinden ein Segment mit seinen unmittelbar abhängigen Segmenten. Physical Twin Pointer verbinden alle von einem bestimmten Segment abhängigen Segmente einer Art. Bei logischen Verknüpfungen können ebenfalls Pointer zur Verbindung von Segmenten unterschiedlicher Datenbanksätze verwendet werden.

- Ein Datenblock kann Segmente von verschiedenen Datenbanksätzen enthalten.

- Beim Löschen von Segmenten wird der Speicherplatz unmittelbar freigegeben und kann für beliebige andere Segmente verwendet werden.

  Es gibt eine Speicherplatzverwaltung, die mit Hilfe von "Bit-Maps" und "FSE" (Free Space Elemente beschreiben den freien Platz in der Datenbank) arbeitet und einen Algorithmus verwendet, der die Anzahl von Zugriffen auf die Datenbank minimiert.

- Gespeicherte Segmente ändern ihre RBA (Relative Byte-Address) nie.

- HDAM (Hierarchic Direct Access Method, siehe Abbildung
  17)
  verwendet einen Umrechnungsalgorithmus (Randomizing Routine), um aus dem Schlüssel eines Root-Segmentes den Speicherplatz am externen Speichermedium zu errechnen. Syno-
  nymsätze werden von ihrem errechneten Speicherplatz weg
  verkettet und im nächstmöglichen freien Bereich gespeichert. Es gibt einen durch die Randomizing Routine adressierbaren Bereich und einen Überlaufbereich, der für De-
  pendent-Segmente oder ganze Datenbanksätze verwendet wird,
  die im adressierbaren Bereich keinen Platz mehr finden.

  HDAM bietet sehr schnell direkten Zugriff auf alle
  Segmente. Bei einer sequentiellen Verarbeitung werden
  die Datenbanksätze gemäß ihrer Speicherreihenfolge geliefert. Als Basiszugriffsmethode kann OSAM oder VSAM
  verwendet werden.

- HIDAM (Hierarchic Index Direct Access Method)
  verwendet eine eigene Indexdatenbank zur Indexierung aller
  Root-Segmente mittels Pointer. Siehe Abbildung 18. HIDAM
  ist eine häufig verwendete universelle Implementierungs-
  art, die mittels Index einen schnellen direkten Zugriff
  erlaubt. Bei sequentieller Verarbeitung werden die Datenbanksätze nach aufsteigendem Schlüssel des Root-Segmentes
  zur Verfügung gestellt. HIDAM verwendet wahlweise OSAM
  oder VSAM.

Allgemeine Vorteile der hierarchisch direkten (HD) Imple-
mentierungsarten:

- Schneller direkter Zugriff mittels Pointer auf alle
  Segmente, daher günstig für stark strukturierte Datenbanken und logische Verknüpfungen.

- Speicherplatzverwaltung ermöglicht optimale Segmentspei-
  cherung und gute Speicherplatzausnutzung durch unmittelbare Wiederverwendbarkeit des externen Speicherplatzes
  für beliebige Segmente.

- Geringer Reorganisationsbedarf und für starke Bewegungen
  geeignet.

- Möglichkeit, beim Laden oder Reorganisieren freien
  Speicherplatz über die ganze Datenbank zu verteilen.

- Jede HD-Datenbank kann physisch auf mehrere OS-Data-
  Sets mit unterschiedlichen physischen Eigenschaften
  (z.B. Blockgröße, reservierter freier Platz usw) aufgeteilt werden. Diese für alle Benutzer transparente
  Aufteilung erlaubt eine bessere Gruppierung von Segmenten nach Speicherattributen oder Zugriffsprofilen.

Mit diesen Implementierungsmethoden ist eine leichte Anpassung
an Benutzererfordernisse ohne negative Auswirkungen auf Anwendungsprogramme möglich.

LOGISCHE DATENBANKVERKNÜPFUNGEN

Hierarchische Datenstrukturen eignen sich gut zur Darstellung
von Datenrelationen der Art:

- 1 : vielfach (z.B. Vater - Sohn): Ein Vater kann mehrere
  Söhne haben, jeder Sohn kann nur einen Vater haben.

- 1 : 1 (Sonderfall von 1 : vielfach)

Bei Datenrelationen der Art "vielfach : vielfach" ergeben sich
jedoch gewisse Nachteile:

- Redundante Speicherung und dadurch Wartungsprobleme
- Unnötige Komplexität der Zugriffe
- Probleme beim Hinzufügen und Löschen

Beispiel:
Beziehung Lehrer - Schüler (siehe Abbildung 19 a). Ein Lehrer
kann mehrere Schüler unterrichten, ein Schüler kann von mehreren
Lehrern unterrichtet werden. Werden nun Schüler als abhängige
Segmente eines Lehrersegmenttyps (Root-Segment) dargestellt
(Abbildung 19 b oben), ergeben sich folgende Probleme:

- Datenredundanz bei Schülern, die von mehreren Lehrern
  unterrichtet werden
- Komplexe Zugriffe, falls für einen bestimmten Schüler
  alle seine Lehrer gesucht sind
- Ein Schüler ohne Lehrer kann nicht existieren.
- Wird ein Lehrer gelöscht, werden auch alle seine
  Schüler mitgelöscht.

Um diese Probleme zu vermeiden, bietet IMS/VS die Möglichkeit,
hierarchische Datenstrukturen miteinander zu verketten, wodurch
Daten, die in einer Datenbank gespeichert sind, von einer anderen Datenbank direkt angesprochen werden können. Auf diese
Weise können komplexe Netzwerkstrukturen in IMS/VS dargestellt
werden, ohne daß der Benutzer auf seine hierarchische Sicht
der Daten verzichten muß.

Die Implementierungsmethode dieser logischen Verknüpfungen
sei kurz anhand des Lehrer- - Schüler-Beispieles beschrieben
(siehe Abbildung 20 a).

Es wird eine physische Lehrer-Datenbank definiert, welche alle
Lehrer als eigenen Segmenttyp (Root-Segment) enthält. Alle
Schüler werden als eigener Segmenttyp in einer zweiten phy-
sischen Datenbank definiert. Die logische Verknüpfung dieser
beiden Datenbanken kann auf folgende Art definiert werden:
Als abhängiges Segment des Lehrer-Segmenttyps wird ein Pointer-
Segment definiert, welches die Verbindung zum Schüler-Segment
in der anderen Datenbank herstellt. Jedes Pointer-Segment zeigt
auf einen Schüler in der Schüler-Datenbank, welcher von diesem
Lehrer unterrichtet wird (Abbildung 20 b).

Das Pointer-Segment wird als "Logical Child"-Segment bezeichnet, das Schüler-Segment heißt "Logical Parent"-Segment. Ein "Logical Child"-Segment hat immer genau zwei Parent-Segmente: einen Physical Parent (Lehrer) und einen Logical Parent (Schüler). Bei unserem Beispiel geht die Verbindung vom Lehrer zu allen Schülern, die von ihm unterrichtet werden, und wird daher "unidirectional" genannt. Falls notwendig, kann auch die Gegenrichtung vom Schüler zu allen Lehrern, die diesen Schüler unterrichten, definiert werden (Abbildung 20 a und b). Diese Verknüpfungsart wird als "bidirectional" bezeichnet. Dabei wartet IMS/VS automatisch die Gegenrichtung, falls der Benutzer eine Seite der Verknüpfung ändert. Es gibt zusätzliche im DBD definierte Regeln für das Löschen, das Einfügen und das Ändern von logisch verknüpften Segmenten.

Mit Hilfe der logischen Verknüpfungen können nun neue Datenstrukturen, sogenannte "Logische Datenbanken", mittels DBDs beschrieben werden, wobei jeder Datenbanksatz Segmente aus den logisch verknüpften, physischen Datenbanksätzen enthält.

Um die Anwendungsprogrammierung nicht unnötig zu komplizieren, werden Netzwerke, welche durch logische Verknüpfungen von mehreren Datenbanken entstehen, immer als mehrere, hierarchisch strukturierte, logische Datenbanken dargestellt.

Eine logische Datenbankstruktur kann wie folgt definiert werden: Ausgehend vom Root-Segment einer (logisch verknüpften) physischen Datenbank kann jedes Segment unverändert übernommen werden, mit Ausnahme von "Logical Child"-Segmenten. Stattdessen wird ein neuer Segmenttyp definiert, der aus der Verkettung von "Logical Child" und zugehörigen "Logical Parent" besteht. Damit wird der Übergang zur logisch verknüpften Datenbank definiert. All dem "Logical Parent"-Segment in seiner physischen Datenbank über- und untergeordneten Segmente können in der logischen Datenbank als abhängige Segmente des "Logical Parents" definiert werden. Dabei wird die physische Datenstruktur teilweise invertiert.

In unserem Beispiel können zwei logische Datenstrukturen definiert werden (siehe Abbildung 20 c):

   - Lehrer als Root-Segment und Schüler als abhängiges
     Segment (ausgehend von der physischen Lehrer-Datenbank)
     Ein Datenbanksatz enthält alle Schüler, die von einem
     Lehrer unterrichtet werden.

   - Schüler als Root-Segment und Lehrer als abhängiges
     Segment (ausgehend von der physischen Schüler-Daten-
     bank). Ein Datenbanksatz repräsentiert alle Lehrer,
     von denen ein Schüler unterrichtet wird.

Das Beispiel zeigt, daß die gleichen physischen Daten in zwei völlig unterschiedlichen (inversen) logischen Datenstrukturen dargestellt werden können.

Logische Datenbanken werden wie physische Datenbanken mittels
Data Base Descriptions (DBD) definiert.

Die vom Benutzer benötigtenDatenstrukturen werden wieder mittels
PCB definiert, wobei sich ein PCB bei logischen Datenbanken auf
die im logischen DBD beschriebene Struktur bezieht.

Logische Datenbanken können beliebig viele logisch verknüpfte,
physische Datenbanken umfassen. Interessante Möglichkeiten bieten
sich auch durch Definition von logischen Verknüpfungen innerhalb
einer physischen Datenbank, wobei verschiedene Datenbanksätze
miteinander verknüpft werden. Diese Möglichkeit wird z.B. bei
Fertigungsindustrie-Anwendungen genutzt, um in einer Produktda-
tenbank einerseits alle Komponenten eines Produkts zu finden,
andererseits Teileverwendungsnachweise des Produkts zu erstellen.

Zusammenfassend noch einmal die Vorteile von logischen Verknüpfungen:

- Wesentliche Erweiterung des hierarchischen Datenmodelles
  in Richtung Netzwerke
- Beseitigung von Datenredundanzen
- Bessere Anpassung an Benutzererfordernisse durch logi-
  sche Datenstruktur
- Automatische Wartung durch IMS/VS

Weitere Beispiele für logische Verknüpfungen siehe Abbildung 21
bis 23.

SEKUNDÄR-INDIZES

Bei einem integrierten Datenbanksystem greifen viele Anwendungen
auf die gleichen Daten zu. Oft besteht dabei der Bedarf, über
unterschiedliche Suchkriterien direkt zuzugreifen oder sequentielle Verarbeitungen in mehreren verschiedenen Reihenfolgen
durchzuführen. Beim Entwurf einer IMS/VS-Datenbank wird mit der
Auswahl eines Schlüsselfeldes für das Root-Segment (Key) sowohl die Reihenfolge der Datenbanksätze für sequentielle Verarbeitung bestimmt, als auch das Suchargument beim direkten
Zugriff auf einen Datenbanksatz festgelegt.

Besteht nun der zuvor erwähnte Bedarf nach mehrfachen Sortierfolgen oder ist der Hauptordnungsbegriff nicht bei allen
Anwendungen bekannt, können beliebige Sekundär-Index-Datenbanken
definiert werden, welche folgenden Aufbau haben:

- Jedes Indexsegment indexiert ein bestimmtes Segment
  in einer physischen oder logischen Datenbank. Das
  indexierte Segment wird auch "Target-Segment" genannt.

- Die zur Indexierung verwendeten Felder, welche Bestandteil des Schlüsselfeldes des Sekundär-Indizes

sind, können im "Target-Segment" oder in einem beliebigen, davon abhängigen Segment enthalten sein.
Dieses Segment wird "Source-Segment" genannt.

- Je Index-Source-Segment existiert ein Segment in
  der Index-Datenbank, welches das Target-Segment
  indexiert.

- Ein Index-Segment in der Index-Datenbank besteht aus
  dem sekundären Ordnungsbegriff (aus dem Source-Segment), einem Pointer zum Target-Segment und wahlweise
  Benutzerdaten aus der indexierten Datenbank.

Sekundär-Index-Datenbanken bieten folgende Möglichkeiten:

- Direkter Zugriff auf das Target-Segment in der physischen oder logischen Datenbank, wobei das Suchargument sich aus Daten zusammensetzt, welche im
  Source-Segment enthalten sind.

- Sequentielle Verarbeitung in der dem Sekundär-Index
  entsprechenden Sortierfolge. Dabei arbeitet der Benutzer mit einer logischen Datenstruktur, in der
  das Target-Segment als Root-Segment fungiert, auch
  wenn es in der physischen Datenbank ein abhängiges
  Segment ist. Ähnlich wie bei logischen Datenbanken
  wird damit eine Strukturinversion erreicht.

- Automatische Erstellung und Wartung der Sekundärindex-
  datenbanken durch IMS/VS.

- Effiziente Indexierung von nicht eindeutigen Ordnungsbegriffen durch internes Eindeutigmachen.

- Selektive Unterdrückung von Indexeintragungen durch
  Benutzer-Exits.

- Automatisches Führen und Warten von zusätzlichen Daten
  in der Indexdatenbank, welche aus der indexierten Datenbank übernommen werden. Diese Einrichtung kann nützlich
  sein, um häufig benützte Daten schneller in der Index-
  datenbank als in der indexierten Datenbank zu verarbeiten.

Für die Benutzer einer Datenbank sind Sekundär-Indizes transparent. Die durch einen Sekundär-Index repräsentierte Datenstruktur wird mittels PCB dem Benutzer zur Verfügung gestellt. Jedes
Anwendungsprogramm kann daher für die gleiche physische oder logische Datenbank mehrere PCBs benutzen, abhängig von der gewünschten Verarbeitungsfolge oder von dem Sucharqument, mit dem
das Programm auf die Daten direkt zugreifen will. Anwendungsbeispiele siehe Abbildung 24.

DATENSICHERHEITS- UND WIEDERANLAUFEINRICHTUNGEN

Das IMS/VS-Datenbank-Recovery-System basiert im wesentlichen auf
einem Protokoll aller anfallenden Datenbankveränderungen auf dem
IMS/VS-Logband. Am Logband werden automatisch alle Datenbankveränderungen (Status vor und nach der Veränderung) aufgezeichnet.

Es können wahlweise ein oder zwei Logbänder ("Dual Logging") geführt werden. Zwei Logbänder bedeuten im Falle eines permanenten
Schreibfehlers auf einem Logband, daß IMS/VS ohne Unterbrechung
mit dem verbleibenden Logband weiterarbeiten kann.

IMS/VS und das Betriebssystem besitzen Einrichtungen, die die
Vollständigkeit des Logbandes in jeder Situation gewährleisten
(z.B.: bei IMS/VS-Absturz, Betriebssystemfehlern, Programmschlei-
fen, Hardware-Fehlern, irrtümlichem Abbruch durch Operator, Strom-
ausfall usw.).

Das Logband wird für zwei Funktionen benötigt:

1.   Zur Rekonstruktion einer zerstörten Datenbank oder eines
      Teiles davon. Dazu werden eine sequentielle Kopie der Da-
      tenbank und alle seit dem Erstellen der Kopie angefallenen
      Datenbankveränderungen herangezogen.

2.   Zum Rückgängigmachen von bereits durchgeführten Datenbank-
      veränderungen. Diese Funktion wird bei Anwendungsprogramm-
      fehlern gebraucht, wenn falsche oder unvollständige Ände-
      rungen aus einer Datenbank wieder entfernt werden müssen.

Folgende Datenbank-Recovery-Hilfsprogramme stehen zur Verfügung:
(siehe Abbildung 25)

   - Datenbank-Image-Copy-Programm:

     Erstellt Datenbankkopien auf Band oder Platte zu Rekon-
     struktionszwecken (wahlweise eine oder zwei Kopien und
     Checkpoint-Restart-Möglichkeit).

   - Datenbank-Change-Accumulation:

     Komprimiert die auf den Logbändern gespeicherten Datenbank-
     veränderungen und sortiert sie in der physischen Speicher-
     reihenfolge, so daß eine möglichst schnelle Rekonstruktion
     einer zerstörten Datenbank möglich ist.

   - Datenbank-Recovery:

     Rekonstruiert mit Hilfe von Datenbankkopien und wahlweise
     mit akkumulierten oder nicht akkumulierten Logbändern den
     letzten Stand einer Datenbank. Prüfpunkt- und Wiederanlauf-
     funktionen sind vorhanden. Eine Datenbank kann datenbe-
     stands- oder spurweise rekonstruiert werden (z.B. bei
     Plattenlesefehlern ist meist nur eine Spur unbrauchbar).

Bei spurweiser Recovery ist automatische Zuordnung einer
Ersatzspur möglich.

- Datenbank-Backout:

  Rückgängigmachen von bereits erfolgten Datenbankveränderungen, z.B. bei Anwendungsprogrammfehlern oder Programm-
  abbruch. Die Veränderungen werden entweder vollständig
  oder nur bis zu einem vom Anwendungsprogramm bestimmten
  Prüfpunkt rückgängig gemacht.

- Log-Terminator:

  Abschließen bzw. Vervollständigen des Logbandes mit Hilfe
  eines Speicherauszugs in jenen Fällen, in denen IMS dazu
  nicht mehr in der Lage war (z.B. CPU-Fehler).

- Log-Recovery-Utility:

  Korrektur und Abschluß von unbrauchbaren Logbändern (z.B.
  kann beim "Dual Logging" aus zwei mit Lesefehlern behaf-
  teten Logbändern ein fehlerfreies Logband erstellt werden).

Ein Monitor für alle Utility-Funktionen ermöglicht den halbauto-
matischen Betrieb bzw. Prüfpunkt/Wiederanlauf für alle Hilfsprogramme.

Prüfpunkt/Wiederanlauffunktionen sind auch für Anwendungsprogramme
vorhanden. Bei Abbruch ist meist ein Datenbank-Backout bis zum
gewünschten Prüfpunkt nötig. Dann kann das Programm an diesem
Prüfpunkt wieder aufgesetzt werden.

IMS bietet mit diesen Funktionen ein komplettes integriertes
Recovery-Restart-System an, welches vom Benutzer ohne zusätzlichen Programmieraufwand problemlos verwendet werden kann.

DATENBANKREORGANISATION

Datenbanken, bei denen Neuzugänge oder Abgänge erfolgen, tendie-
ren zur nicht optimalen Speicherung, d.h. Segmente eines Datenbanksatzes liegen an externen Speichermedien nicht mehr nebeneinander. Freier Platz wird fragmentiert und fallweise für Zugänge
zu klein. Bei HISAM-Datenbanken belegen gelöschte Segmente weiter
Platz und verursachen unnötige Überläufe. Das Ausmaß der nicht
optimalen Speicherung ist von der Bewegungshäufigkeit der Daten-
bankimplementierungsart und anderen Design-Parametern abhängig.
Bei richtiger Auslegung einer Datenbank wird nur selten eine
Reorganisation aus diesen Gründen notwendig sein.

IMS/VS bietet für alle Reorganisationsaktivitäten fertige Hilfsprogramme, welche die zu reorganisierenden Datenbanken entladen
und wieder neu erstellen.

Durch die Reorganisation gelangen alle Datenbanksegmente wieder
in die optimale (hierarchisch sequentielle) Reihenfolge, Spei-
cherplatzfragmentierungen werden bereinigt und bei HISAM werden
gelöschte Segmente eliminiert und Segmente aus dem Überlaufbereich in den Primärbereich übertragen.

Zusätzlich können mit den Hilfsprogrammen folgende Datenbank-
änderungen ohne Auswirkungen auf Anwendungsprogramme durchgeführt werden:

- Strukturänderungen
- Änderungen der Implementierungsmethode und OS/VS-Zugriffs-
  methoden
- Änderungen von Datenbank-Design-Parametern, wie z.B.
  Größe des über eine Datenbank verteilten freien Speicher-
  platzes, Verteilung auf Data-Set-Groups, Pointer-Arten,
  Blockgrößen usw.
- Logische Verknüpfungen können neu definiert oder eliminiert
  werden.
- Sekundär-Indizes können definiert, geändert oder eliminiert
  werden.
- Bestehende Segmente können gelöscht, neue eingefügt werden.

Alle Reorganisationsprogramme besitzen eingebaute Prüfpunkt/
Wiederanlaufroutinen und können wahlweise zwei Kopien der Daten-
bank erstellen, so daß bei einem permanenten Schreibfehler kein
Abbruch erfolgt.

Die Programme können auch jederzeit unterbrochen und zu einem
späteren Zeitpunkt wieder aufgesetzt werden.

DATENSCHUTZEINRICHTUNGEN

In einem Datenbanksystem kommt der Gewährleistung einer ange-
messenen Systemsicherheit eine besondere Bedeutung zu. Den Forderungen nach Daten-SICHERHEIT, Daten-INTEGRITÄT und Daten-SCHUTZ
kann als Systemleistung nur eine systematische Daten-SICHERUNG
gegenüberstehen.

Datensicherungsüberlegungen betreffen alle Funktionen eines Systems und müssen daher in allen Phasen der Planung und Realisierung einer Anwendungslösung kontinuierlich und gewissenhaft
bedacht werden. Datensicherung ist keine Zusatzfunktion eines
Systems!

IMS/VS bietet in verschiedenen Ebenen Möglichkeiten zur Spezifikation von folgenden Sicherungsfunktionen:

    Identifikation
    Autorisierung
    Integrität
    Protokollierung (Logging)

    Überwachung
    Administration
    Wiederherstellung
    Prüfpunkt/Wiederanlauf

Die Realisierung dieser Sicherungsfunktionen erfolgt teilweise
automatisch und teilweise durch abgestimmte Definitionen in den
einzelnen Systemteilen.

Die im Datenbankteil von IMS/VS enthaltenen Datensicherheits- und
Datenintegritätseinrichtungen wurden bereits im Kapitel "Daten-
sicherheits- und Wiederanlaufeinrichtungen" vorgestellt.

Folgende Datenschutzeinrichtungen stehen im Datenbankteil zur
Verfügung:

  - Die Befugnisse jedes Benutzers einer Datenbank werden
    außerhalb des Anwendungsprogrammes im PSB definiert.
    Die kleinste Dateneinheit, die geschützt werden kann,
    ist ein Segment. Mittels PSB werden für jedes Programm
    die verfügbaren Datenbanken, die "sensitiven" Segmente
    dieser Datenbanken und je Segment die erlaubten Verar-
    beitungsarten definiert. Damit werden nicht autorisierte
    Zugriffe verhindert und es wird gleichzeitig dokumentiert,
    wie die Benutzer die Daten verwenden.

  - Die zentrale Verwaltung aller DBDs und PSBs durch die
    Datenbank-Administratorfunktion ermöglicht unter Verwen-
    dung von weiteren betriebssystemspezifischen Schutzmaß-
    nahmen, wie z.B. Kenntworten, einen effizienten Daten-
    schutz.

  - In der Data Base Description (DBD) kann ein Kennwort
    für eine physische Datenbank definiert werden. Damit
    wird ein Zugriff ohne Kontrolle durch IMS/VS verhindert.

  - IMS/VS bietet Möglichkeiten, Datenbanksegmente am externen
    Speichermedium zu verschlüsseln. Für IMS/VS-Anwendungspro-
    gramme ist diese Verschlüsselung transparent. Sie verhin-
    dert jedoch den unbefugten Zugriff auf Datenbanken, Log-
    bänder und Backup-Kopien von Datenbanken ohne Kontrolle
    durch IMS/VS.

Der Datenfernverarbeitungsteil von IMS/VS bietet zusätzliche
Schutzmaßnahmen:

  - Für jede Transaktionsart wird zentral festgelegt, von wel-
    chen Datenstationen sie verwendet werden darf.

  - Zusätzlich können Kennworte für Transaktionen und Steuer-
    befehle festgelegt werden.

- Jeder Versuch eines nicht autorisierten Zugriffes wird
  von IMS/VS am Logband aufgezeichnet. Zusätzlich wird der
  Master Terminal Operator davon in Kenntnis gesetzt.

ARBEITSABLAUF BEI IMS/VS

Bei der Durchführung eines Batch-IMS/VS-Anwendungsprogrammes wird
IMS/VS über Job-Control-Steuerkarten aufgerufen. Beim Aufruf werden, neben anderen Parametern, auch der Name des Anwendungsprogrammes und des PSBs mitgegeben. Im Rahmen der Initialisierungs-
phase werden alle benötigten IMS/VS-Module geladen (falls sie nicht
im Betriebssystem resident sind). Der PSB, alle benötigten DBDs
und das Anwendungsprogramm werden von den entsprechenden Bibliotheken geladen und ein Datenbank-Ein-/Ausgabepufferbereich angelegt.

Das Anwendungsprogramm bekommt die Kontrolle und ruft bei jedem
DL/1-Call über das Language Interface IMS/VS auf. IMS/VS-Module
verarbeiten die Anforderung und greifen mit Hilfe von OS-Zugriffsmethoden auf die Datenbanken zu.

Bei jedem DL/1-Call wird geprüft, ob sich der benötigte Datenbank-
block nicht bereits im Pufferbereich befindet ("Look Aside Buffe-
ring"). Die Verwaltung der einzelnen Puffer erfolgt nach Benütz-
zungshäufigkeit, d.h. bei einer neuen Pufferanforderung wird jener
Puffer verwendet, der bisher am seltensten angesprochen wurde
("Least recently used" Algorithmus).

Durch diese Pufferverwaltung wird eine Minimierung von Ein-/Aus-
gabeoperationen erreicht.

Bei Veränderungen von Datenbanksegmenten werden die Veränderungen
automatisch auf dem IMS/VS-Logband protokolliert.

Eine Datenbank kann von mehreren Batch-Programmen parallel gelesen werden, darf jedoch nicht parallel verändert werden. Pa-
rallele Veränderungen der gleichen Datenbank von mehreren Programmen aus ist unter der Kontrolle des IMS/VS-DC-Systems in vol-
lem Umfang möglich. Dabei können On-line- und Batch-Anwendungspro-
gramme gleichzeitig Segmente derselben Datenbank verändern. Die
Zugriffskontrolle erfolgt auf Segmentebene. IMS/VS-DC besitzt
auch Einrichtungen, die einen Interlock zwischen zwei Anwendungsprogrammen erkennen und beheben können. Ein Interlock wird durch
Abbruch und neues Aufsetzen eines beteiligten Programmes gelöst.

BESONDERE VORZÜGE VON IMS/VS

1.   Hohe Betriebssicherheit:

     IMS/VS enthält ein ausgefeiltes System von Sicherheitsein-
     richtungen, die für eine hohe Verfügbarkeit der Datenban-
     ken sorgen und im Fehlerfall eine rasche und vollständige
     Rekonstruktion der Daten ermöglichen.

Im Datenfernverarbeitungsbetrieb ist die hohe Betriebssicherheit besonders wichtig, da bei einem Ausfall ein
großer Benutzerkreis betroffen ist. IMS bietet mit dem integrierten Logging, der Programmisolation und den Prüfpunkt/
Wiederanlauffunktionen alle Voraussetzungen für einen siche-
ren Betrieb.

2.   Einfache Anwendungsprogrammierung:

DL/1 ist dank seines einfachen Aufbaues leicht erlernbar
und kann in allen gebräuchlichen Programmiersprachen verwendet werden.

DL/I ist auf die Behandlung von hierarchischen Datenstrukturen ausgelegt, trotzdem ist die Verarbeitung von Netzwerken und der Zugriff über sekundäre Ordnungsbegriffe genauso leicht wie die Handhabung einfacher hierarchischer
Strukturen.

Im Datenfernverarbeitungsbetrieb wird DL/I nicht nur für
die Datenbankzugriffe, sondern auch für die Kommunikation
mit den Terminals verwendet. Aus diesem Grunde unterscheidet sich die TP-Programmierung nur unwesentlich von der
Batch-Programmierung.

3.   Gute Anpassung an die Betriebssysteme:

IMS kann als ein integrierter Bestandteil der Betriebsyste-
me angesehen werden und nützt daher alle gebotenen Möglichkeiten optimal aus. Vielfach wurden Betriebsfunktionen nur
für IMS entwickelt.

An Beispielen wären zu nennen:

. Verwendung spezieller, privilegierter Schnittstellen
  zum Betriebssystem, wie:

        - OSAM I/O Driver in MVS
        - VSAM shared resources
        - VTAM authorized path
        - parallel DL/1

. Gemeinsamer Prüfpunkt für OS Dateien und Datenbanken bei Verwendung von GSAM

. VSAM KSDS als Datenbank verwendbar

. Log Terminator Programm lokalisiert Logdaten
  in OS Dumps.

. IMS Fast Path Feature verwendet viele spezielle
  Betriebssystemfunktionen

. IMS-Multiprozessor und -Anschlußprozessor-Unter-
  stützung

ANWENDER

IMS/VS-Datenbanksysteme haben sich dank ihrer universellen Ver-
wendbarkeit weltweit in vielen Anwendungsbereichen bewährt.

In Österreich wird IMS/VS in den Bereichen Banken, Versicherungen, öffentliche Dienste, Verwaltung, Sozialversicherung, Schwerindustrie und IBM-intern verwendet.

Dazu einige Beispiele:

- Die Erste Allgemeine Versicherung speichert Kunden-, Polizzen-, Kraftfahrzeugkennzeichen- und Vermittlerdaten in logisch verknüpften IMS/VS-Datenbanken.

  Alle österreichischen Niederlassungen benützen im Datenfernverarbeitungsbetrieb (IMS/VS DB/DC) die zentral gespeicherten Datenbanken für folgende Anwendungen:

    - Auskünfte, Änderungen und Neuzugänge bei Versicherungsverträgen
    - Auskünfte von Kundendaten
    - Schadensabwicklung

- Das Bundesministerium für Bauten und Technik benutzt IMS/VS zum Verwalten einer Grundstücksdatenbank, die im Rahmen des Projektes "Automation des Grundbuches, Modellversuch Wien" aufgebaut wurde und alle Wiener Grundstücke umfaßt.

- Die Österreichische Post- und Telegraphenverwaltung hat mit Hilfe von IMS/VS-DB/DC zentrale Auskunftssysteme aufgebaut, welche einen On-line-Zugriff auf Informationen über Postämter und den Autobusverkehr ermöglichen.

  Weiters werden Rundfunkbewilligungen über ein alle Landeshauptstädte umfassendes Leitungsnetz on-line verarbeitet. Ein Personalinformationssystem ist ebenfalls im Einsatz und ein Telefonanmeldesystem steht kurz vor der Fertigstellung.

  Die Erste Allgemeine Versicherung und die Österreichische Post- und Telegraphenverwaltung verwenden neben konventionellen Programmiersprachen auch die Abfragesprache GIS/VS für Datenbankanwendungen.

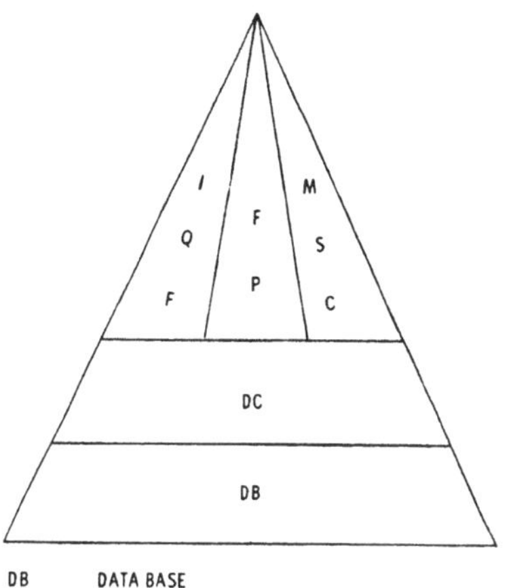

Abbildung 1

LOGICAL DATA STRUCTURE

- A DATA BASE CONSISTS OF 1 TO N DATA BASE RECORDS
- A DATA BASE RECORD CONSISTS OF 1 TO N SEGMENTS
- MAXIMUM OF 255 SEGMENT NAMES
- MAXIMUM OF 15 SEGMENT LEVELS
- 1 ROOT SEGMENT PER DATA BASE RECORD
- DEPENDENT SEGMENTS -- 0 TO N PER PARENT

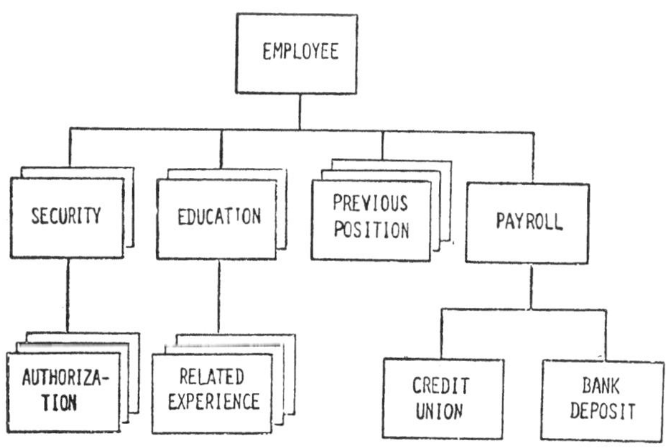

Abbildung 2

Datenbankbeschreibung
DBD

(DATA BASE DISCRIPTION)

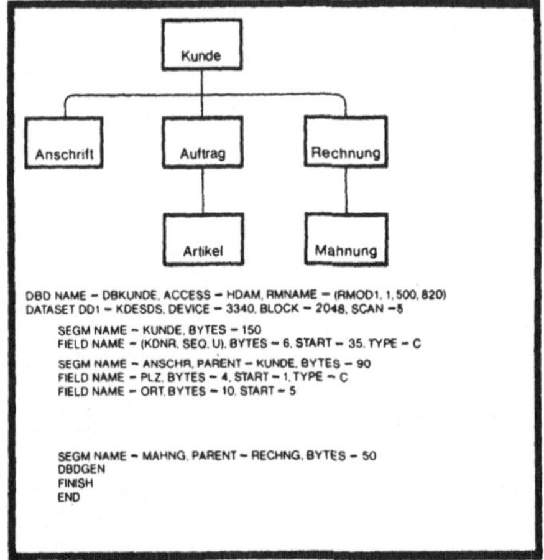

Abbildung 3

Programmbeschreibung
PSB

(PROGRAM SPECIFICATION BLOCK)

Abbildung 4

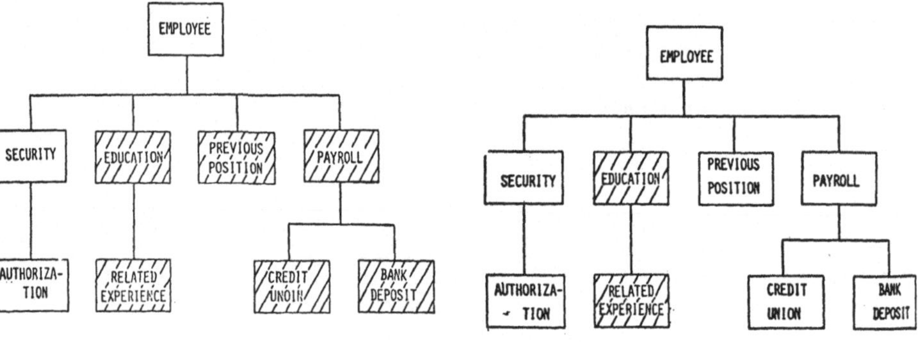

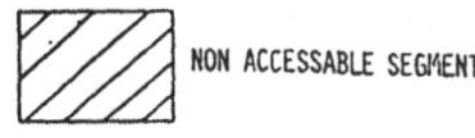

Abbildung 5

Abbildung 6

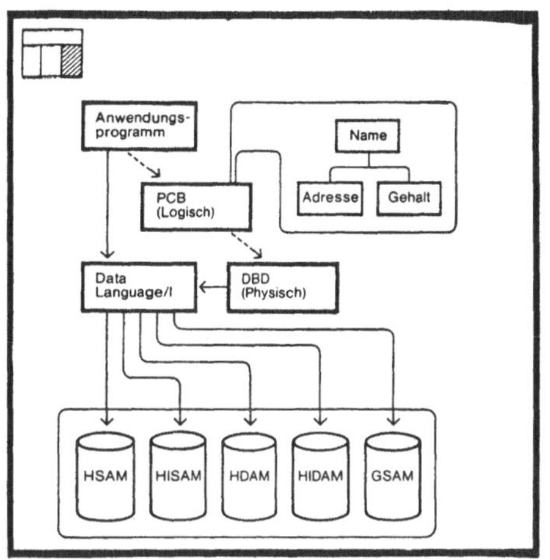

Abbildung 7

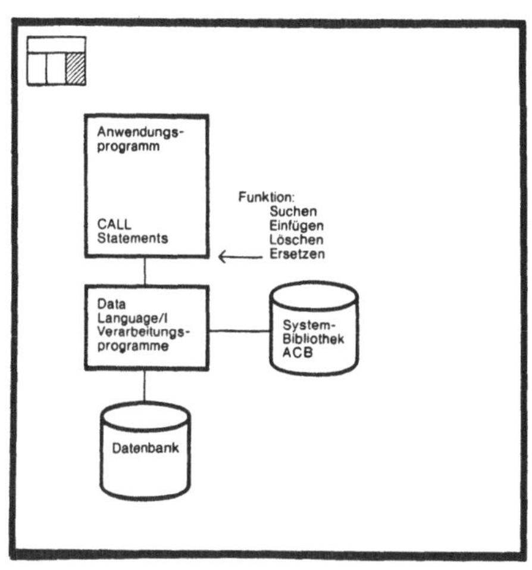

Abbildung 8a

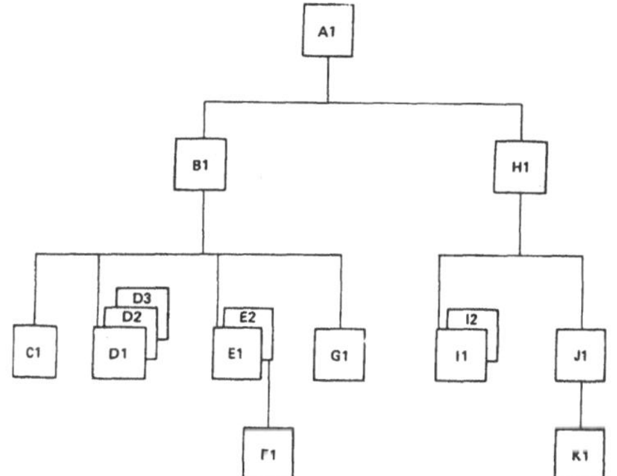

Hirarchische Reihenfolge:

A1 B1 C1 D1 D2 D3 E1 E2 F1 G1 H1
I1 I2 J1 K1 A2 usw.

Abbildung 8b

CALL STATEMENTS

```
1.  FUNCTIONS (ON A SEGMENT BASIS)

     o  GET UNIQUE (HOLD)
     o  GET NEXT (HOLD)
     o  GET NEXT IN PARENT (HOLD)
     o  INSERT
     o  DELETE
     o  REPLACE

2.  SEGMENT SEARCH ARGUMENTS

     o  SEGNAME (CONDITIONS)
```

PL/I	CALL PLITDLI (PARM-COUNT,FUNCTION,DATA-BASE-PCB, IO-AREA,SSA1,SSA2,SSAN);
COBOL	CALL 'CBLTDLI' USING FUNCTION,DATA-BASE-PCB, IO-AREA,SSA1,SSA2,SSAN.
ASSEMBLER	CALL ASMTDLI, (FUNCTION,DBPCB, IOAREA,SSA1,SSA2,SSAN)

Abbildung 9

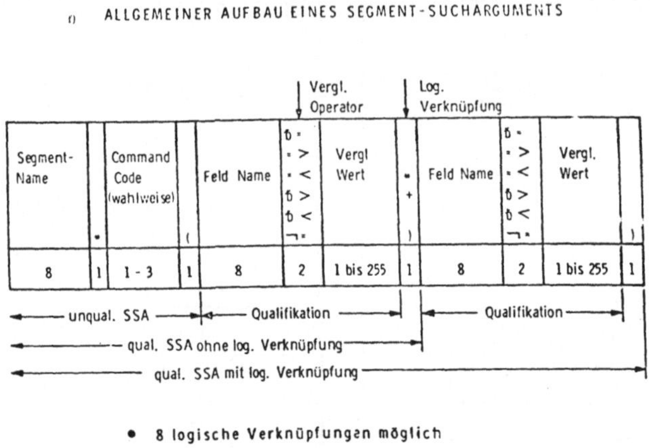

ALLGEMEINER AUFBAU EINES SEGMENT-SUCHARGUMENTS

		Vergl. Operator			Log. Verknüpfung						
Segment-Name	Command Code (wahlweise)	Feld Name	฿ = = > = < ฿ > ฿ < ¬ =	Vergl Wert	Feld Name	฿ = = > = < ฿ > ฿ < ¬ =	Vergl. Wert				
8	1	1 - 3	1	8	2	1 bis 255	1	8	2	1 bis 255	1

←—— unqual. SSA ——→|←—— Qualifikation ——→|←—— Qualifikation ——→

←———— qual. SSA ohne log. Verknüpfung ————→

←———————— qual. SSA mit log. Verknüpfung ————————→

● 8 logische Verknüpfungen möglich

Abbildung 10

```
/* ------------------------------------------------ */
/*.                  ENTRY POINT                     */
/* ------------------------------------------------ */
    DLITPLI: PROC(MAST_PTR,DETAIL_PTR) OPTIONS (MAIN);

DCL   FUNC_GU CHAR(4) STATIC INIT ('GU');
DCL   FUNC_GHU CHAR(4) STATIC INIT ('GHU');
DCL   FUNC_REPL CHAR(4) STATIC INIT ('REPL');
DCL   FUNC-GHN CHAR(4) STATIC INIT ('GHN');

DCL   SSA_NAME...;

DCL   DET_SEG_IO_AREA...;

DCL   1 DB_PCB_MAST     BASED(MAST_PTR),...;
DCL   1 DB_PCB_DETAIL   BASED(DETAIL_PTR),....;

DCL   THREE FIXED BINARY(31) STATIC INITIAL(3);
DCL   FOUR FIXED BINARY(31) STATIC INITIAL(4);

CALL PLITDLI(FOUR,FUNC_GU,DETAIL_PTR,DET_SEG_IO_AREA,
     SSA_NAME);

CALL PLITDLI(FOUR,FUNC_GHU,MAST_PTR,MAST_SEG_IO_AREA,
     SSA_NAME);

CALL PLITDLI(THREE,FUNC_GHN,MAST_PTR,MAST_SEG_IO_AREA);

CALL PLITDLI(THREE,FUNC_REPL,MAST_PTR,MAST_SEG_IO_AREA);

END DLITPLI;


PL/I LANGUAGE INTERFACE
```

Abbildung 11

OS Zugriffs-methoden	IMPLEMENTIERUNGSARTEN					
	Hierarchisch Sequentiell		Hierarchisch Direkt		Verträglich zu OS Files	
	HSAM	HISAM	HDAM	HIDAM	SHISAM	GSAM
ISAM		X		X		
OSAM		X	X	X		
VSAM		X	X	X	X	X
SAM	X					X

Abbildung 12

Speicherung von DL/I-Datenbanksätzen

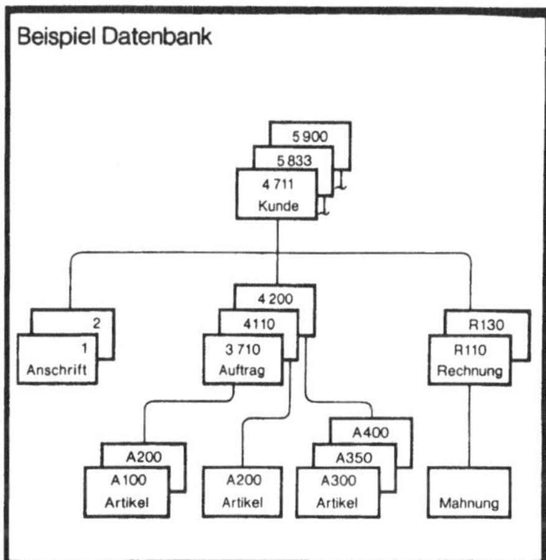

Abbildung 12a

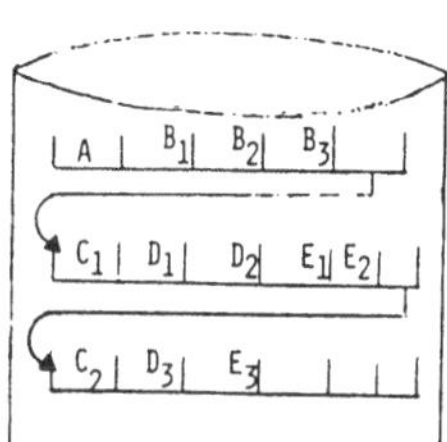

Abbildung 13

Zugriffsmethode hierarchisch sequentiell

HSAM

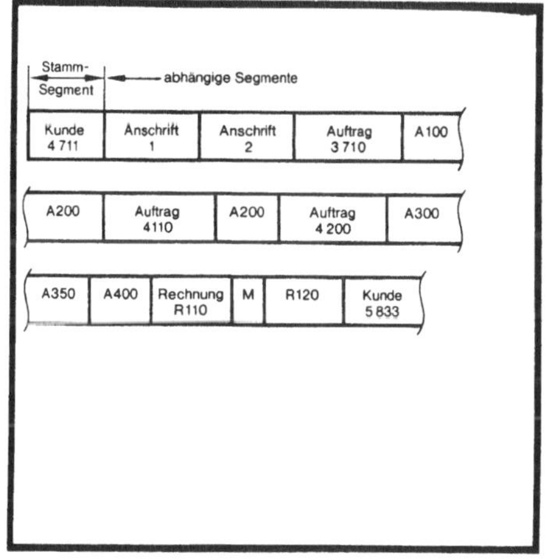

Abbildung 14

Zugriffsmethode
hierarchisch index sequentiell
HISAM

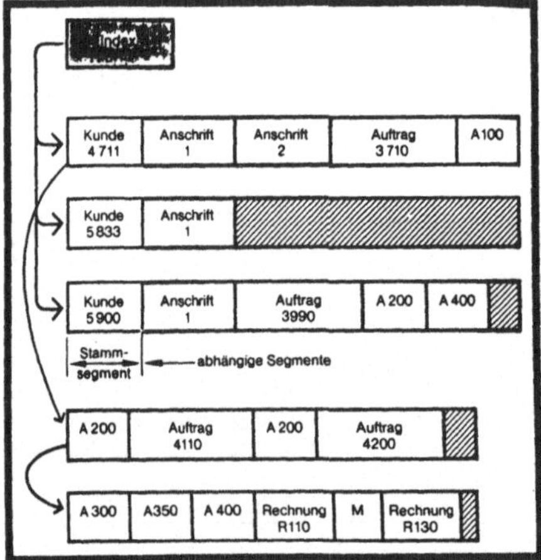

Abbildung 15

Speicherung von
DL/I-Datenbanksätzen

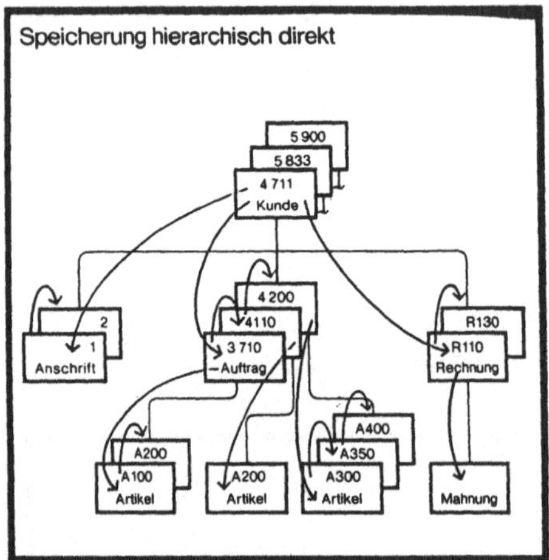

Abbildung 16

Zugriffsmethode
hierarchisch direkt
HDAM

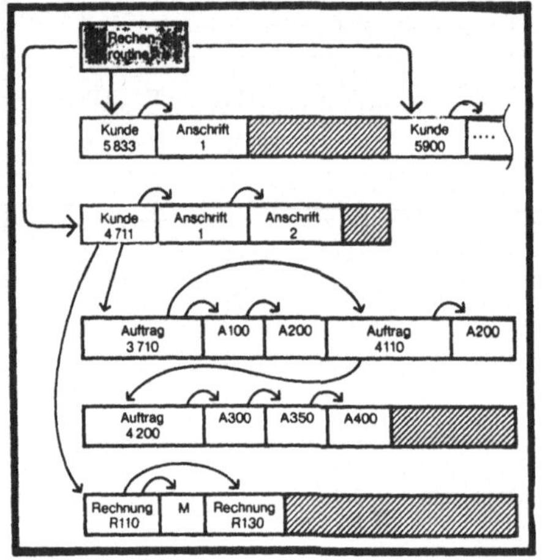

Abbildung 17

Zugriffsmethode
hierarchisch index direkt
HIDAM

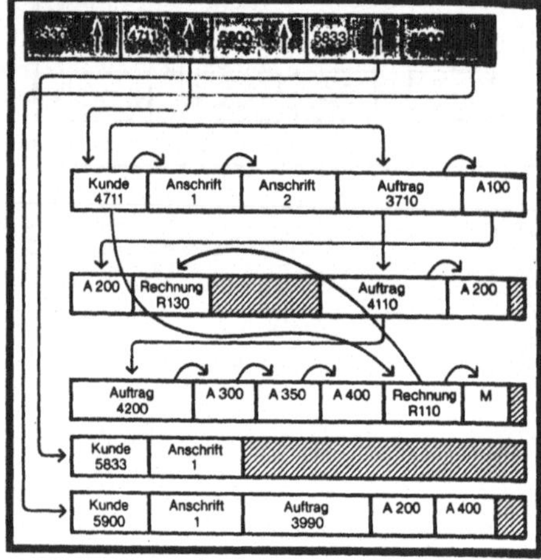

Abbildung 18

LOGISCHE DATENBANKVERKNÜPFUNGEN

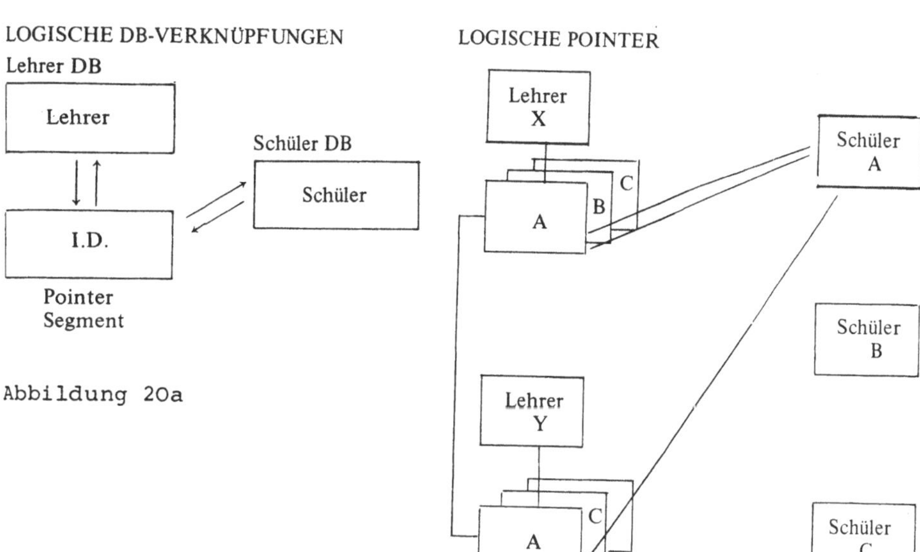

LOGISCHE DATENBANKSTRUKTUREN

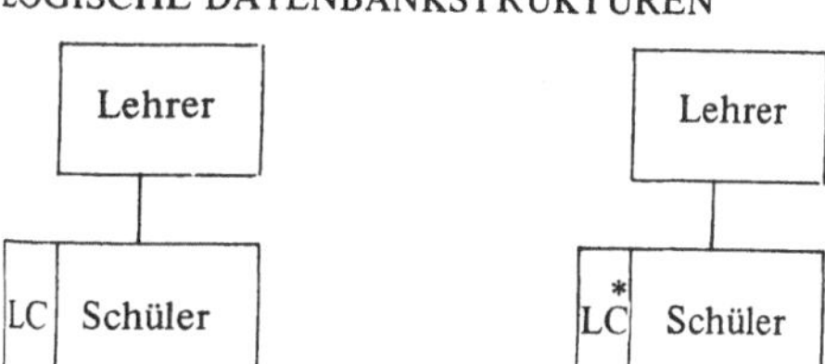

Abbildung 20c

DL/I Datenorganisation

Logische Verbindungen
Minimierung der Datenredundanz

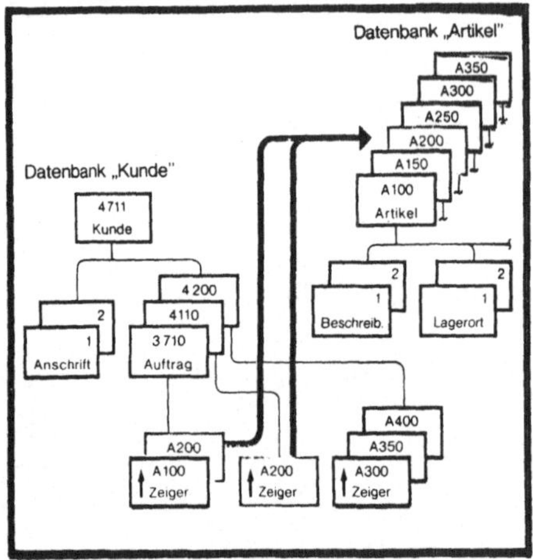

Abbildung 21

DL/I-Datenorganisation

Einseitig gerichtete logische Verbindung

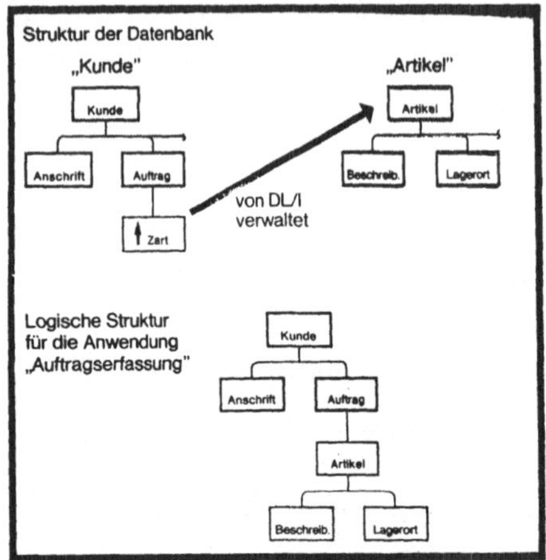

Abbildung 22

DL/I-Datenorganisation

Zweiseitig gerichtete logische Verbindung

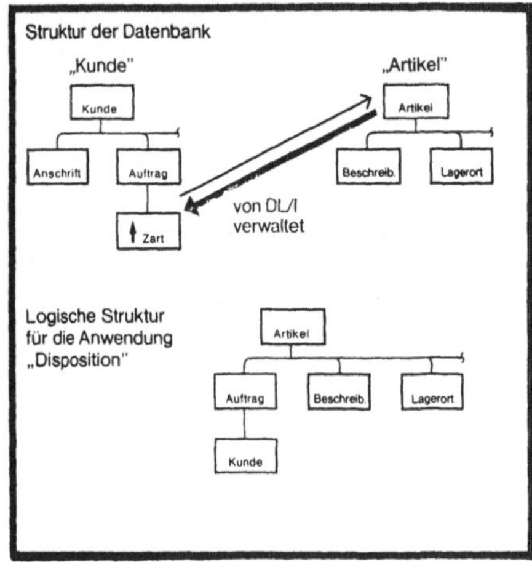

Abbildung 23

DL/I Datenorganisation

Mehrfachindizierung

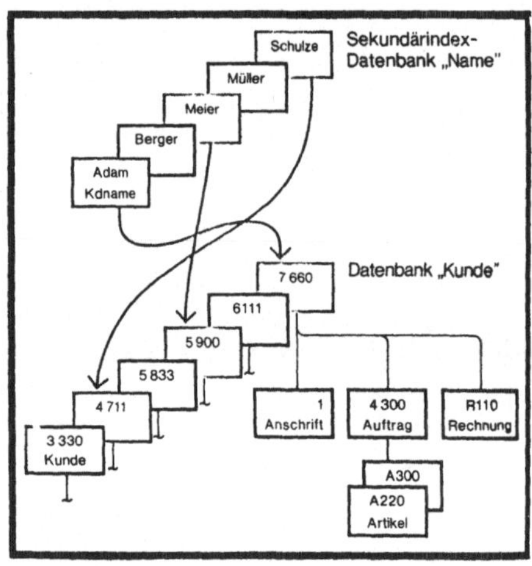

Abbildung 24a

DL/I-Datenorganisation

Mehrfachindizierung

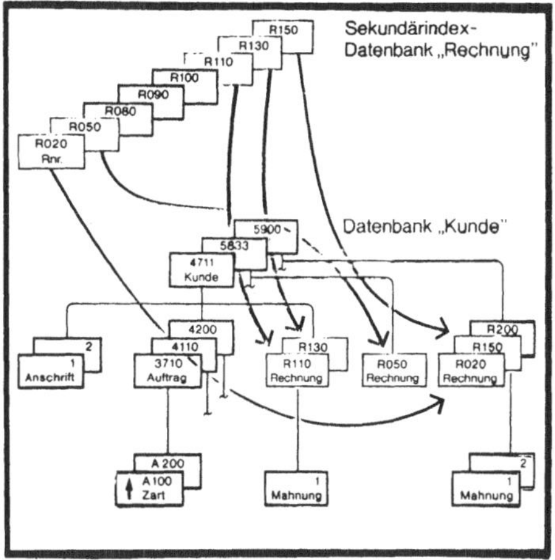

Abbildung 24b

DL/I-Datenorganisation

Mehrfachindizierung

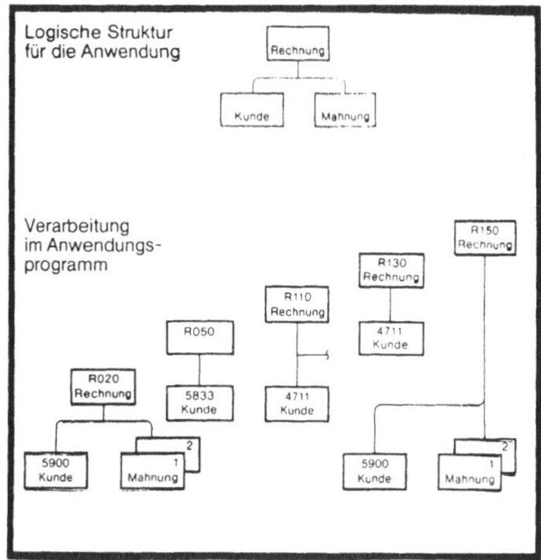

Abbildung 24c

Datenbank
Recovery-Hilfsprogramme

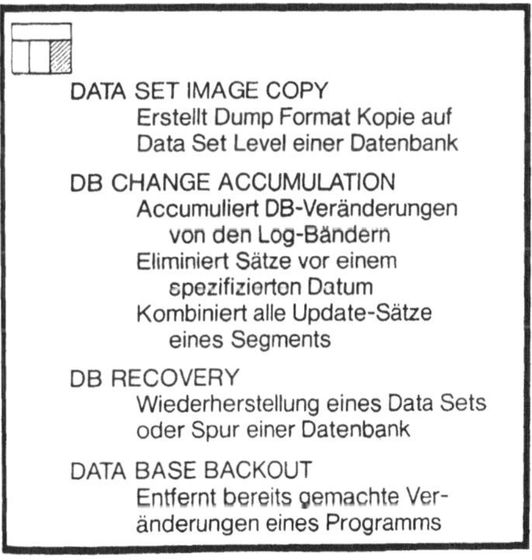

Abbildung 25

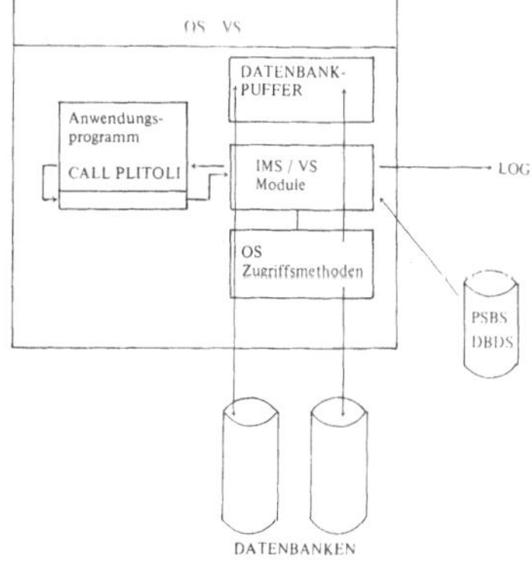

Abbildung 26

Eine volkswirtschaftliche Datenbank unter FMS-8

Erich Wang
WSR-Wien

Gliederung

1. Einleitung
2. System Design
    2.1. Information Management System IMS-8
    2.2. File Design
    2.3. Interne Datenorganisation
3. User Interface
    3.1. Datenbankfunktionen für den Benützer
    3.2. Sprachinterface
    3.3. Filereferenzierung in einem Benützerprogramm
    3.4. Erstellen eines durchführbaren Benützerprogramms
    3.5. Privilegierte Datenbankfunktionen
4. System Utilities
    4.1. File naming
    4.2. Sicherheitssystem
    4.3. Logging
    4.4. Dump und Load
    4.5. Restore
    4.6. Prüfprogramme
    4.7. Sonstige Utilities
5. Schlußwort

1. Einleitung

Der Computerhersteller Sperry UNIVAC hat zwei Datenbanksysteme für die
Produktserie U 1100 konzipiert: FMS-8 und DMS 1100.

DMS 1100 lehnt sich an die CODASYL-Empfehlungen an und wird von der Firma als universelles Datenbanksystem angeboten; hingegen basiert FMS-8 auf einer indexsequentiellen, hierarchischen Datenorganisation. Es besitzt Eigenschaften, die in den folgenden Paragraphen erläutert werden, die FMS-8 zu einem hervorragenden System machen. Mit diesem System wurde die volkswirtschaftliche Datenbank des Institutes für Wirtschaftsforschung errichtet.

2. System design

2.1 Information Management System IMS-8

FMS-8 ist die Abkürzung vom

  File

  Management

  System

  |

  8

`-8` sollte anzeigen, daß es unter der Kontrolle des Betriebssystems EXEC-8 arbeitet. FMS-8 ist ein Prozessor des Systems IMS-8, die Abkürzung von

  Information

  Management

  System

  |

  8

IMS-8, wie der Name schon zeigt, sollte nicht nur die Daten verwalten können, sondern aus diesen Informationen gewinnen. Dazu gehören noch zwei Prozessoren: der Interactive Prozessor und der Report Writer, eine Art Query Language Processor. Das Zusammenspiel zwischen den Prozessoren und Benützerprogrammen kann aus dem folgenden Diagramm entnommen werden.

2.2 File design

1) Index- und Datenfile
Die dem FMS-8 zugrunde liegende Datenorganisations- und Verarbeitungsform ist eine indexsequentielle.

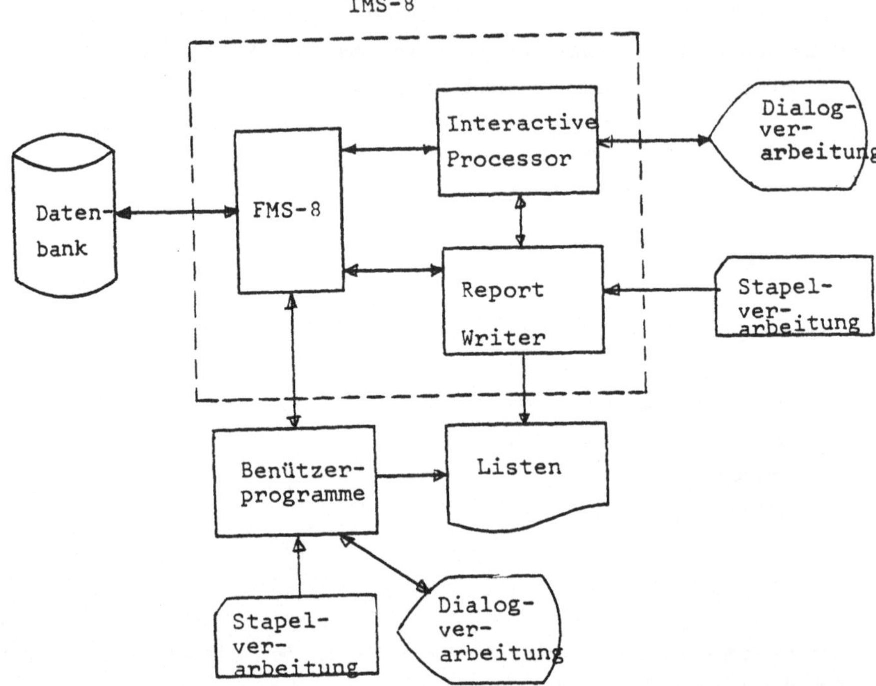

Die Datenbank, genannt Database, besteht aus dem Index- und dem Datenteil. Der
Indexteil wird benützt, um die Datensätze in den Datenteil einzuordnen. Physisch
sind sie auf zwei Files gespeichert. Das hat den Vorteil, das Indexfile auf eine
schnelle Speichereinheit, etwa auf einen flying head mit fixen Lese- und Schreib-
köpfen legen zu können, um einen schnellen Zugriff auf den Index zu erzielen.

2) FMS-8 Files

Die Datenbank kann in bis zu 1000 FMS-8 Files aufgeteilt werden. Da sie von 1 bis
1000 numeriert sind, werden sie auch als numbered files bezeichnet. Zunächst kann
man sich mit der Aussage begnügen, daß sich zu einer Anwendung, logisch zusammengehörige Datensätze in einem FMS-8 File befinden.

3) FMS-8 Subfiles

Ein FMS-8 File kann man weiter in FMS-8 Subfiles aufgliedern. Ein numbered file
kann bis 64 Subfiles enthalten. Da die Subfiles namentlich vom Benützerprogramm
angesprochen werden, nennt man sie im FMS-8 auch named Files. Die Datensätze, die

in einem Subfile gespeichert sind, müssen vom gleichen Typ sein und die
gleiche Wortlänge aufweisen.

4) Search Key

a. Primary Search Key (PSK)

Zur Identifikation eines Datensatzes gibt es einen Schlüssel, z.B. eine Kontonummer. Diesen Schlüssel nennt man im FMS-8 Primary Search Key. In einem FMS-8
File muß die Länge der Primary Search Keys gleich sein. Die Datensätze in verschiedenen Subfiles, die zu einem FMS-8 File gehören, müssen einen gemeinsamen
Schlüssel haben.

b. Secondary Search Key (SSK)

Ein Datensatz in einem Subfile kann einen Hilfsschlüssel haben, der wiederum in
5 Teilschlüssel zerlegbar ist. Diesen Hilfsschlüssel nennt man im FMS-8 Secondary
Search Key. Er dient dazu, die Datensätze in einem Subfile unter einem Primary
Search Key zu differenzieren.

Von der Anwendung her kann man die Beziehung zwischen SSK, PSK, Subfile und FMS-8
File so betrachten, daß ein Subfile eine Datei darstellt. Hier werden Datensätze
gleichen Typs gespeichert. Mehrere Dateien, die zu einer Anwendung gehören, deren
Datensätze mit einem gemeinsamen Schlüssel (PSK) angesprochen werden können,
werden einem FMS-8 File zugeordnet.

Ein Beispiel soll diese Beziehung illustrieren. Eine Verkaufsfirma wird von
m Firmen mit n Waren beliefert.Jede Ware wird mit einer Warennummer versehen,
die als PSK dient. Es gibt für jede Lieferfirma ein Subfile mit dem Namen F1,
F2,..., FM. Ein Subfile mit dem Namen BEZ ist für die Warenbezeichnung gedacht.
Alle diese Subfiles gehören zu einem FMS-8 File, weil alle Datensätze in den
Subfiles einen gemeinsamen Schlüssel (die Warennummer) im FMS-8 File haben. Jede
Lieferung von einer Firma wird mit einem 6-stelligen Datum als Hilfsschlüssel
in die zugehörige Datei (Subfile) gespeichert.

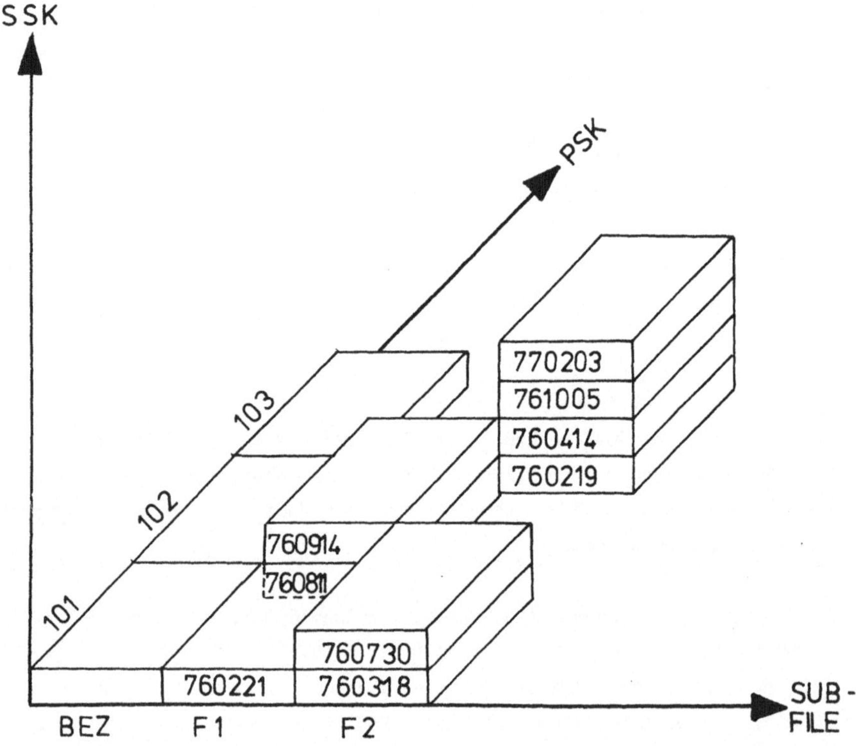

In der volkswirtschaftlichen Datenbank befinden sich Daten in Form von Zeitreihen. Eine Zeitreihe setzt sich aus Beschreibungen und Beobachtungen zusammen. Zur Identifikation wird der Zeitreihe eine eindeutige Benennung
(Label) zugeordnet. Die Benennung wird als PSK verwendet. In einem FMS-8 File
kann man jetzt die Beschreibung einer Zeitreihe in ein Subfile speichern. Die
Beobachtungen der Zeitreihen weisen verschiedene Längen auf, wie aus dem
ersten Teil des Vortrages hervorgeht. Wenn man die Satzlänge nach der längs-
sten Zeitreihe richtet, würde viel Platz unbenützt bleiben. Der SSK bietet
eine ideale Lösung dieses Problems. Die Satzlänge wird mit 60 Wörtern für
60 Beobachtungen gewählt. Der Beobachtungsteil einer Zeitreihe wird in eine
oder mehrere Datensätze zerlegt. Jeder Datensatz mit der Länge 60 Wörter
erhält einen SSK. Die SSKs sind aufsteigend durchnumeriert.

Eine Zeitreihe mit der Benennung ABCXYZ mit 150 Beobachtungen wird wie folgt mit dem FMS-8 Filekonzept realisiert:

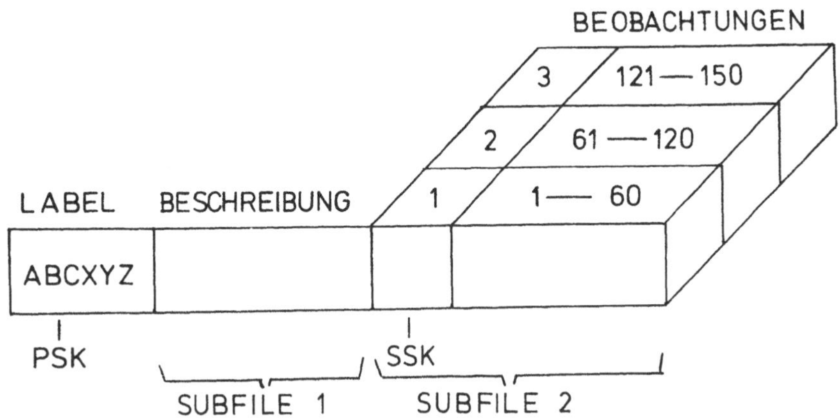

5) Lock

Bei Durchführung bestimmter Datenbankoperationen, insbesondere wenn ein Datensatz verändert wird, wird während der Operation der zu verändernde Datensatz gesperrt. Im FMS-8 heißt es: es wird ein Lock am Primary Search Key gesetzt. In dieser Zeit wird zum Schutze kein anderer Benützer auf den Datensatz zugreifen können.

6) Level

Je nach Wichtigkeit und nach Beschaffenheit kann man die FMS-8 Files in übereinanderstehende Ebenen einstufen. Die Ebenen werden im FMS-8 Levels genannt. Es gibt 4 Levels hierarchisch von oben nach unten angeführt: 0,1,2,3,.

Durch undiszipliniertes Setzen oder zum Aufheben vergessener Locks in einem Programm kann eine Deadlock-Situation entstehen. Viele Sätze werden dadurch für Eigen- und Fremdbenützung bockiert.

Um diese Situation von vornherein auszuschließen, ist das Level-Konzept vor allem gedacht.

Der Datenbankadministrator ordnet die FMS-8 Files in logische Kategorien ein, indem er den einzelnen Files Levels zuordnet.

Ist ein Datensatz auf einer niedrigen Ebene gesperrt und setzt das Programm einen
PSK Lock auf einen Satz in einer höheren Ebene,so werden alle Sperren auf niedrigeren Ebenen aufgehoben, um eine Hinderung der Operation auf einer höheren Ebene
zu vermeiden.

Ein File auf einer höheren Ebene kann z.B. Primärdaten und ein File auf einer
niedrigeren Ebene ableitbare Daten enthalten.

Ein Programm kann nur einen Lock auf einer Ebene setzen, sobald es einen zweiten
setzt, wird der erste aufgehoben.

Ein Beispiel:

```
          CALL OPEN-DB Funktion
          .

          .

          .

     1000 READ (Inputunit, 1, END = 2000) PSK, neuer Wert
        1 FORMAT (...)
          CALL READ-LOCK-Funktion
          CALL MODIFY-Funktion
          GO TO 1000
     2000 CALL CLOSE-FILE-Funktion
          .

          .

          .

          END
```

Wenn der Lock nicht durch Setzen eines anderen Locks aufgehoben wäre, würden alle
verarbeiteten Datensätze gesperrt bleiben. Durch den Level-Lock-Mechanismus wird
die willkürlich gesetzte Sperre aufgehoben.

Will man jedoch in einem Programm mehrere Locks auf verschiedenen Ebenen setzen,
so muß man sie von der obersten Ebene beginnend setzen. Das gleichzeitige
Setzen von Locks auf inhaltlich zusammenhängende, durch ihre hierarchische Struktur auf verschiedenen Ebenen befindliche Datensätze, schützt die Benützer in einem

Multiprocessing Betrieb vor Irrtümern und Fehlinformationen. Ein Beispiel soll die
Verwendung des Levels veranschaulichen. Es gibt 3 Datensätze, die inhaltlich abhän
gig sind:

1.Satz	Preis für PKW Marke 1
2.Satz	PKW-Preisindex
3.Satz	Verbraucherpreisindex

Jetzt sei der Preis für PKW Marke 1 gestiegen; der Datensatz wird modifiziert.
Aus dem Preis wird der PKW-Preisindex abgeleitet, der wiederum den Verbraucher-
preisindex bestimmt. Wenn die letzten zwei Datensätze während der Modifikation
des ersten Datensatzes nicht gesperrt würden, so würden andere Benützer auf die
zwei alten Datensätze zugreifen können.

Durch ihre hierarchische Struktur ist es daher notwendig, die 3 Datensätze in über-
einander stehenden Ebenen anzuordnen. Bei Veränderung des 1. Datensatzes sollen
die anderen zwei gesperrt und anschließend auch verändert werden.

Level	Datensatz
0	Preis für PKW Marke 1
1	PKW-Preisindex
2	Verbraucherpreisindex

2.3 Interne Datenorganisation

1) Data Track und Data Track Split
Ein Data Track ist eine Speichereinheit in dem Datenteil der Datenbank. Die Daten-
sätze werden auf Data Tracks geschrieben. Man kann ihn auch als Datenseite oder
Page bezeichnen.

Das Format eines Data Tracks zeigt, wie die Datensätze angeordnet sind (siehe
nächste Seite).
Die PSK und SSK sind aufsteigend angeordnet.

Man kann durch das Format erkennen, daß zusammengehörige Datensätze stets nebeneinander stehen. Sie können ohne Pointer mit einem Zugriff in den Hauptspeicher ge-
holt werden. Das ist der Vorteil der hierarchischen, indexsequentiellen Anordnung.

FILE NR.	Anz. d.W. in DT	1. PSK	1.Sub file	1.SSK	1.Satz	2.SSK	2.Satz	-----	2.Sub file	1.SSK

1.Satz	2.SSK	2.Satz	---------	2.PSK	1.Sub file	1.SSK	1.Satz	---------

Ergibt sich beim Einfügen eines Datensatzes der Umstand, daß auf dem entsprechenden Data Track kein ausreichender Platz vorzufinden ist, so wird ein Track Split vorgenommen, d.h. dem vorhandenen Data Track wird ein zusaetzlicher Data Track hinzugefügt.   Ein Teil der am Ende befindlichen Eintragungen auf dem alten Data Track wird auf den neuen Data Track geschrieben. Es gibt einen Track Split Parameter (TSP), der das Verhältnis zwischen dem belegten und freien Platz im alten Data Track bestimmt. Die Wahl des Parameters richtet sich nach der Art der hinzukommenden Daten. Wenn sie gestreut anfallen, so wird der Split in der Mitte des alten Data Track am geeignetsten sein, hingegen wenn die Daten am logischen Ende der alten Datei anfallen, wie z.B. Datensätze mit laufenden Nummern als Schlüssel, wird sich der Split am Ende des Data Tracks als günstig erweisen.

Meines Erachtens bietet der Track Split-Mechanismus gegenüber der herkömmlichen Behandlung des Overflowproblems im zentralen oder dezentralen Overflowbereich eine elegante Lösung.

2) Index Control

So wie der Datenteil aus Data Tracks besteht, so setzt sich der Indexteil der Datenbank aus Index Pages mit fixen Größen zusammen. Für jedes FMS-8 File gibt es eine Primary Index Control (PIC) Page. Hier sind Informationen über PSK - Laenge, Level, TSP des FMS-8 Files eingetragen. Weiters ist hier die Satzlänge und SSK-Länge der FMS-8 Subfiles zu finden.

Zu jedem Data Track im Datenteil gibt es eine Eintragung im Indexteil, die sich index entry nennt. Darin steht der erste PSK und die Adresse des Data Tracks. Kann eine Primary Index Control Page kein weiteres index entry mehr erfassen, so wird eine Secondary Index ControlPage (SIC) zugeordnet. Ein Pointer gibt die Adressen der weiteren SIC´ s an.

3) B-Baumstruktur

Die Speicherstruktur im FMS-8 entspricht der eines B-Baumes. Ein B-Baum erfüllt die folgenden Bedingungen:

i   Jeder Knoten hat $\leq$ m untergeordnete Knoten

ii   Jeder Knoten, ausgenommen die Wurzel und die Blätter, hat $\geq$ m/2 untergeordnete Knoten

iii   Alle Blätter befinden sich auf gleicher Ebene

iv   Ein Knoten, der kein Blatt ist, enthält k-1 Schlüsseln und hat k untergeordnete Knoten

v   Die Wurzel hat mindestens 2 untergeordnete Knoten

m nennt sich die Ordnung des B-Baums.

Wenn N die Anzahl der Schlüssel und l die Anzahl der Ebenen (die Tiefe des Baumes) darstellt, so gilt, daß sich N+1 Blätter auf der Ebene l befinden. Die Anzahl der Knoten auf den Ebenen 1,2,3,.... ist mindestens 2, 2(m/2), $2(m/2)^2$ ... Mathematisch dargestellt:

$$N + 1 \geq 2(m/2)^{l-1}$$

oder

$$l \leq 1 + \log_{(m/2)} \left(\frac{N+1}{2} \right)$$

l ist die Anzahl der Zugriffe zum Auffinden eines Blattes.
Ist N = 1.000.000 und m = 100, so ergibt sich aus der Formel l $\leq$ 3.

Die B-Baum-Struktur garantiert nicht nur ein schnelles Auffinden eines Endknotens,

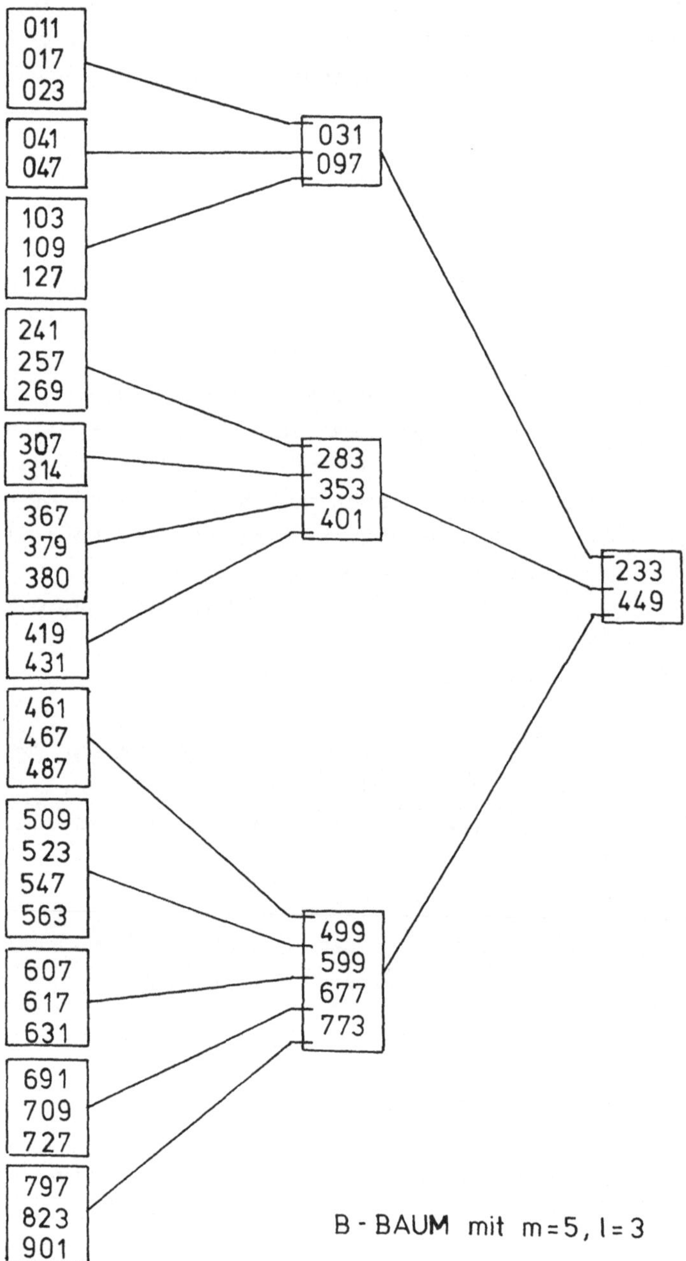

B - BAUM mit m = 5, l = 3

sie macht das Einfügen von einem Schlüssel auch sehr einfach.

Ein neuer Schlüssel wird auf der niedrigsten Ebene eingefügt. Nehmen wir einen
Endknoten als Beispiel, in den wir den Schlüssel 251 einfügen:

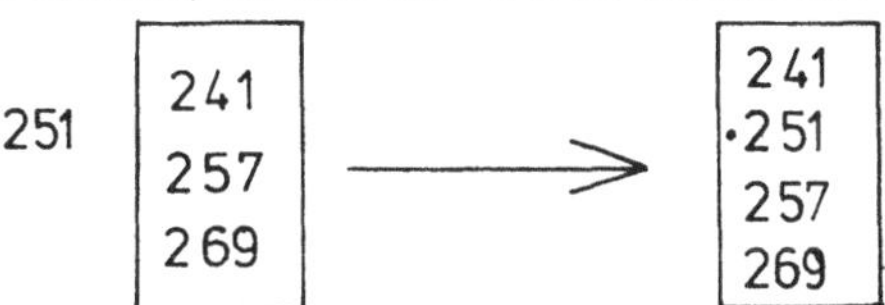

Wird aber beim Einfügen eines Schlüssels die Größe $m-1$ in einem Knoten über-
schritten, so wird der Knoten in 2 Knoten aufgespalten (wie z.B. beim Einfügen des Schlüssels 262):

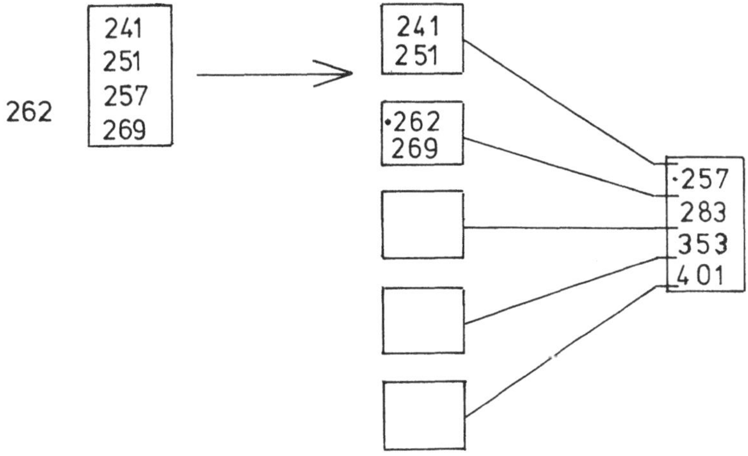

Generell gilt:

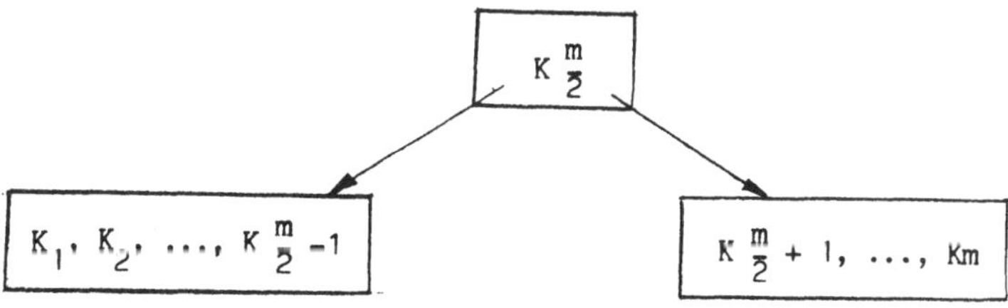

Der Schlüssel K $\frac{m}{2}$ wird auf eine Ebene höher gesetzt. Erweist sich in der höher Ebene ein Split für notwendig, so wandert ein Schlüssel nach oben ab. Wenn sch lich die Wurzel aufgespalten wird, dann wird eine neue Wurzel aufgestellt, der Baum vertieft sich um eine Ebene.

3. User Interface

3.1 Datenbankfunktionen für den Benützer

Der Anwendungsprogrammierer hat die Möglichkeit,die Datenbankfunktionen zu ver wenden, damit die gewünschten Datenbankoperationen durchgeführt werden können. FMS-8 bietet ihm 18 Funktionen an:

1. OPEN - DB	10. CHAIN-KEY1
2. CLOSE - DB	11. CHAIN-KEY2
3. INSERT	12. CHAIN-KEY3
4. ENQUIRE	13. CHAIN-KEY4
5. MODIFY	14. CHAIN-KEY1-LOCK
6. DELETE	15. CHAIN-KEY2-LOCK
7. READ-LOCK	16. CHAIN-KEY3-LOCK
8. CHAIN	17. CHAIN-KEY4-LOCK
9. CHAIN-LOCK	18. FILE-CLOSE

Interessant sind die Funktionen
.CHAIN
.CHAIN-KEYn (n= 1,...,4)
.CHAIN-LOCK
.CHAIN-KEYn-LOCK (n= 1,...,4)
.READ-LOCK

a) CHAIN
CHAIN liest die Datensätze eines FMS-8 Subfiles nach PSK´s in aufsteigender Ordnung.

b) CHAIN-KEYn

Wie bereits erläutert, kann ein SSK in 5 Teilschlüsseln zerlegt werden. n gibt di
Anzahl der Teilschlüssel an, die bei einer CHAIN-KEYn-Funktion berücksichtigt
werden. CHAIN-KEYn funktioniert wie CHAIN, eben mit der Ausnahme, daß die n Teilschlüssel gleich bleiben.

c) CHAIN-LOCK

Sie funktioniert wie CHAIN. Nur der gelesene Datensatz wird gesperrt.

d) CHAIN-KEYn-LOCK

Analog zu CHAIN-LOCK.

e) READ-LOCK

Soll ein Datensatz mit der MODIFY-Funktion verändert werden, wird er nicht durch
MODIFY gesperrt. Die Sperre wird durch Verwendung von READ-LOCK bewirkt. In der
Praxis wird der Lock so lange gehalten, bis der Benützer, der den Datensatz verändert, von der Richtigkeit der Veränderung überzeugt ist. Das ist auch der Grund
warum eine Sperre nicht von MODIFY gesetzt wird.

3.2 Sprachinterface

FMS-8 hat ein Sprachinterface für COBOL (FD und ASCII) FORTRAN und ASSEMBLER.
Der Funktionsaufruf in einem Benützerprogramm ist äußerst einfach.

In FORTRAN z.B.
        CALL FMS-8-Level   (Parameter).

3.3 Filereferenzierung in einem Benützerprogramm

Bevor ein Benützerprogramm die Datenbankfunktionen benützt, muß der Programmierer
angeben, auf welche FMS-8 Subfiles er mit dem Programm zugreift. Das geschieht
in einem FORTRAN-Programm mit einem CALL.

        CALL FSTART (Filetabelle, Zähler)

Die Filetabelle enthält die Namen der gewünschten Subfiles (named Files). Der

210

Zähler gibt an, wieviele Subfiles insgesamt angesprochen werden.

Meiner Meinung nach ist das eine ausgezeichnete Einrichtung. Denn ohne diese
Spezifikation ist ein Zugriff auf die Datenbank nicht möglich. Ferner braucht
der Datenbankadministrator dem Programmierer nur diejenigen Filenamen bekannt
zu geben, von denen er Gebrauch macht. Die Idee dieser Einrichtung entspricht
etwa der Philosophie des Subschemas in den CODASYL-Empfehlungen.

3.4 Erstellen eines durchführbaren Benützerprogramms

Der Vorgang zur Erstellung eines durchführbaren Benützerprogramms ist sehr einfach:

    i   Ein Programm mit Datenbankfunktionsaufruf in einer der vom FMS-8
       unterstützten Programmiersprache codieren

   ii   Das Programm compilieren

  iii   Das Programm mit MAP-Prozessor (Collector) in eine durch-
       führbare Form bringen.

Hier sind ein Precompiler und andere Prozessoren überflüssig.

3.5 Privilegierte Funktionen

Außer den bereits bekannten Datenbankfunktionen für die Benützer gibt es noch
privilegierte Funktionen, die vom Systemprogrammierer verwendet werden, um bestimmte systembezogene Arbeiten durchzuführen. Die Benützerfunktionen beziehen
sich hingegen nur auf die Manipulation eines Datensatzes. Es gibt insgesamt 27
privilegierte Funktionen.

z.B.:

FILE-LOCK	sperrt ein FMS-8 File
DATABASE-LOCK	sperrt alle FMS-8 Files
DELETE-FILE	löscht den Inhalt eines FMS-8 Files
CHAIN-DT	liest Data-Tracks in einer aufsteigenden Reihenfolge
LOAD-DT	lädt Data-Tracks in die Datenbank

Man kann daraus erkennen, daß sie die Datenbank durch Mißbrauch oder falsche An-

wendung gefährden können, daher dürfen sie nur kontrolliert verwendet werden.
FMS-8 hat ein Sicherheitssystem eingebaut, das nur bestimmten Personen das
Recht einräumt, von den privilegierten Funktionen Gebrauch zu machen.

4. FMS-8 System Utilities

FMS-8 System Utilities sind Programme, die dazu dienen, ein laufendes System zu
pflegen. Sie sind ein wichtiges Werkzeug in der Hand des Datenbankadministrators.

4.1. File naming

Dem Sachbearbeiter, der mit einem Programm auf die Daten in der Datenbank zugreift, genügt es,zu wissen, daß er einen Datensatz mittels einer Kennung an-
spricht. Der Anwendungsprogrammierer muß die Datensätze in FMS-8 Subfiles zuordnen. Er referenziert die Subfiles mittels der Subfilenamen. Es ist die Aufgabe des Datenbankadministrators , die Verknüpfung der externen Filenamen mit
den internen Subfilenummern (0-63) vorzunehmen und die Subfiles den FMS-8 numbered Files zuzuordnen. Diese Aufgabe kann er mit der File naming utility lösen.

4.2. Security System

Wie bereits erwähnt, verfügt FMS-8 über ein Sicherheitssystem, das die Berechtigung der Benützung von privilegierten Funktionen überwacht. Das System kontrolliert auch die Zugriffsberechtigung auf FMS-8 Files.
Das Security System ist vom Konzept her sehr interessant, daher einer näheren
Erläuterung wert.

1) Programm Security File (PSF)
Das Sicherheitssystem prüft die Runidentifikation gegen unerlaubten Zugriff auf
die Datenbank. Die Run-bezogenen Daten sind in einzelnen Datensätzen im Program
Security File gespeichert, welches ein Subfile in einem FMS-8 File darstellt.
(Teil der DAtenbank).
Ein PSF-Datensatz beinhaltet folgende Daten:

    i Runidentifikation
   ii Lese- und Schreibberechtigung auf FMS-8 Files
  iii Division, eine Klassenzuteilung der Runidentifikation

iv Level. Innerhalb einer Division werden noch unter den Runidentifikationen Gruppen gebildet. Der Level stellt das minimale
Sicherheitsniveau dieser Gruppe dar.

v Status, der angibt, ob die Runidentifikation privilegierte
Funktionen verwenden darf.

2) Corporate Security File (CSF)

Das Sicherheitssystem prüft auch die Benützeridentifikation (Account number)
gegen unerlaubten Zugriff. Die Benützer-bezogenen Daten sind in einzelnen Datensätzen im Corporate Security File gespeichert. Diese Datei liegt in einem Subfile eines FMS-8 Files.
Ein CSF-Datensatz beinhaltet:

i Benützeridentifikation
ii Division. Entspricht Division im PSF-Datensatz
iii Klassifikation. Entspricht Level im PSF-Datensatz
iv Position. Entspricht Status im PSF-Datensatz

3) Vorgang bei der Sicherheitsprüfung

i Die Prüfung beginnt, wenn ein Run eine OPEN-DB-Funktion absetzt.
ii Die Runidentifikation und Benützeridentifikation des Runs wird vom
FMS-8 gelesen.
iii Die Benützeridentifikation wird im CSF gesucht. Wird sie dort nicht
gefunden, wird der Run mit einer Fehlermeldung terminiert.
iv Die Runidentifikation wird im PSF gesucht. Wird sie nicht gefunden,
wird der Run mit einer Fehlermeldung terminiert.
v Das Status -Feld im PSF-Datensatz wird mit dem Position-Feld im CSF-
Datensatz verglichen. Deutet ein Feld auf die Zulassung der Verwendung von privilegierten Funktionen hin, so muß das andere dies auch,
wenn nicht, wird der Run beendet.
vi Das Klassifiktions-Feld im CSF-Datensatz wird mit dem Level-Feld
im PSF-Datensatz verglichen. Ist der Wert im CSF-Satz kleiner,
wird der Run terminiert.
vii Das Divisionfeld im CSF-Datensatz und das Divisionfeld
PSF-Datensatz werden verglichen. Sind die Werte ungleich, wird
der Run beendet.

viii   Die Zugriffsberechtigung auf ein Subfile wird mittels der Ein-
       tragung im PSF-Datensatz geprüft. Run mit unerlaubtem Zugriff
       wird terminiert.

In der volkswirtschaftlichen Datenbank wird jeder Institution,die die Datenbank
benützt, eine Division zugeteilt, damit die Institutionen untereinander nicht in
Konflikt kommen. Weiters gibt es innerhalb einer Division verschiedene Klassi-
fikationen von Benützern,davon können manche gewisse Runs nicht durchführen.
Ein Beispiel soll diesen Sachverhalt veranschaulichen:

In PSF sei eingetragen:

Runidentifikation	Level	Division	Lese-Schreib-Berechtigung
INQ1	01	005	File 1 (R)
INQ2	02	005	File 2 (R)
MOD1	03	005	File 1 (R/W)
MOD2	04	005	File 2 (R/W)

In CSF sei eingetragen:

Benützeridentifikation	Klassifikation	Division
USER1	01	005
USER2	02	005
USER3	03	005
USER4	04	005

Der Benützer USER2 kann sowohl File 1 als auch File 2 lesen, kann sie aber nicht
modifizieren. USER4 hat die höchste Klassifikation und kann alle vier der angegebenen Runidentifikationen verwenden.

4.3 Logging

FMS-8 führt während des Betriebes ein Logbuch in Form eines Files. Hier werden
die Datensätze vor und nach einer Veränderung eingetragen. Ferner werden auch
Performance-Informationen über Datenbankoperationen und Checkpoint Records
hineingeschrieben.
Das Logfile hat eine fundamentale Bedeutung bei der Datensicherung und bei der
statistischen Auswertung des Datenbankbetriebes.

4.4 Dump und Load

Zur Sicherung der Datenbank wird die Dump-Utility des FMS-8 benützt, um die gesamte Datenbank oder auch nur Teile davon (numbered Files) auf ein Backup-Band zu kopieren.

Sollte die Datenbank oder Teile davon aus irgendeinem Grund nicht vorhanden sein, so kann man sie durch die Load-Utility von einem Dump-Band laden.

Der Datenbankadministrator hat hier zwei Möglichkeiten, das Laden vorzunehmen:

i 1 zu 1 laden. So wie die Datenbank oder Teile davon hinaus-
geschrieben wurden, werden sie wieder zurückgeladen.

ii Laden mit Neuorganisation. Die Data Tracks und die Index
pages werden während des Ladevorgangs neu organisiert.

4.5 Restore

Ein Datenbanksystem muß Sorge für Datensicherung tragen. Die Dump- und Load-programme dienen dazu, die Datenbank in den Zustand vor dem Dump zu ver-setzen. Mit der Restore-Routine ist es möglich, den Zustand der FMS-8 Files bis zu einem bestimmten Zeitpunkt wiederherzustellen.

Der Datenbankadministrator hat die Möglichkeit, die folgenden Befehle einzeln oder kombiniert im RESTORE-Programm abzusetzen.

RESTORE UNTIL	Zeitpunkt
RESTORE ONLY	Filenummern
RESTORE EXCEPT	Filenummern
USE ONLY	Runidentifikation
USE EXCEPT	Runidentifikation

Macht ein Programm Fehler, so kann man durch USE EXCEPT den Zustand vor dem Einsetzen des fehlerhaften Programms wieder herstellen.

4.6   Prüfprogramme

FMS-8 verfügt über ein Programm CHECK, welches die Datenanordnung auf Plausibilität prüft. Bei Prüfung eines FMS-8 Files setzt das Programm ein File Lock ab, um die Integrität des Files zu garantieren. Das Programm TAPCHK prüft die Dump- und die Log-Bänder auf ihre Gültigkeit. Ungültige Dump- und Log-Bänder würden das LOAD und RESTORE zunichte machen.

Im WSR wird CHECK vor jedem Dump und TAPCHK nach jedem Dump und nach Erstellung eines Log-Bandes vorgenommen.

4.7   Sonstige Utilities

FMS-8 verfügt über einige wichtige Utilityprogramme, die dem Datenbank-administrator die Möglichkeit geben, den Datenbankbetrieb besser in den Griff zu bekommen. Hier werden drei Utilityprogramme kurz vorgestellt.

Um eine Übersicht über die Aktivitäten mit der Datenbank zu gewinnen, wie z.B. wieviele Insert, Delete, Track Split an einem Tag vorgenommen werden, dient ein Instrumentation Informations-Programm, das die auf dem Log-Band geschriebenen diesbezüglichen Daten auswertet.

Ein anderes Programm erlaubt dem Datenbankadministrator, an der Konsole in die File Control Table Einsicht zu nehmen. Es zeigt die aktiven Runs, die zur Zeit auf die Datenbank zugreifen. Der Datenbankverantwortliche kann entscheiden, ob der Run weitergeführt oder beendet wird.

Der Systemverantwortliche kann auch mittels einer FMS-8 Utility einen DATABASE HOLD setzen. Jeder Run, der die Datenbank eröffnen will, bringt eine Konsol-meldung, die auf eine Antwort wartet. Der Datenbankadministrator bestimmt, ob der Run zugelassen wird. Dies bietet einen maiximalen Schutz gegen unerlaubten Zugriff auf die Datenbank. Mit der gleichen Utility kann der Systemverantwort-liche auch diesen DATABASE HOLD aufheben.

Für den Fall,daß die Datenbank in einem unrecoverable read error auf dem Massenspeicher involviert ist, hat FMS-8 Maßnahmen zur Datensicherung in Form von Bad
Track Recording und Bad Track Recovery getroffen.

Die meisten Utility-Runs können durch ST Keyin gestartet werden. Alle diese
Utilities werden für den Datenbankbetrieb im WSR benützt.

5. Schlußwort

Die Volkswirtschaftliche Datenbank des österreichischen Institutes für Wirtschaftsforschung ist seit 1973 in Betrieb. Sie ist Bestandteil des betriebenen
Informationssystems, welches zum unentbehrlichen Werkzeug in der Hand der
Wirtschaftswissenschaftler geworden ist. Von einfacher Abfrage bis zur
komplizierten Wirtschaftssimulation und Wirtschaftsprogrnose wird stets auf
die Daten in der Datenbank zugegriffen.

Der Datenanschluß des Instituts für Höhere Studien, der österreichischen Natio-
nalbank und der Bundeskammer der Gewerblichen Wirtschaft via Terminals gibt
ein gutes Beispiel für das distributed processing. Besonders die beiden letzte-
ren zeigen, daß eine Institution ihre speziellen Bedürfnisse auf einer fremden
Anlage mit minimalem Aufwand befriedigen kann.

Das Datenbanksystem FMS-8, auf dem die Errichtung der volkswirtschaftlichen
Datenbank basiert, zeigt in seinem Filekonzept, in der internen Datenorganisation, in seiner Benützerfreundlichkeit, in seiner Komplexität der Verwaltungs-
programme, in den Maßnahmen zum Datenschutz und Datensicherung seine große
Qualität, wodurch der Aufbau, Betrieb und Pflege sehr erleichtert wurden.

Das File Management System ist ein ausgetestetes, stabiles und bewährtes
System, das erfolgreich auf vielen Anlagen angewendet wird.

Data Management System II (DMS II)

Ing. Karl Petreczek
Burroughs Wien

Der Ausdruck "Datenbank" hat heute in der Industrie viele, zum
Teil voneinander sehr abweichende Bedeutungen. Im Sinne von
DMS II ist eine Datenbank eine Sammlung von zusammengehörigen
Daten, wobei Speicherung der Daten und Zugriff auf die Daten
durch Systemsoftware durchgeführt wird. Für diese Aufgaben -
Speicherung und Zugriff - ist daher keines der Benützerpro-
gramme verantwortlich.

<u>DMS II Designziele</u> - (Die Ordnung der Ziele stellt nicht unbe-
dingt eine Wertung dar)

1. Unabhängigkeit der Applikationsprogramme von der Strukturierung
   der Daten und von der Art des Zugriffes auf die Daten.

2. Mehrere Applikationsprogramme müssen gleichzeitig und mit
   absoluter Sicherheit, sowohl im Multiprogramming als auch
   im Multiprocessing, auf die Datenbank zugreifen können. Dieser Zugriff beinhaltet auch den "concurrent update" der Datenbank.

3. Folgernd Punkt 2 muß voller Schutz gegen "multiplen" bzw.
   "concurrent" update auf Satzebene gegeben sein.

4. Sicherungsaufzeichnungen und Wiederanlauf sind Basiseigenschaf-
   ten des Systems. Sie müssen soweit wie möglich automatisiert
   sein, um einen kontinuierlichen Betrieb in einem "real-time"
   System zu garantieren.

5. Für eine optimale Effizienz des Datenbanksystems sollen alle
   Eigenschaften der Systemarchitektur und des Betriebssystems
   voll genutzt werden.

6. Das Benutzerinterface, sowohl in der Definitionsphase als
   auch in der programmatischen Zugriffphase, soll so einfach
   wie möglich sein.

7. Der Anwender kann volle Kontrolle über den Speicherplatz-
   Zugriffzeit-Konflikt haben, um so für sein Problem die
   optimale Lösung zu erreichen.

Ziel von DMS II ist ein gemeinsamer Zugriff auf gemeinsame
Daten über Batch, Transaction Processing, Remote Job Entry und
Time Sharing.

DMS II Komponenten

1. Zur Beschreibung der Datenbank wird die "Data and Structure
   Definition Language" (DASDL) verwendet.

2. Eine Skeletondatei von Zugriffsroutinen, welche für die Generierung der aktuellen Zugriffsroutinen verwendet wird.

3. Als Erweiterung der Standardkompiler stehen Sprachkonstruktionen zum Zugriff auf die Datenbank in COBOL, PL/1 und ALGOL
   zur Verfügung.

4. Erweiterungen des Betriebssystems (MCP) abgestimmt auf die
   Anforderungen von DMS II.

5. Eine Bibliothek von Hilfsprogrammen für Datenschutz, Datensicherung, Plattenrekonstruktion usw.

Data and Structure Definition Language (DASDL)

DASDL wird vom Datenbankadministrator zur Beschreibung der
Datenbank verwendet. Er kann mit Hilfe von DASDL

  - die Informationen in der Datenbank beschreiben
  - die logischen Verknüpfungen der Informationen in der Daten-
    bank beschreiben
  - den Durchsatz für die gewählten Datenstrukturen optimalisieren
  - die Bedingungen und die verschiedenen Ebenen des Datenschutzes

definieren

- die Integritätsbedingungen der Datenbank festlegen.

Im Folgenden soll am Beispiel einer Datenbank einer fiktiven
Universität die Möglichkeiten von DMS II gezeigt werden. Unsere
fiktive Datenbank "UNIVERSITÄT" soll Informationen über "VOR-
LESUNGEN", "PERSONAL", "STUDENTEN", "BÜCHER" usw beinhalten.

Die Basisstruktur zur Speicherung von Daten ist der "DATA SET".
Die Beschreibung des Data Sets für die Daten von "VORLESUNGEN"
könnte z. B. folgendermaßen aussehen:

```
VORLESUNGEN                 DATA SET
( INSTITUT                  ALPHA (4)
  LEVEL                     NUMBER (3)
  VORLESUNGSNUMMER          NUMBER (4)
  WOCHENTAG FIELD
  ( MO                      BOOLEAN
    DI                      BOOLEAN
    MI                      BOOLEAN
    DO                      BOOLEAN
    FR                      BOOLEAN)
  WOCHENSTUNGEN             NUMBER (2)
  MAX-TEILNEHMER            NUMBER (3)
```

INSTITUT wäre hier ein alphanumerisches Feld der Länge 4,
VORLESUNGS-NUMMER ein numerisches Feld der Länge 4 und MO ein
Boolsches Feld.

Für unsere Vorlesungen könnten als Studienmaterial_ einige
Bücher notwendig sein. Diese Beziehung kann in DASDL wie folgt
dargestellt werden.

```
VORLESUNGEN                    DATA SET

            .

            .

            .

    WOCHENSTUNDEN              NUMBER  (2)
    MAX-TEILNEHMER             NUMBER (3)
    BÜCHER                     DATA SET
     (BUCHNUMMER               NUMBER (12)
      TITEL                    ALPHA (30)
      AUTHOR                   ALPHA (30))
```

Graphisch dargestellt:

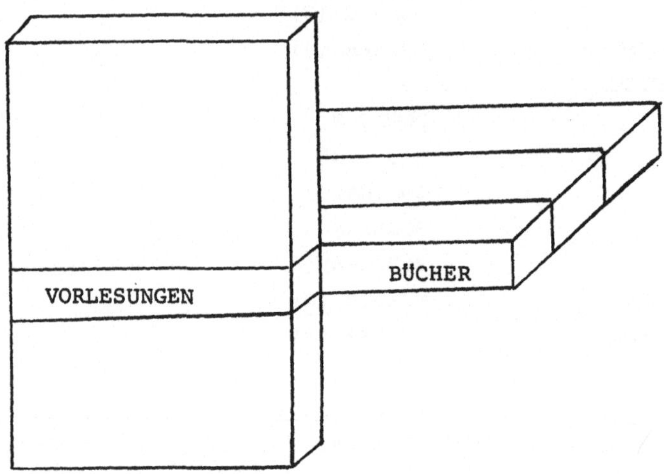

d.h. Elemente eines Data Sets können selbst ein Data Set sein.
Diese eingebetteten Data Sets werden "embedded data set" genannt.

Die Vollständigkeit der Daten kann in DMS II auf Feldebene geprüft werden. z.B.

```
PERSONAL                   DATA SET
(FAMILIENNAME              ALPHA(15) REQUIRED
 VORNAME                   ALPHA(10) REQUIRED
 SEX                       BOOLEAN
 ALTER                     NUMBER(2)
 SV-NUMMER                 NUMBER(10) REQUIRED
 GEHALT                    NUMBER (7,2)
        .
        .
        .
)
```

Ein neuer Personalsatz wird nur dann in die Datenbank eingefügt,
wenn zumindest die Felder FAMILIENNAME, VORNAME und SV-NUMMER
mit Daten beschickt wurden. Das Feld GEHALT stellt übrigens ein
numerisches Feld mit sieben Stellen, davon zwei Dezimalstellen,
dar.

Daten können vor dem Einfügen in die Datenbank vom DMS II System
logisch geprüft werden.
z. B.:

```
VORLESUNGEN                DATA SET
(      .
       .
 LEVEL                     NUMBER (3)
       .
       .
 WOCHENSTUNDEN             NUMBER (2)
       .
 MAX-TEILNEHMER            NUMBER (3)
)
VERIFY (WOCHENSTUNDEN GREATER 0 AND MAX-TEILNEHMER LESS 150)
```

Ein neuer oder geänderter Satz des Data Set Vorlesungen wird
nur dann in die Datenbank eingefügt bzw. zurückgeschrieben, wenn
die in der VERIFY-Klausel gestellten Bedingungen erfüllt sind.

Datenelemente eines Data Sets können automatisch auf einen "NULL"-
Wert initialisiert werden.
z.B.:

```
VORLESUNGEN                      DATA SET
(    .
     .
     .
HÖRSAAL                          ALPHA(4) INITIAL VALUE IS "LEER"
     .
     .
     .
)
```

Wenn das Feld HÖRSAAL mit keinem Wert beschickt wurde, wird beim
Einfügen in die Datenbank anstelle des Systemnullwertes LEER
in das Feld gestellt.

Weiters können in DASDL globale Felder definiert werden. Globale
Felder sind nicht Teile eines Data Sets, sie sind eher als Felder
die gesamte Datenbank betreffend anzusehen.
z.B. in unserer fiktiven Datenbank wollen wir jederzeit wissen,
wie hoch der Personalstand und die Gehaltsumme ist.

```
GESAMT-PERSONAL                  POPULATION (10000) OF PERSONAL
GEHALTSUMME                      NUMBER (11,2)
```

Im Feld GESAMT-PERSONAL würde, vom DMS II System gewartet, die
Anzahl der lebenden Sätze im Data Set PERSONAL stehen. Die von
uns erwartete größte Zahl ist hier 10000. Im Feld GEHALTSUMME
könnte vom Applikationsprogrammierer die Summe des Feldes GEHALT
aus dem PERSONAL Data SET geführt werden.

DMS II erlaubt auch das Speichern von Sätzen mit variabler Länge.
Zur Beschreibung eines Data Sets mit variabler Satzlänge gibt es
zwei Möglichkeiten:

1. Der Data Set besteht aus einem fixen Teil und aus alternativ
   mehreren variablen Teilen. Die variablen Teile haben jeder für
   sich wieder eine fixe Länge.
   z. B.: In unserem Data Set STUDENTEN haben wir einen embedded
   Data Set STUDIENFORTSCHRITT welcher einerseits Information
   über besuchte Lehrveranstaltungen und andererseits Auskunft
   über durchgeführte Arbeiten geben soll.

```
STUDENTEN                       DATA SET
( NAME ...
   STUDIENFORTSCHRITT           DATA SET
   ( ( INFO-TYPE                TYPE(2)           fixer Teil
       NOTE                     NUMBER(1) )
     1: ( WOCHENSTUNDEN         NUMBER(2) )       variabler Teil 1
     2: ( THEMA                 ALPHA(30)
          BEWERTUNG             NUMBER(1) ) )     variabler Teil 2
          .
          .
          .
)
```

Das Feld INFO-TYPE stellt eine Satzart dar (mit maximal zwei
Satzarten). Beim Erstellen des Satzes muß in der CREATE-Anweisung
die Satzart angegeben werden: CREATE STUDIENFORTSCHRITT(2).
Beim Lesen des Satzes kann dann INFO-TYPE wie ein normales Feld
abgefragt werden: IF INFO-TYPE = 2 ....

2. Einzelne Felder im Data Set haben eine variable Länge (z.B.
   Namensfelder) oder sie werden nur fallweise mit einem Wert
   beschickt.

224

z.B.:

A   ALPHA(300) SIZE VARYING
Nur die signifikanten Stellen des Feldes A werden gespeichert,
trailing Leerstellen werden unterdrückt.
N1   NUMBER(3)
A1   ALPHA(300) SIZE VARYING WITH N1
Wie vorheriges Beispiel nur wird zusätzlich die aktuelle Länge
automatisch vom DMS II System in N1 gespeichert.
N2   NUMBER(3)
A2   ALPHA(300) SIZE VARYING DEPENDING ON N2
In A2 werden nur so viele Zeichen,wie in N2 angegeben,gespeicher
N3   NUMBER(3)
A3   ALPHA(20) OCCURS 100 TIMES DEPENDING ON N3
A3 ist eine Tabelle - die Anzahl der tatsächlich zu speichernden
Elemente der Tabelle wird N3 entnommen.
A4   ALPHA(40) STORED OPTIONALLY
A4 wird nur,wenn es mit einem Wert beschickt wurde,gespeichert.
B6   BOOLEAN
N6   NUMBER(10,3) STORED DEPENDING ON B6
N6 wird nur dann gespeichert,wenn die bool'sche Variable B6 "TRU
ist.
A7   ALPHA(25) STORED OPTIONALLY WITH B7
B7   BOOLEAN
A7 wird nur dann gespeichert,wenn es mit einem Wert beschickt wu
zusätzlich wird noch vom DMS II System die bool'sche Variable B7
entsprechend gewartet.

Sätze können in DMS II durch SETS, SUBSETS und LINKS logisch
miteinander verknüpft werden. Der Datenbankadministrator kann
Ordnungs- bzw. Zugriffsmethoden für die Datasets definieren.
Diese Informationen werden in eingenen Schlüsseltabellen, SET
genannt, gespeichert. Die Speicherung der Sets erfolgt unabhängig von der Speicherung der Daten im Dataset.

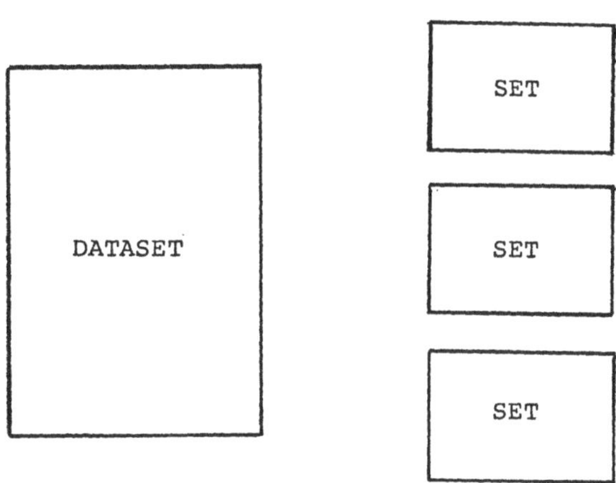

Es können mehrere Zugriffsmethoden auf einen Dataset in DMS II
definiert werden; die Daten werden in jedem Fall nur einmal
gespeichert.

Das Einfügen der S chlüsselinformationen in die Sets (Schlüsseltabellen) erfolgt automatisch beim Einfügen des Satzes in den
Dataset.

z.B. unsere fiktive Universität benötigt:
-    einen täglichen Bericht über das Personal geordnet nach Namen
-    für das Abrechnungssystem Zugriff auf die Personaldaten
     über die Sozialversicherungsnummer.

Die Beschreibung in DASDL des Personal Datasets und seiner beiden
automatischen Sets könnte dann wie folgt lauten:

```
PERSONAL                         DATA SET
(FAMILIENNAME ...
 VORNAME ...
 ALTER ...
 SV-NR. ...
 GEHALT ...

     .
     .
     .

 )
 NAME-SET SET OF PERSONAL KEY IS (FAMILIENNAME, VORNAME)
                     INDEX-SEQUENTIAL DUPLICATES
 SV-SET SET OF PERSONAL KEY IS SV-NR
                     INDEX-RANDOM NO DUPLICATES
```

Auf die Sätze des Dataset Personal kann jetzt sowohl nach Namen
wie auch nach der Sozialversicherungsnummer zugegriffen werden.
Ein Mehrfachvorkommen des gleichen Namens ist erlaubt, ein
Mehrfachvorkommen der gleichen Sozialversicherungsnummer ist
verboten.

DMS II erlaubt eine beliebige Anzahl von Ordnungsbegriffen
für einen Dataset. Die in der Datenbank gespeicherten Information muß daher nicht für jede Auswertung neu sortiert werden.

Die Sets werden automatisch (automatic set) mit dem Dataset
gewartet. In unserem fiktiven Personal Dataset würde dies etwa
so erfolgen:

```
CREATE PERSONAL
MOVE EIN-FAMILIENNAME TO FAMILIENNAME
MOVE EIN-VORNAME TO VORNAME

     .
     .
     .
```

```
MOVE EIN-SV-NR TO SV-NR

     .

     .

     .

STORE PERSONAL
```

Nach dem Einfügen des Satzes in die Datenbank steht automatisch
der Zugriff sowohl nach Namen als auch nach Sozialversicherungsnummer zur Verfügung. Der Programmierer wird in keiner Weise
mit der Wartung der Sets beim Einfügen oder Löschen der Sätze
belastet.

Unsere fiktive Universität benötigt weiters regelmässig Zugriff
auf nur einen Teil der Personaldaten z.B. nur auf die Daten von
Professoren oder auf Daten von Personen welche unter 18 oder
über 65 Jahre alt sind. Diese Datenauswahl kann in DMS II durch
automatische Subsets wie folgt erreicht werden:

```
PERSONAL                 -      DATA SET
(    .

     .

     .

  SV-NR...
  ALTER ...
  RANG ...

     .

     .

     .

 )
PROFESSOREN SUBSET OF PERSONAL WHERE RANG = "P"
                         KEY IS SV-NR
SPEZIAL-ALTER SUBSET OF PERSONAL WHERE ALTER LESS 18 OR

                             ALTER GREATER 65
                     KEY IS ALTER
```

Wird nun mit Hilfe der Sozialversicherungsnummer über den Subset

Professor auf den Dataset Professor zugegriffen, so werden nur
Sätze mit Rang gleich "P" zur Verfügung gestellt. Beim Zugriff
über den Subset Spezial-Alter nur Sätze von Personen unter 18
oder über 65.

Für einen Dataset können mehrere Sets und mehrere Subsets gleichzeitig definiert werden. Die Daten werden auch hier wieder nur
einmal gespeichert. Durch die Definition von mehreren Sets und
Subsets werden Zeit und Kosten für System-Design, Programmierung
und Wartung reduziert und der Durchsatz der Systeme wird erhöht.
Subsets können auch als manuelle Subsets definiert werden, d.h.
ein Satz eines Datasets muß durch eine Insert-Anweisung vom
Programmierer in den Subset eingefügt bzw. herausgenommen werden.
In unserer fiktiven Universität benötigt zum Beispiel die Verwaltung jederzeit Auskunft über Personal auf Urlaub.

```
AUF-URLAUB SUBSET OF PERSONAL KEY IS (FAMILIENNAME, VORNAME)
                                                    DUPLICATES
```

Subsets können auch Elemente eines Datasets sein, Sie sind dann
in den Dataset eingebettet oder "embedded".

```
VORLESUNG                        DATA SET
(    .
     .

     .

VORLESUNGS-BESUCHER SUBSET OF STUDENTEN KEY IS SVNR
     .

     .

     .

)
STUDENTEN                        DATA SET
(    .

     .

     .

SVNR ...
     .

     .

)
```

ÜBer den Subset Vorlesungsbesucher kann jetzt auf alle Studenten
welche eine bestimmte Vorlesung besuchen, zugegriffen werden.
Bei diesem Zugriff kann die Sozialversicherungsnummer des Studenten als Ordnungs- und Zugriffskriterium verwendet werden.

Durch einen embedded Subset kann von einem Mitglied eines Datasets
zu den Mitgliedern eines anderen Datasets eine logische Verknüpfung
auf der Basis einer-zu-viele (1 zu N) hergestellt werden.

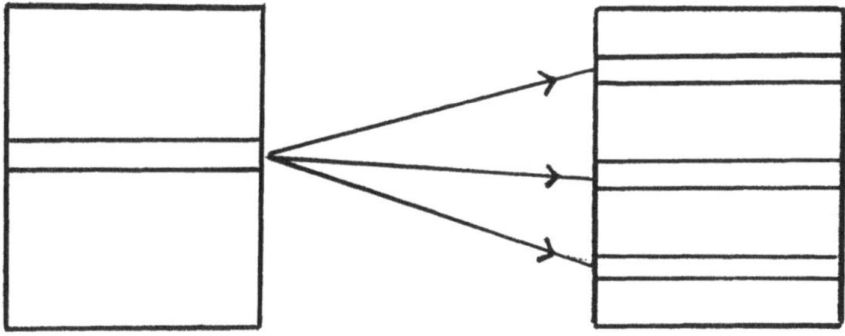

Es gibt hierbei keine Einschränkung über die Anzahl der Subsets
welche von einem Dataset auf einen anderen verweisen. Ein Dataset
kann gleichzeitgig "owner" und "member" von mehereren Subsets
sein. Durch Definition von zwei Datasets kann hier auch eine
N-zu-M Verbindung hergestellt werden.

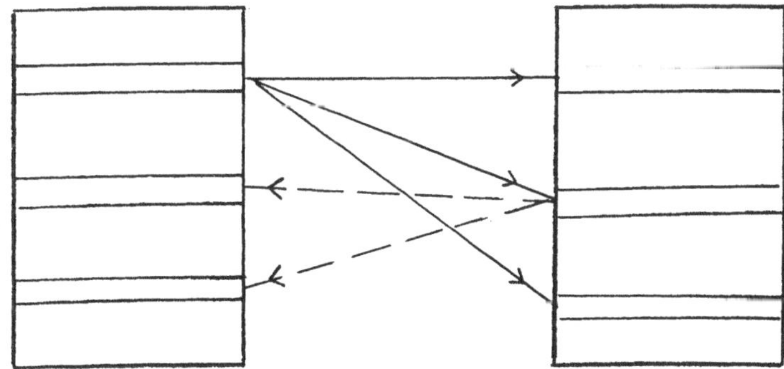

Zur Erhöhung der Durchsatzleistung des Systems können wichtige
und oft benötigte Datenelemente in den Schlüsseltabellen(Sets)
dupliziert gespeichert werden. Auf diese Daten kann damit auch
ohne Zugriff auf den zugehörigen Dataset zugegriffen werden.
Damit kann dann auch entscheiden werden, ob der Satz im Dataset
überhaupt gelesen werden soll.

```
PERSONAL                    DATA SET
(      .

       .

       .

   SV-NR ...

       .

   GEHALT ...

       .

       .

)
```

GEHALTS-SET OF PERSONAL KEY IS SV-NR DATA (GEHALT)
Das Datenelement wird hier bewußt zweimal (redundant) gespeichert.

Wenn für eine Applikation keine 1-zu-N sondern nur eine 1-zu-1
Verbindung zwischen den Mitgliedern zweier Datasets notwendig
ist, so kann dies durch eine LINK-Verknüpfung erreicht
werden.

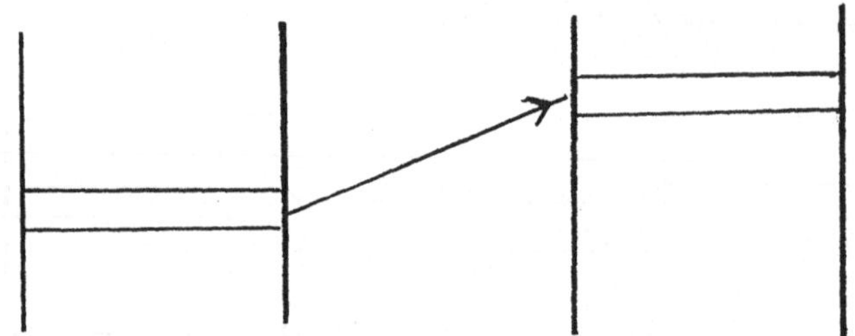

Der Link erlaubt den direkten Zugriff auf die logisch verknüpfte
Information. Der Link stellt somit eine schnelle und effiziente
Zugriffsmethode auf verknüpfte Information dar.

Abhängig von den Vollständigkeitsanforderungen an die Verknüpfung,
der Lebhaftigkeit der verknüpften Informationen und den Zeit-
und Speicherplatzbedingungen, gibt es mehrere Methoden um einen
Link zu definieren.
z.B. Unprotected Link:

VORLESUNG   DATA SET
(.

      .

VORTRAGENDER IS IN PERSONAL WITH NO PROTECTION

      .

      .

)
PERSONAL DATA SET
(.

      .

)

VORTRAGENDER

VORLESUNG

ADRESSE

PERSONAL

Diese Art von Link kann schnell erzeugt und gelöscht werden,
da der verknüpfte Satz hier nicht verändert wird. Der verknüpfte
Satz in Personal ist hier aber nicht geschützt, d.h. er kann
ohne Aufbrechen des Links gelöscht werden. Der Unprotected Link
ist daher nur für"stabile" Datenbanken geeignet.

Wenn der verknüpfte Satz gegen Löschen bei bestehender Link-
verbindung geschützt werden soll, so kann dies durch einen
"counted link" erfolgen.

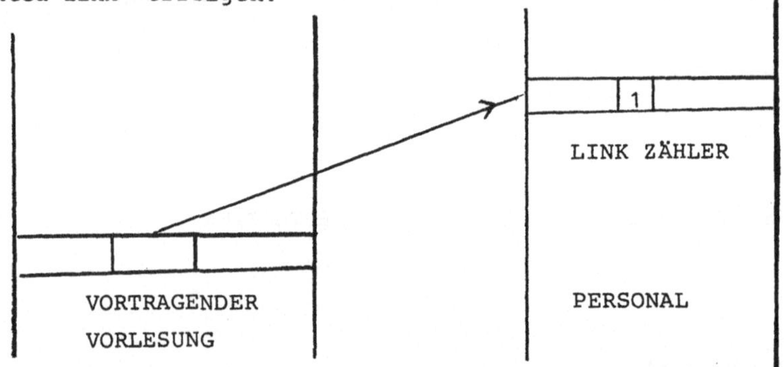

Hier wird jetzt im Personalsatz die Anzahl der Links welche auf
diesen Satz verweisen, gezählt. Der Satz kann nur gelöscht
werden, wenn dieser Zähler auf Null steht, d.h. es b esteht kein
Link auf diesem Satz. Die Integrität der Verknüpfung ist hier
in jedem Fall gewährleistet.

Ein Link kann auch als "symbolisch" d.h. der Link besteht nicht
aus der Adresse, sondern einer symbolischen Referenz (über einen
Set) des Satzes, definiert werden. Weiters ist es noch möglich,
Links als "selbst verifizierend" (über ein Referenzdatenelement)
oder auch als "selbstkorrigierend" (über ein Keyfeld eines Sets)
zu definieren.

DMS II - Physische Optionen

Ein Dataset kann auch auf mehrere physische Dateien aufgeteilt
werden. Die Aufteilung der Sätze in diese einzelnen Dateien
erfolgt dabei aber nach logischen in DASDL definierten Gesichtspunkten.

```
HISTORIE                    DATA SET
(JAHR                       NUMBER (4)

        .

        .

JAHRES-DATEN                DATA SET
(NAME ...

 SALDO ...

        .

        .

)PARTITIONED ON JAHR
)
```

Jahres-Daten ist hier ein embedded Dataset in Historie.
Es wird aber hier für jedes Jahr ein eigener physischer File
für die Jahresdaten angelegt. Die einzelnen physischen Dateien
für den embedded Dataset Jahresdaten müssen aber nicht gleichzeitig auf der Platte zum Zugriff zur Verfügung stehen.

DMS II - Datenschutz

Eine wichtige Funktion eines Datenbanksystems ist der Schutz vor
unbefugten Zugriff.

In DMS II kann einem bestimmten Benutzer der Datenbank
- nur Lesen der Daten
- Lesen und Schreiben der Daten
- kein Zugriff auf die Daten
gestattet werden.

Dieser Schutz kann auf mehrere Ebenen erfolgen:

- physische Datenbank
- logische Datenbank
- Dataset
- Set bzw. Subset
- Satz
- Datenelement innerhalb eines Satzes.

Eine in DMS II definierte Datenbank, als Urform im weiteren als physische Datenbank bezeichnet, kann in mehrere logische Datenbanken geteilt werden. Eine logische Datenbank stellt ganz allgemein eine Teilmenge der physischen Datenbank dar, wobei sich Teilmengen der logischen Datenbank überlappen dürfen. Datenelemente, Sätze, Datasets und Subsets können also gleichzeitig Mitglieder mehrere logischer Datenbanken sein. Die Speicherung der Daten erfolgt auch hier wieder nur einmal. Eine Applikation, welche eine logische Datenbank zum Zugriff auf die Daten verwendet, hat auch nur Zugriff auf die Strukturen dieser logischen Datenbank.

```
PERSONAL                      DATA SET
(       .

        .

TELEFON                       NUMBER (10)
RANG                          ALPHA (1)
FAMILIENNAME                  ALPHA (15)

        .

        .

)
NAME SET OF PERSONAL KEY IS FAMILIENNAME
```

TELEFON-INFO REMPAS PERSONAL READONLY (FAMILIENNAME, TELEFON)
                SELECT RANG NOT EQUAL "0"

Der Dataset Telefoninfo stellt hier eine logische Redefinition
des Datasets Personal dar, allerdings können nur die Datenelemente
Familienname und Telefon gelesen ("readonly") werden. Gleichzeitig
wird auch noch eine Einschränkung im Zugriff auf Sätze mit dem
Feld Rang ungleich "0" definiert.

TELEFONBUCH DATABASE (TELEFON-INFO (SET NAMEN))
                GUARDFILE = "TELEFONBENUTZER"

Die hier definierte logische Datenbank Telefonbuch besteht aus
dem Dataset Telefoninfo und dem Set Namen. Als Datenschutz-
einrichtung wird hier das Standard Burroughs Datenschutzsystem
Guardfile verwendet. Im Guardfile Telefonbenutzer befinden sich
alle Informationen über Usercode, Password und Lese- bzw.
Schreibbeschränkungen.

DMS II - Datenbank-Reorganisation

Datenbanken stellen, als mehr oder weniger vollständiges Abbild
einer lebenden Organisation (Unternehmen, Körperschaft usw.)
lebende Gebilde dar. Organisationen sind im Laufe der Zeit
Änderungen unterworfen, daher muß auch die sie abbildende Datenbank geändert werden. Ein Datenbanksystem muß daher Hilfen für
eine einfache und schnelle Reorganisation der Datenbank zur
Verfügung stellen.

DMS II erlaubt Änderungen an den Strukturen der Datenbank
ohne Neucompilation der Applikationsprogramme (Datenunabhängigkeit!). Neue Daten und Sets können eingefügt, alte gelöscht
Werden. Neue Datenelemente können in existente Datasets eingefügt
werden. Alle physischen Definitonen der Datenbank können

geändert werden. Falls bei einer Änderung an den Datenbankstrukturen eine Reorganisation der Datenbank notwendig wird,
werden die hierfür notwendigen Programme auf Wunsch von DMS II
System generiert. Diese generierten Reorganisationsprogramme
erzeugen, wenn genügend Systemressourcen (Plattenplatz) zur Verfügung steht, direkt aus den alten Datenbankfiles die neuen
reorganisierten Strukturen; wenn nicht genügend Systemressourcen
zur Verfügung stehen, werden erst temporäre Dateien (Banddateien)
erstellt, aus denen dann die neuen, reorganisierten Strukturen
geladen werden. Der Benutzer kann die für die Reorganisation
zur Verfügung stehenden Ressourcen selbst spezifizieren.

DMS II - Physische Optionen

Die physische Organisationform für die Zugriffstabellen (Sets)
kann vom Benutzer definiert werden. Der Datenbankadministrator
kann unter Index-Sequentiell, Index-Random, Random, Direct,
Bit-Vector, geordneten und ungeordneten Listen wählen.
z.B. Index-Sequentiell

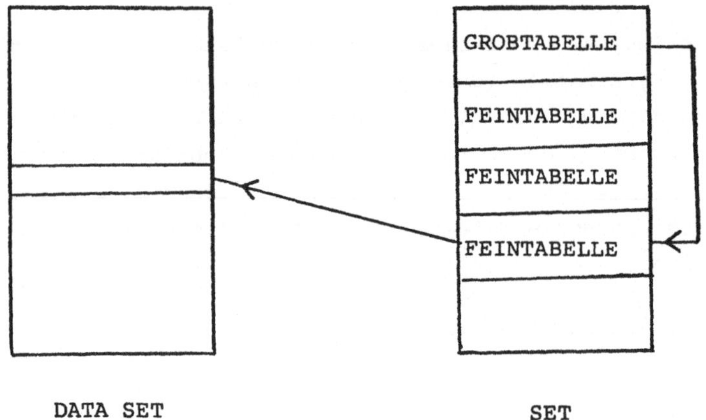

z.B. Direct:

```
STUDENT          DIRECT DATA SET
(         .

          .

  STUDENTEN-NR        NUMBER (5)

          .

          .
)
```

Die direkte Zugriffsmethode erlaubt ohne Tabellen auf die Daten
direkt zuzugreifen. Der Zugriffschlüssel kann hier direkt oder
über ein randomizing Verfahren die Platznummer des Sates im
Dataset ergeben.

Eine weitere, interessante Zugriffsmethode stellt der Bit-Vector
dar. Der Bit-Vector ermöglicht die schnelle Auswahl einiger Sätze
welche einem bestimmten Auswahlkriterium genügen. Diese Methode
wird besonders effektiv, wenn das Auswahlkriterium eine niedrige
Trefferrate ergibt.

```
PERSONAL       DATA SET
(         .

          .

  GEHALT ...

          .

          .
)
```

FREIE MITARBEITER SET OF PERSONAL WHERE GEHALT = 0 BIT VECTOR

Personal		Freie Mitarbeiter	
1000		1	
0		0	Bit-Vector
1200		1	
0		0	
3500		1	

Gehalt

Jedem Satz im Dataset wird ein Bit im Bit-Vector zugewiesen.
Bei Zugriff über den Bit-Vector Freie Mitarbeiter werden nur jene
Sätze mit Gehalt = 0 zur Verfügung gestellt.

Mehrere Bit-Vectoren können auch logisch miteinander zu einem
neuen Bit-Vector verknüpft werden, damit kann rasch und effektiv
eine Auswahl nach komplexen, logischen Kriterien erfolgen.

"Fine Tuning" der Datenbank durch den Datenbank-Administrator

Der Datenbank-Administrator kann natürlich auch Einfluß auf die
physische Speicherungsform der Datenbank nehmen, wobei bei
Burroughs-Plattendateien automatisches "paging" vorhanden ist,
sodaß die Eingriffe auf ein Minimum gehalten werden können.
Wenn bei einer Datei paging erlaubt wird, so werden vom Betriebssystem der Datei dynamisch Palettenbereiche je nach momentaner
Größe der Datei zugewiesen. Diese Plattenbereiche müssen nicht
kontinuierlich auf der Platte stehen.

Der Programmierer wird dadurch von der Notwendigkeit über ein
genaues Wissen von verwendeten, bzw. verfügbaren Plattenplatz
befreit. Die Belegung des Massenspeichers wird verbessert.
Die Notwendigkeit für Reorganisationsläufe wird reduziert.
Der Datenbank-Administrator kann sich in der physischen Beschreibung der Datenbank also auf das "fine Tuning" der Datenbank für
die vorgesehenen Applikationen beschränken.
z.B. BUFFERS = 2 + 2 PER USER
    Für den Dataset werden 2 Puffer vorgesehen plus
    2 je aktiven Benutzer des Datasets.
    TABLESIZE = 100
    Ein Satz einer Zugriffstabelle besteht aus
    100 Tabellenelementen.

DMS II FUNKTIONSABLAUF

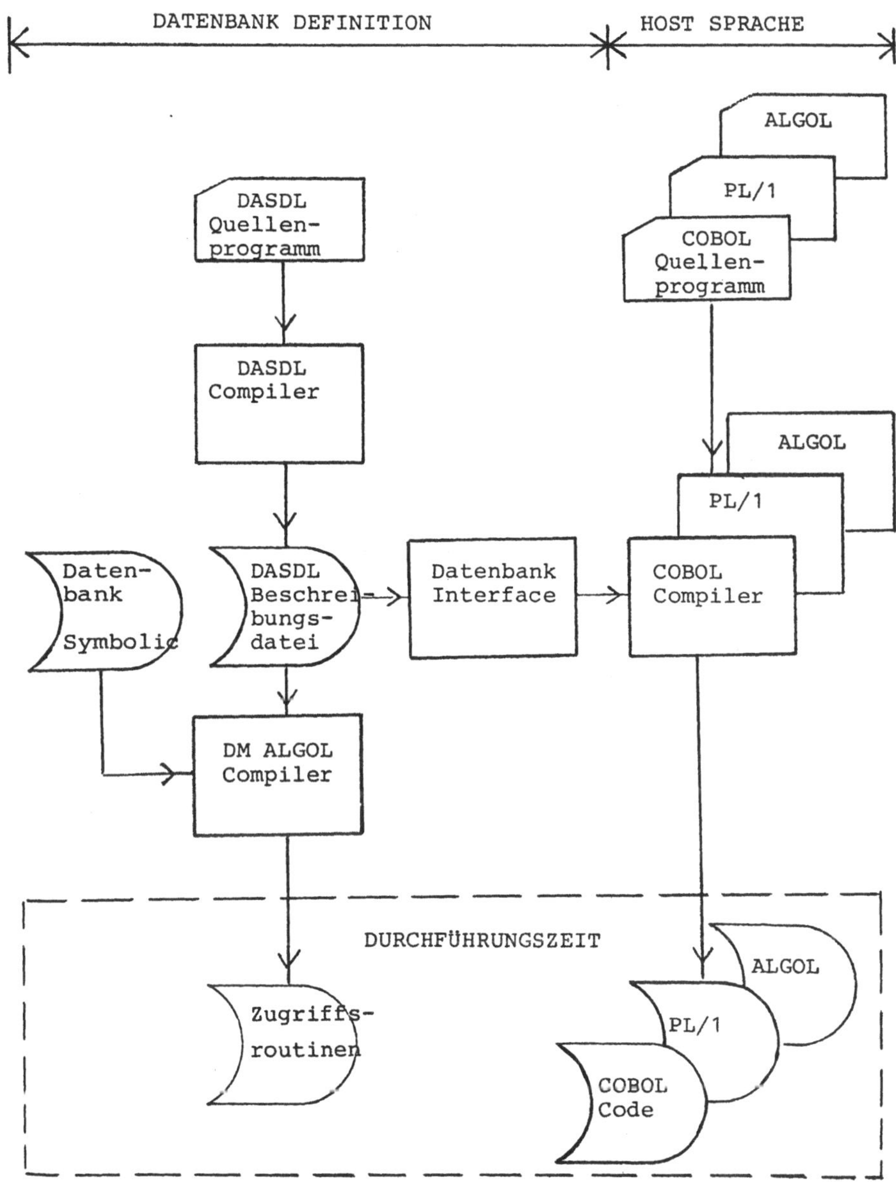

240

<u>DMS II - Spracheninterface</u>

Als Host-Sprachen stehen COBOL, PL/1 und ALGOL zur Verfügung.

Das Spracheninterface besteht aus einfachen, selbsterklärenden
Verben. Der Programmierer ist in keiner Weise für die Datenbeschreibung verantwortlich; er bekommt die vom Datenbank-
Administrator definierten Satzbeschreibungen automatisch sprach-
gerecht zur Verfügung gestellt. Der Programmierer hat auch nicht
mit dem physischen "mapping" der Datenbank zu tun, er arbeitet
immer nur mit den logischen Strukturen. Audit und Recovery ist
ebenfalls ein Teil des DMS II Systems und nicht ein Teil des
Applikationsprogrammes.

Die Datenbanksprache ist voll in die Burroughs Standard Compiler
integriert, es ist daher kein Precompiler oder Preprozessor für
Datenbank-Programme notwendig. Für DMS II Programme sind auch
keine speziellen JCL-Karten notwendig.

Die Interface-Sprache ist so einfach gehalten, daß keine eigenen
Systemprogrammierer hierfür notwendig sind, im Gegenteil sie kan
von einem normalen Applikationsprogrammierer leicht innerhalb
eines Tages erlernt werden.

<u>DMS II Spracheninterface in COBOL</u>

Im folgenden werden die Möglichkeiten des DMS II Spracheninterfa
an Hand des COBOL-Interface erläutert. Für PL/1 und ALGOL
stehen praktisch die gleichen Sprachkonstruktionen mit leichten
Modifikationen zur besseren Anpassung an die Host-Sprache zur
Verfügung.

COBOL Erweiterungen in der Data Division
==

Da der Datenbank-Administrator bereits alle Datenelemente der
Datenbank in DASDL beschrieben hat, kann und muß der Applikationsprogrammierer diese Beschreibungen verwenden. Diese Datenbe-
schreibungen werden durch die "Invoke"-Anweisung in das Programm
kopiert.

```
   DB UNIVERSITAET
   01 INVOKE PERSONAL
$  02 NAME
$  03 VORNAME PIC X(15).
$  03 FAMILIENNAME PIC X(15).
$  02 SEX      BOOLEAN.
   02 ALTER    PIC 9(2) comp.
        .
        .
        .
```

   Die durch den Compiler eingefügten Daten-Beschreibungen werden
   vom Compiler mit "$" gekennzeichnet.

Durch die vom DMS II System erzwungene Verwendung der Invoke-
Anweisung wird die Datenbeschreibung zentralisiert und standar-
disiert.

Ein Applikationsprogramm kann eine Satzbeschreibung auch mehrfach
aufrufen.

```
DB UNIVERSITAET
01 X = PERSONAL
01 Y = PERSONAL
01 Z = PERSONAL
```

Durch den multiplen Aufruf von Satzbeschreibungen stehen einem
Applikationsprogramm mehrere Arbeitsbereiche gleichzeitig für
einen Dataset zur Verfügung. Dadurch kann ein Programm mehrere
Sätze eines Datasets gleichzeitig "current" haben.

COBOL Erweiterungen in der Procedures Division

Vor Zugriff auf die Information in der Datenbank muß die Datenbank eröffent werden.
OPEN UPDATE UNIVERSITAET

    Die Datenbank kann in diesem Programm verändert werden.
OPEN INITIALIZE UNIVERSITAET

    Für dieses Programm wird eine leere Datenbank angelegt.
OPEN INQUIRY UNIVERSITAET

    Die Datenbank wird in diesem Programm nur gelesen.

Lesen eines Satzes:

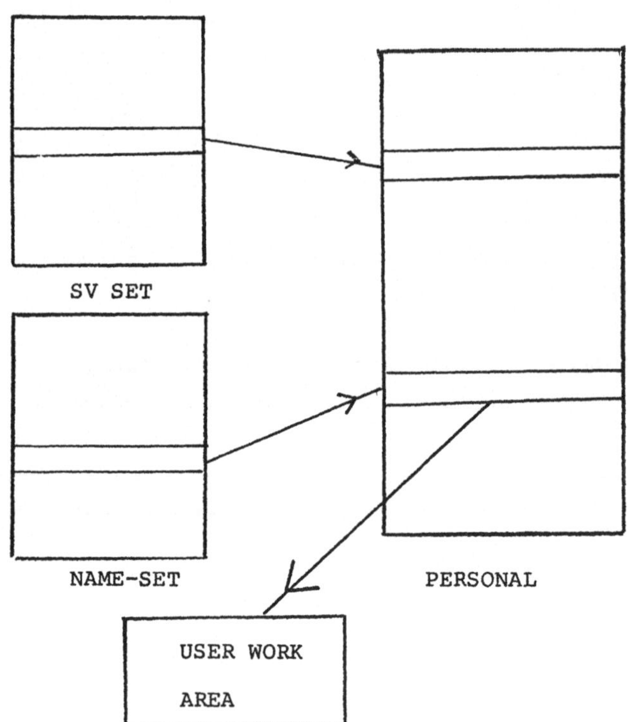

```
FIND SV_SET AT SV-NR = 123456789
FIND NAME-SET AT FAMILIENNAME = "MEIER"
```

Hier wird erst ein Personalsatz mit der spezifizierten Sozialversicherungsnummer gelesen, dann wird ein Personalsatz mit
Familienname = Meier gelesen und in demselben Arbeitsbereich
wie vorher dem Benutzer zur Verfügung gestellt. Dieser letzt-
gelesene Satz ist der "current-Satz" des Datasets.

Serieller Zugriff

Mit der Anweisung:
```
FIND SV-SET
```
kann ein Satz mittels des "current path" wieder aufgerufen werden.

Die Sätze eines Datasets können natürlich auch sequentiell verarbeitet werden.

```
FIND NEXT SV-SET
FIND PRIOR NAME-SET
FIND FIRST NAME-SET
FIND LAST SV-SET
```

Die Sätze werden hier entsprechend den Ordnungskriterien in den
Sets abgearbeitet, Es kann dabei sowohl vorwärts (first, next)
als auch rückwärts (last, prior) gelesen werden.

Random Zugriff

Auf einen Satz kann mit Hilfe der Schlüssel in den Sets random
zugegriffen werden:
```
FIND NAME-SET AT FAMILIENNAME = "MAYER"
FIND ALTERS-SET AT ALTER = 65 or LATER = 75
FIND NEXT ALTERS-SET AT ALTER = 70
FIND NAME-SET AT FAMILIENNAME = "MÜLLER" OR VORNAME = "FRANZ"
```

Wenn ein Schlüssel in einem Set aus mehreren Datenelementen
besteht, so müssen nicht alle Datenelemente zur Auswahl definiert werden. Weiters können auch alternative Bedingungen
angegeben werden. Eine Selektionsanweisung kann daher zu mehreren
Sätzen führen, welche diesen Bedingungen genügen. Diese Sätze
können mit Hilfe der "NEXT"-Klausel gelesen werden.

Der Zugriff über eine Link-Verbindung erfolgt genau gleich wie
über einen Set oder einen Subset:
FIND ADRESSINFO

Einfügen eines Satzes

CREATE PERSONAL
MOVE INFAMILIENNAME TO FAMILIENNAME
MOVE INVORNAME TO VORNAME
MOVE IN-SV-NR TO SV-NR
    .
    .
    .
STORE PERSONAL

Die "Create"-Anweisung initialisiert den Satz auf "Null" oder
die vom Datenbank-Administrator definierten Initialwerte.

Die "Store" Anweisung schreibt dann die "user-work-area" logisch
in die Datenbank.

Die Create-Anweisung kann durch eine "Free" Anweisung oder durch
einen Zugriff auf Dataset storniert werden.

Durch die Store-Anweisung werden auch alle automatischen Sets
und Subsets dieses Datasets automatisch mitgewartet.

Löschen eines Satzes

Ein Satz eines Datasets plus alle seine automatischen Sets und
Subsets werden durch die "Delete" Anweisung gelöscht.

DELETE NEXT NAME-SET
    löscht z.B. den nächsten Satz ausgehend vom "current path".

DELETE SV-SET AT SV-NR = 1234567789
    löscht den mittels der SV-NR spezifizierten Satz.

Ein Satz wird nur dann gelöscht, wenn alle seine Links, manuellen
Subsets und embedded Datasets vorher gelöscht wurden.

Update eines Satzes

MODIFY NAME-SET AT FAMILIENNAME = "MAYER" AND VORNAME = "FRITZ"
MOVE "C" TO RANG
    .
    .
STORE PERSONAL

Die "Modify" Anweisung arbeitet genau wie die "Find" Anweisung,
nur wird zusätzlich der gelesene Satz gegen weiteren Zugriff
gesperrt (Record Level Lockout). Damit können mehrere Programme
gleichzeitig denselben Dataset verändern, ohne Gefahr des
"Multiple update". "Deadlock" Situationen werden vom DMS II System
automatisch erkannt und behandelt. Es kann daher von einem
Programm falls notwendig mehr als ein Satz gesperrt werden.
Für dieses Mehrfachsperren sind keine weiteren speziellen
Anweisungen notwendig.

Satzselektion

Ein Satz kann durch vollständige Angabe eines Schlüssels einer
seiner Sets selektiert werden:
MODIFY NAME-SET AT FAMILIENNAME = "BERGER" AND VORNAME = "PETER"

Ein Satz kann aber auch bei nur teilweise bekanntem Schlüssel
gesucht werden:
FIND NAME-SET AT VORNAME GREATER "KARL"
oder
FIND NAME-SET AT FAMILIENNAME GREATER OR EQUAL "HUBER".

Bei nur teilweiser Angabe der Schlüssel kann es natürlich vorkommen, daß mehrere Sätze dieser Bedingung genügen. Diese Sätze
können dann mit der "next"Klausel gelesen werden.

Diese teilweise Angabe des Schlüssels ist besonders für on-line
Abfragesysteme eine wertvolle und erforderliche Eigenschaft.

Ausnahmen Behandlung

Bei Zugriff auf die Datenbank kann es auch zu Ausnahmen
("Exceptions") wie z.B. Satz nicht gefunden, kommen. Diese
Ausnahmen können mit Hilfe der "On-Exception" Klausel erkannt
und behandelt werden.
MODIFY NAME-SET AT FAMILIENNAME = "BAUER"
     ON EXCEPTION IF DMSTATUS(NOTFOUND)....
               IF DMSTATUS(DEADLOCK)....
               IF DMSTATUS(OPENERROR)...

Die Art der auftretenden "Exception" kann durch Abfrage des
DMS II Resultatfeldes "dmstatus" ermittelt werden.

Die Behandlung und Ermittlung der Ausnahmen kann alternativ auch
in einem "COBOL declarative" erfolgen.

Die gesamte DMS II ZUgriffssprache besteht aus 16 Verben:
OPEN, CLOSE, MODIFY(LOCK), STORE, DELETE, FREE, FIND, SET, CREATE,
RECREATE, GENERATE, INSERT, REMOVE, ASSIGN, BEGIN-TRANSACTION
und END-TRANSACTION.

DMS II - Recovery

DMS II Recovery wurde unter Bedachtnahme auf möglichst einfache
Verwendung, mit minimalen Operator-Eingriffen, entworfen.

Zu den Recovery-Prozeduren gehört auch die Behandlung und
Behebung von Plattenfehlern. Diese Fehlerbehebung führt zu keinem
Stillstand der laufenden Programme sondern nur zu einer minimal
gehaltenen Durchsatzreduzierung ("Graceful Degradation") des
Systems. Das Ziel ist eine kontinuierliche Verarbeitung in
Batch und On-Line zu garantieren.

Die für eine Recovery der Datenbank notwendigen Audit-Aufzeichnungen können sowohl auf Platte, als auch auf Band durchgeführt
werden. Diese Aufzeichnungen können auch dupliziert geführt
werden. Dabei kann primäre und sekundäre Aufzeichnung auf dem
gleichen Medium oder auch auf verschiedenen Medien erfolgen.
Die Recovery Routinenen schalten, falls bei der primären Aufzeichnung ein Fehler erkannt wird, automatisch auf die sekundäre
Aufzeichnung um.

Transaktionsorientiertes Recovery

Eine Batch order On-Line Transaktion kann aus einer Serie von
logisch zusammengehörigen Datenbankoperationen b estehen.
Zur Wahrung der Integrität der Datenbank müssen alle diese
Operationen oder keine durchgeführt werden. Diese gemeinsame
Durchführung der Datenbankveränderungen wird durch Gruppierung
der Veränderungsanweisungen in eine Transaktion (d.h. zwischen
die Anweisungen "Begin-Transaction" und "End-Transaction" erreicht.

```
READ PERSONALB AND
READ VORLESUNGSBAND
         .
MODIFY PERSONAL


         .
MODIFY VORLESUNG
         .
BEGIN TRANSACTION
         .

         .
STORE PERSONAL
         .
STORE VORLESUNG
         .
END-TRANSACTION
```

Alle Veränderungen der Datenbank dürfen nur im Transaktionsstatus
erfolgen. Der Datenbank-Administrator kann dabei die Häufigkeit
und die Ressourcen für die Audit-Aufzeichnungen im DASDL
definieren.

```
PARAMETERS (SYNCPOINT = 5 TRANSACTION,
            CONTROLPOINT = 19 SYNCPOINTS).
```

SYNCPOINT: Kein Programm befindet sich im Transaktionsstatus.
              Alle Audit-Puffer werden auf das Audit-Medium ge-
              schrieben.

CONTROLPOINT:Alle modifizierten Datenbank-Puffer werden innerhalb
              von zwei Controlpoints mindestens einmal auf die
              Platte geschrieben, um so das Absuchen des Audit-
              Trails im Falle von Recovery zu minimalisieren.

Das Recovery-Hilfsprogramm wirt automatisch vom Betriebssystem
ohne Operatoreingriff gestartet. Die benötigten Audit-Dateien
werden automatisch vom Recovery-System gefunden und die Datenbank
wird wiederhergestellt.

Recovery Ablauf

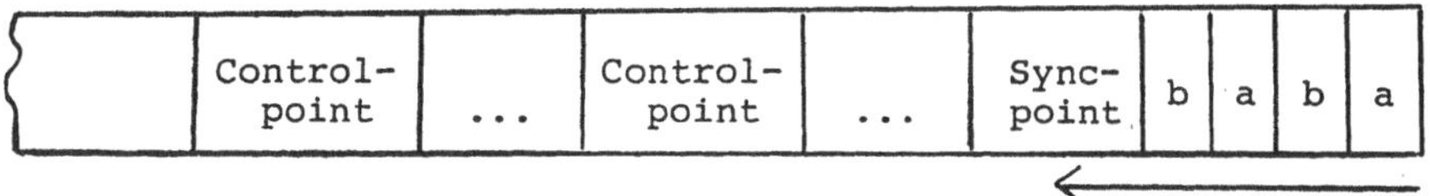

- Die Auditaufzeichnung wird bis zum letzten Syncpoint zurückgelesen. Dies ist der letzte Zeitpunkt, an dem kein Programm
  in der Mitte einer Transaktion war.
- Die auf dem Audit-File aufgezeichneten "before images"
  werden zum Rückgängigmachen der Datenbankveränderung benutzt.

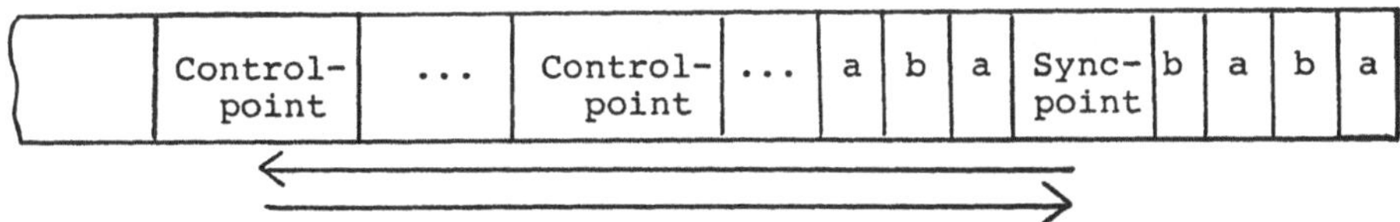

- Die Auditaufzeichnung wird bis zum zweitletzten Controlpoint
  zurückgelesen.
- Vom zweitletzten Controlpoint wird bis zum letzten Syncpoint
  vorwärts gelesen.
- Die "after images" des Audit-Trails werden dabei verarbeitet,
  um sicherzustellen, daß alle Transaktionen bis zum letzten
  Syncpoint ihren Niederschlag auf der Platte gefunden haben.
- Restart-Information über die letzte komplette Transaktion
  wird für jedes laufende Programm im "Restart Dataset"
  gespeichert.
- Recovery ist beendet. Die normale Verarbeitung wird fortgesetzt.

Recovery Ablauf bei unerwünschtem Abbruch

Die Recovery Strategie von DMS II ist in diesem Fall wie folgt:
- Alle Jobs werden neu gestartet.
- Die Integrität der Datenbank wird mit Hilfe der Audit-Aufzeich-
  nungen wiederhergestellt.

- Recovery der Datenbank wird abgeschlossen.
- Die zuletzt laufenden Programme werden automatisch gestartet.
- Die Restart-Informationen werden den Programmen übergeben.

Es besteht keine Notwendigkeit, Dateien zu rekonstruieren oder
Transaktionen zu wiederholen.

Das Betriebssystem startet automatisch alle Programme welche
zur Zeit des Fehlers auf die Datenbank zugegriffen haben.
Die vom Benutzer definierte Restart-Information plus Information
über die Art des Fehlers wird an die Programme übergeben.

Recovery für irreparable Plattenfehler

Strategie:
- Nur die vom Fehler betroffenen Teile der Dateien werden
  gesperrt. Gegen den Rest der Datenbank können weiterhin
  ungestört Transaktionen durchgeführt werden.
- Ein Hilfsprogramm stellt mit Hilfe des letzten Datenbankdumps
  und des Audit-Trails, gleichzeitig mit den laufenden Anwen-
  dungsprogrammen, die zerstörten Teile der Datenbank wieder her.
- DMS II gibt automatisch die gesperrten Teile nach der Re-
  konstruktion wieder frei.
- Es besteht auch hier wieder keine Notwendigkeit, den gesamten
  File zu rekonstruieren.
- Die Bennützer können ohne Unterbrechung die guten Teile der
  Datenbank ungestört weiterverwenden.

Datenbankabsicherung (Dump)

Die Datenbank kann gleichzeitig mit laufender Abfrage und
Update Programmen abgesichert werden.

Die Absicherung (dump) wird hierbei mit der Audit-Aufzeichnung
synchronisiert.

Statistische Reports über die Datenbankverwendung

Eine der Aufgaben des Datenbank-Administrators ist die laufende
Anpassung und Optimierung der logischen und physischen Strukturen
an die Anforderungen der Datenbank-Benutzer. Diese Anforderungen
können sich im Laufe der Zeit, z.B. beim Übergang von batch-
orientierter Verarbeitung zu einem on-line Betrieb, wesentlich
ändern.

DMS II stellt dem Datenbank-Administrator automatisch einen
Bericht über die wichtigsten Kenndaten der Datenbankverwendung
zur Verfügung. Dieser statistische Bericht umfaßt:
Information über die DMS II Hauptspeicherbelegung,
Zeitdauer der aktiven Datenbankbenützung,
Anzahl der logischen Operationen je Struktur,
Anzahl der physischen Lese- und Schreiboperationen je Struktur,
Ein/Ausgabezeiten und Wartezeiten für die physischen Operationen,
Größe und Verwendung des DMS II Hauptspeicherpuffers.
Mit Hilfe dieses Berichtes kann der Datenbank-Administrator zeit-
gerecht auf die neuen Erfordernisse reagieren, um so stets eine
optimale Systembenützung zu ermöglichen.

Berichtsprogrammgenerator (REPORTER)

Eine der Hauptaufgaben der EDV ist es heute immer noch gedruckte
Berichte zu liefern. Um diese Aufgabe zu vereinfachen und kosten-
günstiger zu gestalten, steht für die Generierung von Bericht-
programmen das Burroughs REPORTER System zur Verfügung.

Mit diesem Burroughs REPORTER System können Berichtsprogramme,
welche sowohl DMS II Datenbanken als auch normale Dateien als
Eingabe verwenden, generiert werden. Die vom REPORTER System
verwendete Defintionssprache ist eine COBOL-ähnliche
"free form" Sprache. REPORTER generiert COBOL-Programme,

welche dann mit dem Standard-Compiler compiliert werden.
Zur Vereinfachung der Programmierung wird vom Datenbank-Administrator ein Vokabular, welches die verfügbaren Datenelemente,
ihre Struktur und Beschreibung beinhaltet, generiert.
Für eine Datenbank können mehrere Vokabulare, geschützt über
Usercode und Password, bestehen. Die einzelnen Vokabulare
können jetzt verschiedene Teile bzw. Datenelemente für den
Programmierer sichtbar oder unsichtbar machen, um so auch hier
wieder Schutz gegen unbefugten Zugriff zu bieten.

Unsere fiktive Universität benötigt z.B. einen Bericht über
alle Beschäftigten, deren Name mit "MAC" oder "MC" beginnt.
Das entsprechende REPORTER-Programm könnte etwa folgendermaßen aussehen:

```
VOCABULARY = PERSONAL,
SET PAGE-WIDTH TO 60.
INPUT PERSONAL-DATEN AT NAME = "MAC" OR "MC",
TITLE "AUSGEWAEHLTES PERSONAL",
REPORT NAME ASCENDING, ADRESSE, TELEFON.
```

Mit Hilfe dieses Programmes ergibt sich dann folgender Bericht:

```
        AUSGEWAEHLTES PERSONAL
NAME            ADRESSE                 TELEFON
MAC DONALD      1248 12TH ST.           417-2159
MAC KENZIE      346 ELM ST.             316-1191
MAC HANUS       10 BEACH DR.            417-1211
MC ALPINE       1919 HOLL RD.           417-1109
MC CAMMAN       1847 PARK PLACE         417-3387
```

Seitenvorschubsteuerung, Einteilung der Kolonnen und Seiten,
Seiten und Kolonnenüberschriften werden automatisch generiert.
Weiters kann auch, wie in diesem Bericht, mit Hilfe der
"Ascending"-Klausel automatisch nach einem oder mehreren Datenelementen sortiert werden. Innerhalb einer Berichtszeile kann
mit den Datenelementen gerechnet werden, wobei sowohl arithmetische, als auch boolesche Operationen zur Verfügung stehen.

Reports können auch Gruppenbrüche beinhalten, die entsprechende
Programmlogik wird ebenfalls vom System generiert. Über einzelne
Gruppenbrüche, bzw. über den gesamten Bericht können auch Totale
und verschiedene statistische Auswertungen gebildet werden.

Mit Hilfe des REPORTER-Systems können somit schnell, einfach
und kostensparend Berichte, sowohl für die permanente Verwendung,
als auch als Einzelbericht zur Beantowrtung von Sonderfragen,
erstellt werden.

DMS II Inquiry System

Für die interaktive Abfrage und Veränderung der Daten einer
DMS II Datenbank über Terminals steht das DMS II Inquiry System
zur Verfügung. Abfragen, welche mit Hilfe des DMS II Inquiry
Systems durchgeführt werden, sind wieder voll gegen unbefugten
Zugriff geschützt. Dieser Schutz kann sich auf Datenstrukturen,
einzelne Sätze und einzelne Datenelemente erstrecken. Die einzelnen Abfragen werden in einer einfachen Datenmanipulationssprache definiert, wobei sich diese Abfragen auf einen einzelnen
Satz oder auch auf Gruppen von Sätzen beziehen kann. Die Abfragesprache kann mit den extrahierten Daten auch arithmetische und
boolesche Operationen durchführen und so die gewünschten
Informationen in der für den Anwender am besten geeigneten Form
zur Verfügung stellen. z.B.:

```
RUN DMINQ/PERSONAL          Aufruf des DMS II Inquiry Systems
$ READY                     Prompting durch das System
SELECT NAME = "MC"          Auswahl eines Satzes
$                           Satz steht zur Verfügung
DISPLAY NAME, TELEFON       Diese Felder sollen jetzt ausgegeben
                            werden
NAME = MC CLINTOCK   TELEFON = 316-2358
```

```
DISPLAY NAME, TELEFON FOR NAME = "MAYR"     Select and Display
                                            kombiniert
NAME = MAYR B.    TELEFON = 123456
NAME = MAYR H.    TELEFON = 3456788
NAME = MAYR M.    TELEFON = 2233445


DISPLAY (SUM OF GEHALT) FOR ALL          Totale über alle Gehälter
SUM GEHALT = 1,007,423.20
```

DMS II Kompatibilität

Burroughs DMS II wurde ursprünglich auf den Systemen der
Serie B 6000/7000 implementiert. Ausgehend von dieser Implementierung wurde kompatible Systeme für die Systemfamilien B 1700/
B 1800 und B 2800/B 3800/B 4800 geschaffen. Burroughs stellt
somit seinen Kunden ein kompatibles Datenbanksystem von der
kleinsten bis zur größten EDV-Anlage zur Verfügung. Damit wird
dem Anwender von DMS II ungestörtes Wachstum, ohne Programm-
änderungen oder Änderungen in der Datenbankbeschreibung, über
den gesamten Burroughs Produktbereich ermöglicht.

ISIS-Statistische Datenbank des ÖSTZ

Dr. Herbert Pilat
Österreichisches Statistisches Zentralamt

Datenverarbeitung in der Statistik, so könnte man sagen, ist
Datenverarbeitung par exellence, es sind ja alle Kriterien
gegeben, die den Einsatz der EDV sinnvoll erscheinen lassen.
Die Statistik erfaßt den gesamten sozioökonomischen Raum in
möglichst vielen Details, was wiederum einen enormen Daten-
anfall nach sich zieht, dessen Bewältigung nur mit EDV-tech-
nischen Mitteln möglich ist.

So nimmt es nicht wunder, daß die Statistik und hier gerade
die Österr. Statistik eine Tradition in der Datenverarbeitung
aufweist, auf die wir stolz sein können. So wurden in Österreich bereits um die Jahrhundertwende elektrische Lochkarten-
zählgeräte eingesetzt. In der Nachkriegszeit arbeitete man
mit Tabelliermaschinen, seit über 1o Jahren verfügt das
Österr. Statistische Zentralamt über ein leistungsfähiges
EDV-System.
Das Amt ist zur Einhaltung des gesetzlichen Publikations-
auftrags verpflichtet, was im letzten Jahrzehnt durch die
ständige Ausweitung des Informationsbedürfnisses immer
schwieriger wurde. Da die 'Manpower' nicht mehr vermehrbar
ist, sind wir bereits heute in der Situation, daß die pro-
grammierte Auswertung zur Deckung der Informationswünsche
nicht mehr ausreicht, 1971 hat man mit der Planung des ISIS,
'Integriertes statistisches Informationssystem', begonnen.
Organisatorisch gesichert war das Projekt durch die Existenz
des Referats 'Forschung und Entwicklung' im Rahmen des
Rechenzentrums, als dessen Leiter ich mich vorstellen darf.

Ich werde nun versuchen, die statistische Datenbank ISIS
in ihren Silhouetten anzudeuten. Es handelt sich um eine
Makrodatenbank, das Datenmanagement verwaltet also ausschließlich aggregiertes Material.

Das Zahlenmaterial liegt systemimmanent in Form einer großen
Anzahl von multidimensionalen Matrizen vor, die hinsichtlich
ihrer Größe stark variieren. Die Datenbank ist nicht als sek-
torielles System ausgelegt (z.B. Regionalsysteme), sondern
umfaßt die gesamte Breite statistischer Erhebungen.
Die Ergebnisse sollen vorzugsweise online an den Arbeits-
platz geliefert werden, der sich im Haus oder in einer
fremden Organisation befinden kann. Damit ist auch schon an-
gedeutet, daß der Benützer keine speziellen EDV-Kenntnisse
besitzen muß und sich bei der Formulierung seiner Datenwünsche
nur einer sehr einfach gehaltenen Abfragesprache bedient.
Dazu steht ihm ein Benützungshilfensystem zur Verfügung, auf
das später noch kurz eingegangen werden soll.
Lassen sie mich jetzt einige Aspekte des ISIS im einzelnen
betrachten.
Hier wäre zunächst die sachliche Struktur, wie sie sich dem
Benutzer gegenüber darstellt.
Der Begriff 'System' liefert eine sektorielle Einteilung des
gesamten Datenbankinhalts. Die Systemstruktur ist im Prinzip
hierarchisch und führt über die 'Hauptsysteme' zu den 'Sub-
systemen letzter Ordnung' (Abb.1). Sie dient letztlich nur
dem Hinfinden zu Details im Datenkörper und könnte auch weit
sphistischer angelegt sein, als sie derzeit implementiert
ist.

An den Enden des 'Systembaums' hängen die eigentlichen Datenträger, die 'Segmente'.
Jedes Segment besteht aus einem verbalen Segmenttitel, der
intern in formalisierter Form derart vorliegt, daß Ver-

wandtschaften für das System erkennbar sind und einer Reihe
von Merkmalen, die die Gliederungsgesichtspunkte der im
Titel beschriebenen Materien sind.
Durch die allgemeine Regel, daß alle sinnvollen Verkreuzungen
zwischen den vorgegebenen Segmentkriterien erlaubt sind,
spannt ein Segment eine Menge von Martizen (variabler Dimension) auf.

Was das inhaltlich bedeutet, kann am besten an Hand eines
Beispielsegments aus der Regionalstatistik illustriert
werden (Abb.2).
Wie sich die Segmentforumulierung inhaltlich rund um den
semantischen Kreis des Subsystems letzter Ordnung gruppiert,
entnimmt man beispielhaft einer Seite des Segmentkatalogs
(Abb.3). Eine hinsichtlich ihrer Einspeisung besondere
Spezies von Segmenten sind die Zeitreihensegmente, die entweder längs der Zeitachse gleiten oder wachsen können.

Der Aspekt der <u>Organisation der Dateneinspeisung</u> verdient
bei einer Großdatenbank wie ISIS besondere Beachtung. Viel
oder wenig speichern macht zwar qualitativ wenig Unterschied. Das technische Konzept muß aber ein anderes sein,
wenn man mit großen Datenmengen operiert.

ISIS umfaßt derzeit 411 Systeme,
                    3180 Segemente,
           über 1oo ooo Matrizen mit
                     45 Md. logischen Datenzellen

Die der Dateneinspeisung vorgelagerte Arbeit ist so automatisiert, wie sonst nicht üblich. Die formale Zerlegung der
Segmente in Matrizen, die Erzeugung der Programmiervorgabe
für die Basisbänder, in die das statistische Urmaterial umgesetzt werden muß, erfolgt automatisch.

258

Da ISIS ja keine Einzeldaten enthält (bzw. aus Datenschutz-
gründen enthalten darf) ist die Aggregierung ein zentrales
Problem. Auch im Zeitalter extrem leistungsfähiger EDV-Systeme
ist die technische Aggregierungsarbeit aufwandsmäßig sehr
erheblich und wird im ISIS durch ein hochspezialisiertes
Produkt, den Aggregator, geleistet.

Die <u>Möglichkeiten der Abfrage</u> zeigt das Schema der Abb.4.

Die Benutzung des Systems erfolgt online und offline. Die
aggregierten Daten sind in stark komprimierter Form im
'Datenkörper' zu finden, der 'Adreßkörper' enthält die Meta-
daten.

Diese beiden Dateien werden via Datenbanknukleus durch die
Programmprodukte DB/1, DB/2, DBAUSZUG, die sequentielle Datenbasis durch TABGEN angezapft.

DB/1:
Heißt das reine on-line Abfragesystem, das durch seine
sehr konzisw und einfache Sprache den online Datenzugriff
ermöglicht.

Wie die Formulierung erfolgt, zeigt am besten das folgende
einfache Beispiel:

: C9F F50 1 C11 ALLE B19 1 BIS 9

Ausgangspunkt der Datenspezifikation ist immer ein Segment
mit seinem Angebot an Gliederungsmöglichkeiten.
Durch Anführen des Segmentcodes und der relevanten Merk-
malscodes, versehen mit einer Ausprägungsliste baut man in
einfacher Weise einen Datenquader auf, der von DB/1 in der
in Abb.5 gezeigten Form auf das Terminal gebracht wird.
DB/1 besitzt darüber hinaus eine Reihe von Dialoghilfen,
die zu besprechen den Rahmen des Referats sprengen würde.

DB/2:

Ist die um Analysekomponenten angereicherte online Abfrage-
komponente und gestattet die Anwendung arithmetischer
Operationen auf Matrizen.
DB/2 verfügt darüber hinaus über einen begrenzten Vorrat
an mathematischen, statistischen und manipulativen
Funktionen, etwa die Möglichkeit auf eine fremdsprachliche
Textierung umzuschalten.
Sprachlich vorgesehen, aber noch wenig entwickelt sind die
Möglichkeiten, optisch verbesserte Ausgaben zu erhalten,
etwa graphische Ausgabe oder das Delegieren längerer Aus-
wertungen an den Batch.
In Vorbereitung ist ein Direktanschluß von APL an das
Abfragesystem, der komplexere Auswertungen der Datenbank-
materie möglich machen soll. Gelöst wird dies durch Modus-
umschaltung APL-DB/2 bzw. durch Datentransfer DB/2 in die
APL-Umgebung im APL-Dialog.

DBAUSZUG:
Ist die offizielle Version der Abfrage.
Die Bedienung des Benützers erfolgt via 'Automatauftrag'.
Auf einem Formblatt spezifiziert der Benützer seine Daten-
wünsche in der Sprache des DB/1.
Rechenhaftigkeit wie in DB/2 ist im jetzigen Entwicklungs-
stadium nicht inkludiert. DBAUSZUG besitzt gewisse
Möglichkeiten, die Form der Tabellendarbietung zu beein-
flussen.
TABGEN: -
Schließlich gestattet es, ad hoc-Auswertungen aus dem
Datenbasisfundus offline abzuwickeln und entspricht in
seiner Funktion etwa DBAUSZUG.
Der Vorteil des Automatauftrages liegt ja einerseits darin,
daß keine statistisch- oder EDV-technisch versierte Fach-
kraft benötigt wird, andererseits aber ein Response in
vertretbarer Zeit erfolgen kann.
Die Responsezeit liegt unter einer Woche und setzt sich
aus Durchführungszeit, Zeit für den organisatorisch be-
dingten internen Lauf und den Postversand zusammen.

Entscheidend, ob eine Datenbank beim Endbenützer ankommt oder
nicht, sind die Benützungshilfen. ISIS stellt den numerischen
Daten ein Kommentarsystem zur Seite, das zur Interpretation
der Daten unerläßlich ist, das etwa Erhebungsspezifikation
Datenqualität oder Ungereimtheiten in den Zahlen erklären
kann. Die Kommentare sind für online Benützung gedacht und
somit integrierter Bestandteil des Abfragesystems.

Als off-line Benützungshilfen existieren Kataloge, die im
Loseblattverfahren ständig gewartet werden,
ein Mitteilungsdienst zur Datenbank und
ein Schulungsdienst, der die notwendige Kenntnis zur Benützung
der Datenbankprodukte vermitteln soll.

Diese etwas eingehendere Darstellung der Datenbank war notwendig, um die Überlegungen zu rechtfertigen, die bei der
Projektrealisierung angestellt wurden.
Die offizielle Freigabe des ISIS fand im Frühjahr 1974 statt,
die Planungs- und Implementierungsphase dauerte 2 1/2 Jahre.

Das System läuft auf einer IBM 370/158 unter VS2 mit TSO.
Die Programmierung erfolgte komplett in eigenen Haus, es wurde
kein am Markt erhältliches Datenmanagementsystem verwendet.

Warum das? Der Hauptgrund dafür war - man schrieb 1972 - einfach das Nichtvorhandensein eines brauchbaren komerziellen
Systems und die Ungewißheit, ob ein adäquates System in der
notwendigen Zeit erhältlich sein wird. Es war nicht erhältlich,
wie wir jetzt, fünf Jahre später wissen.

Der Datenumfang der etwa $1o^5$ null - bis sechsdimensionalen
Matrizen liegt in einem Streuungsbereich von 1 bis $1o^8$ Zellen.
Jedes Einzeldatum muß im Direktzugriff in akzeptabel kurzer
Zeit bei der online-Abfrage vorhanden sein. Andererseits
können aus Gründen des beschränkten Speicherplatzes auf Platte

nicht alle Matrizen physisch realisiert werden. Man muß also
vom System verlangen, den Datenfundus nicht lediglich als
Symmlung voneinander isolierter Komplexe zu sehen, sondern die
zwischen den Komplexen bestehenden Verwandtschaftsbeziehungen
zu verwerten und im einzelnen zu entscheiden, was physisch zu
speichern ist und was bei der Abfrage online erzeugt werden
kann.

Ein weiterer Grund ist das Unbehagen, im zentralen Teil unseres
automatisierten Datensystems eine 'black bix' zu haben mit
allen ihren Konsequenzen bei fehlerhafter Funktion.

Zum Thema 'theoretisches Datenbankmodell' ist zu sagen, daß für
ISIS eine praxisnahe Eigenentwicklung gewählt wurde. Während
der Planungsphase 1972 standen im wesentlichen noch die hierarchischen Datenbankmodelle im Vordergrund der Diskussion.
Diese erscheinen aber nicht praktikabel, wenn man an ein
speziell statistisches System die Forderung stellt, zigtausende
mehrdimensionale Matrizen mit ungeheurer Schwankungsbreite hinsichtlich ihrer Größe zu speichern. Man muß aus Gründen der
rascheren Auffindbarkeit der Daten ein kartesisches Daten-
konzept aufgreifen, modifiziert für große Matrizen durch Einsatz binärer Suchformen. Die Organisation der Metdaten zu ISIS
könnte man als eine dem relationalen Datenbanksystem nahe-
stehende Form bezeichnen.

Die verwendeten Programmiersprachen sind Assembler und PL/1,
wobei die wesentlichen Teile des Datenbanksystems in Assembler
gehalten sind, da der Nachteil der etwas aufwendigeren
Programmierung und Programm-Wartung durch Performancevorteile
im Maschinenlauf überkompensiert wird.
Zur Realisierung einer Datenbank gehört neben der Implementierung
des Softwareinstruments vor allem auch die organisatorische
Einbettung in die Umgebung der potentiellen Benützer.

Ein System, das wie ISIS jene Datenaggregate aufnehmen soll,
die zu einem späteren Zeitpunkt interessieren sollen, das
also das Auswertungsprogramm einer Erhebung möglichst vor-
wegnehmen soll, ist auf die Mitarbeit aller Endbenützer an-
gewiesen.

Dazu wurde das Instrument des 'Fachbeiräts für Datenbanken'
geschaffen, der jährlich einmal im Plenum zusammentritt. Das
Plenum legt die zu behandelnden Themenkreise fest, sichtet
konkurrenzierende Wünsche, legt Prioritäten fest und delegiert
die weitere Untersuchungsarbeit an Arbeitsgruppen, Die Arbeitsgruppen übernehmen die Segmentformulierung, überarbeiten
diese in 2 Lesungen und übergeben die konkreten Arbeitser-
gebnisse zwecks Formalisierung an das Österreichische Stat.
Zentralamt.

Da der Fachbeirat allen Benützern und Interessenten der Datenbank offensteht - vertreten sind Fachleute aus Instituten,
Ministerien, Ländern, Städten und Privatinstitutionen, kann
man hier von einem gesamtösterreichischen Projekt sprechen.
Das Kapitel <u>Datenschutz</u> darf in einen Referat über Datenbanken
nicht fehlen. ISIS enthält nur aggregierte Daten, reagiert
also in der Regel nicht so sensibel auf die Datenschutz-
problematik.

Es kann jedoch - beispielsweise in der Industriestatistik -
zu einem so hohen Aggregationsniveau kommen, daß auch aus
aggregiertem Material Rückschlüsse auf Einzelfälle gezogen
werden können.
ISIS kennt den Begriff der Benützermenge, der dem Benützer
den Zugriff auf eine Untermenge aller Segmente einschränkt.
Weiters gibt es Schutzfunktionen, die auf Segmente angewandt
werden, die einen Schutzfilter der Ausgabe vorschalten.
Dieser Filter veranlaßt dann die Ausgabe maskierter Meldungen
(etwa 'geheim'), beispielsweise wenn die Anzahl der bei-
tragenden Einzelfälle auf 3 oder weniger sinkt.

Unbefugte Inbetriebnahme des Abfragesystems soll durch Kennworte und einen Magnetausweis verhindert werden.

Der Ausbau des Systems ISIS erfolgte stufenweise, sowohl inhaltlich als auch konzeptionell. Diese Vorgangsweise soll auch in Zukunft beibehalten werden.

Verfolgt man die weltweiten Bemühungen um ein umfassendes statistisches Datenmanagementsystem, so merkt man, daß man sich hier am Wege von einer eher naiven Sicht der Dinge zu einer realistischen Betrachtungsweise erst am Anfang befindet.

In der Tat weiß man jetzt noch nicht, was wirklich erreicht werden kann und um welchen Preis. Daher glaube ich, daß das Design eines mächstigen Datenmanagementsystems in einem Schritt ein zweifelhaftes Unterfangen wäre.

Immerhin, die bisherigen Planungsstufen des ISIS wurden erfüllt. Die weiteren Ausbaustufen zielen in Richtung Aufbau einer umfassenden Metadatenbank als Vorstufe eines automatisierten Systems, das den überwiegenden Prozentsatz von ad-hoc-Auswertungen leisten kann, ohne Kapazität an Fachpersonal zu binden. Mit anderen Worten, es geht darum, die Datenbeschreibungssprache in die statistische Arbeit zurückzuziehen. Der Engpaß an Fachpersonal bei wachsendem Informationsbedarf zwingt zu einer tiefgreifenden Rationalisierung.

Auch auf dem Sektor der Statistik bedeutet nämlich Stehenbleiben Zurückfallen.

BILDUNG
DEMOGRAPHIE
SOZIALSTATISTIK
WIRTSCHAFT NACH INSTITUTIONEN
WIRTSCHAFT NACH FUNKTIONEN
GESUNDHEIT
STEUERN
REGIONALSTATISTIK
INDIZES UND INDIKATOREN
VOLKSWIRTSCHAFTL. GESAMTRECHNUNG
INTERNATIONALE DATEN
BILDUNG
DEMOGRAPHIE
SOZIAL-STATISTIK
WIRTSCHAFT NACH INST.
WIRTSCHAFT NACH FUNKT.
BERUFS-TÄTIGKEIT
WOHUNGS-WESEN
STRUKTUR
WANDERUNG
BERUFSPENDEL-WANDERUNG

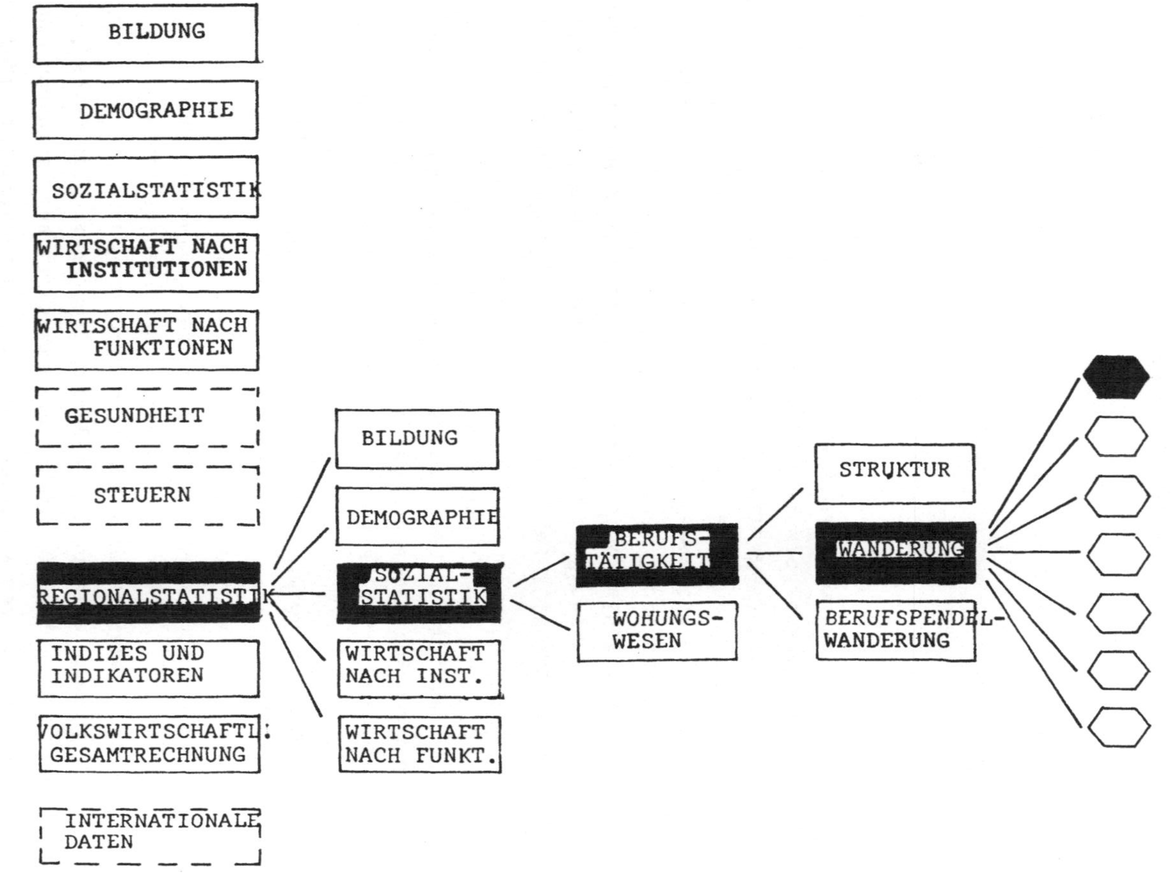

Abb.1

C9F ANZAHL DER GEWANDERTEN BERUFSTAETIGEN, AM 12.5.1971

   1 F50 POLITISCHER BEZIRK DES WOHNORTES <98>

   1 F32 BUNDESLAND DES WOHNORTES <9>

   2 B19 POLITISCHER BEZIRK DES HERKUNFTSORTES BZW.AUSLAND <99>

   2 B28 BUNDESLAND DES HERKUNFTSORTES BZW: AUSLAND <10>

     C11 GESCHLECHT <2>

: C9F F50 1 C11 ALLE B19 1 BIS 9 =

Abb. 2

C9F ANZAHL DER GEWANDERTEN BERUFSTAETIGEN, AM 12.5.1971

   F50 POLITISCHER BEZIRK DES WOHNORTES <98>

       1 EISENSTADT   <101>

  C11 GESCHLECHT <2>

     B19 POLITISCHER BEZIRK DES HERKUNFTSORTES BZW.AUSLAND <99>

   1 MAENNLICH

1 EISENSTADT	<101>.	0
2 RUST	<102>.	3
3 EISENSTADT - UMGEBUNG	<103>.	48
4 GUESSING	<104>.	4
5 JENNERSDORF	<105>.	5
6 MATTERSBURG	<106>.	18
7 NEUSIEDL AM SEE	<107>.	22
8 OBERPULLENDORF	<108>.	12
9 OBERWART	<109>.	12

   2 WEIBLICH

1 EISENSTADT	<101>.	0
2 RUST	<102>.	2
3 EISENSTADT - UMGEBUNG	<103>.	42

  C11 GESCHLECHT <2>

     B19 POLITISCHER BEZIRK DES HERKUNFTSORTES BZW.AUSLAND <99>

4 GUESSING	<104>.	5
5 JENNERSDORF	<105>.	2
6 MATTERSBURG	<106>.	19
7 NEUSIEDL AM SEE	<107>.	17
8 OBERPULLENDORF	<108>.	15
9 OBERWART	<109>.	13

Abb. 5

```
BERUFSTAETIGKEIT - WANDERUNG  HALPISYSTEM REGIONALSTATISTIK
*************************************************************************

C9F ANZAHL DER GEWANDERTEN BERUFSTAETIGEN, AM 12.5.1971

   1  F50  POLITISCHER BEZIRK DES WOHNORTES     98
   1  F32  BUNDESLAND DES WOHNORTES      9
   2  B19  POLITISCHER BEZIRK DES HERKUNFTSORTES BZW. AUSLAND    99
   2  B28  BUNDESLAND DES HERKUNFTSORTES BZW. AUSLAND   10
      C11  GESCHLECHT     2
---------------------------------------------------------------------

C8G ANZAHL DER ZUGEZOGENEN BERUFSTAETIGEN, AM 12.5.1971

   1  F41  GEMEINDE DES WOHNORTES   2345
   1  F50  POLITISCHER BEZIRK DES WOHNORTES     98
   1  F32  BUNDESLAND DES WOHNORTES     9
      C11  GESCHLECHT     2
---------------------------------------------------------------------

C7H ANZAHL DER ZUGEZOGENEN BERUFSTAETIGEN, AM 12.5.1971

   1  F50  POLITISCHER BEZIRK DES WOHNORTES     98
   1  F32  BUNDESLAND DES WOHNORTES      9
      D50  ALTER IN 5-JAHRESGRUPPEN     12
      B26  ENTFERNUNGSKATEGORIE    4
      C11  GESCHLECHT     2
---------------------------------------------------------------------

C61 ANZAHL DER ZUGEZOGENEN BERUFSTAETIGEN, AM 12.5.1971

   1  F50  POLITISCHER BEZIRK DES WOHNORTES     98
   1  F32  BUNDESLAND DES WOHNORTES      9
      C23  ZUSAMMENGEFASSTE WIRTSCHAFTSKLASSEN    27
      B26  ENTFERNUNGSKATEGORIE     4
      C11  GESCHLECHT     2
---------------------------------------------------------------------

DON ANZAHL DER WEGGEZOGENEN BERUFSTAETIGEN, AM 12.5.1971

   1  B37  GEMEINDE DES HERKUNFTSORTES BZW. AUSLAND    2350
   1  B19  POLITISCHER BEZIRK DES HERKUNFTSORTES BZW. AUSLAND    99
   1  B28  BUNDESLAND DES HERKUNFTSORTES BZW AUSLAND      10
      C11  GESCHELCHT     2
---------------------------------------------------------------------

D2L ANZAHL DER IN EINEN ANDEREN POLITISCHEN BEZIRK GEZOGENEN BERUFSTAETIGEN
    AM 12.5.1971

   1  B19  POLITISCHER BEZIRK DES HERKUNFTSORTES BZW. AUSLAND     99
   1  B28  BUNDESLAND DES HERKUNFTSORTES BZW. AUSLAND     10
      D50  ALTER IN 5-JAHRESGRUPPEN    12
      B62  ENTFERNUNGSKATEGORIE      3
      C11  GESCHLECHT     2
---------------------------------------------------------------------
```

Abb.3

ISIS in graphischer Darstellung

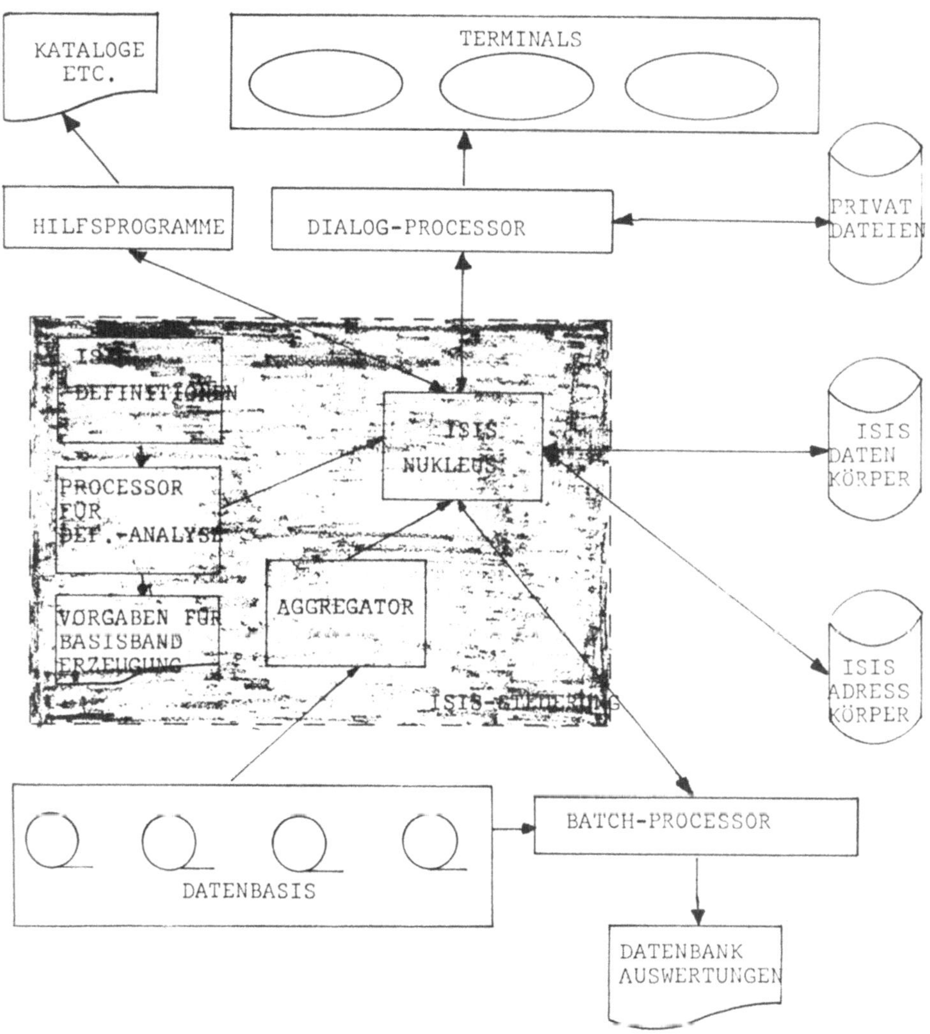

Abb.4

UDS
Das Universelle Datenbank-System von Siemens

Dipl.-Ing. Hermann Kudlich
Siemens Data Wien

Prognosen über den zu erwartenden Zuwachs der EDV in den
nächsten 15 Jahren lauten, daß nach diesem Zeitraum weltweit
5o bis 75 % aller Menschen ein Terminal mit Zugriff zu Datenbanken haben werden oder aktiv benutzen können. Diese
Schätzung wurde von C.W.Bachmann, einem der führenden Wissen-
schaftler auf dem Datenbanksektor und geistigem Vater der
"Codasyl-Normen" für Datenbanken anläßlich der letzten SICOB
in Paris abgegeben.

Einer der wesentlichen Gründe für diese Entwicklung liegt in
der Wandlung des Datenbegriffes. In der ersten Phase der EDV
bildeten die Daten die Basis für einzelne Verarbeitungs-
routinen und bezogen daraus ihre Bedeutung: die konventionellen
ablauf- bzw. verfahrensorientierten Dateikonzepte sind Beispiele für diese Betrachtungsweise.

Mit zunehmendem Informationsbedürfnis in Zusammenhang mit
immer leistungsfähigeren Speichertechnologien kam es zu einer
Wertverschiebung des Datenbegriffes. Die Bedeutung der Daten
liegt nun in ihrer Verfügbarkeit für jede Form der Verarbeitung
und Auswertung. Diese Auffassung der Daten als eigenständige
Größe, z.B. ein Material mit bestimmten Eigenschaften, ein
Mitarbeiter mit speziellen Kenntnissen, erfordert eine in der
DB integrierte Datenbeschreibung. Daher stellt die selbstbe-
schreibende Eigenschaft der Daten, d.h. die Datenbeschreibung
- bis auf Feldebene - ist Bestandteil der Daten selbst, die
wichtigste Voraussetzung für Transparenz und Hantierbarkeit
der Daten dar.

Der Aufbau entsprechender Datenbeschreibungskataloge mittels
geeigneter Datenbeschreibungssprachen, sogenannter DDL's,
ermöglicht die Datenunabhängigkeit der Programme. Basierend
auf diesen Vorstellungen haben die Arbeiten der "data-base-
task-group" (DBTG) im Rahmen von CODASYL die Entwicklung der
modernen Datenbank-Technologie entscheidend beeinflußt.

Siemens sieht in diesen Normierungsbetrebungen erhebliche
Vorteile für einen immer breiter werdenden Anwenderkreis
komplexer Datenbanken, angefangen von einer einheitlichen
Terminologie bis hin zu objektiven Leistungskriterien von
"DB-software" unterschiedlicher Hersteller.

Aus diesen Gründen hat die Firma Siemens das Datenbank-System
UDS auf den Markt gebracht, das auf den Normierungsvorschlägen
von "DBTG" inklusive des "Journal of development 1976" basiert.

1. Grundstruktur von UDS

Die Abb.1 zeigt die dreistufige Systemarchitektur von UDS, bestehend aus der physikalischen, der logischen und der externen
Ebene.

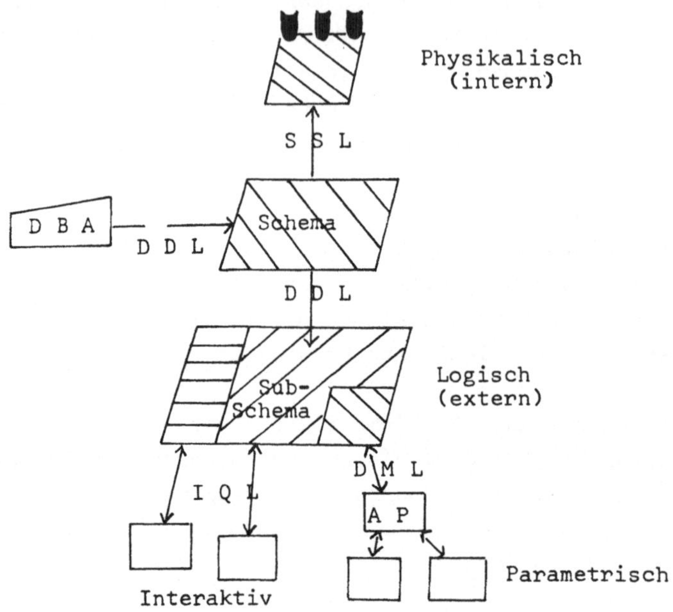

Abb.1 Struktur von UDS

Mit der Datendefinitionssprache (DDL) legt der Datenbankadministrat
die gewünschte Struktur der Datenbank auf rein logischer
Ebene fest. Das Schema, als Ergebnis dieses Prozesses, enthält
die Satzbeschreibung auf Feldebene, die Definition der einzelnen
Satzbeziehungen (sets) und Zugriffspfade sowie die Festlegung
der Datenbankbereiche (areas). Diese logische Ebene wird
niemals direkt benutzt, sondern sie dient als zentrale Verbindung zwischen der externen und der internen Ebene.

1.1 Externe Ebene

Mit der "Subschema-DDL" werden von der Gesamtbeschreibung der
Datenbank Untermengen festgelegt, die bestimmten Anwendungen
zugeordnet werden. Jede Datenbank-Anwendung arbeitet mit einem
bestimmten Subschema und sieht folglich nur den erforderlichen
Ausschnitt der Datenbank. Dieses Konzept gewährleistet den
Schutz der Daten vor unberechtigtem Zugriff.

1.2. Interne Ebene

Die tatsächliche physikalische Datenspeicherung auf der
Geräteebene kann durch Anwendung der Speicherstruktur-Sprache
(SSL) stark beeinflußt werden. Zum Beispiel kann durch Auswahl unterschiedlicher Kettungstechniken die physikalische
Datenstruktur optimal an die entsprechende Verarbeitungs-
charakteristik (seriell, gestreut, geringe oder große Daten-
bewegung) angepaßt werden.

Mit den Funktionen dieser Systemkomponente, die über den
Umfang des CODASYL-Vorschlages weit hinausgehen, können sehr
wirklungsvolle Tuning-Maßnahmen bei Laufzeit- und Speicherplatzproblemen ergriffen werden.

1.3. Benutzerkreise - DB-Schnittstellen

Da der Benutzer mit einer UDS-Datenbank über das Subschema
auf rein logischer Ebene verkehrt, hat er sich ausschließlich
mit seiner zentralen Frage zu beschäftigen, was mit welchen
Daten getan werden soll. Wo die Daten stehen, wie sie gespeichert sind usw. ist für den Benutzer der Datenbank nicht
von Interesse.

Als Endbenutzer kristallisieren sich grob 2 Gruppen mit unter-
schiedlichem Anforderungsprofil heraus. Der "interaktive Benutzer" läßt sich charakterisieren als EDV-Unkundiger, der
Sachbearbeiter oder Manager. Er formuliert spontan Anforder-

ungen an die Datenbank, wobei er sich einer höheren, mengen-
orientierten Abfragesprache, der IQL (interactive-query-
language) bedient.

Im Gegensatz dazu steht der "parametrische Benutzer", der
vorgegebene Probleme mittels Parameter definiert, d.h. über
Anwenderprogramme mit der Datenbank zusammenarbeitet.

1.3.1. COBOL-DML

Für die Kommunikation mit der Datenbank steht eine Daten-
manipulations-Sprache (DML) zur Verfügung. Es handelt sich
hierbei um eine Erweiterung des Sprachumfangs von ANS-COBOL
um 13 Befehle für den Datenbankzugriff gemäß der Spezifikation
des "Journal of development 1976". Die Datenbankschnittstelle
wird direkt vom Compiler aufgebaut, eine Vorübersetzung ist
nicht erforderlich.

1.3.2. CALL-DML

Um auch den Anschluß höherer Programmiersprachen an UDS zu
ermöglichen, wurde über den CODASYL-Vorschlag hinausgehend
eine "CALL-DML" implementiert. Der Benutzer verkehrt auf
Unterprogrammbasis mit der Datenbank, wobei erst zur Ablauf-
zeit mittels eines Converter-Bausteins eine Umsetzung dieser
Schnittstelle auf das interne Format erfolgt ("run-time-system").

1.3.4 Kompatible DB-Schnittstelle (KDBS)

Die systemneutrale und kompatible Datenbankschnittstelle
(KDBS) erlaubt es, den Anwendern unterschiedlicher Datenbanksoftware übertragbare Programme zu entwickeln.

Der Funktionsumfang der Schnittstelle, der in Zusammenarbeit
mit großen deutschen Behörden festgelegt wurde, beinhaltet
eine gemeinsame Untermenge der Datenbanksysteme IMS und UDS.
Wegen des gemeinsamen Funktionsvorrates bei UDS und IMS er-

geben sich bei Anwendern dieser Variante funktionelle Einschränkungen für UDS. Das hat zur Folge, daß Anwenderprogramme mit KDBS-Befehlen z.B. Netzstrukturen nicht abarbeiten können.

2. Datenstrukturen

2.1. Grundbausteine

Einer der wesentlichsten Systemaspekte von UDS ist der Aufbau unterschiedlichster Datenstrukturen in Abhängigkeit vom jeweiligen Einsatzfall.

Als Grundelement jeder Struktur dient der "set", eine logische Verbindung zweier unterschiedlicher Satzarten.

Ein "set" wird durch drei Parameter beschrieben, einer übergeordneten Satzart (owner), einer untergeordneten Satzart (member) und der bezeichneten Verbindung (set-name) beider Satzarten. Jeder owner-Satz kann mit beliebig vielen member-Sätzen verkettet sein, wobei diese zyklisch owner-member-Kette als "set-occurrence" bezeichnet wird (Abb.2).

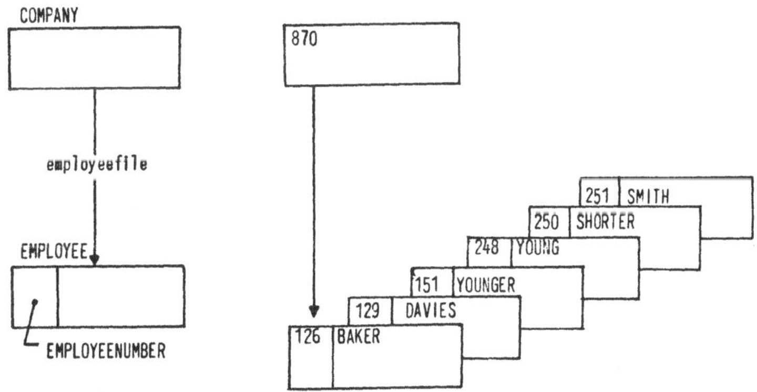

Abb.2: Der set EMPLOYEEFILE mit einer "set-occurrence"

2.2. Strukturierung

Durch Zusammenfügen unterschiedlichster sets lassen sich bausteinartig beliebig komplexe Datenstrukturen aufbauen, angefangen von <u>linearen Strukturen</u> über <u>Baumstrukturen</u> bis zu Netzwerken.

Mit dem "set-Baustein" hat der Anwender von UDS ein sehr leistungsfähiges Werkzeug in der Hand, das ihm ermöglicht, seine meist recht komplexen, hierarchischen Organisationstrukturen mit reringem Aufwand auf die Ebene der EDV abzubilden.

2.3. Stückliste als Beispiel einer Netzstruktur

Als Beispiel für einen Strukturierungsvorgang soll die Stücklistenverwaltung dienen. Diese sicherlich schon recht komplexe Organisationsstruktur wird dabei mittels UDS in zwei Satzarten umgesetzt, den Teilestamm- und den Struktursatz, die durch zwei "set-Beziehungen" logisch miteinander verbunden sind (Abb.3).

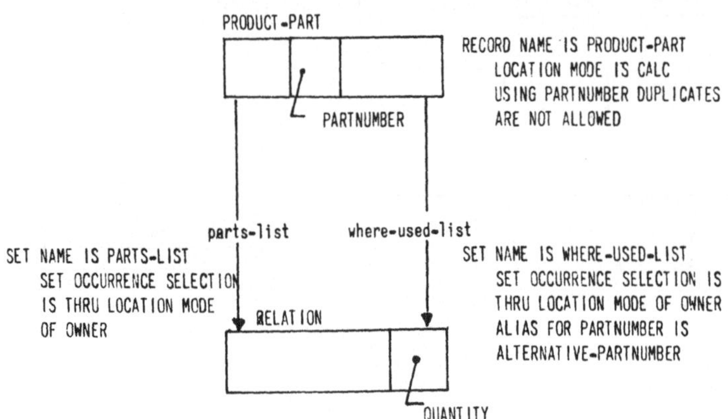

Abb.3: Strukturierung eines Netzwerkes am Beispiel einer

Bei Auflösung eines Teiles wird vom Teilestammsatz ausgehend
über den set "A", den Struktursatz und den Satz "V" die
Struktur abgearbeitet, während bei dem Vernwendungsnachweis
die Abarbeitung mit dem set "V" beginnt. Mit diesem einfachen Strukturprogramm in Form eines Netzwerkes beherrscht
man die Stücklistenproblematik, wobei das gewünschte Resultat
nur mehr durch die Auswahl der Zugriffspfade bestimmt wird
("navigierendes System").

3. Datenorganisation

Die vielfältigen Strukturierungselemente der DDL geben dem
Anwender einer UDS-Datenbank die Möglichkeit, unterschiedlichste
Datenorganisationen verwenden zu können. Aus Gründen des Über-
blicks über die DDL erscheint es zweckmäßig, die Darstellung der
konventionellen Datenorganisationen mit UDS zu betrachten.

3.1. Sequentielle Datenorganisation

Eine **sequentielle Datei** wird durch einen "singulären Set" dargestellt, d.h. durch Angabe von "OWNER IS SYSTEM" wird vom
System ein "virtueller owner-record" eingerichtet, der als
Verbindung zu den "Member-Sätzen" dient Mit der sogenannten
"ORDER-Klausel" werden auf sehr einfache Weise der Sortier-
modus (auf- oder absteigend) und den Sortierbegriff festgelegt, wobei beliebige Felder zu einem Begriff zusammengezogen
werden können.

3.2. Index-sequentielle Datenorganisation

Die Erweiterungen der "ORDER-Klausel" um den Eintrag INDEXED
bewirkt den Aufbau einer "indexsequentiellen Datenorganisation".
Zum Unterschied von einer konventionellen "IS-Datei" können
wahlweise doppelte Schlüsselbegriffe zugelassen werden und
durch Anwendung der "SEARCH-KEY-Klausel" beliebig viele Schlüsselfelder definiert werden.

3.3. Direkte Datenorganisation

Die vom Zugriff her optimale Datenverwaltung bietet sicherlich
die "Random-Organisation". Durch Angabe von"CALC" in der
"LOCATION-MODE-Klausel" der DDL wird bei Speicherung und
Wiedergewinnung eines Satzes der Inhalt des "random-Feldes"
von einer systeminternen Hash-Rountine in einen externen
Speicherplatz umgerechnet. Bei Mehrfachbelegung eines Platzes
wird versucht, den Satz in der gleichen "page" unterzubringen,
der Transporteinheit zwischen Arbeits- und Plattenspeicher.
Ist in der errechneten page kein Platz mehr frei, werden
"overflow-pages" angelegt. Mit einem Dienstprogramm kann der
Zustand einer geladenen Datenbank ausgegeben werden. Auf
Grund dieser Informationen, wie z.B. der mittleren Anzahl von
"overflow-pages" sowie der im Durchschnitt erforderlichen Zugriffe für Speicherung oder Wiedergewinnung eines "random-
Satzes", können entsprechende Tuning-Maßnahmen eingeleitet
werden.

Dabei kann entweder durch Vergrößerung des für die "random-
Sätze" vorgesehenen externen Speicherplatzes oder durch
Implementierung eines anwendereigenen Hash-Algorithmus eine
bessere Verteilung der Sätze und damit ein optimales Zeitverhalten erreicht werden. Im Gegensatz zu einer konventionellen
"DA-Datei" sind wahlweise identische Random-Begriffe zugelassen.

3.4. Integrationsmöglichkeiten

Diese angeführten Datenorganisationen können beliebig gemischt
in einem set oder mehreren sets einer Datenbank verwendet
werden. Das gibt dem Anwender die Möglichkeit, entsprechend
den jeweiligen Erfordernissen für bestimmt Informationen unterschiedliche Zugriffswege zu kombinieren.

Die gewünschte Struktur der DB wird durch Auswahl der entsprechenden Elemente der DDL ausschließlich auf logischer Ebene

festgelegt, die erforderlichen Zugriffsmethoden werden von
UDS automatisch bereitgestellt und sind daher für den UDS-
Anwender nicht von Interesse.

4. Zugriffsmöglichkeiten

Der Zugriff auf Informationen innerhalb der Datenbank erfolgt
immer satzweise, wobei ein Satz ("record") aus beliebig vielen
Feldern ("item") aufgebaut ist. Dabei kann der Zugriff entweder direkt oder in Abhängigkeit von der jeweiligen Struktur
erfolgen ("via set").

4.1. Direkte Zugriffsmöglichkeiten

Durch Angabe eines Kennbegriffes, eines primären, sekundären
oder direkten Schlüssels wird die gewünschte Information unabhängig von der Datenbank-Struktur bereitgestellt. Diese
Vorgangsweise ist immer dann notwendig, wenn entweder der
Aufsatzpunkt einer Verarbeitungsfolge, d.h. der Einstieg in
die DB, festzulegen ist oder schnell ohne Zuhilfenahme der
Verkettungen eine Information gefunden werden soll.

4.1.1. Direkter Zugriff über "calc-key"

Wurde eine Satzart in der DDL als "CALC" definiert, kann nach
Versorgung des "calc-Feldes" mit dem DML-statement FIND-2
direkt zugegriffen werden.

4.1.2. Direkter Zugriff über den "data-base-key"

Jedem Satz wird vom System für seine gesamte Lebensdauer eine
interne Identifikation zugeteilt, der sogenannte "logical-
data-base-key". Wurde für eine Satzart in der DDL "DIRECT"
festgelegt, bekommt der Anwender in einem Feld seiner Wahl
den Datenbank-Schlüssel hinterlegt. Soll auf diesen Satz
später wieder zugegriffen werden, ist das Feld mit dem ent-

sprechenden Schlüssel zu versorgen und ein FIND-1 Statement
abzusetzen.

4.1.3. Direkter Zugriff über den "search-key"

Alle Sätze einer bestimmten Satzart werden zu einem "impliciten
set" zusammengefaßt, ohne daß der Anwender dies explizit in der
DDL erklären muß. In der DDL können für jeden "impliciten set"
beliebig viele Schlüsselbegriffe definiert werden, wobei ein
Begriff aus beliebig vielen Datenfeldern zusammengesetzt sein
kann. Für jeden Schlüsselbegriff wird intern ein Vollindex
aufgebaut, der das Zugriffsverhalten optimiert.

Dieses Funktionselement von UDS bietet die Möglichkeit, die
Datenbank bzw. Teile davon ohne Berücksichtigung von Strukturen
zu bearbeiten und stellt damit als lineare Datenstruktur die
entscheidende Brücke zu relationalen DB-Modellen dar.

Als "universelles DB-System" ermöglicht UDS die Koexistenz
von linearen (relationalen) sowie Baum- und Netzstrukturen in
einem System.

4.1.4. Direkter Zugriff mit komplexer Suchlogik

Alle Sätze eines impliciten sets können nach bestimmten
Kriterien durchsucht werden. Dabei erfolgt die Datenwiedergewinnung mit dem DML-statement FIND-7A derart, daß Sekundär-
merkmale eines Satzes über Boolesche Operatoren beliebig verknüpft werden können. Dieses Statement, das im Kapitel DML
noch eingehender besprochen wird, ist das einzige, das zu
einem Zeitpunkt mehr als einen Satz auswählen kann ("multi-
record-selecting-facility). Die Ergebnissätze werden "member"
in einen "dynamischen set", der in der DDL zu definieren ist
und mit DML-statements weiter bearbeitet werden kann.

4.2. Zugriffsmöglichkeiten in Abhängigkeit von der DB-Struktur

4.2.1. Direkter Zugriff in einer "set-occurrence"

Das DML-statement FIND-7 bietet die Möglichkeit, in einer
vorher ausgewählten "set-occurrence" einen bestimmten member-
Satz aufzusuchen. Als Suchbegriff kann hierbei jedes beliebige
Feld bzw. jede beliebige Feldkombination des Satzes dienen.
Die Festlegung erfolgt als Operand im Statement FIND. Wurde
in der DDL auf "Set-Ebene" ein Sekundärindex festgelegt, erfolgt durch den direkten Suchweg eine Zugriffsbeschleunigung.

4.2.2. Direkter Zugriff in einer "set-occurrence" mit komplexer Suchlogik

Im Gegensatz zu der im Pkt.4.1.4 besprochenen komplexen Suchfrage stellen nicht alle Sätze einer Satzart sondern die
member-Sätze einer bestimmten "set-occurrence" die zu durch-
suchende Satzmenge für das FIND-7A-statement dar. Sonst
funktioniert der Ablauf wie schon vorher besprochen.

4.2.3. Direkter Zugriff mit Hilfe der "currency-Information"

Eine Folge von DML-statements, die von einem OPEN ("READY")
und einem CLOSE ("FINISH") eingerahmt ist, wird als "run-unit"
(RU) bezeichnet. Dabei kann ein Batch-Programm eine "run-unit"
darstellen oder es können in einem on-line-Programm so viel
"run-units" existieren, wie Terminals angeschlossen sind. Der
letzte von einem DML-statement betroffene Satz wird als
"current of run-unit" (CRU) bezeichnet.

Weiters ist der Begriff "area" zu definieren. Eine "area" ist
als logischer Behälter für Sätze aufzufassen, wobei eine Satzart oder mehrere Satzarten in einer "area" enthalten sein oder
die Sätze einer Satzart auf mehrere "areas" verteilt werden
können. Diese Festlegung erfolgt innerhalb der DDL, die Zuordnung der "area" zu den externen Speicherbereichen erfolgt
dynamisch beim Ablauf von DB-Dienstprogrammen bzw. DB- Anwenderprogrammen.

Je "run-unit" existieren für jede "area" ein "current-record-of area" (CRA), für jeden set ein "current-record-of set" (CRS) und für jede Satzart ein "current-record-of record-type" (CRR).

CRA: letzter Satz einer "area", der von einem DML-statement einer bestimmten RU betroffen wurde.

CRS: letzter Satz eines "sets", der von einem DML-statement einer RU betroffen wurde.

CRR: letzter Satz einer Satzart, der von einem DML-statement einer RU betroffen wurde.

Das DML-statement FIND-5 ermöglicht die Wiedergewinnung eines Satzes unter Zuhilfenahme dieser "currency-Informationen". Je nach Operandenangabe im DML-statement wird der CRA einer bestimmten "area" oder der CRS eines bestimmten "sets" oder der CRR einer bestimmten Satzart bereitgestellt und somit CRU.

4.2.4. Direkter Zugriff auf den owner-Satz einer "set-occurrence"

In einer vom Anwender vorher auszuwählenden "set-occurrence" kann mit dem DML-statement FIND-6, ausgehend von den member-Sätzen, auf den zugehörigen owner-Satz zugegriffen werden.

4.2.5. Sequentieller Zugriff unter Vernwendung der "currency-Informationen"

Ausgehend von den "currency-indicators" wird der erste oder letzte oder nächste oder vorherige oder einer absoluten Position entsprechende "member" eines "sets", einer "area" oder einer bestimmten Satzart bereitgestellt.

5. Datenschutz

Den erhöhten Anforderungen an Datenschutz, Datensicherung und
Datensicherheit wird in UDS bereits weitgehend Rechnung ge-
tragen. Die unbeabsichtigte Zerstörung und Veränderung von
Daten wird durch entsprechende DML-Aufrufe (READY bzw.
KEEP: Satzschutz) sowie vom Data-Base-Handler (DBH) durch
Blockschutz und Schutz des CRU verhindert.

Der Schutz der Daten vor unbefugtem Zugriff ist in UDS auf
3 Ebenen realisiert:

- Das Schema-/Subschema-Konzept bewirkt, daß dem Anwender
  nur die Daten zur Verfügung gestellt werden, die Bestandteil des jeweiligen Subschemas sind. Einzelne Anwenderprogramme können somit vom Zugriff sowohl auf ganze
  Bereiche der DB wie auch auf einzelne Felder einer Satzart
  ausgeschlossen werden.

- Der Schutz der Datendefinition im Schema und in den
  einzelnen Subschemata wird durch einen LOCK/KEY-Mechanismus
  gewährleistet.

- Mittels eines Dienstsprogrammes werden im Datenbank-Katalog-
  Datenschutztabellen angelegt, die dem Data-Base-Handler die
  Möglichkeit geben, den Zugriff zur DB über die Benutzeridentifizierung und die Art der Zugriffsberechtigung zu
  kontrollieren.

5.1. Benutzeridentifizierung

Die Benutzeridentifizierung, die im Programm vor dem ersten
DML-statement (READY) dem System zu übergeben ist, besteht aus
der Angabe einer Benutzergruppe, eines Benutzernamens und eines
Paßwortes.

Der DBH überprüft die Angaben mit den entsprechenden Einträgen
der Datenschutztabellen, die zur Laufzeit in den Arbeitsspeicher
geladen werden. Kann bei falscher Angabe ein Benutzer nicht
identifiziert werden, wird das Programm mit einem Fehlercode
zurückgewiesen.

5.2. Zugriffsberechtigung

Mit dem vorher erwähnten Dienstprogramm definiert der Benutzer
zusätzlich, welche Daten mit welchen Funktionen abgefragt bzw.
bearbeitet werden dürfen.

Während des Ablaufes eines Anwenderprogramms wird bei jedem
DML-Aufruf überprüft, ob der jeweilige Aufruf mit den für die
Benutzergruppe spezifizierten Rechten vereinbar ist oder nicht.
Wenn dies nicht der Fall ist, bekommt der Anwender einen ent-
sprechenden Fehlercode mit der Auswirkung, daß der Aufruf von
UDS nicht durchgeführt wurde.

Zusätzlich zu der Möglichkeit, Zugriffsrechte auf Typebene
zu definieren, kann der Anwender Zugriffsrechte auf Programm-
ebene vergeben. In diesem Fall laufen die als "erlaubt" ge-
kennzeichneten Programme nach der Benutzeridentifizierung ohne
anweisungsgebundene Überprüfung der Zugriffsrechte ab.

Bezogen auf die einzelnen Daten-Ebenen sind folgende Zugriffsrechte von Bedeutung und unterliegen somit der Kontrolle des
Data-Base-Handlers:

Zugriffsrechte auf Area-Ebene:

   Festlegung des zugelassenen Zugriffsmodus je "area" beim
   Statement READY (volle - eingeschränkte - ausschließliche
   Wiedergewinnungs- bzw. Änderungsberechtigung).

Zugriffsrechte auf Set-Ebene:

   Festlegung der Einkettung (INSERT) eines Satzes je "set" bzw.
   der Auskettung (REMOVE) je "set".

Zugriffsrechte auf Satzart-Ebene:

Festlegung der Aufnahme, Modifikation, Löschung sowie
Wiedergewinnung (bis auf Feldebene) einer bestimmten
Satzart. Die Zugriffsrechte können für jede dieser
4 Funktionen einzeln oder für beliebige Kombinationen
vergeben werden. Es kann also für den Benutzer "X" einer
Benutzergruppe "Y" die Aufnahme, Änderung und Löschung
einer Satzart "Z" verboten, das Lesen hingegen erlaubt
sein.

6. Speicherstruktursprache - SSL

Im "DBTG-report" wurde auf die Notwendigkeit einer Sprache
zur Speicherstrukturierung hingewiesen. Normvorschläge wurden
jedoch nicht erarbeitet. Die in UDS enthaltene Speicherstruktur-
Sprache bietet erhebliche Vorteile bei der Lösung von Laufzeit-
und Speicherplatzproblemen. Mit dem wahlweisen Einsatz der
SSL kann die physikalische Abbildung der DB-Struktur auf der
internen Geräteebene unabhängig von der logischen Schema-Beschreibung beeinflußt werden.

6.1. Verkettungsmöglichkeiten

Eine Komponente der SSL bietet dem Anwender die Möglichkeit,
unter mehreren Verkettungstechniken zu wählen. Dadurch wird
die physikalische Darstellung eines sets an seine Verarbeitungs-
charakteristik optimal angepaßt.

6.1.1. Kettung-"chain"

Wird in der SSL für einen bestimmten set die Verkettungsart
"CHAIN" angegeben, werden alle Sätze einer "set-occurrence"
durch Verweisadressen ("pointer") in der logischen Reihenfolge miteinander verknüpft. Die Verweisadressen bestehen aus
den "data-base-keys" der entsprechenden Sätze. Es ist möglich,
Verweisadressen auf den logisch nächsten Satz und den logisch

vorherigen Satz zu definieren. Diese Kettungstechnik ist dann
zu wählen, wenn ein set vorwiegend seriell bearbeitet wird
(Abb. 4).

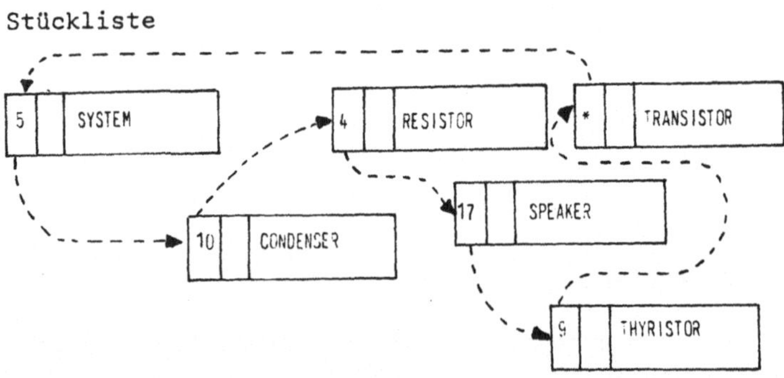

Abb.4: Implementierung der Kettungstechnik "chain"

6.1.2. Kettung-"pointer-array" (Adreßtabelle)

Bei dieser Speicherungsart wird für jede "set-occurrence" eine
Indextabelle aufgebaut. In dieser Tabelle stehen die Schlüsselfelder der member-Sätze in der logischen Reihenfolge, die in
der DDL angegeben wurde, zusammen mit der jeweiligen physikalischen Adresse in der Datenbank.

Ist die Abarbeitung in einem set vorwiegend gestreut, wird
diese Art der Speicherung die besten Ergebnisse bringen (Abb.6).

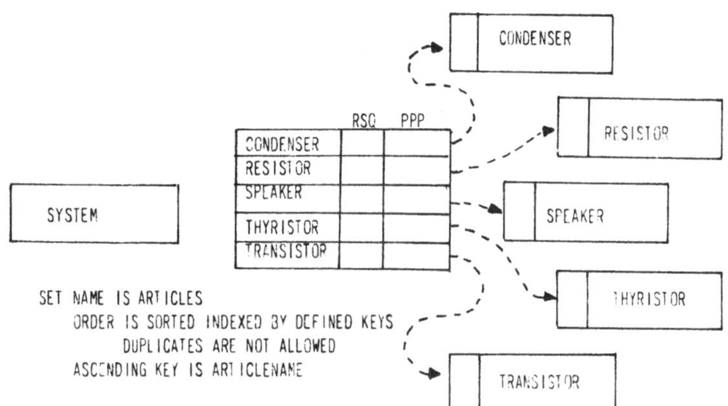

Abb.6: Implementierung der Kettungstechnik "pointer-array"

6.1.3. Kettung-"list"

Bei der Listenmethode entspricht die physikalische Reiehnfolge
der member-Sätze ihrer logischen Reihenfolge. Eine "set-
occurrence" entspricht somit einer sequentiellen Datei.

Diese Listenmethode ist dann einzusetzen, wenn ein set über-
wiegend seriell abgearbeitet wird und wenig Neuaufnahmen bzw.
Löschungen auftreten (Abb.5).

Die drei erläuterten Möglichkeiten der Verkettung können grundsätzlich für jeden einzelnen set gesondert angegeben werden,
ohne dadurch die Speicherung anderer sets zu beeinflussen.

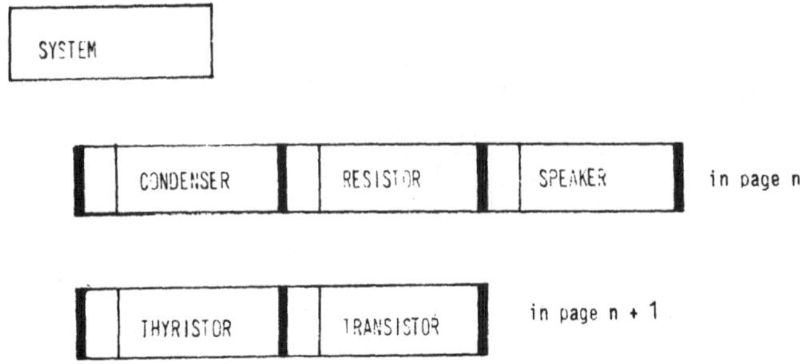

Abb 5: Implementierung der Kettungstechnik "list"

6.2. Möglichkeiten der Platzoptimierung

Der Datenbankverwalter kann durch einen Eintrag in der SSL die
Speicherung einer Adreßtabelle oder Liste so steuern, daß der
Index bzw. die Liste der member-Sätze in der physikalischen
Nähe des owner-Satzes gespeichert wird. Die Zugriffsgeschwindig-
keit vom owner zu den zugehörigen member-Sätzen kann damit
wesentlich erhöht werden.

Eine andere Anweisung der SSL gibt die voraussichtliche durchschnittliche Zahl von member-Sätzen je "set-occurrence" an.
Dadurch wird auf dem Datenträger ausreichend Platz reserviert,
um die zusammengehörigen member-Sätze physikalisch in enger
Nachbarschaft zueinander abspeichern zu können. Der Zugriff
auf alle member-Sätze einer "set-occurrence" wird dadurch
wesentlich beschleunigt.

Über diese Grundanweisungen hinaus enthält die SSL eine Reihe
von Komponenten, die es dem Benutzer ermöglichen, die Speicherstruktur der Datenbank an seine spezifischen Bedürfnisse anzupassen. Es würde über den Rahmen dieses Vortrages hinausgehen,
alle diese Möglichkeiten im Detail zu behandeln.

7. Kommunikation mit der Datenbank

Das UDS-Benutzerprogramm kann seine Datenbankaufträge über drei
verschiedene Benutzerschnittstellen formulieren:

- COBOL-DML
- CALL-DML
- KDBS

In diesen Sprachen sind Funktionen, wie Eröffnen und Schließen
der Datenbank, Änderung und Wiedergewinnung der Daten sowie
Schutz der Daten gegen Beeinflussung durch gleichzeitig ab-
laufende Programme enthalten. Die Unabhängigkeit der Programme
von den gespeicherten Daten sowie die Möglichkeit des ständigen
Wachstums der Datenbasis werden in hohem Maße dadurch erreicht,
daß sich die DML nicht auf die physikalische, sondern auf die
logische Struktur der Daten bezieht.

7.1. COBOL-DML

Die COBOL-DML besteht aus Befehlen für die Bearbeitung der
Datenbank, die in die Gastgebersprache ANSCOBOL eingebettet
sind. Da die COBOL-DML die Normierungsvorschläge des "Journal
of development 1976" voll berücksichtigt, sollen die einzelnen
Sprachelemente überblickartig betrachtet werden.

7.1.1. Befehle für die Steuerung der Datenbank

Die Datenbank wird mit READY eröffnet und mit FINISH abgeschlossen. Durch die Angabe des Zugriffsmodus im READY-state-
ment erfolgt der Schutz auf Bereichsebene, d.h. die Festlegung,
ob gleichzeitig andere Benutzer in den angesprochenen "areas"
lesen oder ändern dürfen.

7.1.2. Befehle für Wiedergewinnung

Zum Auffinden von Datensätzen in der Datenbank dient die FIND-
Anweisung, die innerhalb der DML eine fundamentale Bedeutung
besitzt.

Es existieren 7 unterschiedliche FIND-Formate:

- direktes Auffinden eines Satzes über den "data-base-key"
  bzw. den "calc-key",

- serielle Abarbeitung einer "set-occurrence",

- Auffinden des einem member zugehörigen owner-Satzes,

- Auffinden eines Satzes über die "currency-indicators"
  und

- direkte Positionierung eines member-Satzes innerhalb
  einer "set-occurrence".

Diese letzte Anweisung wurde über den CODASYL-Vorschlag hinausgehend um die Möglichkeiten der komplexen Suchlogik erweitert
(FIND-7A). Dabei werden aus einer "set-occurrence" jene member-
Sätze gesucht, welche die vom Benutzer festgelegten Suchkriterien erfüllen. Sie werden durch die Angabe von logisch
verknüpften Feldern definiert, denen konkrete Vergleichsbedingungen zuzuordnen sind.

Die Ergebnissätze werden in Form ihrer "data-base-keys" member
in einem set, der "result-set" bezeichnet wird und in der abgespe
RESULT-Option angegeben wird,

Durch Angabe eines sets in der LIMITED-Option wird das Suchkriterium auf jene Sätze eingeschränkt, die member in diesem
set sind. Wiederholte Anwendung dieses statements auf die jeweils zuvor ermittelte Ergebnismenge mit zunehmender Ver-
schärfung des Suchkriteriums ermöglicht eine schrittweise
Suche nach gewünschten Informationen (Browsing).

Weiters kann dem Benutzer die Anzahl der Sätze übergeben werden,
welche die Suchbedingung erfüllen.

Das Format der Suchbedingung entspricht den Regeln eines zusammengesetzten Ausdruckes in ANSCOBOL. Die Felder eines Satzes können mit den Vergleichsoperatoren "gleich", "größer" und "kleiner" behandelt werden. Diese Ausdrücke können über die Boolsche Logik mittels AND, OR und NOT miteinander verknüpft werden.

Zusätzlich kann durch Angabe einer Maske in der Suchbedingung definiert werden, welche Stellen eines Feldes bezüglich der Erfüllung des Suchkriteriums getestet werden sollen.

Die Anweisung GET liefert dem Benutzer einen gewünschten Satz aus der Datenbank zur weitern Bearbeitung ab. Das Statement FETCH beinhaltet sowohl die Funktion Positionierung als auch die Funktion Bereitstellung eines bestimmten Satzes.

7.1.3. Befehle für die Änderung der Datenbank

Mit STORE wird ein Satz physisch in die DB aufgenommen und, falls in der DDL gefordert, in die entsprechenden sets logisch eingekettet.

Dieser Vorgang der Einkettung kann auch getrennt mit CONNECT ausgelöst und mit DISCONNECT rückgängig gemacht werden.

Ein Satz wird mit ERASE physisch aus der DB gelöscht, wobei wahlweise auch die Löschung sämtlicher mitverketteter member-Sätze veranlaßt werden kann.

Änderungen werden satz- oder feldweise mit der Anweisung MODIFY durchgeführt.

7.1.4. Befehle für den Satzschutz

Es kann vorkommen, daß sich Programme beim gleichzeitigen Zugriff auf die DB gegenseitig beeinflussen bzw. stören, was zu

falschen Ergebnissen und Folgefehlern in der DB führen kann.
Mit dem Satement KEEP kann eine "run-unit" den CRU gegen
den Zugriff anderer Benutzer sperren und diesen mit FREE
wieder freigeben. Bei dead-look-Situationen enthält die
verursachende run-unit einen Fehlercode und kann mit FINISH
die Änderungen in der Datenbank bis auf den Startpunkt zu-
rücksetzen. Für die andere RU wird dadurch die Sperre aufgehoben.

7.2. CALL-DML

Für Assembler, COBOL und FORTRAN, die der Anwender von UDS
als "host-language" benutzt, wird auf Unterprogrammbasis
der volle Funktionsumfang der vorher beschriebenen Schnittstelle angeboten.

Über einen Interpreter-Baustein werden die gewünschten DB-
Funktionen zum Ablaufzeitpunkt interpretiert und ausgeführt.

7.3. KDBS

Zur Unterstützung einer systemneutralen Anwendungsprogrammierung
können die Zugriffsfunktionen zu Datenbanken über die kompatible
Datenbankschnittstelle abgewickelt werden. Das Konzept dieser
Schnittstelle wurde von mehreren großen deutschen Behörden in
Zusammenarbeit mit EDV-Herstellern, darunter auch die Firma
Siemens, erstellt.

Bei der Festlegung des Funktionsumfanges dieser Schnittstelle
wurde davon ausgegangen, sowohl die wichtigsten Elemente des
CODASYL-Vorschlages miteinzubeziehen als auch eine weitgehende
Verträglichkeit mit IMS anzustreben.

Bei Verwendung dieser Schnittstelle ergibt sich eine vierschich-
tige Struktur, bestehend aus dem Anwenderprogramm mit der systemneutralen DB-Schnittstelle und den 3 herstellerspezifischen
Komponenten KDBS, DB-System und Betriebssystem. Der Schnitt-

stellen-Umsetzer transformiert die invariante Anwenderschnitt-
stelle auf das interne Format des jeweils verwendeten Daten-
bank-Systems.

KDBS ist so konzipiert, daß die Bearbeitung von linearen Datenstrukturen eine echte Untermenge der Anweisungen für die Bearbeitung von komplexen Datenstrukturen (außer Netzstrukturen)
darstellt.

Die Schnittstelle teilt sich in 3 Funktionsgruppen, u.zw.

- Organisationsanweisungen
- Anweisungen zur Datenwiedergewinnung
- Anweisungen zur Direktänderung

8. Datensicherung

Tritt während des Ablaufs eines Anwenderprogramms, das den Inhalt
einer oder mehrerer "areas" verändert, ein Hardware- oder Soft-
warefehler auf, ist der Zustand der Datenbank nicht mehr gesichert. Bevor das Programm weiterlaufen kann, müssen Rekonstruktionsprogramme ausgeführt werden. Diese Programme setzen die
Datenbank auf einen definierten Stand zurück. Erst dann kann ein
Wiederanlauf durchgeführt werden. Die Rekonstruktionsprogramme
müssen sicherstellen, daß die Datenbank unter minimalen Zeit-
verlust wieder auf einen definierten Stand gesetzt werden kann.

UDS bietet 2 unterschiedliche Rekonstruktionsmöglichkeiten an:

die "Back-up-Methode" und die "Back-out-Methoden".

Der Wiederholungsprozeß kann als Ablauf zweier getrennter
Phasen gesehen werden. Die erste Phase besteht aus dem Zu-
sammentragen der Information, die zur Wiedereinrichtung der
Datenbank und zur Neusynchronisierung der auf sie zugreifenden
Benutzerprogramme erforderlich ist. Die zweite Phase besteht aus
der Verwendung dieser Information, um eine Wiederherstellung von

einer tatsächlichen Zusammenbruchsituation aus zu bewirken.
Die erste Phase wird als eine stetige und oftmals wiederholte
Reihe von Operationen ausgeführt, die eine sorgfältige Über-
wachung verlangt.

8.1. Informationen für den Wiederanlauf

Im Rahmen der vorher mit "Phase 1" bezeichneten Tätigkeit können
für einen eventuellen Zusammenbruch folgende Informationen bereitgestellt werden:

- Kopien der Datenbankbereiche
- Protokolle veränderter Bereiche (before- and after-images)
- Wiederanlaufpunkte der Anwenderprogramme

Mittels eines Dienstprogrammes (BCOPY) können die Datenbank-
Bereiche in vom Anwender frei wählbaren Zeitabschnitten auf
Platte oder Band abgezogen werden. Die Bereitstellung von
Kopien der Datenbank bildet den grundlegenden Bestandteil der
Datensicherheit. Was auch immer an Fehlern passieren kann, der
Benutzer hat stets ein Duplikat seiner Datenbank zur Verfügung,
das als Ausgangspunkt und Grundlage zur Wiederherstellung des
Originals verwendet werden kann.

Die Protokollierungsmöglichkeit von UDS, als ein Bestandteil
des Wiederherstellungsprozesses, erlaubt dem Benutzer, eine
Auswahl zu treffen aus dem Protokollieren der geänderten Blöcke
vor (before images), nach (after images) oder vor und nach
diesen Änderungen. Die gesamte protokollierte Information
wird auf Band oder Platte abgelegt. Bei einem Wiederanlauf
können entweder die in der Datenbank vorgenommenen Änderungen
mit den "before images" rückgängig gemacht werden ("Back-out-
Methode") oder die Kopie der Datenbank wird mittels der
"after images" aktualisiert ("Back-up-Methode").

Wenn Stapelprogramme Datenbank-Bereiche verändern, besteht für
den Benutzer die Möglichkeit, Wiederanlaufpunkte zu schreiben.

Dies ist jedoch nur dann möglich, wenn die zentrale Zugriffs-
komponente von UDS, der DBH, nicht als eigenes Programm
existiert ("independent version"), sondern direkt an das
Anwenderprogramm gebunden wird ("linked version").

Dadurch ist es ausgeschlossen, daß ein Datenbank-Bereich von
mehreren Programmen gleichzeitig verändert wird, so daß beim
Wiederanlauf keine Probleme bezüglich der Synchronisation der
Programme existieren.

Da die Synchronisierung zwischen Programm- und Datenbank-Wieder-
anlaufpunkt Voraussetzung für den Wiederherstellungsprozeß ist,
muß der Anwender sicherstellen, daß der Schreibbefehl für den
Datenbank-Checkpoint so nahe wie möglich beim Schreibbefehl für
den Wiederanlaufpunkt des Benutzerprogramms positioniert ist.

8.2. Wiederherstellungsalternativen bei On-line-Betrieb

Tritt während eines Laufs von UDS ein schwerwiegender Fehler auf,
der die Datenbank-Bereiche in einen inkonsistenten Zustand ver-
setzt, können die Bereiche wieder in einen konsistenten Zustand
rücküberführt werden, indem alle Transaktionen ("run-units"),
die zum Zeitpunkt des Zusammenbruchs nicht beendet waren,
auf ihren jeweiligen Anfang zurückgesetzt werden. Diese Funktion
des DBH wird automatisch durchgeführt, wenn ein entsprechender
Parameter angegeben wird. Da die Transaktionen zu unterschiedlichen
Zeiten in der Datenbank Veränderungen bewirken, geben die Bereiche der Datenbank nach einem Wiederanlauf nicht den Stand zu
einem bestimmten Augenblick wieder. Dieser Zustand wird als
"Konsistenzpunkt" bezeichnet.

Der automatische Roll-Back-Mechanismus benützt die "before-
images" der Blöcke, die von den nicht beendeten Transkationen
verändert wurden.

294

Zu Beginn und Ende eines DBH-Laufs und nach einem Warmstart
wird ein Konsistenzpunkt in den Protokollbereich geschrieben.
Datum und Uhrzeit dieses Punktes werden dem Benutzer mitgeteilt, der diese Angaben als Referenzpunkte für weitere
Dienstprogramme verwenden kann.

Bei Zerstörung von Datenbereichen kann, ausgehend von einer
aktuellen Kopie der Datenbank, mit dem Dienstprogramm BMEND
unter Zuhilfenahme der "after-images" auf jeden beliebigen
Konsistenzpunkt vorgesetzt werden. Prinzipiell ist es auch
möglich, nach einem System-Zusammenbruch die Datenbank mit
dem Dienstprogramm BBCKOUT mittels der "before images" auf
einen Konsistenzpunkt zurückzusetzen und danach einen Kalt-
start von UDS zu veranlassen.

8.3. Wiederherstellung bei Batch-Betrieb

Batch-Programme, bei denen der DBH ein integrierter Bestandteil ist ("linked-version"), können Datenbank-Checkpoints
schreiben. Nach einem Zusammenbruch wird die Datenbank mit
den bereits erwähnten Dienstprogrammen auf einen wählbaren
Checkpoint entweder mit den "before images" rückgesetzt oder
mit den "after images" vorgesetzt. Danach kann das Programm
auf den entsprechenden Programm-Wiederanlaufpunkt aufgesetzt
und gestartet werden.

9. Verwaltung und Reorginaisation einer UDS-Datenbank

UDS beinhaltet für den Aufbau und die Wartung einer Datenbank
eine Reihe von Dienstprogrammen, die sich grob in folgende
Funktionsgruppen unterteilen lassen:

- Datenbankaufbau
- Diagnoseunterlagen
- Reorganisation
- Rekonstruktion

Auf die erste Gruppe wird im nächsten Abschnitt bei der Skizzie-
rung eines Arbeitsablaufes eingegangen.

Die zweite Gruppe beinhaltet utilities zur Ausgabe bestimmter Datenbank-Informationen, entweder zu Diagnosezwecken im Fehlerfall oder zur Einleitung von Tuning-Maßnahmen, die von Veränderungen der Struktur bis zur Reorganisation der Datenbank-Bereiche reichen können.

Überblick über ein bestimmtes Subschema, Ausdruck eines bestimmten Benutzerbereiches oder eines Datenbank-Blockes sowie die Bereitstellung unterschiedlichster Statistiken sind nur einige der Möglichkeiten.

Die tägliche Arbeit mit der Datenbank kann zu starken Veränderungen des Datenbestandes führen. UDS besitzt eine dynamische Verwaltung des externen Speicherplatzes. Nach Löschen eines Satzes aus der Datenbank kann der freigewordene Platz jederzeit wieder von einem anderen, neuaufgenommenen Satz belegt werden. Dieser Mechanismus vermeidet eine allzu häufige Rekonstruktion der Datenbank.

Es können jedoch Situationen auftreten, in denen sich die beim Aufbau der Datenbank geschätzte Anzahl der Sätze als zu klein oder zu groß erweist. Daher besteht die Möglichkeit, die voraussichtliche Satzanzahl pro Satztyp zu erhöhen oder zu verringern und damit die Benutzerbereiche zu vergrößern oder zu verkleinern.

Weiters kann die Reorganisation von "calc-Sätzen" veranlaßt werden, um die Speicherung dieser Sätze in Überlaufbereichen zu minimieren. Entsprechend der Benutzerangabe wird für die "calc-Sätze" eine bestimmte Anzahl neuer "pages" reserviert und die Sätze werden in diesen Bereich transferiert. Die zuvor belegten Primär- und Überlaufbereiche werden für andere Zwecke freigegeben. Ob eine Reorganisation von "calc-Sätzen" notwendig ist, kann anhand der Statistikausgabe eines Dienstprogrammes festgestellt werden.

Eine weitere Funktion besteht im Updating und Reorganisieren
der Verbindung innerhalb eines sets. Die zu reorganisierende
Information kann bestehen aus "search-key" - bzw. "ascending/
descending-key"-Tabellen, die physikalisch in Form von
"pointer-arrays" oder "lists" aufgebaut sind. Wenn member-
Sätze aus einer "set-occurrence" gelöscht werden, können
die Tabellen beträchtlich mehr Platz als tatsächlich notwendig
belegen. Spezifiziert der Benutzer eine Belegungsrate, werden
die Tabellen entsprechend der Anzahl der existierenden member-
Sätze neu aufgebaut und der reservierte Speicherplatz wird
zum festgelegten Prozentsatz gefüllt. Zusätzlich enthält UDS
eine dynamische, während der Verarbeitung permanent tätige
Tabellenreorganisation.

Ein genaueres Eingehen auf die Problematik würde eine intensive
Erläuterung der physikalischen Speicherstruktur von UDS erfordern und damit den Rahmen dieses Vortrages sprengen.

1o. Skizzierung eines Arbeitsablaufes

Die Prozeduren für den Einsatz von UDS gliedern sich in zwei
Stufen:
- Generierung der Datenbank
- Generierung der Anwenderprogramme

1o.1. Generierung der Datenbank

Diese Stufe setzt sich aus den Arbeitsgängen zum Aufbau eines
Schemas und den notwendigen Abläufen zur Übersetzung einer Sub-
Schema-Beschreibung zusammen.

1o.1.1. Schema-Generierung

Das Schema wird sich als logisches Resultat von Entwurfstudien
des Benutzers ergeben mit der Beschreibung der Bereiche, Sätze
und sets seiner Datenbank. Die gesamte Beschreibung der Datenbank ist selbst wieder in einer Datenbank, der COMPILER-DB,
abgelegt, die aus 2 Bereichen DBDIR und DBCOM besteht.

Nach Reservierung der erforderlichen Plattenbereiche muß die
COMPILER-DB eingerichtet und formatiert werden. Anschließend
erfolgt die Übersetzung des Schemas (DDL-Compiler) und wahlweise der Speicherstruktur (SSL-Compiler).

Danach erfolgen der Aufbau und die Formatierung der Benutzer-
Datenbank-Bereiche sowie der Eintrag der Datenschutz-Angaben
in den Datenbank-Katalog.

1o.1.2. Sub-Schema-Generierung

Dieser Vorgang besteht aus der Übersetzung der Sub-Schema-
Beschreibung des Benutzers und ihrer Abspeicherung in der
Compiler-Datenbank.

1o.2. Generierung der Anwenderprogramme

Ist die Generierung der Datenbank abgeschlossen, können die
Programme, die mit der Datenbank zusammen arbeiten, übersetzt
werden. Dabei ist sicherzustellen, daß die Compiler-Datenbank
des im Programm angesprochenen Subschemas bereitgestellt wird.

Wird die "linked-in"-Variante von UDS verwendet, muß anschließend
das Programm mit der zentralen Systemkomponente, dem DBH, zu
sammengebunden werden. Danach ist das Programm ablaufbereit.

Wird die "independent"-Variante von UDS verwendet, ist der DBH
ein eigenständiges Programm und übernimmt die zentrale Daten-
behandlung für alle Progrmme, die mit der Datenbank arbeiten.
Durch diese zentrale Stellung des DBH wird die Integrität der
Datenbank bei gleichzeitiger Bearbeitung durch mehrere Programme
sichergestellt. Nach dem Bindevorgang des Anwenderprogrammes ist
vor dem Beginn des Ablaufes der DBH zu laden, wobei sämtliche
Betriebsmittel, die von den Logging-Funktionen benötigt werden,
bereitzustellen sind.

11. Zukünftige Datenbank-Strategie

Als CODASYL-System hat sich UDS bisher bei über 2o Einsatzfällen
im In- und Ausland sehr gut bewährt. Mit UDS bietet Siemens
über den CODASYL-Ansatz hinausgehend ein System, das mit seinem
erweiterten Funktionsumfang auf langjährige Erfahrung mit den
Systemen SESAM und PRISMA aufgesetzt. Die Firma Siemens wird
auch in Zukunft die Entwicklung von UDS verstärkt in jene
Richtung vorantreiben, die es dem Anwender jeder Größenordnung
ermöglicht, alle denkbaren Problemlösungen bei der Verwaltung
formatierter Daten mit <u>einem</u> System abzudecken.

Rückblick auf 5 Jahre Erfahrung mit dem
Datenbanksystem ADABAS

Dipl.-Ing. Hans Mittheisz
Gemeinde Wien

. Kurzfassung

Es werden die für die Entscheidung der Stadt Wien maßgeb-
lichen Anforderungen an ein Datenbanksystem erläutert.
Diese Anforderungen erfüllte das DB-System ADABAS (<u>A</u>dap-
tierbares <u>D</u>aten <u>B</u>ank <u>S</u>ystem) am besten.Das Konzept und die
Anwendung dieses Systems im Bereich der Stadt Wien bei Verarbeitung von Massendaten mit Identifizierungs- und Zugriffs-
problemen werden dargestellt.

. Anforderungen an ein Datenbanksystem:

Die Notwendigkeit Datenbanksysteme einzusetzen ergab sich
wie in anderen Organisationen so auch im Bereich der Stadt
Wien durch die Leistungssteigerung der EDV-Anlagen, die sich
vor allem in der Organisation neuer Anwendungen auswirkte.
Die auf EDV übernommenen Gebiete wurden immer umfangreicher
und komplexer und die konventionellen Datenorganisationen
erwiesen sich in zunehmendem Maße als Restriktion.

Die Schwerpunkte bei der Auswahl, die 1970/71 durchgeführt
wurde, waren Anforderungen auf dem Gebiet Speicherung und
Zugriff; die angeführten Forderungen sind nicht nach ihrer
Wichtigkeit gereiht:

- DBMS muß Datenkomprimierungsroutine zur Reduzierung des
  externen Speicherplatzes enthalten. Diese Funktion ist
  sehr wichtig durch die Größe der im On-line-Betrieb zu
  führenden Datenbestände, sie soll wahlweise durchzuführen
  sein und darf bei der Verarbeitung keine Performanceschwie-
  rigkeiten bringen.

- Keine Reorganisations- und Umordnungsläufe für bestehende
  Datenbestände nach intensiven Updates, es ist eine sehr
  gute Speicherbelegungstechnik des Datenbanksystems notwendig, um die Massendatenverarbeitung (Personenwesen mit etwa
  1,9 Mio. Personensätzen) bewältigen zu können.

- Zugriff auf Einzelinformation bzw. feldweise Verarbeitung
  soll möglich sein (mit Subschema = Definition des Teilaus-
  zugs aus der Datenbank für ein einzelnes Anwendungsproblem).

- Bei einem Suchvorgang müssen mehrere Suchbegriffe zu einem
  Suchkriterium logisch verknüpfbar sein - mit den Operatoren
  und ($\wedge$), oder (v), nicht ($\neg$). Phonetisierungsmodul muß vorhanden sein, um auch phonetisiert suchen zu können.

- Die Anzahl der durch ein Suchkriterium logisch definierten
  Sätze muß als Information vom Datenbanksystem geliefert
  werden können.

- Strukturerweiterungen bzw. -änderungen müssen leicht möglich sein, etwa das Hinzufügen neuer Datenfelder zu bestehenden Sätzen.

- Die Verknüpfung von Dateien muß möglich sein, da im On-line
  auf Daten mehrerer Dateien nach unterschiedlichsten Gesichts
  punkten zugegriffen werden muß.

- Physisch serielles und logisch serielles (nach einem gewissen Deskriptor) Verarbeiten eines Bestandes muß mit ge-
  ringem Overhead gegenüber serieller Bandverarbeitung möglich
  sein.

- TP-Betrieb muß möglich sein
  Das DB-System muß
  . einen Multi-User-Betrieb ermöglichen
  . Verträglichkeit mit eingesetztem TP-Monitor ergeben
  . Veränderung derselben Datei durch mehrere Programme ermöglichen
  (Zugriffsschutz zur Sicherung eines laufenden UPDATE-Vor-
  ganges auf den einzelnen Satz - Problematik des konkur-
  rierenden Datenbankzugriffs).

. korrekten Abschluß der Datenbank bei Programmabbrüchen
  bzw. Abbruch einer On-line-Update-Transaktion garantieren
  (absturzsichere Speicherung !)
- Dienstprogramme müssen vorhanden sein:
  . Laden Datei
  . Löschen Datei
  . Sichern Datei / Datenbank
  . Restore von Dateien / Datenbank
  . Logbandmöglichkeit für Regenerate bzw. Backout von
    Dateien bzw. der Datenbank
- IBM-Verträglichkeit
  Es gibt kein 'bestes' Datenbanksystem, sondern von den ver-
  schiedenen Anforderungen hängt die Auswahl eines diesen An-
  sprüchen am besten entsprechenden Datenbanksystems ab. Im
  Falle der Stadt Wien wurden die gestellten Anforderungen
  durch das Datenbanksystem ADABAS am besten erfüllt und
  dieses System nach Benchmarks ausgewählt.

3. Das Datenbanksystem ADABAS

Um die später angeführten Problemlösungen verständlicher zu
machen, ist ein kurzer Überblick über das DB-System ADABAS
notwendig.

ADABAS liefert heute seinem Benutzer eine komplette Datenverwaltung, die unter anderem folgende Vorteile besitzt:

- eine Daten-Definitionssprache, mit der sich beliebige Datenstrukturen und Datenverknüpfungen herstellen lassen

- die Technik der invertierten Listen, deren Anwendung eine
  wirksame Methode zum schnellen Wiederauffinden von Daten
  und zur Beantwortung von Fragen an die Datenbank innerhalb
  von Millisekunden darstellen

- umfassende Möglichkeiten der Datenmanipulation, wobei dem
  Benutzer eine Vielzahl verschiedener Zugriffsstrategien
  zum Wiederauffinden und Modifizieren von Daten zur Verfü-

gung stehen, aus denen er je nach Art der Anwendung die effizientesten auswählen kann,

- eine komplette Serie von Datenbank-Dienstprogrammen, die es dem Benutzer ermöglichen, die Datenbank mit minimalem Aufwand aufzubauen, zu pflegen und zu überwachen.

Zusätzlich zu den bereits genannten Datenverwaltungsfunktionen bietet ADABAS

- ADASCRIPT (eine Dialogsprache)

- Mehrfach-Benutzer-Unterstützung, wobei ein einmalig geladenes ADABAS gleichzeitig On-line- und Batch-Verarbeitungen mehrerer Benutzer zuläßt

- komplette Datensicherung; die physische und logische Integrität der Datenbank ist im Falle von Hardwareausfällen oder Programmfehlern absolut gesichert

- Datenschutz, der unerlaubten Zugriff auf die Datenbank und/oder unerlaubte Änderung durch einzelne Benutzer in der Datenbank verhindert.

Das Datenbankverwaltungssystem ist sehr flexibel:

- es ermöglicht, eine Vielzahl verschiedener Datentypen und Datenstrukturen innerhalb der Datenbank zu definieren

- mit ADABAS können Daten sowohl auf Feldebene als auch auf Satzebene aufgefunden und angesprochen werden.

- ADABAS kann neue Felder in bereits existierende Dateien einfügen, Nichtdeskriptoren in Deskriptorfelder umwandeln, komp-lexe logische Kopplungen zwischen Dateien dynamisch aufbauen oder auflösen, alle Speicherbereiche der Datenbank dynamisch erweitern – ohne jegliche Reorganisation oder Neuladen der Datenbank.

Diese Flexibilität erlaubt dem Benutzer, eine aufgebaute Datenbank mit minimalem Aufwand und problemlos anzupassen und/ oder zu erweitern, um so den Anforderungen der Datenbankanwendungen wirkungsvoll gerecht zu werden.

ADABAS nützt optimal die Möglichkeiten der EDV-Anlage aus

– Datenkompression

– Adressierungs- und Speichertechniken, die keine Kettungen
  enthalten, frei werdende Speicherbereiche sind sofort
  wieder für die Einspeicherung neuer Daten verfügbar;
  periodische Reorganisationen sind nicht erforderlich.

– dynamische Pufferverwaltungstechnik minimiert durch
  Verwaltung und Wiederbenutzung von kernspeicherresi-
  denter Information die Zugriffe auf die Externspeicher.

<u>ADABAS Datenbank – Struktur und Datenverwaltung:</u>

Eine ADABAS Datenbank ist physikalisch und logisch in zwei
Bereiche unterteilt, und zwar in

DATENSPEICHER

und

ASSOZIATOR

Diese Trennung wurde vollzogen, um die Kontrollinformationen (invertierte Listen) konsequent von den Datensätzen zu
trennen. Zum Suchen in der Datenbank wird lediglich gezielt
auf Ausschnitte der invertierten Listen zugegriffen und
nicht der Datenbestand durchsucht. Der zu einer Datenbank
gehörende Arbeitsbereich beinhaltet nur temporäre Daten,
die für die Verarbeitung von ADABAS-Befehlen benötigt werden (AUTORESTART-Routine, Datensicherungsbereich, ISN-Listen).

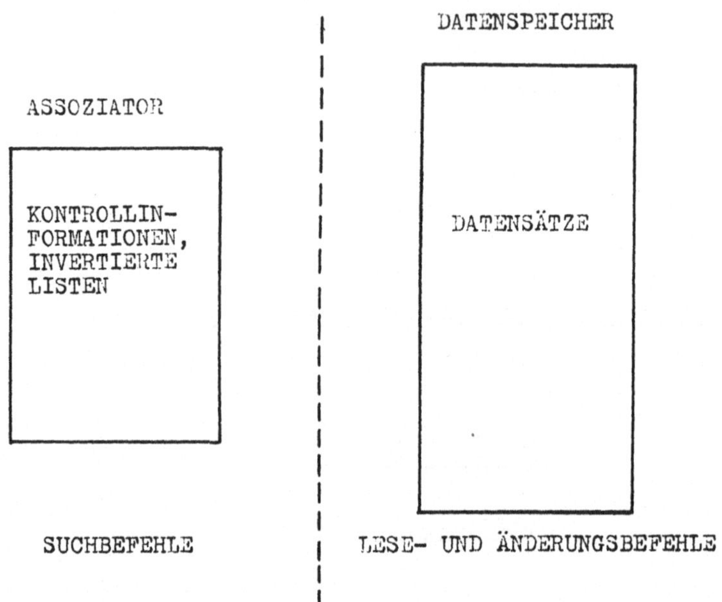

DATENSPEICHER

Der Datenspeicher - Teil der Datenbank enthält die Datensätze
aller Anwendungen.

ADABAS speichert in jedem Datensatz nur relevante Informationen. Leerfelder, führende Nullen in numerischen Feldern sowie
nachstehende Blanks in alpha-numerischen Feldern werden nicht
gespeichert.

Der komprimierte Datensatz im Datenspeicher enthält weder
Feldnamen noch Adreßverweise noch Kettungsverweise, sondern
nur relevante Informationen in Form von Byte-strings. Diese
Kompressionstechnik hat die Aufgabe, die erforderliche Speicher-
kapazität für die Daten so klein wie möglich zu halten.

<u>ASSOZIATOR</u>

Die Kontrollinformationen für die ADABAS-Datenbank werden -
logisch und physikalisch von den Datensätzen getrennt - im
ASSOZIATOR gepflegt und gewartet.

Die wichtigsten Komponenten des ASSOZIATORS sind:

- DIE FELDBESCHREIBUNG
- DIE SPEICHERVERWALTUNGSTABELLEN
- DER ADRESS-KONVERTER
- DAS ASSOZIATIONS-NETZ

DIE FELDBESCHREIBUNG

Die Feldbeschreibung definiert den logischen Inhalt einer
Datei innerhalb einer Datenbank.

Die kleinste logische Einheit innerhalb der Datei ist das
Feld.

Die logische Reihenfolge sowie die Eigenschaften der Felder
werden festgelegt, wenn eine Datei in die Datenbank geladen
wird.

Der Datenaustausch zwischen Benutzerprogramm und Datenbank
kann auf Feldebene durchgeführt werden, wobei das System
die Daten in beliebiger Form aufbereitet.

Jeder Benutzer kann Informationen aus der Feldbeschreibung
durch einen speziellen LESE-Befehl erhalten (LF = Lesen
Feldbeschreibung).

Es ist mit ADABAS leicht möglich, die Feldbeschreibung einer
bereits geladenen Datei zu erweitern. Diese Erweiterung erfordert kein Neuorganisieren der Datenbank.

ADABAS ASSOZIATOR

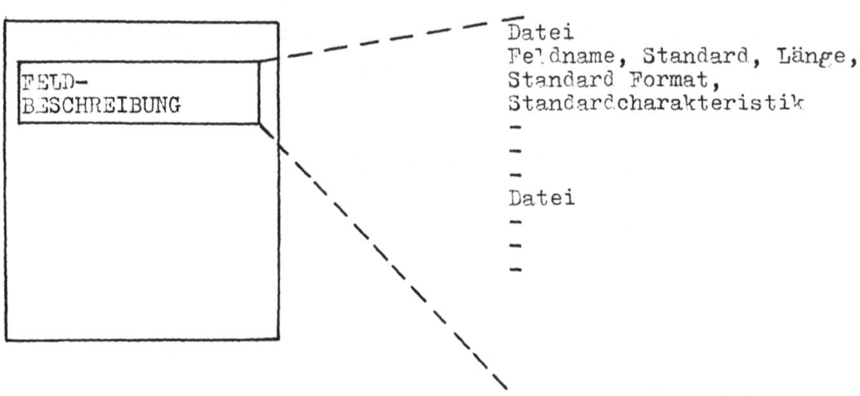

DIE SPEICHERVERWALTUNGSTABELLEN

Die Speicherverwaltungstabellen werden zur Einteilung und zur
Verwaltung beider Teile der Datenbank, des ASSOZIATORS und des
DATENSPEICHERS benötigt.

Der Speicherplatz wird jeder Datei zum Zeitpunkt ihres Ladens
zugewiesen. Speicherplatz, der durch das Löschen von Sätzen
oder durch das Löschen einer ganzen Datei frei wird, wird zur
sofortigen Wiederbenutzung zur Verfügung gestellt.

Wächst eine Datei während der späteren Verarbeitung über den
ihr anfangs zugewiesenen Speicherplatz hinaus an, so weisen
die Speicherverwaltungsroutinen von ADABAS dieser Datei automatisch zusätzlichen Speicher aus einem allgemeinen Speicherbereich zu. Dieser allgemeine Speicherbereich wird vom Benutzer
beim Einrichten der Datenbank definiert.

Sollten die zugewiesenen Speicher der gesamten Datenbank er-
schöpft sein, so ist es möglich, die Zuweisung für die gesamte Datenbank zu erweitern, ohne daß ein Neuladen oder eine
Reorganisation erforderlich ist. Mit Dienstprogrammen ist es
auch möglich, den Speicherraum einer Datei, der durch automatische Erweiterungen gestreut angelegt wurde, wieder zusammenzufassen oder beliebig zu manipulieren.

DER ADRESS-KONVERTER

Jedem Datensatz, der mit ADABAS in den DATENSPEICHER geladen wird, wird eine interne Satz Nummer (ISN) zugewiesen, die danach vom Anwender zum logischen Ansprechen des Datensatzes benutzt wird.

Die ISN eines Datensatzes bleibt diesem Datensatz zugewiesen, bis er vom Benutzer aus der Datenbank gelöscht wird.

Die physikalische Blocknummer des Blockes, in dem der einzelne Datensatz mit seiner ISN gespeichert ist, ist ebenfalls in eine Liste eingetragen, die Bestandteil des Assoziators ist. Diese Liste ist der ADRESS-KONVERTER.

Alle logischen Referenzen zu einem Datensatz laufen über die ISN. ADABAS erreicht die richtige physikalische Blocknummer des Blockes, in dem der gesuchte Datensatz gespeichert ist, einfach durch die Benutzung der ISN als Index für den ADRESS-KONVERTER.

Die Trennung zwischen logischer Identifizierung und physikalischem Speicherplatz eines Datensatzes bringt dem Benutzer folgende, bedeutende Vorteile:

- Extrem schnelles Auffinden und Ändern der Daten

- Absolute Geräteunabhängigkeit

- Absolute Unabhängigkeit des logischen Datei-Inhalts von der physik-alischen Datenorganisation

ADRESS KONVERTER

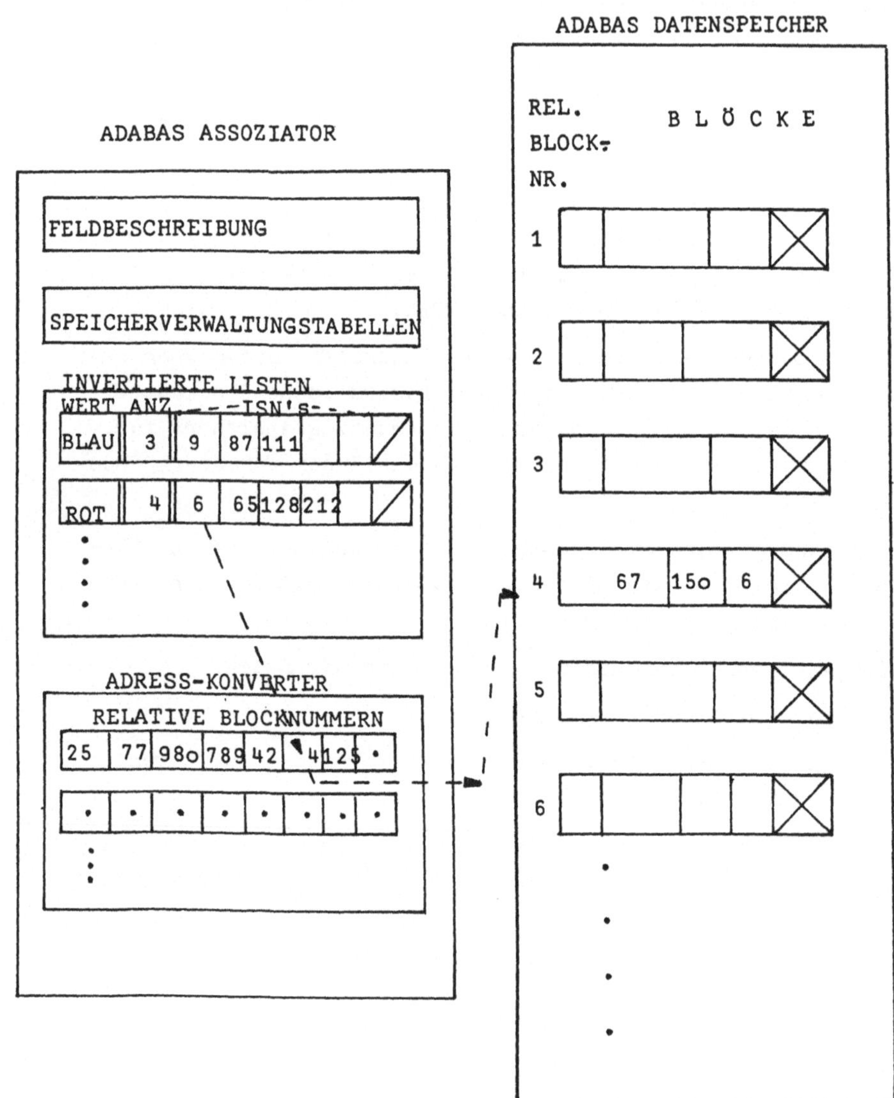

DAS ASSOZIATIONSNETZWERK

Das ASSOZIATIONSNETZWERK enthält die invertierten Listen, die
für die optimale Verarbeitung von Suchanfragen an die Datenbank erforderlich sind.

Eine beliebige Anzahl von Feldern einer Datei können vom Benutzer als Suchschlüssel ausgewählt werden. ADABAS nennt ein
solches Feld Deskriptor-Feld.

Für jedes Deskriptorfeld wird eine ivertierte Liste aufgebaut
und gewartet. Diese Liste (Normalindex) enthält für jeden Wert
des Deskriptors eine Liste aller Sätze (ISN's), in denen dieser Wert vorhanden ist und ist über eine 3-stufige Adressie-
rungshierarchie (Hyperindex, Superindex, Hauptindex) ansprech-
bar. Jede Indexstufe steht in getrennten Blöcken des Assozia-
torbereichs.

PHYSISCHE SPEICHERVERWALTUNG

Das Basiselement, das von ADABAS zur physischen Speicherver-
waltung verwendet wird, ist der physische Block.

Die verwendete Blocklänge ist direkt von dem benutzten Speicher-
typ abhängig. Ein einzelner Block enthält mehrere variable
lange, logische Sätze (in komprimierter Form). Für jeden Block
ist ein bestimmter Puffer reserviert, der eventuelle Ausdeh-
nungen der logischen Sätze innerhalb des Blockes leicht ermöglicht. Die Größe des zu reservierenden Puffers kann vom Benutzer für jede Datei bestimmt werden.

Da ADABAS intern nur fixe Blocklängen verwendet, kann die Datenbank auf verschieden externen Speichergeräten, die vom Benutzer ausgewählt werden, sehr optimal organisiert werden.

Der freie Speicherplatz wird dynamisch verwaltet, so daß
Speicherplatz, der durch das Löschen von Sätzen verfügbar
wird, sofort für die Wiederbenutzung freigegeben wird.

Durch diese dynamische Speicherplatzverwaltung und durch die
Tatsache,daß ADABAS keine Kettungstechniken verwendet,wird die
Notwendigkeit einer period.Reorganisation der Datenbank ausge-
schlossen.

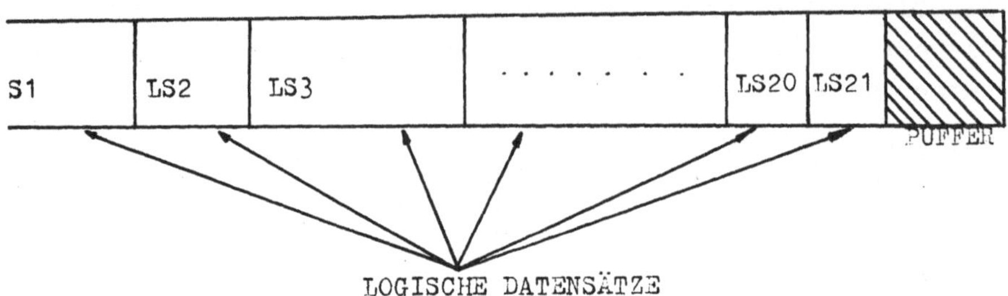

DATEI-STRUKTUR

Die Hauptkomponente einer ADABAS-Datenbank ist die Datei.
Eine einzelne ADABAS-Datenbank kann bis zu 255 verschiedene
Dateien aufnehmen (Obergrenze ist bei Laden der 1.Datei in
die Datenbank angebbar).

Eine Datei in ADABAS besteht grundsätzlich aus:
- Feldbeschreibung, Adreßkonverter
- Invertierte Listen für Deskriptorfelder
- Logischen Datensätzen

Die Feldbeschreibungen aller Dateien sind im Feldbeschrei-
bungsteil des ASSOZIATORS (4 Blöcke pro Datei) enthalten.
Die Feldbeschreibungen definieren und beschreiben die
Reihenfolge und die Eigenschaften der Datenfelder eines
logischen Satzes.

Die invertierten Listen für jedes Deskriptorfeld der Datei
werden benötigt für:
- Beantwortung von Suchanfragen
- Logisch sequentielle Verarbeitung
- Aufbau von Verknüpfungen zwischen Dateien

Die logischen Datensätze enthalten alle existierenden Werte für
alle Felder und sind im DATENSPEICHER-Teil der Datenbank abgelegt. Eine einzelne Datei kann maximal aus 16 777 214 Sätzen
bestehen.

DATEI-DEFINITION

Eine Datei-Definition in ADABAS besteht aus Feldbeschrei-
bungs-Eintragungen für jedes Datenfeld der Datei. Eine einzelne ADABAS-Datei kann bis zu 500 Einzelfelder haben.

Jede Feldbeschreibungs-Eintragung besteht aus:

Stufennummer	Elementarfeld, Feldgruppe
Feldname	
Feldtyp	Elementarfeld, Multiples Feld, Gruppenfeld, Periodengruppenfeld
Feldeigenschaften	Deskriptor, Nullwertunter- drückung, Fixe Länge
Standard Länge	
Standard Format	Alpha, dezimal ungepackt, dezimal gepackt, binär, Festpunkt

Die Stufennummer dient zur Definition von hierarchischen Beziehungen der einzelnen Felder untereinander. Alle Felder,
die als Mitglieder (Unterfelder) eines anderen Feldes zu
betrachten sind (Gruppenfeld), müssen mit einer höheren
Stufennummer definiert werden als das Gruppenfeld. Der Feld-
name ist der Schlüssel, durch den der Benutzer auf das von
ihm gewünschte Feld im Datensatz zugreift.

Intern sind die ADABAS-Feldnamen 2 Stellen lang. Wird
ADASCRIPT verwendet, so können externe Feldnamen bis
maximal 80 Zeichen verwendet werden (anstatt der internen
oder zusätzlich).

Die unterschiedlichen Feldtypen ermöglichen die Darstellung
bestimmter logischer Eigenschaften. Folgende Feldtypen
können in einer ADABAS Datenbank definiert werden:

Elementarfeld	Das Feld kann innerhalb eines jeden logischen Satzes nur ei- nen einzigen Wert haben

Multiples Feld	Maximal 191 Werte. Dieser Feldtyp wird meistens benutzt, wenn für ein Feld mehrere synonyme Werte existieren.

Beispiel:
Sprachkenntnisse: Englisch
              Deutsch
              Russisch

Gruppenfeld	besteht aus einer Serie von einem oder mehreren nacheinander liegenden Feldern, die als Teil eines übergeordneten Feldes (Gruppenfeld) betrachtet werden. Die Einzelfelder, die das Gruppenfeld bilden, können Elementarfelder oder multiple Felder sein. Diese Möglichkeit erlaubt die Definition von hierarchischen Strukturen innerhalb eines Datensatzes.

Beispiel:
01 Adresse   Gruppenfeld
   02 Stadt
   02 Straße
   02 Hausnummer

Periodengruppenfeld	Als Periodengruppenfeld wird ein Gruppenfeld bezeichnet, das sich innerhalb eines logischen Satzes mehrfach – maximal 99mal – wiederholt.

Im Falle multipler Felder oder Periodengruppenfelder werden nur existierende Werte physikalisch gespeichert.

Den einzelnen Feldern können folgende Eigenschaften und Merkmale zugewiesen werden:

- Deskriptor-Status

- Nullwert-Unterdrückung

- Fixe Länge (keine Datenkompression)

Die wesentlichen Aufgaben der Deskriptorfelder liegen in ihrer Verwendung als

- Such-Kriterium

- Sortier-Kriterium

- Kriterium für logische sequentielle Verarbeitung

- Kriterium für logische Dateikopplung

Deskriptorfelder können zur Formulierung von Suchkriterien
bei Anfragen an die Datenbank verwendet werden. Eine einzelne
Anfrage kann aus verschiedenen Teilsuchkriterien bestehen,
die wiederum verschiedene, mit logischen Operatoren verknüpfte
Deskriptorfelder enthalten (AND (und), OR (oder), FROM-TO
(von-bis), BUT-NOT (aber-nicht)).

Über ein Deskriptorfeld kann die Reihenfolge bestimmt werden,
mit der die auf eine Anfrage gefundenen Datensätze an den Benutzer ausgegeben werden. Darüberhinaus kann über ein Deskriptorfeld die logische Reihenfolge bestimmt werden, in der
die Datensätze sequentiell von einer Datei zu lesen sind.

Deskriptorfelder dienen auch dazu, logische Verknüpfungen
und Kopplungen zwischen verschiedenen Dateien einer Datenbank herzustellen.

Jedes Elementarfeld und jedes multiple Feld kann zum Deskriptor bestimmt werden, ebenso alle Felder, die Mitglieder einer
Periodengruppe sind.

Es ist darüberhinaus möglich, einen Teil eines Feldes als
Deskriptor zu definieren oder zwei oder mehrere Felder,
oder Teile von Feldern zu einem Deskriptor zu kombinieren.
(Bildung von Matchcodes mit automatische Pflege des Matchcodes im Assoziator).

Die Nullwertunterdrückung hat eine Bedeutung sowohl für die
Speicherung der Daten im Datensatz als auch bei Deskriptor-
feldern für den Aufbau der invertierten Listen. Wird für ein
Feld Nullunterdrückung definiert, so wird es im Datensatz
als Leerfeld behandelt (völlig unterdrückt), wenn sein Wert
Null (bei numerischen Feldern) oder Blank (bei alphanumerischen Feldern) ist. Ist das Feld ein Deskriptorfeld, so wird
für den Nullwert keine invertierte Liste im Assoziator angelegt, damit können Sätze mit Nullinformation in dem gegebenen
Feld nicht über Suchanfragen aufgefunden werden. Wird keine
Nullunterdrückung definiert, so bleibt im Datensatz jeweils
ein Byte der Nullinformation enthalten und im Assoziator

wird eine invertierte Liste für den Nullwert aufgebaut. Sätze
mit Nullinformation in dem gegebenen Feld können mit Suchanfragen aus der Datenbank selektiert werden.

Ein Feld kann mit fixer Länge definiert werden. In diesem
Fall wird das Feld nicht durch ADABAS komprimiert, sondern
immer mit einer festen Anzahl Bytes gespeichert.

Ohne besondere Angabe wird ein Feld immer in variabler Länge
mit vorangestelltem Längenbyte gespeichert. Beim Ansprechen
eines Feldes werden Standardlänge und Standardformat (aus
der Feldbeschreibung) von ADABAS als Default-Werte benutzt,
wenn durch den Benutzer explizit keine Längen- oder Format-
Definitionen für dieses Feld vorgenommen werden.

Der Benutzer kann zu jeder Zeit Standardlänge und Standard-
format eines Feldes überschreiben, indem er in einem ADABAS-
Befehl die Länge und das Format des betreffenden Feldes
explizit angibt. Alle notwendigen Konvertierungen werden
automatisch von ADABAS durchgeführt.

DATEI-KOPPLUNG

Die Kopplung von Dateien in ADABAS bietet eine weitere Möglichkeit der logischen Strukturierung einer Datenbank.

Mit der Dateikopplungstechnik kann eine logische Netzwerk-
struktur aufgebaut werden. Zwei beliebige Dateien können
über einen gemeinsamen Deskriptor gekoppelt werden. Ist die
Kopplung zwischen zwei Dateien vollzogen, können Anfragen
formuliert werden, die Suchkriterien aus beiden Dateien
enthalten.

Dateien können zu beliebigen Zeitpunkten gekoppelt oder entkoppelt werden. Vor dem Laden der Datenbank sind hierzu keinerlei Definitionen oder Vorbereitungen erforderlich. Das erlaubt dem Benutzer eine größere Flexibilität und den Aufbau
von logischen Netzwerken, wenn eine Dateikopplung für den
Benutzer sinnvoll und notwendig wird.

Eine Datei kann mit maximal 80 anderen Dateien gekoppelt werden. Die logische Beziehung zweier gekoppelter Dateien besteht in beiden Richtungen gleichzeitig. Erst zum Zeitpunkt der Anfrage wird vom Benutzer bestimmt, welche Datei als Primär-Datei und welche als Sekundär-Datei behandelt wird.

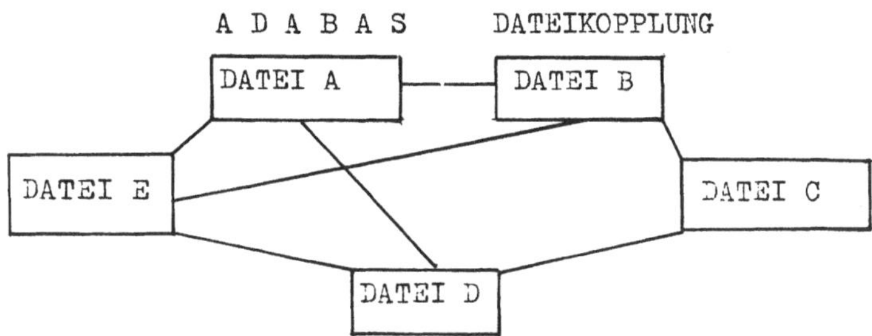

ADABAS-BEFEHLE

Alle ADABAS—Befehle werden durch den ADABAS-Nukleus ausgeführt. ADABAS führt folgende allgemeine Befehle aus:

FIND	(assoziatives Suchen)
READ	(random, physikalisch sequentiell, logisch sequentiell, Deskriptorwerte-Lesen, Lesen Feldbeschreibung)
UPDATE	(Feldwerte ändern, Feldwerte löschen, Feldwerte hinzufügen)
ADD	(Neuzugang eines logischen Satzes)
DELETE	(Löschen eines logischen Satzes)
OPEN/CLOSE	(logisches Open und Close)
CHECKPOINT	(Setzen eines logischen Restart-Punktes)

Der ADABAS Nukleus besteht aus zwei bzw. drei Teilen

ADAMPM (Multi-user) + ADAEMO + ADADAK

ADAMPM	. Warteschlange von asynchron ankommenden Befehlen
	. ISN-Hold-Funktion
	. Interregion-Kommunikation
	. Benutzerwarteschlange

ADAEMO hat folgende Aufgaben

. syntaktische Interpretation der Befehle

. Aufbereitung aller Puffer

. Kompression und Dekompression von Sätzen

. Datenschutz

. Zerlegung der ADABAS-Befehle in Einzel-ADADAK-Befehle

. Verwaltung von Internen Formatpuffern

ADADAK regelt

. alle Ein/Ausgaben

. Datensicherung

. eigentliches Durchführen der Suchbefehle, Sequenzlogik bei Lesebefehlen

. 'Bufferpool'

Ein Benutzerprogramm, das in COBOL, PL1, FORTRAN oder ASSEMBLER geschrieben ist. kann Datenoperationen durch das Aufsetzen von ADABAS-Standardaufrufen durchführen.

Ein einfaches Beispiel einer Datei:

    Feldbeschreibung einer Personendatei
    Ø1,AA,2Ø,A,DE,NU   FAMILIENNAME
    Ø1,AB,1Ø,A,MU(ØØ5),DE,NU   VORNAMEN
    Ø1,AC,7,U,DE,NU   GEBURTSDATUM

wobei definiert wurde:

AA   (ADABAS-Feldname für den Familiennamen) ist 20-stellig   als Deskriptor mit eingeschalteter Komprimierung definiert, d.h. nach Leerfeld kann nicht gesucht werden, da für den Deskriptorwert Ø keine invertierte Liste aufgebaut wird.

AB   (Vornamen) ist ein 10-stelliger alphanumerischer Deskriptor, der max.5x vorkommen kann, mit Komprimierung.

AC   (Geburtsdatum) ist ein 7-stelliges numerisches Feld Deskriptor und zu komprimieren.

<u>Datenbereich</u>

Datei-Personen (keine exakte interne Darstellung)

ISN1	ABEL FRANZ HANS 9461Ø15
ISN2	ADAM ANTON 9472Ø13
ISN3	ADAM ELISABETH 9Ø1Ø1Ø1
ISN4	ADUNA ANTON

<u>Assoziatorbereich:</u>

Deskriptorname	Deskriptorwert	Invertierte Liste (ISN)	
FAMILIENNAME (AA)	ABEL	1	
	ADAM	2,3	Zugriff über Adreß-
	ADUNA	4	konverter auf richtigen Daten-Block
VORNAMEN(AB)	ANTON	2,4	⟹
	ELISABETH	3, . . .	
	FRANZ	1, . . .	
	HANS	1, . . .	
GEBURTSDATUM(AC)	9Ø1Ø1Ø1	3	
	9461Ø15	1	
	9471Ø13	2	

Familienname = ABEL und Vorname = FRANZ oder HANS oder ANTON
und Geburtsdatum = von 945Ø1Ø5 (d.h. 1.1.1945) bis 9481231,
aber nicht 9562Ø18. Diese Anfrage würde bei unserem Beispiel
zumindest das Ergebnis – 1 Satz, nämlich der mit der internen Satznummer 1, gefunden – liefern, nachdem die Satznummern
bei den verwendeten Deskriptorwerten abgeglichen wurden. Für
das Suchen wird nur der Assoziatorbereich benötigt und nach
dem Suchvorgang wird die Anzahl der Datensätze, die den angegebenen Spezifikationen entsprechen, geliefert und auch die
Adressen zur Verarbeitung (ISN-Liste) bereitgestellt.

4. Praktischer Einsatz des DB-Systems ADABAS

Die Stadt Wien hat sich 1971 für ADABAS entschieden und
war damit einer der ersten ADABAS-Anwender überhaupt.
Statt mit CALL-Schnittstelle und damit dem Aufbau der
verschiedenen Steuerblockpuffer zu arbeiten, wurde eine
eigene Datenbanksprache - angelehnt an den CODASYL-For-
malismus (Vorschlag 1969) - konzipiert, die als Befehle

OPEN	Eröffnen Datei
CLOSE	Schließen Datei
FIND	Suchen Satz
GET	Lesen Satz bzw. Felder
MODIFY	Verändern Satz bzw. Felder
DELETE	Löschen Satz
STORE	Speichern neuen Satz

und Befehle für die CHeckpoint/Restart-Probleme enthält,
entwickelt und in COBOL eingebettet. Mit dem INVOKE-Be-
fehl wird dem Programmierer der für die jeweilige Anwendung notwendige Teilauszug (Subschema) zur Verfügung gestellt. Als Problem ergab sich, daß der CODASYL-Formalis-
mus nicht ohne Eigenentwicklung geeignet war, die im Datenbanksystem ADABAS liegenden Möglichkeiten zu nützen.
Es wurde etwa der FIND-Befehl so definiert, daß die Anzahl der eine komplexe Suchanfrage erfüllenden Sätze
(ADABAS-Suchbefehl) als Lösung geliefert wird.

Die Entscheidung für das Datenbanksystem ADABAS, die 1971
file, war keineswegs unproblematisch. Die Weiterentwicklung
des Produktes, die verstärkte Einsatzmöglichkeit im Rahmen
der Stadt Wien und die steigende Anzahl der ADABAS-Installa-
tionen - weltweit - zeigen, daß die Entscheidung richtig war.
Die Notwendigkeit einer eigenen DB-Sprache mit Precompiler
für die Batchprogramme und einer Online-Schnittstelle wurde
erkannt und da diese Schnittstelle von der SAG 1971 noch
nicht angeboten wurde, wurde eine eigene TP-Sprache - aus
einem COBOL-Subset und den Befehlen der DB-Sprache bestehend -
entwickelt und TCAM als TP-Monitor eingesetzt.

<u>ADV-Systemkonzept:</u>

In der MD ADV wird die ADABAS-Version 3.2.1 im Singel-Use-
Mode eingesetzt (wobei eine eigene ADV-Schnittstelle die
Mehrfach-Benutzung der Datenbank(en) erlaubt). Es laufen
im Rechenzentrum auf zwei Anlagen (370/158 mit 2MB und
370/158-3 mit 3MB) zwei ADABAS-Nuclei, wobei auf der Maschine 370/158 mit 2MB eine auf 333∅-liegende Datenbank,
auf der schnelleren Anlage eine 335∅-Datenbank bearbeitet
wird. ADABAS läuft unter dem Betriebssystem OS/VS2, beide
Datenbanken werden gleichzeitig mit ONLINE- und Batch-
programmen bearbeitet.

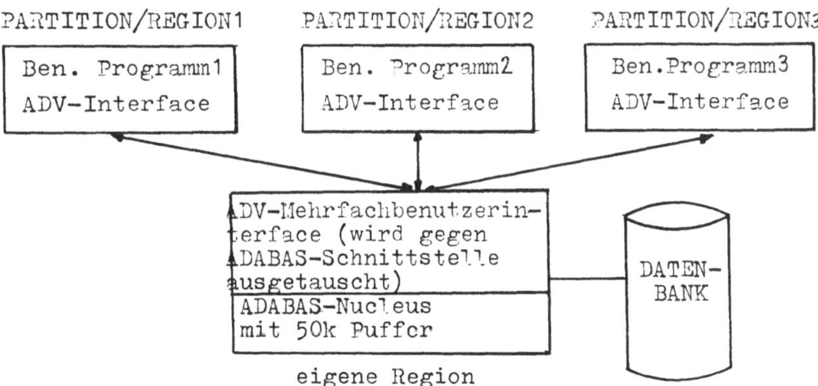

Die Datenbanken werden von den Benutzern nur über Inter-
region-angesprochen. Alle Utilities sind in Prozeduren,
in denen die relevanten Angaben ersetzt werden, eingebettet. Die verschiedenen Einheiten (333∅, 335∅) erfordern, zwei Bibliotheken für ADABAS-Nucleus und ADABAS-
Dienstprogramme, da mit Hilfe eines Patch die Zuordnung
auf die Type des Direktzugriffsspeichers erfolgt. ADABAS
verwendet ausschließlich Speichermedien mit Direktzugriff
für die Abspeicherung der Daten, wobei die einzige Voraussetzung ist, daß das Gerät auf der logischen Ebene des Betriebssystems adressierbar ist.

Standardmäßig werden unterstützt:

23Ø5	Trommelspeicher
2314	Plattenspeicher
333Ø	– " –
334Ø	– " –
335Ø	– " –
458Ø	– " –

In der auf dem Plattentyp 333Ø liegenden Datenbank werden
nur Dateien zum Testen (wenige Sätze, geringer Datenspeicherbedarf – 1 bis 2 Zylinder; der Datenspeicherbedarf,
wird beim Komprimierlauf ermittelt und ist in Zylindern
beim Ladevorgang anzugeben, der Assoziatorplatz wird von
ADABAS aus den Eingabedaten hochgerechnet (10.000 Sätze
oder 1/8 des Eingabestandes) oder er kann bei nicht relevanten Eingabedaten durch Einsatz der manuellen Allocation
gesteuert werden) gespeichert. Die auf 335Ø liegende Datenbank umfaßt 4 Platten à 555 Zylinder mit zwei Fixköpfen und
stellt die Produktionsdatenbank dar.

An einigen Applikationen sollen nun die Möglichkeiten des
DB-Systems ADABAS gezeigt werden.

Die größte Datei, die in der EDV der Stadt Wien als ADABAS-
Datei aufgebaut wurde, ist die Personendatei mit 1,9 Mio
Sätzen und einer max. Satzgröße von 1950 Bytes. Als Grund-
datei dient die Datei der wahlberechtigten Wiener, die
Wählerevidenz (1,3 Mio Personen). Die Wählerevidenz war ursprünglich in 2 Karteien nach den Gesichtspunkten 'Personen-
namen' bzw. 'Adressen' vorhanden. Diese Karteien wurden dann
auf EDV übernommen, wobei sich bei Einsatz der EDV folgende
Probleme ergaben:

- welche Begriffe werden als Suchbegriffe definiert ?
- welche Verknüpfungen sind möglich, bzw. sinnvoll, sodaß
  akzeptables Antwortzeitverhalten über Online und gute
  Verarbeitungszeiten im Batch erreicht werden?

Die Trennung der Information in einen Satz mit Personen-
stammdaten und in Adreßsätze erwies sich als günstigste
Lösung. Der einzelne Personensatz enthält mehrere Verweise
zu Adreßsätzen,da ja eine Person mehrere Wohnsitze haben
kann. Als Verbindung der Personendatei und Adreßdatei
wurde nicht die Kopplungsmöglichkeit, die ADABAS bietet,
gewählt. Die logische Kopplung von Dateien im ADABAS geschieht mittels einer invertierten Datei. 2 Sätze aus 2
verschiedenen Dateien werden über den Inhalt eines bestimmten, in beiden Sätzen definierten Feldes gekoppelt,
wobei für den Fall der Wählerevidenz eine n:m-Kopplung,
d.h. mehrdeutige Kopplung in beide Richtungen vorliegt.

Da im Verlaufe der Realisierung der Applikation Wählerevidenz einige Male die Datenstruktur völlig geändert
wurde, erwies sich die von ADABAS angebotene Kopplung
(Utility-Läufe) damals bei den Datenmengen 1,3 Mio Personen
und 113.000 Adressen als nicht praktikabel. Bei jeder Umstellung mußte die Kopplung aufgehoben werden (was sehr
schnell geht), die betroffene Datei neugeladen und die
Kopplung wieder durchgeführt werden, was bei den riesigen
Datenmengen sehr zeitaufwendig war.

Um die Möglichkeit des DB-Systems zu nützen, das auf der
exakten Verwaltung der ISN basiert, wurden alle Adressen
Wiens durchnummeriert, wobei die vom DB-System intern
vergebene Satznummer als Adreßcode gewählt wurde und in den
Daten als erstes Feld gespeichert ist. Der Adreßcode identifiziert eine Adreßangabe mit allen Identadressen eindeutig
und ist auch als Deskriptor in den entsprechenden Personensätzen vorhanden.

Weiters wurden die Datei der Straßenbezeichnungen Wiens
als ADABAS-Datei aufgebaut, wobei der schon übliche Straßencode als interne Satznummer verwendet wurde. Diese Datei
enthält zu einem Straßencode den aktuellen Straßen- bzw.
Verkehrsflächennamen in verschiedenen Schreibweisen,

übliche Varianten und auch historische Angaben. Mit dieser
Lösung ist eine Umschlüsselung von beliebigen Adreßangaben
über Straßen- bzw. Adreßdatei und das Auffinden der zu dieser Adresse gehörenden Person möglich.

Personendatei (1,9 Mio)

. Stammdaten - Zunamen (bis zu vier)
              Vornamen
              Geburtsdatum ...

. Adreßangaben
  Familienstand und Familienangehörige

. Wählerevidenzdaten ("Wahlrecht")

. Standesamtsdaten

. Staatsbürgerschaftsdaten

. Erwerbstätigkeit .....

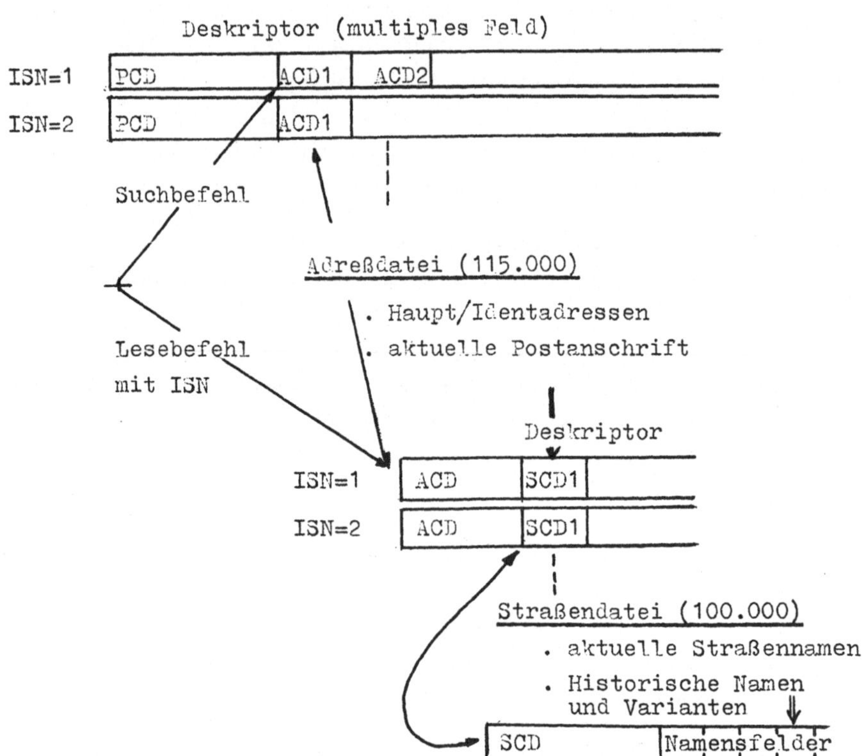

In den Personensätzen selbst werden die internen Satznummern
"verwandter" Personensätze gespeichert, womit das Problem
der Familienbeziehung gelöst ist und alle notwendigen Anfragen befriedigt werden können. Das Kind trägt den Verweis
(ISN) zu dem Vaterpersonensatz, der Vaterpersonensatz den
Verweis zu seinem Vater, zu seinen Kindern und seiner Gattin
usw. Es ist damit die Herstellung einer Familienstruktur
möglich.

Die Probleme bei den einzelnen Suchvorgängen auf der Personendatei waren folgende:

Um eine Einzelperson rasch zu finden, ist eine Verknüpfung
der Begriffe Familienname + Vorname + Geburtsdatum zu einem Suchkriterium zwar möglich, diese Verknüpfung ist wegen
des doch sehr aufwendigen Suchvorgangs aber nur in Ausnahme-
fällen sinnvoll. Die Suchzeit ist vom Wertevorrat der einzelnen Deskriptoren abhängig, deren ISN-Liste abgeglichen werden.
Als kritische Deskriptorwerte sind bei den Vornamen FRANZ,
ANNA (ca. 100.000), MARIA (ca. 80.000) bzw. bei den Familiennamen BAUER zu nennen.

Am effektivsten wäre natürlich die Verwendung eines eindeutigen Personenkennzeichens zur Personenidentifikation. Da es
in Österreich ein allgemeingültiges Personenkennzeichen nicht
gibt und nach dem derzeitigen Stand nicht geben wird, gilt
für die Wählerevidenz als Grundlage der Auskunft bzw. des
Änderungsdienstes der Meldezettel mit allen ausgeschriebenen
Stammdaten. Für eine sinnvolle EDV-Lösung war es notwendig,
ein Suchfeld zu definieren, das - aus den Stammdaten zusammengesetzt - fast eindeutig ist, d.h. bei jeder Anfrage nur einen gefundenen Satz ergibt, sodaß ein gutes Antwortzeitverhalten garantiert wird. (Schnellster Suchalgorithmus im ADABAS!)
Bei der Planung der Personendatenbank war bald klar, daß ein
geeignetes Kriterium für den Hauptsuchvorgang sich aus Teilen
des Familien- und des Vornamens, dem Geschlecht und dem Geburtsdatum zusammensetzen müßte. Das führte zur Definition

eines "Superdeskriptors", der physisch in den Daten als
multiples Feld vorgesehen wurde, also gespeichert wird.
Der ADABAS-Superdeskriptor ist in der jetzigen Version
3.2.1 realisiert, wobei der Superdeskriptor nicht
physisch in den Daten, sondern nur im Assoziator aufgebaut wird. Er erlaubt außerdem nur die Beteiligung _eines_
multiplen Feldes beim Aufbau des Superdeskriptors, während bei der ADV-Lösung Familienname und Vorname multiple
Felder darstellten. Es wurden zur Bestimmung eines
günstigen 'Superdeskriptors', der eine hohe Rate eindeu-
tiger Zuordnungen garantiert, 3 Varianten untersucht,
wobei es darum ging, wieviele Stellen von den Grundfel-
dern für den Aufbau zu nehmen sind.

Variante A	Familienname	10	
	Vorname	5	und zusätzlich
B	Familienname	8	Geschlecht 1
	Vorname	4	Geburtsjahr 3
C	Familienname	6	
	Vorname	3	Geburtstag 4

Wenn man die Sätze, die unvollständige oder keine Geburtsdaten enthielten, außer acht läßt, so ergab sich bei den
Sätzen mit genauen Geburtsdaten für alle 3 Varianten fast
Eindeutigkeit (ca. 99,97%). Diese Untersuchungen führten
zur Annahme der Variante B, d.h. zur Definition eines
20-stelligen Suchfeldes, eines fast eindeutigen Identifi-
kationsmerkmales, sodaß nur in Sonderfällen die Verknüpfung
mehrerer Begriffe wie Familien-, Vorname, Adresse zur Identifikation benötigt werden.

Das Problem der schnellsten Identifizierung einer bestimmten
Person, würde sich natürlich nicht stellen, gäbe es ein Personenkennzeichen. Pro Personensatz wird die von ADABAS vergebene interne Satznummer als Quasipersonenkennzeichen in jedem Satz abgespeichert und kann für Wartungsarbeiten benützt
werden, womit die sicherlich schnellste Verarbeitung erreicht
wird (= Lesen einer bestimmten ISN).

In der Personendatenbank kann standardmäßig im On-line nach
folgenden Kriterien gesucht werden (Anfragen auf =); für
Pflegearbeiten (DBA) und Auswertungen stehen noch andere
Möglichkeiten zur Verfügung (Bereichsanfragen!).

```
A,'FAMILIEN-NAME','VORNAME','GEBURTSDATUM(JJJMMTT)','GESCHLECHT'
B,'FAMILIEN-NAME','GEBURTSDATUM(JJJMMTT)','GESCHLECHT'
C,'STR-NAME/CODE','HAUSNUMMER','STIEGE','KATEGORIE','SONDERNUMMER'
D,'FAMILIENNAME','VORNAME'
E,'PERSONENCODE'
F,'FAMILIEN-NAME'
G,'VORNAME'
H,'WAHLRECHT','FAM-NAME','VORNAME'
I,'FAM-NAME','STR-NAME/CODE','HAUSNR','STIEGE','KATEGORIE','SONDERNR'
K,'ADRESSCODE'
L,'FAMILIENNAME','ADRESSCODE'
```

Die Möglichkeiten, die das DB-System ADABAS auf dem Sektor
'Verarbeitung von Massendaten mit Identifikationsproblem'
bietet, erleichtern wesentlich die organisatorische Arbeit.

Ein nicht zu unterschätztender Vorteil des Systems liegt in
der Datenkomprimierung. Die Notwendigkeit der Komprimierung
ist sicher bei den Daten im kaufmännischen Bereich (viele
Schlüssel, Rechenfelder, num.Informationen) nicht so gegeben;
bei Strukturen mit vielen Adreßdaten, Erklärungen, Texten,
ist eine sinnvolle Komprimierung erst Grundlage einer möglichen organisatorischen Realisierung, vor allem, wenn rie-
sige Datenmengen über On-line im Zugriff sein müssen. Die
Komprimierregel - wahlweise

. Unterdrückung führender Nullen bei
  numerischen Feldern

. Unterdrückung nachstehender Leerstellen bei alphanumerischen Feldern

. Unterdrückung bei Leerfeldern

bringt je nach Struktur, die verarbeitet wird, eine Speicher-
platzersparnis für den Datenbereich von 30 - 80 %, da ja ein
Großteil der in fixer Länge definierten Felder oft nicht gefüllt bzw. kürzere Information, als der reservierte Bereich
aufnehmen könnte, enthält. Es ist natürlich klar, daß das
Komprimieren von Daten bei Veränderungsbefehlen (MODIFY,
STORE) bzw. das Entkomprimieren von Daten beim Lesen je nach
der Anzahl der beim Laden definierten ADABAS-Felder einen gewissen Overhead ergibt. Es ist daher bei der Erstellung einer
Datei darauf zu achten, welche Felderanzahl bzw. welche Anordnung der Felder eine günstige Komprimierung, aber auch keinen
zu großen System-Overhead ergibt. Bei kleinen Dateien ist es
nicht wichtig, Datenspeicher zu ersparen, bei der Personendatei war es aber notwendig, auf höchstmögliche Datenkomprimierung zu kommen. Bei einer max. auf 1950 Bytes ausgelegten
Struktur wurde eine durchschnittliche komprimierte Satzlänge
von 350 Bytes erreicht, es wird also bloß etwas mehr als 1/5
der bei fixer Speicherung benötigten Speicher gebraucht. Bei
Verwendung einer 3350-Konfiguration würden bei unkomprimierter
Speicherung mehr als 7 Platten statt wie jetzt 890 Zylinder
für den Datenspeicher und insgesamt 2 Platten für Assoziator
und Daten benötigt werden.

Bei der Verarbeitung von Massendaten kommen auch die Vorteile

- kein Reorganisieren trotz häufiger Veränderungen
- absturzsichere Speicherungsform (AUTORESTART)
- verschiedenste Auswertungsmöglichkeiten

voll zum Tragen.

Bei allen Applikationen im Rahmen der Stadt Wien, bei den
Dateien des räumlichen Bezugssystems, in der Mietzinsver-
rechnung, im Gesundheitswesen, im Abgabenbereich, tritt
das Problem der Verarbeitung großer Daten über On-line und
das Problem der Identifizierung von Personen, auch juristischer Personen, auf. Da sich durch den Einsatz der On-line-
Möglichkeit die Entwicklung weg von Zugriff über verschie-
dene Schlüssel zu Zugriff über Adresse bzw. Namen zeigt,
liegen die Schwierigkeiten bei der Lösung des Suchvorganges.
Die Namen juristischer Personen sind etwa aus verschiedenen
Teilen zusammengesetzt. Als Lösung bot sich hier die Verwendung eines multiplen Feldes als Deskriptor an, d.h. einer
Tabelle mit den verschiedenen Namensteilen Titel, Zunamen,
Vornamen, Firmennamen als Elemente. Damit können beliebige
Suchvorgänge unterstützt werden, während ein Feld in der
Datenstruktur die richtige Schreibweise zur Adressierung
enthält, z.B.

| DR. | MAYER | HANS | UND | SOEHNE .... |

Die Suchvorgänge
Dr. Mayer, Dr. Hans Mayer, Dr. Mayer Hans, Dr. Hans Mayer
und Söhne, Mayer und Söhne
liefern das richtige Ergebnis.

Der Vorteil des multiplen Feldes als Deskriptor ist an diesem
Beispiel leicht zu sehen, da die verschiedenen Anfragen erfolgreich sind, weil die Stellung der Einzelwerte innerhalb
der Tabelle unwichtig ist. Für jeden der möglichen Deskriptorwerte ist ja eine Indexliste im Assoziator aufgebaut, die

Suchanfrage wird durch Abgleichen der Indexlisten bei den
entsprechenden Deskriptorwerten gelöst.

Bei Dateien, die großen Veränderungen unterliegen, ist die
Definition der Deskriptoren genau zu diskutieren, da ja bei
Änderungsbefehlen auch die notwendigen Veränderungen im
Assoziatorbereich (Löschen des Verweises bei einem Deskriptorwert, Eintragen Satznummer bei anderem Deskriptorwert)
durchgeführt werden müssen. Bei Dateien, wo die Auswertungsmöglichkeiten das wesentliche sind und kaum Veränderungen erfolgen, kann jede nur erdenkliche Abfragemöglichkeit unterstützt werden, indem fast alle Felder einer Struktur zu
Deskriptoren (Suchbegriffen) erklärt werden. Das trifft
für alle Formen von Dokumentationen, die formatierte Informationen enthalten bzw. bei Einsatz des Datenbanksystems
zur Kontrolle von Daten und zur Datenbereinigung zu.

ADABAS ist ein System zur Be- und Verarbeitung formatierter
Daten, kann aber mit einem gewissen organisatorischen Aufwand auch für eigentlich unformatierte Daten eingesetzt
werden. Bei Speicherung und auch beim Aufsuchen von Dokumen-
ten gibt es Grundinformationen mit fixer Struktur (Ersteller,
Erstellungsdatum, Fachgebiet), Beschlagwortung, einen Text-
teil, der eine Beschreibung des jeweiligen Dokuments darstellt, und einen Verweis zur Ablagestelle. Die Speicherung
des Dokuments, des Artikels, der Buchbesprechung oder der
Verordnung direkt auf DA-Speicher ist ja wenig sinnvoll und
außerdem sehr kostspielig. Um das Problem des Thesaurusauf-
baues zu lösen, können wir wieder das multiple Feld nehmen,
das uns das Abspeichern von 191 gleichwertigen Begriffen ermöglicht. Das Problem der Synonyme, der Deklinations- bzw.
Konjungationsformen ist vom Benutzer zu lösen. Das DB-System
ermöglicht eine platzsparende Speicherung und gute Erfolge
bei Suchvorgängen.

Beispiel:

Autor	− 10-stellig, Deskriptor	
Datum	− 6-stellig, Deskriptor	formatiert
Fachgebiet	− 20-stellig, Deskriptor	
Schlagwörter max. 191 à xx Stellen (multiples Feld und Deskriptor)		

Beliebiger Text bzw. Verweis auf Externspeicher

Texte bis max. 253 Byte können in Feldern mit alphanumerischem Inhalt gespeichert werden. Längere Texte müssen unterteilt werden, wobei sich als Möglichkeiten

- Abspeichern in einem multiplen Feld
- Abspeichern als Periodengruppe

anbieten. Die einzelnen Schlagwörter können mit ADABAS Utilitys ausgewertet und geprüft werden. Beliebige Zugriffsmöglichkeiten sind bei dieser Lösung gegeben.

Ein Problem, das schon immer in der elektronischen Datenverarbeitung Bedeutung hatte, jetzt verstärkt durch die Diskussion des bald zu erwartenden Datenschutzgesetzes ins Rampenlicht rückte, ist der Datenschutz. ADABAS bietet als System mit feldweiser Verarbeitung die Möglichkeit, für jede Anwendung nur den genau benötigten Auszug aus der Gesamtdatei (=Subschema) zu definieren, was neben erhöhtem Datenschutz auch zu besseren Durchführungszeiten führt. Zusätzlich zu der Feldauswahl sind Securitymöglichkeiten einfacher Form auf Datei- und Feldbasis vorhanden. Jede Datei ist über einen Schutzschlüssel geschützt. Die Felder einer Datei sind ebenfalls über je einen Schutzschlüssel pro Feld geschützt, wobei zwischen Lese- und Schreibberechtigung unterschieden wird.

5. <u>Zusammenfassung</u>

Die im Rahmen des Magistrats der Stadt Wien eingesetzte DB-Software hat bei den derzeit realisierten EDV-Applikationen ihre Güte und Flexibilität gezeigt und wird auch allen voraussehbaren Anforderungen entsprechen.

Die Datenbank des Wiener Allgemeinen Medizinischen Informationssystems WAMIS

Dr. H. Grabner
Medizinisches Rechenzentrum Wien

1. EDV im Krankenhaus

In den letzten zwei Jahrzehnten gab es einen enormen Zuwachs
an betriebswichtigen Daten in den verschiedenen Ebenen des
Krankenhausbetriebes, daß ab einer gewissen Größe solcher
Institutionen die Bewältigung der gestellen Aufgaben - sowohl administrativ als auch die Medizin selbst betreffend -
mit konventionellen Mitteln nicht mehr möglich ist. Ver-
schärft wird die Situation dadurch, daß die einzelnen Auf-
gabengebiete immer komplizierter und spezialisierter werden,
so daß generell ein Mangel an erfahrenem Personal herrscht.

Die steigenden Kosten im Gesundheitswesen machen eine
Rationalisierung nicht nur im Sinne einer Kostenersparnis,
sondern überhaupt mit dem Ziele einer Bewältigung der gestellten Aufgaben notwendig.

Im Krankenhaus kann man zwischen zwei voneinander verschiedenen Aufgabengebieten unterscheiden

- die administrativen Aufgaben, die für den Betrieb eines
  Spitals notwendig sind

- die ärztliche und pflegerische Betreuung des Patienten.

Beide Komplexe haben naturgemäß Verbindungspunkte. Eine
EDV-gerechte Bearbeitung kann jedoch für jedes einzelne
Aufgabengebiet getrennt erfolgen.

Entsprechend den Intentionen des Kuratoriums des Fonds
"Kampf dem Krebs", das durch seine Spende den ersten
Keim zur Schaffung eines Medizinischen Rechenzentrums
im Jahre 1966 gab, und entsprechend den Aufgaben des
Bundesministeriums für Wissenschaft und Forschung, das
den eigentlichen Ausbau und die fortlaufende Arbeit
am Rechenzentrum erst ermöglicht, liegen die Hauptziele
des Instituts für Medizinische Computerwissenschaften
in der Lehre und Forschung und selbstverständlich in
der hochspezialisierten Patientenbetreuung. Unsere Erfahrungen erstrecken sich daher vornehmlich auf die Erfassung, Verarbeitung und wissenschaftliche Asuwertung
von medizinischen Patientendaten.

Das zentrale Thema des Medizinischen Rechenzentrums lag
in den letzten Jahren in der Entwicklung des Wiener
Allgemeinen Medizinischen Informationssystems WAMIS.
Das Hauptziel dieses Informationssystems ist die Speicherung aller Informationen, die an allen Patienten gewonnen werden, die das Allgemeine Krankenhaus der Stadt
Wien passieren, und die wissenschaftliche Auswertung dieses
enormen Datenmaterials. Daneben ergibt sich die Möglichkeit,
die Arbeit des am Krankenbett tätigen Arztes sowie der
Krankenschwester durch verschiedenste EDV-spezifische
Methoden und Maßnahmen zu erleichtern.

Das Fundament des Informationssystems WAMIS stellt dabei
die zentrale patientenbezogene medizinische Datenbank dar.
In dieser Datenbank laufen alle Informationen zusammen, die
am Patienten erhoben werden.

2. Medizinisches Informationssystem und Datenbank
Allgemeine Betrachtungen

Zunächst ist es notwendig eine Begriffsbestimmung vorzunehmen.

332

Datenbanken sind Systeme von Datenkollektiven (Dateien), die
nach logischen und/oder formalen Kriterien organisiert sind
mit dem Zweck die gesammelten Daten geordnet zusammenzustellen
und wiederzugeben.

COLLEN (San Frnacisco) hat ein Medizinisches Informationssystem (MIS) definiert als "A system that utilizes electronic
data processing and communication equipment to provide on-line
processing with realtime responses for patient data within one
or more general medical centers including both hospital and
outpatient services" (5). Diese eher pragmatische Definition
beinhaltet die On-line Datenverarbeitung, die allerdings nicht
Voraussetzung für ein medizinisches Informationssystem, sondern
lediglich ein Attribut darstellt.

REICHERTZ (Hannover) hat deshalb ein Medizinisches Informationssystem allgemeiner definiert als ein System zur Verwaltung von
organisierten Datenbeständen und Datenbanken zur

- Eingabe und Kontrolle der Bestände unter Verwendung von
  Prüfkriterien

- Verfügungsstellen der Daten nach vordefinierten Kriterien (16)

Die Hauptfunktion eines medizinischen Informationssystems
ist dabei die Entscheidungsunterstützung. Diese wird gewährleistet durch Berichte, Analysen und Trenderkennung und zwar
in regelmäßiger und angeforderter Weise. Unter Berichter-
stattung versteht man dabei die Wiedergabe von Daten, die
im allgemeinen nach Qualifikatoren geordnet sind. Die Analyse
gewinnt Informationen sekundärer Art aus den gespeicherten
Daten unter Verwendung vergleichender mathematischer und/oder
statistischer Verfahren. Die Analyse ist deshalb meistens die
Grundlage für Entscheidungen auf der Ebene des Spitalmanagements
sowie auf Seiten des Mediziners bei epidemiologischen Untersuchungen, diagnoseunterstützenden Verfahren, etc..

Die Trenderkennung ist die eigentliche auf das Management
ausgerichtete Funktion eines medizinischen Informationssystems. Dazu gehören

- Prognosen

- Warnung bei Grenzwertüberschreitung

- Erkennung von Regelabweichung

- Ermittlung von Korrektur- und Steuerparameter

Zu allen genannten Punkten der Trenderkennung lassen sich
sowohl für den administrativen als auch für den medizinisch-
wissenschaftlichen Sektor konkrete Anwendungsbeispiele nennen.

Viele Versuche der Errichtung von medizinischen Informationssystemen sind daran gescheitert, weil zu großer Wert auf die
Speicherung von Fakten - also die historische Funktion eines
Informationssystems - gelegt wurde und der Tatsache zu wenig
Beachtung geschenkt wurde, daß von einem Informationssystem
meistens Managementfunktion, also Entscheidungshilfen erwartet werden.

Ein medizinisches Informationssystem ist heutzutage ohne ein
entsprechendes Dialogsystem nicht mehr vorstellbar, da die
dafür notwendigen Geräte, wie Bildschirme, Drucker, Schreib-
maschine von der Computerindustrie preisgünstig angeboten
werden. Ein Dialogsystem bietet auf Grund seiner interaktiven
Möglichkeiten eine breite Palette von Vorteilen, wie rasche
Entscheidungsmöglichkeit, Auswahlmöglichkeit, Fehlerprüfungen,
etc..

Erst der Einsatz von Dialogtechniken in Verbindung mit einer
adäquaten Hardware-Ausstattung erlaubt die unmittelbare
formale und logische Überprüfung eines eingegebenen Daten-
elements. Allerdings hat jede noch so umfassende Plausibilitäts-
prüfung seine Grenze. Ein syntaktisch und **semantisch** fehlerfrei

eingegebenes Geburtsdatum zum Beispiel muß nicht unbedingt
den tatsächlichen Gegebenheiten entsprechen.

Von GUIDE und SHARE (13) sowie von CODASYL wurden Empfehlungen für die Entwicklung von Datenbanken und der zugehörigen Software herausgegeben. Die wesentlichsten Punkte
dabei sind:

- Unabhängigkeit der Datenspeicherung in bezug auf
  Darstellung und Format

- Unabhängigkeit von den Speichermedien und Zugriffsmethoden

- die Daten müssen in Relation zueinander gebracht werden
  können

- die Redundanz muß minimal gehalten werden

- eine dynamische Umstrukturierung muß möglich sein

- auf den verschiedenen Ebenen muß eine Datensicherheit
  und ein Datenschutz gewährleistet sein

- ein ausreichendes Zeit/Leistungsverhalten muß gegeben sein

- Interfacemöglichkeiten zu anderen Kollektiven müssen
  möglich sein.

Hinsichtlich der Anforderungen besteht kein wesentlicher
Unterschied zwischen medizinischer Datenbank und kommerzieller
Datenbank. Im medizinischen Bereich jedoch sind die kritischen
Datenelemente im allgemeinen von vornherein nicht erkennbar.
So weiß man zum Beispiel nicht, welche Befunde in Zukunft
wichtig sind. Dadurch ergeben sich Probleme bei der Auslagerung
oder beim Löschen von Daten. Naturgemäß stellt der administrative
Bereiche andere Anforderungen an eine medizinische Datenbak als
der wissenschaftliche Bereich. Als Beispiele seien genannt:
die Verordnung, Durchführung, Registrierung und Abrechnung von
Leistungen, verschiedene Lagerhaltungsprobleme (Apotheke, etc.),

wodurch sich beim administrativen Sektor gänzlich andere
Probleme stellen.

Charakteristisch für ein medizinisches Informationssystem
ist die Verwendung eines einheitlichen Ordnungsbegriffes,
also eines patientenbezogenen verwechslungsfreien Schlüssels.
Dieses Problem wurde weltweit auf verschiedene Weise mehr
oder minder gut gelöst. Die computergerechte Identifikation
eines Patienten muß folgende Bedingung erfüllen:

- der Patient muß über nur ihm eigene Kriterien erkennbar
  sein, wobei die Verwechslungsmöglichkeit auf ein Minimum
  herabgedrückt werden soll

- der individuell zugeordnete Ordnungsbegriff soll im
  Alltagsbetrieb gut zu handhaben und maschinell prüfbar
  sein

- eine Zusammenführung zu anderen persönlichen administrativen
  Kennzeichnungen, wie Versicherungsnummer, Personalnummer,
  etc. soll möglich sein

- der Patient soll auch im regionalen und überregionalen
  Gesundheitsinformationssystem über seinen Ordnungsbegriff
  auffindbar sein.

Diese idealisierte Bedingungen lassen sich nicht immer erfüllen, weil im einzelnen Fall die kompletten Identifikations-
kriterien möglicherweise nicht erhebbar sind. So kann das
Geburtsdatum unbekannt sein (Patienten aus den Entwicklungs-
ländern), oder der Name nicht eruierbar sein (Patient im
Koma), etc..

Infolge der komplexen Struktur medizinischer Daten ergibt
sich die Notwendigkeit neben einer formatierten Datenbank auch
nichtformatierte Elemente zuzulassen.

Die formatierte Datenbank benützt eine feste Zuordnung von
Qualifikatoren zu Positionen in den gespeicherten Strukturen.
Das nichtformatierte Datenelement ist dagegen entweder selbst-
beschreibend, oder durch Zusatzinformationen gekennzeichnet,
wodurch die weitere Verarbeitung möglich wird. Zu den
formatierten Datenelementen in der Medizin gehören die meisten
Resultate von Laboruntersuchungen, die therapeutischen Maß-
nahmen (Schlüsselsystem des Austria-Codes-Spezialitätenregisters),
Diagnosen (WHO,SNOMED,...) sowie ein Großteil der medizinischen
Daten, die in Form von Alternativentscheidungen erfaßbar sind.
Formatfreie Elemente gibt es bei vielen röntgenologischen
Untersuchungen sowie diversen Spezialbefunden, wo es nicht
oder nur schwer gelingt, das Begriffsvolumen von vornherein
abzugrenzen. Die formatierte Datenbank hat unzweifelhaft den
Vorteil der kompakten Aufzeichnungsmöglichkeit, wobei einzelne
Merkmale invertiert werden können und so einen schnellen Zu-
griff gewährleisten. Als nachteilig wird manchmal die Tatsache
angesehen, daß Speicherplatz vergeudet wird, wenn große Anteile
des möglichen Datensektors nicht vorhanden sind bzw. nicht erhoben wurden. Ein formatfreies Speichersystem hat zwar den
Vorteil der vereinfachten Aufzeichnung, man muß allerdings die
Wartung und Pflege eines je nach Problem mehr oder weniger umfangreichen Thesaurus in Kauf nehmen.

Neben diesen Möglichkeiten Daten abzuspeichern besteht im
medizinischen Bereich sehr oft die Notwendigkeit in zusätzlichen
Einheiten Relationen zwischen den Eintragungen festzulegen. In
formatierten Datenbanken wird man also zusätzlich logische
Datenstrukturen definieren, wenn es darum geht, Daten für ein
bestimmtes klinisches Problem zu definieren. Rein theoretisch
kann ein ganzes Datenbankkonzept aus Relationen aufgebaut sein.
Im medizinischen Bereich ist ein derartiges Konzept zur Zeit
noch nicht realisiert.

Ein Grundproblem des medizinischen Informationssystems und
seiner Datenbank ist mit dem Schlagwort "Record Linkage" zu

benennen. Bei umfangreichen Datenstrukturen, wie sie im
medizinischen Bereich vorkommen sowie der Möglichkeit der
in Zeit und Ort variierenden Datenerfassung kann das Zu-
sammenführen von Daten zu einem Patientendatensatz
Schwierigkeiten bereiten, wenn

- die bereits zitierte Identifikation des Patienten nicht
  umfassend und maximal eindeutig gelöst ist

- die Technik der Dateneingabe ein gewisses Maß an Fehlern
  nicht ausschließt

Auf diese Umstände hat besonders ACHESON in seinem Artikel
"Medical Record Linkage" (1) hingewiesen. Insbesonders bilden
die bereis erwähnten Validisierungstechniken in Zusammenhang
mit einer medizinischen Datenbank einen essentiellen Baustein
des Gesamtsystems.

3. WAMIS und Datenbank

Das Wiener Allgemeine Medizinische Informationssystem (1o,11)
kommt im Bereich der Universitätskliniken der medizinischen
Fakultät Wien zu Einsatz. In erster Linie handelt es sich dabei
um eine wissenschaftliche Applikation, das heißt es soll dem
Arzt ein Hilfsmittel für seine Forschung geboten werden. Naturgemäß ist dem Pflege- und Behandlungsbereich ein breiter Sektor
gewidmet. Dagegen ist der Verwaltungsbereich nahezu gänzlich
ausgeklammert.

Die Idee im Rahmen der Kliniken ein Informationssystem zu
installieren reicht bereits bis zum Jahr 1970 zurück. Damals
wurden die ersten Gehversuche in dieser Richtung mit Hilfe von
einfachen Bildschirmen (IBM 2260) unternommen. Das Informationssystem WAMIS basiert einerseits auf diesen Versuchen einer
Realzeitverarbeitung, andererseits auf den Erfahrungen, die
mit den im Jahre 1967 eingeführten Stapelbetrieb gewonnen wurden.

In der Planungsphase, die 1971 begann, stand dem Medizinischen
Rechenzentrum eine IBM-Rechenanlage der Serie 37o/145 mit
256 K zur Verfügung. Die periphere Ausrüstung bestand in
6 Plattenspeicher IBM 333o mit insgesamt 6oo Mio Bytes,
3 Bandeinheiten 341o, 1 Lochkartenleser 35o5, 1 Stanzer 3525,
1 Schnelldrucker 14o3, 35 Terminals (Bildschirmgeräte 3277
und Matrixdrucker 3286) sowie 1 Prozeßrechner 5/7 mit 24 K
Kernspeicher.

Für die Installation der Terminals an 11 Kliniken war ein
Stufenplan beginnend mit dem praktischen Einsatz des Informationssystems im Jahre 1975 vorgesehen.

Nach dem erfolgreichen Einsatz von nun 2 1/2 Jahren ergaben
sich etliche Probleme bei der Abstimmung der Systemparameter
sowie bei der Anpassung der Benützeraktivität an die zur
Verfügung stehende Hardware. Besonders der letze Punkt hat
dazu geführt, daß einerseits durch eine Aufstockung der Kernspeicher der Zentraleinheit zunächst auf 384 K, schließlich
auf 512 K erweitert wurde unter gleichzeitigem Abbau des
Stanzers und Anmietung eines bescheideneren Lesers (IBM 25o1),
andererseits eine totale Umrüstung des Zentralrechners auf
ein System 148 mit 1o24 K vorgenommen werden muß (geplant
für November 1977).

Das eingesetzte Informationssystem läßt sich durch eine
Reihe von Parametern beschreiben:

- Das System ist konventionell, also interaktiv aufgebaut

- Es handelt sich um ein gerichtetes System. Es existiert
  also ein vorgegebenes Repertoire an Programmen, das
  den Benützern zur Verfügung steht.

- Es existiert neben der rein informationell organisierten
  Datenbank auch eine operationelle Komponente. Es besteht
  dabei die Möglichkeit die während des Arbeitstages ange-
  fallenen Daten noch bestimmten Korrekturprozeduren (darunter

auch vollständiges Löschen) zu unterwerfen, was bei der rein
informationell orientierten Datenbank nicht mehr gestattet
ist.

Die patientenorientierte Datenbank bildet den zentralen Teil
des Systems WAMIS. Die Datenbank selbst ist primär formatiert
aufgebaut. Unformatierte Elemente sind zwar zugelassen, sie
werden jedoch in einem übergeordneten formatierten Datenelement
gespeichert und so der allgemeinen Struktur angepaßt. Der Grund
für diese Vorgangsweise ist darin zu suchen, daß am Medizinischen
Rechenzentrum seit dem ersten Einsatz der EDV praktisch nur mit
formatierten Daten gearbeitet wurde. Eine reine Klartextver-
arbeitung wurde nicht forciert. In allen Fällen (zum Beispiel
Röntgenbefundung) wurde stets der Versuch unternommen das
Begriffsvolumen von vornherein festzulegen, sodaß der Weg über
den Klartext entfallen konnte.

Die Datenbank des WAMIS ist hierarchisch datei-orientiert
aufgebaut. Es gibt dabei 4 Stufen. Die Verknüpfung der
einzelnen Stufen erfolgt durch Pointer entsprechend der
logischen Struktur des ganzen Systems.

Der zentrale Ordnungsbegriff ist die 15-stellige Identi-
fikationszahl, kurz I-Zahl, des Patienten. Die I-Zahl setzt
sich zusammen aus den ersten 6 Buchstaben des Geburtsnamens,
dem Geburtsdatum, dem Geschlecht und der Geburtsreihung im
Falle von Mehrlingsgeburten. Für den Fall, daß eine Doppel-
belegung auftritt, wird durch eine Formulierung die Eindeutigkeit sichergestellt. Mit Hilfe dieses Ordnungsbegriffes
ist es möglich, alle anfallenden Daten in einem Patientendatensatz zusammenzuführen, womit das Problem des "Medical
Record Linkage" zumindest für diesen Bereich hinreichend
gelöst ist. Im täglichen Gebrauch ist die I-Zahl auf Grund
ihrer Länge etwas umständlich zu handhaben. Aus diesem Grund
wurde eine wesentliche kürzere Arbeitsnummer eingeführt.
Es handelt sich dabei um eine fünfstellige Nummer, die unter

Hinzuziehung einer Prüfziffer modulo 11 zu einer sechs-
stelligen Nummer erweitert wird. Die Arbeitsnummer dient
in erster Linie für den täglichen Arbeitsablauf zur
leichteren Identifizierung des Patienten. Die I-Zahl
ist auf Grund ihrer Eindeutigkeit gewissermaßen "ewig"
in der Datenbank registriert, die Arbeitsnummer hingegen
findet nur temporäre Verwendung, da der pro Klinik zur
Verfügung stehende Nummernkreis begrenzt ist.

Sowohl mit der I-Zahl als auch mit der Arbeitsnummer
kann eine Anfrage an die Datenbank gestartet werden.
Die beiden Ordnungsbegriffe werden in getrennten ISAM-
Dateien in der ersten Stufe der File-Hierarchie gespeichert.

Um Übertragungs- und Schreibfehler bei der Arbeitsnummer
auszuschalten, wird im Spitalsbereich eine Metallfolie
benützt, die alle relevanten personenbezogenen Daten enthält. Das Beschriften dieser Folie erfolgt dabei voll-
automatisch mittels konventionellen elektrischen Kugel-
kopfschreibmaschinen, die über eine Zusatzeinrichtung an
den Prozeßrechner S/7 und somit an das Zentralsystem 37o
angeschlossen sind.

Der Datenbankzugriff sieht nun folgendermaßen aus (siehe
Abb. 1). Beginnend mit der Arbeitsnummer (in etwa 9o% aller
Zugriffe der Fall) werden zunächst die personenbezogenen
Daten eingelesen. Daraufhin wird die Sammeldatei gelesen
und nach dem gewünschten Resultat zunächst global gesucht.
Ist eine entsprechende Eintragung vorhanden und stimmt diese
auch in bezug auf die gewünschte Zeit, dann wird je nach
Problemstellung beginnend mit dem zeitlich ersten Resultat
der Verlauf bis zum letzten Wert gelesen oder sofort das
Letztergebnis ausgewählt, wobei noch die Möglichkeit besteht, die zeitlich unmittelbar davor liegenden Resultate
zu Vergleichszwecken heranzuziehen. Beide Zugriffsarten also

beginnend mit dem zeitlich ersten bzw. mit dem letzten
Ergebnis, kommen in der Praxis häufig vor. Daraus
resultiert die Notwendigkeit einer sogenannten evolu-
torischen Pointerverkettung der Daten, also einer Verkettung in beide Richtungen, zeitlich aufsteigend sowie
absteigend.

Die in der Sammeldatei registrierten "Resultat-Ordnungs-
begriffe" lassen sich natürlich günstig invertieren.
In der medizinischen Praxis kommt es sehr oft vor, daß
man für wissenschaftliche Studien alle Patienten mit einer
bestimmten Diagnose bearbeiten möchte, was dann natürlich
leicht zu bewerkstelligen ist.

Auf der zweiten Stufe befinden sich die Dateien für alle
personellen und referenz-bezogenen Daten, das heißt, neben
den personenbezogenen Daten, wie Name, Adresse, usw. befinden sich hier die Angaben über die Spitalsaufenthalte,
Ambulanzbesuche sowie die kritischen Daten, wie Blutgruppe,
usw.. Ausgehend von der I-Zahl bzw. von der Arbeitsnummer
erreicht man über Pointeradressen die zugehörigen Datensätze.

Auf der dritten Stufe befindet sich eine Datei, die eine
Zusammenfassung aller am Patienten erhobenen Daten enthält.
Dieser Teil der Datenbank ist besonders wichtig für den
täglichen Arbeitsablauf. Es gelingt so sehr leicht - d.h.
mit nur einem Zugriff - , ein umfassendes Bild über den
gegenwärtigen Stand der durchgeführten Untersuchungen,
therapeutischen Maßnahmen, registrierten Krankheiten zu bekommen, ohne den mühsamen Weg über die Beurteilung und Be-
wertung der Einzelresultate, die in der Datei der vierten
Stufe gespeichert sind, gehen zu müssen. Im konkreten enthält eine Eintragung in dieser Sammeldatei der dritten Stufe,
z.B. bei einer Laboruntersuchung, neben einem Code, der die

Tatsache "Laborresultat" kennzeichnet, das Datum der letzten
Durchführung, weiters zwei Pointeradressen zum Anfang bzw.
Ende der Kette der Resultate zu dieser Laboruntersuchung.
Die Resultate sind dann in einer Datei auf der vierten Stufe
registriert (siehe Abb.2).

Es wurde eingangs erwähnt, daß neben der informationellen
Datenbank eine operationelle Komponente existiert. Im
täglichen Routinebetrieb - insbesondere auf dem Labor-
sektor - besteht die Notwendigkeit die Resultate einer
abschließenden visuellen Prüfung zu unterziehen. Das
Eliminieren fehlerhafter Ergebnisse bzw- Ändern einzelner
Werte bei besonderen Konstellationen ist unumgänglich
notwendig. Da das Hinzufügen und Eliminieren von Resultaten
in einer Datenbank aus Sicherheitsgründen während des On-
line-Betriebes möglichst unterbleiben soll, wurde folgender
Weg eingeschlagen. Alle Resultate des Arbeitstages werden
in ein eigens dafür vorgesehene Datei sequentiell eingetragen.
Gleichzeitig wird im Vorgängerelement des gleichen Typs der
Pointer der zum Nachfolger zeigt, gesetzt und somit die Verbindung hergestellt. Desgleichen erfolgt die Eintragung der
Pointers in der Sammeldatei der dritten Stufe bzw. wird ein
neues Element in der Sammeldatei eingetragen, falls es das
erste Resultat überhaupt ist. Grundsätzlich besteht also die
Strategie darin, daß in der informationellen Datenbank
während des On-line Betriebes nur Pointer zu Nachfolger-
elementen eingetragen werden. Für diese Pointer ist bereits
ein fixer Platz vorgesehen. Neuzugänge oder Streichungen
kommen dabei nicht vor. Eine Streichung ist nur bei den
Daten in der Tagesdatei möglich. Die Übernahme der Tages-
daten in die informationelle Datenbank erfolgt dann im
Stapelbetrieb nach Abschluß der On-line Verarbeitung. Sollte
trotzdem ein Datenelement übernommen werden, dann besteht
nur die Möglichkeit einen Deleatur-Kode an einer vordefinierten
Stelle zu setzen.

4. CICS, DB-Zugriff, DB-Schreiben, DB-Sicherheit

Wie aus den Ausführungen des letzten Abschnittes hervorgeht, ist die Datenbank des Systems WAMIS speziell den medizinischen Bedürfnissen angepaßt und dementsprechend strukturiert, es handelt sich also nicht um eine Standarddatenbank sondern um ein selbstprogrammiertes System. Die Steuerung des Teleprocessing-Netzes erfolgt dabei mit Hilfe des Betriebssystems CICS. Der Gund für die Wahl des operierenden Systems CICS lag einerseits an der Größe der Zentraleinheit zur Zeit der Planung, andererseits an der unproblematischen Handhabung der Terminalperipherie. Erst zu einem viel späteren Zeitpunkt - nämlich zu einem Zeitpunkt als das Informationssystem bereits im Rountinebetrieb eingesetzt wurde -, ergab sich die Möglichkeit unter CICS das Datenbankzugriffssystem DL/1 zu verwenden.

Eine auf Basis von DL/1 aufgebaute medizinische Datenbank hat natürlich den Vorteil, daß alle Probleme der Reorganisation, des Restarts, Logging, usw. durch entsprechende Utilities einfach bewältigt werde- können. Die entsprechenden Routinen mußten natürlich bei der "handgestrickten" Datenbank des WAMIS programmiert werden. Weiters läßt sich aus der aufgezeigten Struktur der Datenbank des Systems WAMIS sowie auch an Hand von analogen Systemen im europäischen Raum leicht erkennen, daß eine medizinische Datenbank segment-hierarchisch strukturierbar ist. Zum gegenwärtigen Zeitpunkt werden bereits Systeme, wie zum Beispiel das System HCS (Health Care Support), mit einer solchen Struktur angeboten.

Es gibt allerdings einige Punkte, die für die handgestrickte Datenbank sprechen. Darunter sind zu erwähnen

- die Minimierung der Filezugriffe für die Schwerpunkts-
  anwendungen

344

- die optimale Anpassung an die medizinischen Gegebenheiten

- die effiziente Ausnützung des Speicherplatzes

Zusammenfassend läßt sich zum gegenwärtigen Zeitpunkt die
Idee der handgestrickten medizinischen Datenbank jedoch
nicht mehr vertreten, weil die zur Verfügung stehenden
Softwarepakete den Aufwand an Manpower nicht mehr rechtfertigen, auch dann nicht, wenn man einzelne Abstriche
in der Zieldefinition für das Gesamtsystem machen muß,
weil vielleicht die lokalen Gegebenheiten nicht anpaßbar
sind oder ein anderer Grund vorliegt.

Angepaßt an das Konzept der Datenbank für das System WAMIS
wurden entsprechende zentrale Routinen für das Schreiben,
den Zugriff sowie für das Logging verfaßt. In allen An-
wendungs-Programmen werden diese Zentralroutinen in Form
von Unterprogrammen verwendet. Die Struktur der Datenbank
ist somit unabhängig von den Anwendungsprogrammen. Darüberhinaus sind die Anwendungsprogramme praktisch unabhängig
von der Datenspeicherung. Die großen zentralen Routinen
des Systems arbeiten auf "Anonym-Basis", das heißt losge-
löst von eigentlichem Dateninhalt. Strukturänderungen innerhalb
der medizinischen Daten haben deshalb keinerlei Einfluß auf
die Verarbeitungsprogramme. Betrachtet man die eingangs
zitierten Empfehlungen von GUIDE und SHARE, dann ergeben sich
bei der Datenbank des Systems WAMIS nur Probleme, wenn man
Daten auf der untersten Stufe miteinander in Beziehung bringen
möchte. Dies ist dann nur mit Hilfe von übergeordneten Pointern
möglich, die natürlich in allen Reorganisationsprogrammen
Veränderungen nach sich ziehen. Die Anwendungsprogramme selbst
sind zum Großteil in der Assembler-Sprache (etwa 7o%) geschrieben, der Rest in PL/1.

Im folgenden soll nun auf jene Probleme hingewiesen werden,
die mit den Schlagworten "security" und "confidentiality"
beschrieben werden können. Es handelt sich hier um zwei
verschiedene Formen der Sicherheit, nämlich einerseits
um eine innere Sicherheit, worunter man den korrekten Betrieb des Informationssystems versteht, und andererseits um
eine äußere Sicherheit, womit der Schutz gegen unbefugtes
Benützen des Informationssystems, vor allem seiner Datenbank,
gemeint ist. Gerade bei einem medizinischen Informationssystem handelt es sich bei diesen beiden Formen der Sicherheit um immens wichtige Punkte. Die innere Sicherheit, also
die "security" im engerer Sinne, besteht ihrerseits aus drei
Komponenten: Zuverlässigkeit, Verfügbarkeit und technische
Sicherheit (sog.RAS-Feature). Die Zuverlässigkeit ist einerseits durch die entsprechenden Hardwareeinrichtungen gegeben,
wird jedoch andererseits bei den Daten durch geeignete progra,,-
technische Maßnahmen, wie prüfbarer Ordnungsbegriff (Prüfziffer modulo 11), Kennsätze etc. gewährleistet.

Die technische Sicherheit des Systems WAMIS basiert auf
einer Journaldatei auf einem Magnetband, wo alle zulässigen
Veränderungen in der informationellen Datenbank sowie alle
Neuzugänge in der entsprechenden operationellen Komponente
ein zweites Mal registriert werden. Die Datenbank selbst
wird in einen Tripelsystem geführt. Der sich daraus ergebende
relativ hohe Aufwand ist in jedem Fall gerechtfertigt.

Die Verfügbarkeit von Informationen richtet sich in erster
Linie nach Fragen der Wirtschaftlichkeit und damit der zur
Verfügung stehenden Hardware. Der Einsatz eines Duplexsystems
verbunden mit einem 24-Stundenbetrieb wäre zum gegenwärtigen
Zeitpunkt ein ausgesprochener Luxus. Das Informationssystem
WAMIS steht den Benützern etwa 1o Stunden am Tag zur Ver-
fügung.

Die äußere Sicherheit des Systems, also die "Confidentiality", stellt bei einem medizinischen Informationssystem ein besonderes Problem dar, weil der Aufwand, der mit dem Einsatz eines derartigen Systems verbunden ist, nur dann zu rechtfertigen ist, wenn das System extrem benutzerfreundlich ist. Andererseits muß ein gewisser Schutz der Daten gegen unbefugte Zugriffe vorhanden sein. Beim System WAMIS wurde dazu folgender Weg eingeschlagen. Da die Datenbank patientenorientiert ist und das medizinische Auskunftssystem den zentralen Teil des Systems darstellt, werden primär alle damit verbundenenProgramme allen Benützern zur Verfügung gestellt. Dies entspricht auch der üblichen Gepflogenheit, daß der Kliniker eine Krankengeschichte einer anderen Klinik entleihen bzw. einsehen kann, wenn es die ärztlichen Maßnahmen erforderlich machen. Es ist allerdings möglich, daß eine Klinik den Zugriff zu ihren Daten allen Nichtklinikangehörigen teilweise oder ganz verwehrt. Dies ist zum Beispiel bei den psychiatrischen Fächern der Fall, wo der Zugriff grundsätzlich nur an hauseigenen Bildschirmgeräten möglich ist, unter Einhaltung der übrigen Sicherheitsroutine, wie Paßwort, etc..

Handelt es sich um eine wissenschaftliche Auswertung der Datenbank, dann stehen dem Kliniker nur die Daten seiner eigenen Klinikdatenbank zur Verfügung. Ausnahmen davon bilden nur die interklinischen Studien. Es ist also unmöglich, daß die Daten einer Klinik von einer anderen Klinik ausgewertet werden, ohne daß die erste Klinik dazu ihr Plazet gegeben hat.

5. Komponenten des Systems WAMIS

Rund um die Datenbank des Systems WAMIS wurden entsprechend der medizinischen Anforderungen verschiedene Module aufgebaut. Im einzelnen handelt es sich dabei um

a) Programmsystem zur <u>Unterstützung der täglichen Routine-
   arbeiten</u> am Krankenbett bzw. in den Ambulanzen (14,15).

b) Wiener Laborsystem <u>WIELAB</u>. Dieses System dient der voll-
   automatischen Erfassung von Laborresultaten mit Hilfe
   des Prozeßrechners S/7 (3).

c) <u>Medizinisches Dokumentationssystem</u>. Hier werden alle
   medizinischen Daten (Alternativdaten, diverse numerische
   Werte, freie Texte) in einer zentralen Routine erfaßt
   (12,17,18).

d) <u>Auskunftssystem</u>. Dieses System dient der patientenbezogenen
   Auskunft. Dabei ist auch eine Sprachauskunft geplant
   (Bancsich).

e) <u>Computerünterstütztes Dieagnosesystem</u>. Dieses System benützt die Datenbank und baut aus dem Symptombild des
   Patienten einen Diagnose- und Untersuchungsvorschlag
   auf (2,6).

f) <u>Auswertungssystem WAMAS</u>. Neben allgemein gehaltenen Aus-
   zählungsroutinen werden hier die verschiedenen parametrischen bzw. parameterfreien Tests eingesetzt. Hinzu
   kommen noch verschiedene Verfahren zur Prognoseunter-
   stützung (7).

g) <u>Biosignal-Verarbeitungs-Systeme</u>, wie vollautomatische
   Geburtenüberwchung (8,9), Lungenfunktionsüberwachung (4),

6. Erfahrungen

Der Einsatz der EDV in der Medizin, insbesonders der eines
medizinischen Informationssystems, stellt in jedem Fall ein
gewisses Risiko dar, weil der Erfolg nur dann garantiert
werden kann, wenn es zu einer harmonischen Einheit von
klinischer Organisation und Computeranwendung kommt. Nach

Abschluß der Planungsphase wurde praktisch an 11 Kliniken
der EDV-Betrieb über das Informationssystem WAMIS aufgenommen. Während des zweieinhalbjährigen praktischen Einsatzes wurden verschiedenste Erkenntnisse gewonnen, sowie
einzelne Kritiken geäußert, die Auswirkungen auf die
Organisation und den Routinebetrieb haben. Im wesentlichen
ergeben sich dabei 4 Schwerpunkte:

1. Die EDV-Unterstützung für 11 Universitätskliniken bringt
   eine Vielfalt an organisatorischen Problemen mit sich,
   weil die einzelnen Kliniken unterschiedlich organisatorisch strukturiert sind. Ein Klinikum als Ganzes gesehen ist mit einem lebenden Organismus vergleichbar,
   der seine Dynamik aus dem Wechselspiel verschiedenster
   Einflußgrößen bezieht. Der für die EDV notwendige
   Formatierungsprozeß muß daher soweit gehen, daß selbst
   Änderungen der Organisationsparameter den Computerein-
   satz nicht unmöglich machen. Aus diesem Grund erwuchsen
   bei den Anwendungsprogrammen zum Teil erhebliche Schwierigkeiten und Terminverzögerungen. Zum anderen Teil war für
   für Betreuung der Kliniken das dafür notwendige Personal
   nicht vorhanden. Auf Grund der rechtlichen Stellung der
   EDV-Abteilung konnten organisatorische Konzepte nur auf
   Basis von Beratung und Empfehlung erstellt werden. Die
   Durchführung aller EDV-spezifischen Maßnahmen war deshalb
   vom "Good Will" der Klinik abhängig. Da natürlich die
   Kliniken ein lebhaftes Interesse am Computer haben, konnten
   letztlich alle Schwierigkeiten erfolgreich überwunden werden.

2. Das gesamte Informationssystem ist modular aufgebaut.
   Jede Klinik kann die für ihre Zwecke notwendigen und
   interessanten Bausteine selektieren und einsetzen. Diese
   Tatsache resultiert jedoch in einer großen sachlichen Vielfalt, daß heißt in einer Vielfalt an Transaktionen, Programmen, Tabellen. Dies steht in gewissem Widerspruch zum

zum Steuerungssystem CICS, das bei vorgegebener Anzahl von
Terminals am effizientestes arbeitet, wenn einge wenige
Transaktionen aktiv sind. Für die EDV ensteht ferner bei
beschränktem Personal die Schwierigkeit der Wartung und
Koordination, so daß es günstiger erscheint primär ein
Detailziel beim Einsatz eines medizinischen Informations-
systems anzusteuern als von vornherein eine Gesamtlösung
zu planen.

3) Die weitgehende organisatorische Selbständigkeit der
Kliniken verbunden mit vielfältigen EDV-Applikationen
hatte eine rasche, aber auch unkoordinierte Ausweitung
des EDV-Einsatzes zur Folge. Da nicht zuletzt aus
finanziellen Gründen die Rechnerleistung nicht im gleichen
Umfang wachsen konnte, ergaben sich Engpässe vor allem bei
der Antwortzeit, die bei Spitzenbelastungen des Systems ein
für den Routinebetrieb nicht mehr vertretbares Ausmaß erreicht hat. Durch eine Erweiterung des Kernspeichers
einerseits, aber auch Straffung der Benützeraktivitäten
andererseits konnte hier eine Verbesserung erzielt werden.
Eine vollständige Sanierung des Antwortzeitproblems ist
erst mit Einsatz des Systems 148 zu erwarten.

4) Auf Grund der unterschiedlichen medizinischen Aufgaben der
einzelnen Kliniken ergeben sich stark unterschiedliche Anforderungen bezüglich der Speicherung der Patientendaten.
Als Voraussetzung für einen sinnvollen Routinebetrieb ver-
langten mehrere Kliniken den direkten Zugriff zu Patientendaten, die bisher in Bandarchiven gespeichert waren (zum
Teil zurückgehend bis 1965). Die Übernahme dieser Daten
auf Plattendateien hatte zur Folge, daß eine ungleichmäßige
Verteilung der Belegung entstand, und letzten Endes die für
Neuzugänge vorgesehene Kapazität starken Einschränkungen
unterworfen wurde.

Die weitere Entwicklung des Systems WAMIS läßt sich im
Moment nicht exakt angeben, weil sehr viele Kompoenten
zusammenwirken, deren Konsequenzen im gemeinsamen Zusammenhang nicht restlos geklärt sind. Darunter sind
zu nennen

- Einsatz des Zentralrechners 148

- Umstrukturierung der Datenbank von Datei-hierarchie
  auf Segmenthierarchie

- Einsatz von HCS

- Integration der Verwaltung

- Neubau des AKH

Zusammenfassend läßt sich sagen, daß die ursprüngliche
Zieldefinition des Systems WAMIS in der gegenwärtigen
Ausbaustufe erreicht wurde.

7. <u>Literatur:</u>

1. ACHESON, E.D.:
   Medical Record Linkage
   Meth. Inform. Med. 8 (1969), 1-6

2. ADLASSNIG, K.P., GERGELY, T., GRABNER, H., GRABNER, G.:
   A computer assisted system for diagnostic decision
   making - On line usage of the database of the medical
   information system WAMIS
   Medinfo 77, Toronto, p. 213-218.

3. BANCSICH, J.:
   WIELAB - A New Hardware Concept and its Related Software
   Support for Automatic Sample-identification and Conver-
   sational Input in Clinical Laboratories
   Medinfo 74, p. 969-974

4. BANCSICH, J., GEIER, R.:
   Hierarchical processor structures for on-line computer
   support in lung-function test-labs
   Medinfo 77, Toronto, p. 1067.

5. COLLEN, M.F.:
   General Requirements for a Medical Information System (MIS)
   Proceedings of a Conference on Medical Information Systems,
   San Francisco. 1970, p. 1-16

6. DORAU, F., GRABNER, H., GRABNER, G.:
   A medical information system as aid to computer
   assisted diagnosis
   Medcomp 77, Berlin, p. 659-666

7. DORDA, W., KOGLER, W.:
   WAMAS - statistische Auswertung einer patienten-
   bezogenen Datenbank
   Symposium Schloß Reisenburg, Mai 77

8. GEIER, R.:
   Computer Assisted Perinatal Intensive Care:
   Software concepts and Hardware Requirements
   IRIA-Symposium on Medical Data Processing
   Toulouse 1975, 167-179

9. GEIER, R.:
   Entwurf und Realisierung eines Systems zur rechner-
   unterstützten perinatalen Intensivüberwachung
   EDV in Medizin und Biologie 2 (1976), 47-52

10. GRABNER, H., GRABNER, G.:
    Aims and structure of the Vienna General Medical
    Information system WAMIS
    Medinfo 74, p. 375-379

11. GRABNER, H.:
    Wiener Allgemeines Medizinisches Informationssystem (WAMIS)
    Münch.Med.Wschr. 117 (1975), 1765-1768

12. GRABNER, H., LEJHANEC, J.:
    Das universelle Dokumentationssystem im Rahmen des
    Informationssystems WAMIS
    EDV in Medizin und Biologie 2 (1976), 53-56

13. Joint Guide-Share Data Base Requirement Group
    Data Base Management Systems Requirements
    Share SSD 208 (1970), 43-110

14. MARKSTEINER, A.:
Prerequisits and programs for on-line data
acquisition in clinical laboratories, connected with
the medical information-system WAMIS
EDV in Medizin und Biologie 4 (1974), 106-110

15. MARKSTEINER, A., BANCSICH, J., GRABNER, H.:
Einsatz der EDV im Krankenhaus zur Unterstützung
der täglichen Routine-Arbeiten
Ärztl. Lab. 20 (1974), 426-429

16. REICHERTZ, P.L.:
The Medical System Hannover (MSH) in Collen, M.:
Hospital Computer Systems, New York (1974), 598-661

17. SEIDL, A., KUPKA, S., GRABNER, H., GRING, H.:
Die Dokumentation geburtshilflicher Krankengeschichten
mit Hilfe von Bildschirmterminals im Rahmen des
Informationssystems WAMIS
Wiener Klin. Wochenschrift 88 (1976), 257-261

18. WALEK, H., KOLARZ, G., HOHENECKER, H., CERCELY, T.,
GRABNER, H., THUMB, N.:
Bildschirmdokumentation von Anamnese und physikalischem
Befund bei Rheumakranken
Acta Med. Austriaca 5 (1976), 166-170

8. Anhang

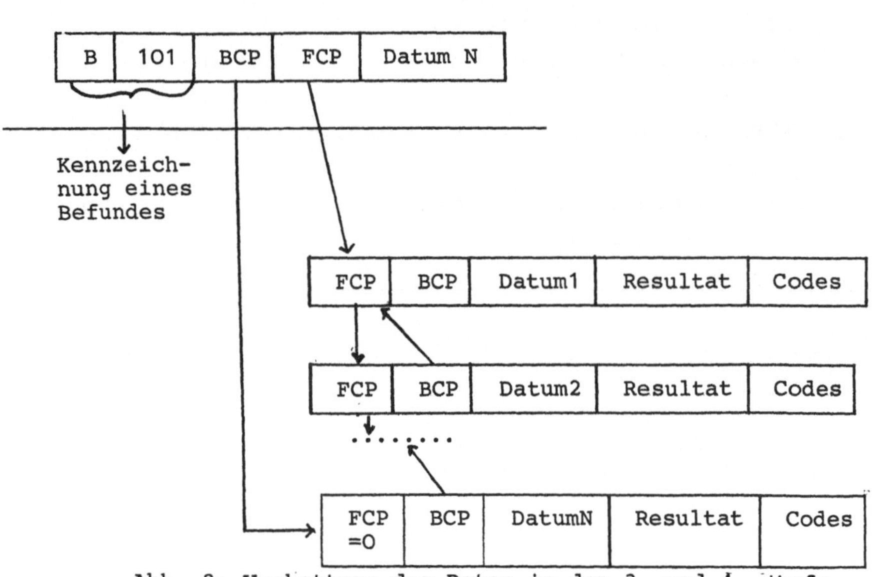

Abb. 1: Schematische Darstellung der Datenbank des Systems WAMIS

Abb. 2: Verkettung der Daten in der 3. und 4. Stufe der Datenbank

FCP.... Vorwärts-Adreßpointer

BCP.... Rückwärts-Adreßpointer

IDMS
Integrated Database Management System

J.P. Schoon
F.A. Mayer KG Wilhelmshaven

Das Datenbanksystem IDMS ist als Kernstück der ADV/ORGA Datenmanagement Systeme zu verstehen (s. Abb. 10).

Abb. 10

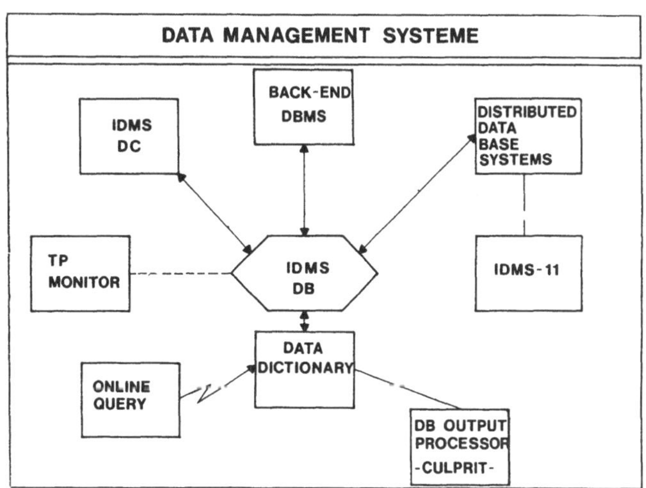

Es läuft für alle IBM-Systeme ab 360/30 und 370/115 für die Betriebssysteme DOS, DOS/VS, OS, OS/VS, MVS. Für Siemens steht das
System für die Betriebssysteme BS1000 und BS2000 zur Verfügung.
Für Univac-Systeme besteht die Möglichkeit, unter VMOS oder VS9
zu arbeiten. Digital Equipment bietet für die PDP11 IDMS unter
dem Betriebssystem IAS/RS an. ICL bietet ebenfalls IDMS für die
Systeme 4/1900/2900 an. Kompatibilität besteht weitgehend zu anderen Codasyl-Systemen, so daß mit IDMS die gewünschte Hardware-
Unabhängigkeit erreicht wird.

In einer DB/DC Umgebung bietet sich der Einsatz des integrierten
IDMS-DB/DC-Systems an. Anwender haben aber ebenfalls die Möglich-
keit, mit den gängigen auf dem Markt verfügbaren TP-Monitoren
(CICS, Interkomn, Shadow, Taskmaster, TICS, TCSS) zu arbeiten.

IDMS stellt eine Realisierung des DBTG-Vorschlages dar. Die
Codasyl-Spezifikationen sind in ihren wesentlichen Funktionen im
IDMS realisiert.

Basis des Systems ist die von Codasyl vorgeschlagene DDL (Data
Definition Language) zur Schema-/Subschema-Beschreibung und außerdem die DML (Data Manipulation Language), deren symbolische Befehle in Cobol, PL1 oder Assembler eingebettet sind. Es handelt sich
um ein Host-Language-System.

Die physische Beschreibung der Datenspeicherung wird durch die
Device Media Control Language durchgeführt.

In der Schemabeschreibung werden die Beschreibungen der Datenstrukturen durchgeführt. Das Subschema - als Untermenge der Schema-
beschreibung - definiert die logische Sicht eines Programmes in
die Datenbank und definiert außerdem Datenschutzklauseln und Zu-
griffsrestriktionen für dieses Programm (s. Abb. 20).

Abb. 20

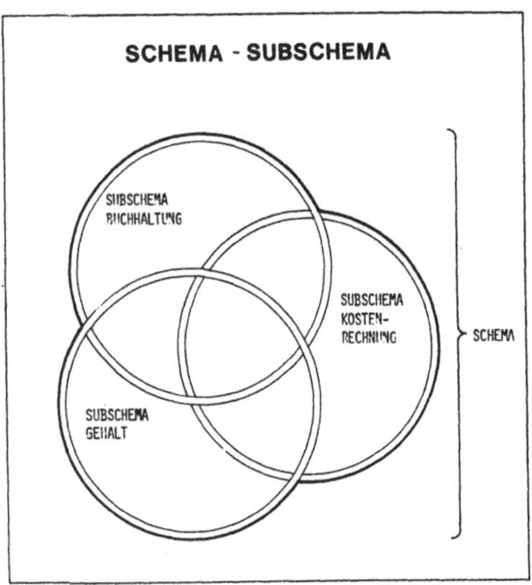

Die kleinste Verknüpfungseinheit innerhalb einer Datenstruktur
ist der Set. Ein Set besteht aus einem bestimmten Exemplar einer
Satzart (Owner) und n-Exemplaren anderer Satzarten (Member).

Abb. 30

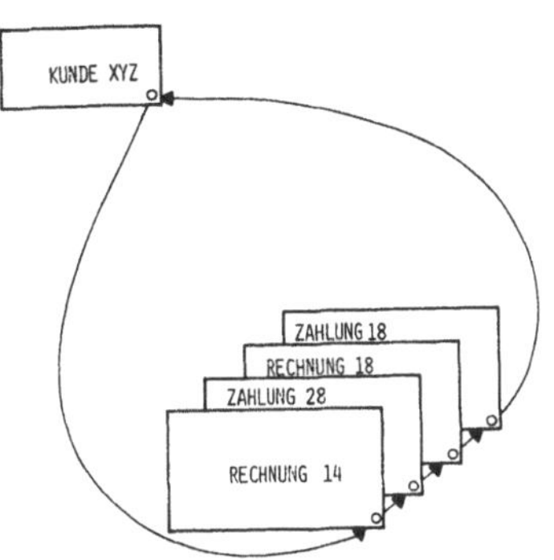

Die formale Darstellung des Sets ist in Abb. 40 gezeigt. Die
Pfeilspitze deutet immer auf den Member und hat keinerlei Beziehung zur Verarbeitungsrichtung. Die Auflösung einer formalen Darstellung des Sets Kunde/Auftrag wird in Abb. 50 gezeigt. Weitere
Beispiele der Set-Verknüpfungen (Darstellung 1: N) sind in Abb. 60
gezeigt.

Abb. 40

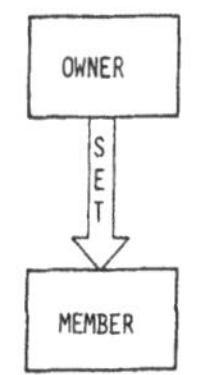

Abb. 50

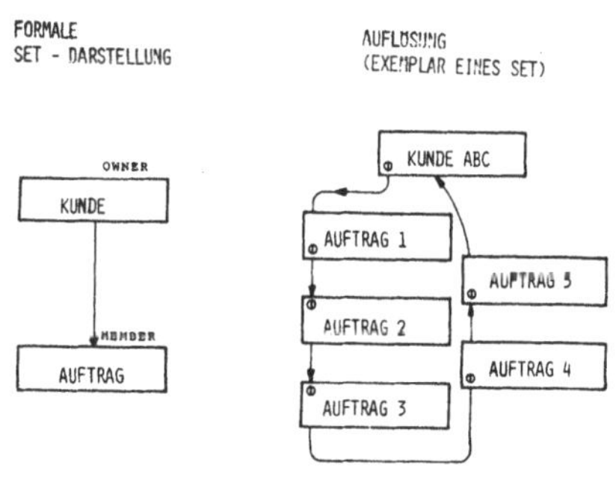

Abb. 60

Beispiele für SET-Verknüpfungen

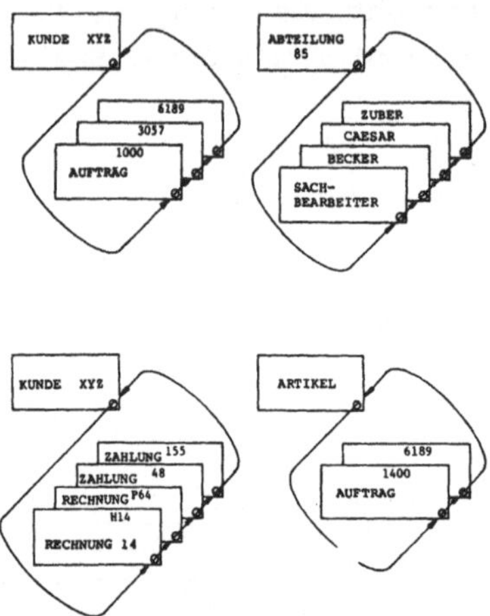

N:N-Darstellungen sind durch Einfügen eines logischen Verbindungs-
segmentes möglich.

Mehrere Sets untereinander verknüpft in beliebiger, anwendungs-
bezogener Ordnung ergeben dann die Datenbankstruktur. Ein Beispiel
einer Datenstruktur (aufgelöste Darstellung) wird in Abb. 70 gezeigt.

Abb. 70

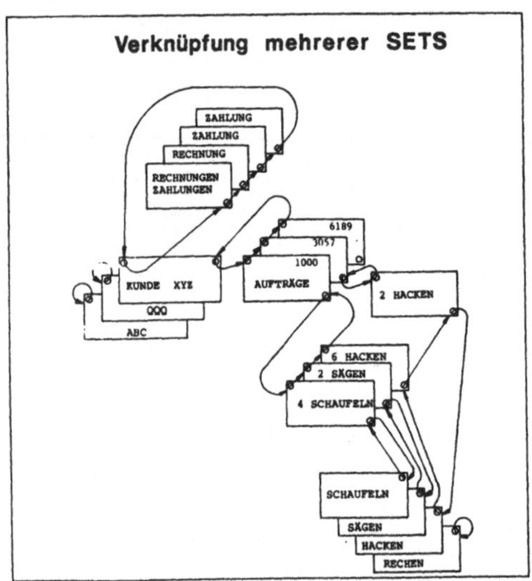

IDMS bietet bezüglich der Strukturdarstellungen keine Restriktionen. Alle Strukturen können anwendungsbezogen ausgewählt werden. Das System paßt sich den Bedürfnissen einer Anwendung an. Es ist nicht erforderlich, Datenstrukturen in die Konvention des Datenbanksystems zu pressen. Die folgende Darstellung der verschiedenen Strukturvarianten mag bei einer ersten Betrachtung keine wesentliche Aussage bringen; erst ein Vergleich unterschiedlicher DB-Systeme zeigt dann in vielen Fällen die nicht ohne weiteres sichtbare Einschränkung einzelner Systeme hinsichtlich einer flexiblen Datenstrukturierung. Die Möglichkeiten der flexiblen Datenstrukturierung erscheint als das wesentliche Kriterium für den Einsatz eines DB-Systems. Im IDMS sind folgende Strukturen denkbar:

Hierarchische Struktur

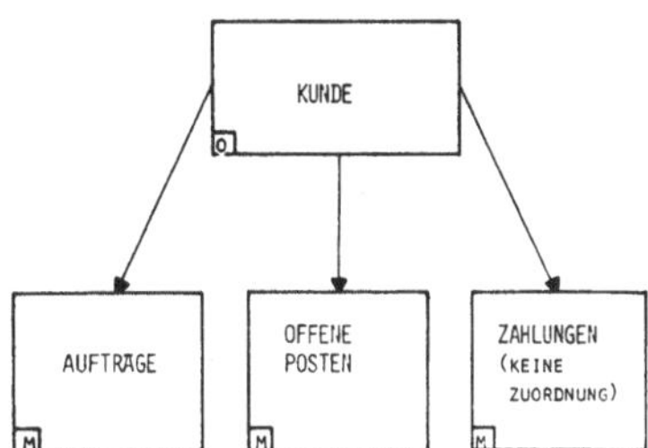

Das Kriterium einer Hierarchie ist die Abhängigkeit mehrerer untergeordneter Sätze von einem übergeordneten Satz.

Hierarchische Struktur mehrerer Ebenen

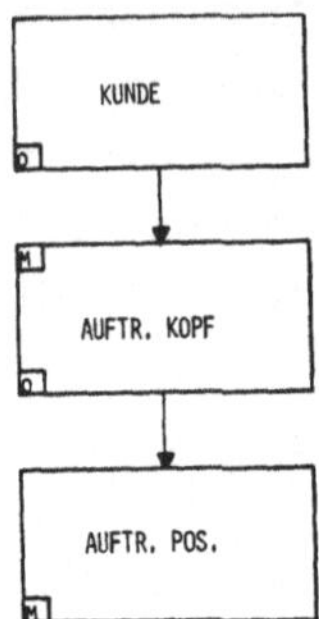

Diese Struktur stellt eine Erweiterung der vorstehend beschriebenen hierarchischen Struktur dar. Sie kann sich über 3 bis n
Stufen erstrecken. Wesentliches Kriterium dieser Struktur liegt
in der Verwendung eines Satzes sowohl in übergeordneter als auch
in untergeordneter Position - eine Variante, die nicht bei allen
DB-Systemen zulässig ist.

Hierarchische Struktur mit unterschiedlichen Satzarten/-Längen

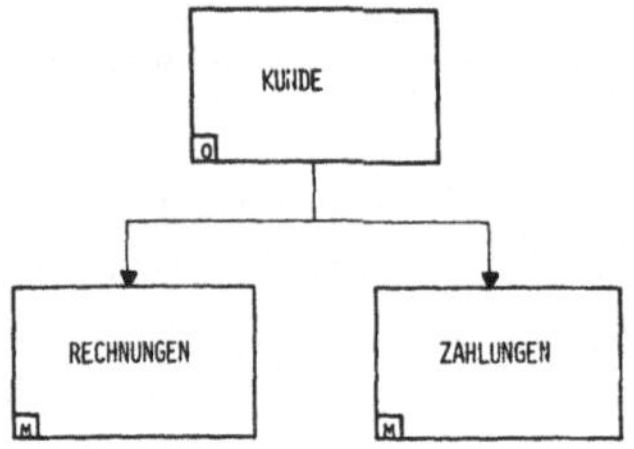

Es ist häufig notwendig, in einer hierarchischen Struktur den
übergeordneten Satz mit Sätzen unterschiedlicher Satzart und
Satzlänge (in der konventionellen Speichertechnik: Sätze aus verschiedenen Dateien) zu verknüpfen. Das gilt ebenfalls für die
Verknüpfung von Sätzen mit variabler Satzlänge.

<u>Mehrfach-Verkettung (z.B. Stücklistenstruktur)</u>

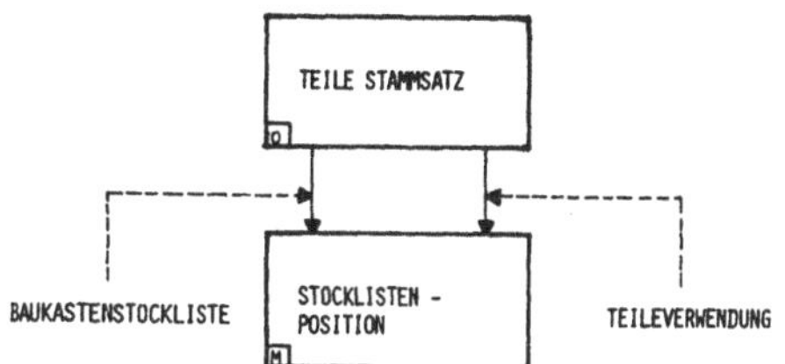

Eine Mehrfach-Verkettung wird z.B. beim Aufbau von Stücklisten (Baukastenstücklisten und Teileverwendung) für die Fertigungs-industrie benötigt.

IDMS kann beliebig viele Verknüpfungen, die nach unterschied-lichen Kriterien aufgebaut wurden, zwischen n-Satzarten dar-stellen.

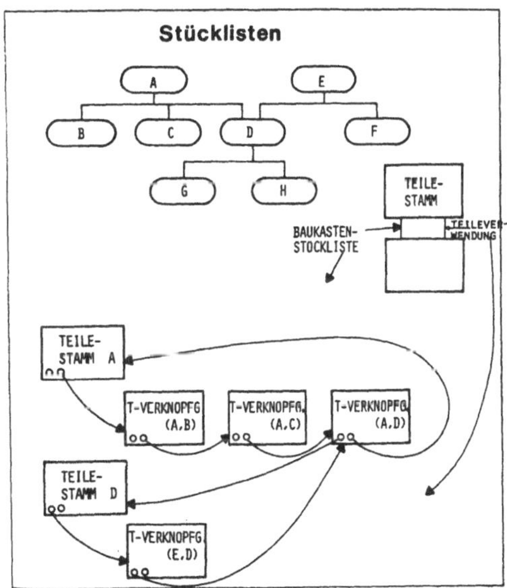

Netzstruktur

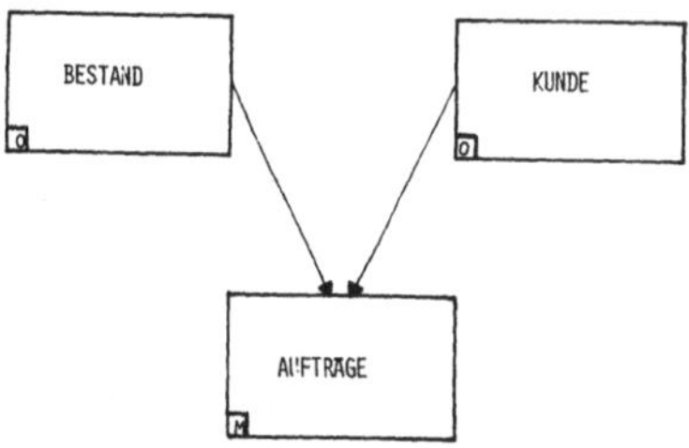

Merkmal einer Netzstruktur ist die Abhängigkeit eines untergeordneten Satzes von 2 bis n übergeordneten Sätzen. Die bisher
gezeigten hierarchischen Strukturen sind als Untermenge der Netzstruktur zu betrachten.

Indexsequentielle Speicherung

IDMS bietet die Möglichkeit, die logische und physische Sequenz
identisch zu halten und eine Adressierung über Primär-Index und
n-Sekundär-Indizes zu verwirklichen. Außerdem besteht die Möglichkeit einer Adressierung über Generic Key.

Temporäre Verknüpfungen

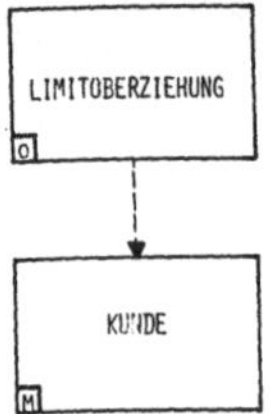

IDMS bietet die Möglichkeit, beliebige Verknüpfungen, die nur
temporär wirksam sind, durchzuführen. Es kann per Anwendungs-

programm eine logische Verknüpfung aufgebaut und aufgrund bestimmter Kriterien wieder gelöscht werden. Diese zusätzlichen Verknüpfungen werden vom IDMS durchgeführt, ohne die Sätze physisch aus der Datenbank zu entfernen und neu aufzunehmen.

Sätze ohne Verknüpfung

Außerdem besteht die Möglichkeit, Sätze ohne Verknüpfung in die Datenbank aufzunehmen, sie direkt zu adressieren und sie später mit beliebigen anderen Sätzen, die bereits in der Datenbank vorhanden sind, nachträglich zu verknüpfen. Diese Verknüpfungen können durchgeführt werden, ohne daß bestehende Anwendungsprogramme davon berührt sind.

Pointer Arrays (Inverted Files)

Invertierte Listen enthalten Satzadressen für vorher definierte Feldinhalte. Diese Satzadressen können auf mehrere Dateien verweisen.

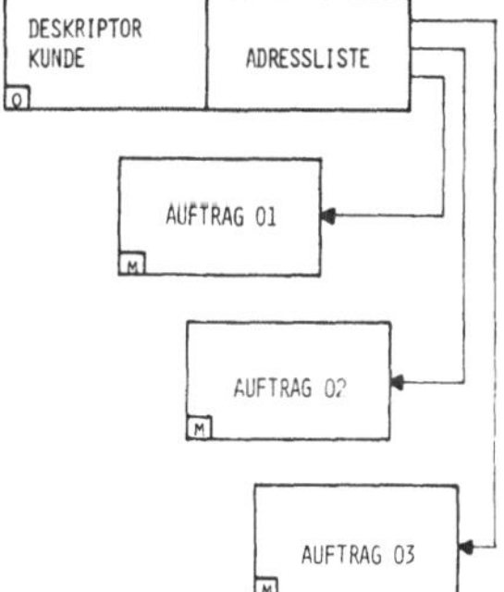

Bei dieser Strukturierungstechnik erfolgt der Zugriff zu den gesuchten Informationen über einen vorgeschalteten Index. Der im Index vorhandene Suchbegriff (im obigen Beispiel: Kundennummer) repräsentiert den Feldinhalt des Feldes Kundennummer.

Innerhalb eines Sets werden die einzelnen Sätze (Owner und n-Member-Sätze) durch Pointer verknüpft. Es besteht die Möglich-keit des Next-Pointer, des Prior-Pointer und des Owner-Pointer. Welche Pointer im speziellen Fall vom IDMS angelegt werden sollen, ist in der DDL (Data Definition Language) für den bestimmten Set zu beschreiben.

SET- Verknüpfung

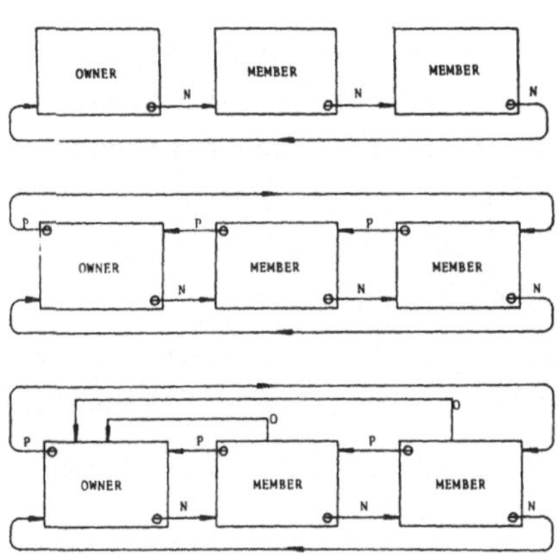

Der Update-Vorgang innerhalb eines Sets kann von der Sequenz in der DDL festgelegt werden. Es besteht die Möglichkeit des First-Updates, des Last-Updates, des Next-Updates, des Prior-Updates oder des Sorted-Updates (Ascending bzw. Descending).

Die im IDMS verwendeten Zugriffsmethoden basieren bei IBM-Syste-men auf BDAM. Bei der DDL-Beschreibung können drei Zugriffsme-thoden festgelegt werden. Die Direktzugriffsmethoden sind einmal über einen im System vorhandenen Algorithmus zur Umrechnung des logischen Keys in den Database-Key (CALC-Algorithmus) und durch einen vom Benutzer vorgegebenen Database-Key (direct) realisiert. Die indirekte Adressierung erfolgt über den VIA-Zusatz. Eine in-direkte Adressierung erfolgt durch den Zugriff über einen zuge-hörigen Owner. Member-Sätze, für die eine direkte Adressierung gewählt wurde, werden physisch benachbart zu ihrem Owner abgelegt. Diese Speicherungsvariante erlaubt die physische Gruppierung von Datengruppen, die einen häufigen Zugriff erfordern. Dadurch wird

erreicht, daß die Zugriffsfrequenz bei IDMS im Mittel unter 1,0
liegt.

Die kleinste adressierbare Einheit innerhalb des IDMS ist eine
Page (eine Page entspricht einem BDAM-Block). Die Größe einer
Page kann vom Benutzer gewählt werden. Eine Page ist identifi-
ziert durch den Database-Key. Innerhalb der Page wird durch einen
'Footer' mittels einer Displacement-Angabe ein einzelner Satz
identifiziert. Wie aus der Abb. 150 ersichtlich, werden durch
Update entstandene Lücken automatisch vom System geschlossen.
Der Freiplatz innerhalb einer Page wird immer geschlossen zur
Verfügung gestellt.

IDMS Freiplatzverwaltung

Abb. 150

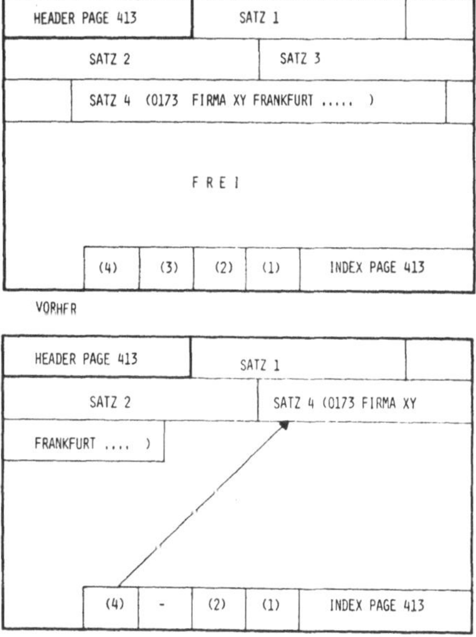

Überlaufbereiche werden nicht angelegt, da der Freiplatz innerhalb des Datenbestandes verwaltet wird. Datensätze, die auf ge-
füllte Pages treffen, werden unter Verwendung einer vom System
geführten Space Management Page in physisch benachbarten Pages
(gleicher Zylinder) abgelegt.

Der Füllungsgrad einer Page kann beim Laden des Bestandes festgelegt werden. Es ist zweckmäßig, bei variablen Sätzen, die im
Laufe von mehreren Abrechnungsperioden sich jeweils verlängern
können, den Füllungsgrad etwas niedriger zu halten. Variable Sätze,
die im Laufe der Zeit innerhalb der Page keinen Platz mehr finden,
werden jeweils in einer Fragmentlänge geteilt und dann teilweise
in physisch benachbarten Pages abgelegt. Sollte in der Home-Page
wieder Platz vorhanden sein, werden die ausgelagerten Fragmente
automatisch zurückgeholt. Der Anwendungsprogrammierer braucht
keinerlei Kenntnisse über die Aufteilung variabler Sätze zu besitzen.

VARIABLE SATZLÄNGE

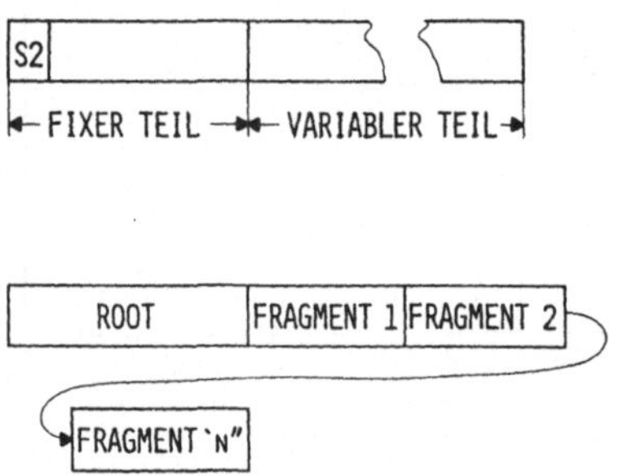

Um eine anwendungsbezogene Gruppierung innerhalb der Datenbank
zu erreichen, werden Pages zu Areas zusammengefaßt. Die Größe
einer Area wird in Anzahl Pages ausgedrückt.

Datenbank - Bereiche

Area

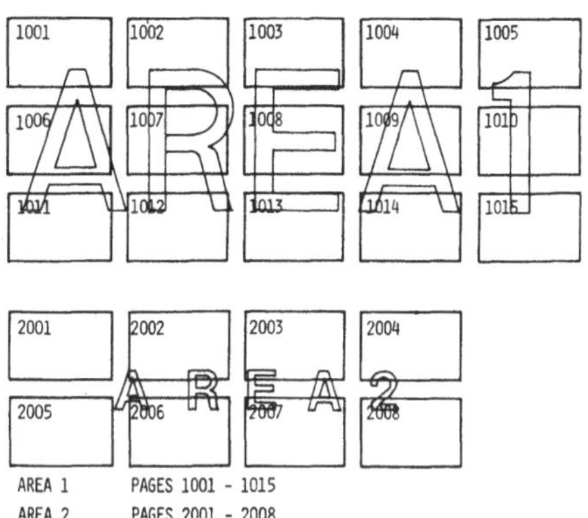

Eine Reorganisation ist bei IDMS in der Regel nicht notwendig.
Diese Aussage bezieht sich auf die Reorganisation aufgrund intensiven Updates. Das Page-Konzept erlaubt eine optimale Verteilung der Datensätze. Ein Reorganisieren einzelner Areas kann notwendig werden, falls der physische Platzbedarf innerhalb einzelner Areas nicht mehr ausreichend ist. In diesem Falle steht ein Dienstprogramm zur Verfügung, das einzelne Areas der Datenbank entlädt, und ein anschließendes Ladeprogramm füllt die Sätze in eine dann vergrößerte Area wieder ein.

In diesem Zusammenhang sollte erwähnt werden, daß die physische Veränderung von Satzformaten (sowohl im Daten- wie auch im Pointer-Teil) durchgeführt werden kann, ohne bestehende Anwendungsprogramme davon in Kenntnis zu setzen.

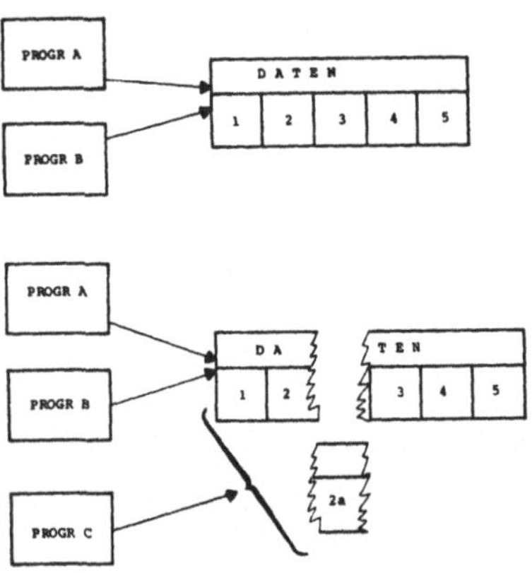

Diese Technik erweist sich als sehr vorteilhaft, wenn bereits in
der Datenbank vorhandene Sätze mit neu hinzukommenden oder anderen
Sätzen der Datenbank nachträglich verknüpft werden sollen. Der für
die Verknüpfung notwendige Platzbedarf für die entsprechenden
Pointer kann mit einem Dienstprogramm (Restructuring Utility) geschaffen werden, ohne daß die Datenbank entladen werden muß. Auch
davon sind bestehende Anwendungsprogramme nicht berührt.

Zur Beschreibung der Datenbank wird die Data Description Language
(DDL) verwendet. Die DDL Syntax ist in ihren wesentlichen Elementen in den folgenden Abbildungen dargestellt.

DDL - SYNTAX

<u>AREA DESCRIPTION.</u>

AREA NAME IS <u>AREA NAME</u>.

    RANGE IS <u>PAGE NO</u> THRU <u>PAGE NO</u>.

<u>RECORD DESCRIPTION.</u>

RECORD NAME IS <u>RECORD NAME</u>.
LOCATION MODE IS

$$\left\{ \begin{array}{l} \text{DIRECT} \\ \text{CALC USING } \underline{\text{IDENTIFIER}}. \\ \text{VIA } \underline{\text{SET NAME}}. \end{array} \right\}$$

    DISPLACEMENT <u>NO OF PAGES</u>.

WITHIN <u>AREA NAME</u>.

    FROM <u>PAGE NO</u> THRU <u>PAGE NO</u>.

<u>SET DESCRIPTION.</u>

SET NAME IS <u>SET NAME</u>.

$$\text{ORDER IS} \left\{ \begin{array}{l} \underline{\text{FIRST}} \\ \underline{\text{LAST}} \\ \underline{\text{NEXT}} \\ \underline{\text{PRIOR}} \\ \underline{\text{SORTED}} \end{array} \right\}$$

MODE IS CHAIN.
LINKED TO PRIOR.
OWNER IS <u>RECORD NAME</u>.
MEMBER IS <u>RECORD NAME</u>.

    LINKED TO OWNER.

$$\left\{ \begin{array}{l} \text{ASCENDING} \\ \text{DESCENDING} \end{array} \right\} \text{KEY IS } \underline{\text{IDENTIFIER}}.$$

Die somit erfolgte Datenbankbeschreibung wird mit Hilfe des Schema-Prozessors im Data Dictionary abgelegt.

Abb. 210

IDMS - COMPILIERUNG

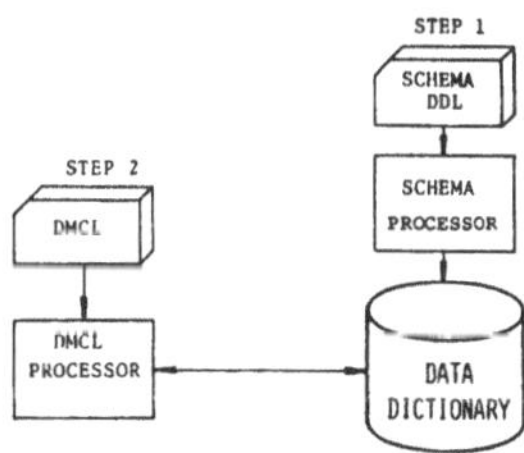

Die physische Beschreibung erfolgt mittels Device Media Control Language (DMCL). Hier wird die Größe einer Page und die Größe des Buffers spezifiziert. Siehe Abb. 210.

Deadlock-Bedingungen werden von IDMS erkannt und nach Wahl des Benutzers folgendermaßen gelöst:

- Abbruch des verursachenden Programmes

- Abbruch des Programmes, das die größere
  Anzahl von Sätzen gesperrt hat

- Abbruch des Programmes, das die kleinere
  Anzahl von Sätzen gesperrt hat

Der Datenschutz ist innerhalb des IDMS in einer sechsstufigen Hierarchie bis auf Feldebene geregelt.

ZUGRIFFS - SCHUTZ

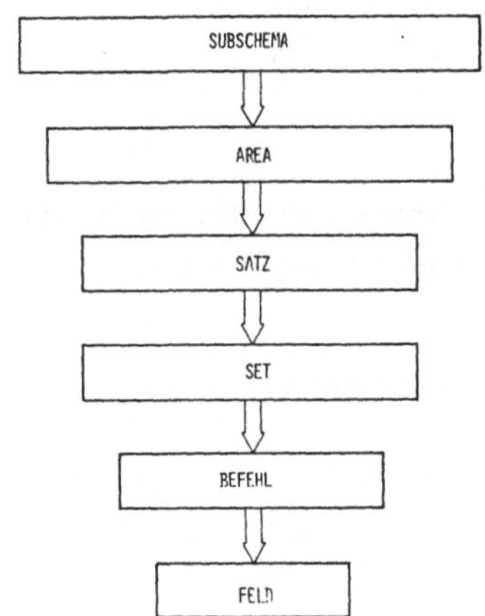

Die Festlegung des Datenschutzes erfolgt in der Subschema-Beschreibung. Das Subschema stellt die Sicht eines Anwendungsprogrammes in die Datenbank dar. Es ist eine Untermenge der Schemabeschreibung, ergänzt um spezielle Programmanweisungen, wie z.B. Datenschutz, und ist ebenfalls im Data Dictionary abgelegt. Das Subschema ermöglicht die feldweise Zurverfügungstellung einzelner Satzelemente. Eine zusätzliche Beschreibung der Datenstrukturen ist nicht erforderlich, da diese Beschreibung bereits in der Schema Description aufgeführt wurde.

SUBSCHEMA

```
AREA SECTION.
     COPY BEREICH - A AREA.
     COPY BEREICH - B AREA.
          PRIVACY LOCK FOR UPDATE IS 'NO'
          PRIVACY LOCK FOR PROTECTED UPDATE IS 'NO'
          PRIVACY LOCK FOR EXCLUSIVE UPDATE IS 'YES'
```

SUBSCHEMA

```
RECORD SECTION.
     COPY ZAHLUNGEN           RECORD.
     COPY PERSONAL            RECORD.
     COPY KONTEN              RECORD.
          PRIVACY LOCK FOR STORE  IS 'NO'
          PRIVACY LOCK FOR MODIFY IS 'NO'
          PRIVACY LOCK FOR ERASE  IS 'YES'

     01  KOSTENSTELLEN       RECORD
          PRIVACY LOCK FOR STORE  IS 'NO'
          PRIVACY LOCK FOR MODIFY IS 'NO'
          PRIVACY LOCK FOR ERASE IS 'NO'

          05 KST - NR
          05 KST - NAME
          05 KOSTENV.J.
          05 KOSTEN LJ
```

```
SET SECTION.
     COPY KOSTENSTELLEN-ZAHLUNGEN      SET.
     COPY KONTEN-ZAHLUNGEN             SET.
     COPY PERSONAL-ZAHLUNGEN           SET.
          PRIVACY LOCK FOR CONNECT  IS 'NO'
          PRIVACY LOCK FOR DISCONNECT IS 'NO'
     COPY KOSTENSTELLEN - PERSONAL     SET.
```

Die vorstehenden Abbildungen zeigen das Beispiel einer Subschema-Beschreibung.

Wie aus Abb. 250 ersichtlich, wird auch die Subschema-Beschreibung in das Data Dictionary durch den Subschema-Prozessor eingefügt.

Abb. 250   **IDMS-COMPILIERUNG**

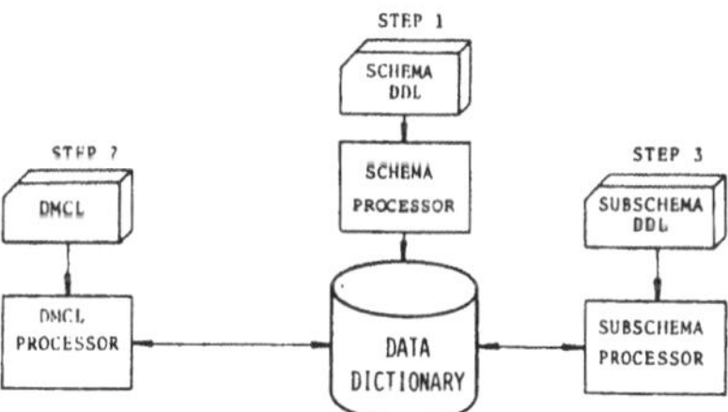

Das Data Dictionary dokumentiert alle Datenstrukturen einer Datenbank. Die Anwendungsprogramme müssen vor Kompilierung über Copy-Anweisung die entsprechenden Beschreibungen aus dem Data Dictio-

nary herausziehen. Das Data Dictionary gibt eine zwangsläufig
ajour gehaltene Dokumentation aller Datenstrukturen. Ein ebenfalls zur Verfügung stehendes erweitertes Data Dictionary erlaubt
weitergehende Dokumentationen. Es können in diesem erweiterten
Data Dictionary Strukturen aller Dateiorganisationen dokumentiert
werden. Außerdem können benutzer- und programmorientierte Dokumentationen aufgenommen werden.

Alle Update-Vorgänge innerhalb einer IDMS-Datenbank werden automatisch auf einem Journal File protokolliert. Das Journal File
ermöglicht eine Rekonstruktion der Datenbank nach System- oder
Programmzusammenbrüchen. Die Sicherung im Online-Betrieb, d.h. bei
Absturz einer Online-Transaktion, erfolgt automatisch ohne Ein-
griff des Operators. Es stehen zu diesem Zweck die Dienstprogramme
Journal Rollback (alten Zustand wieder herstellen), Journal Roll-
forward (neuen Zustand wieder herstellen) und das Autorecovery
zur Verfügung. Außerdem enthält das Journal File noch Informationen über die Zugriffsaktivitäten der einzelnen Anwendungsprogramme.

Das Journal File kann sowohl auf Band wie auch auf Platte geführt
werden. Sind Plattenbereiche zugeordnet, so werden diese im Flip/
Flop-Betrieb bedient und bei gefülltem Bereich auf Band geschrieben.

Die Manipulation der Datenbank durch die Anwendungsprogramme erfolgt durch die Data Manipulation Language (DML). Die wesentlichen
Syntax-Elemente der DML sind aus der Abb. 260 ersichtlich.

Abb. 260

DML-SYNTAX

```
DB SUBSCHEMA NAME.
READY AREA NAME.
FINISH AREA NAME.

STORE RECORD NAME.
MODIFY RECORD NAME.
CONNECT RECORD NAME INTO SET NAME.
DISCONNECT RECORD NAME FORM SET NAME.
DELETE RECORD NAME.

FIND RECORD NAME    ⎫
                    ⎬ USING IDENTIFIER.
OBTAIN RECORD NAME  ⎭

GET RECORD NAME.
```

Abb. 270 zeigt den gesamten Ablauf der Implementierung der Schema- und Subschema-Beschreibung und die anschließende Kompilierung der Anwendungsprogramme. Der DML-Prozessor, der über Copy-Funktionen die für das Anwendungsprogramm relevanten Beschreibungen aus dem Data Dictionary holt, übernimmt neben der Umsetzung der DML-Statements in entsprechende Call-Befehle außerdem die Generierung aller für die Kommunikation mit der Datenbank notwendigen Bereiche und überprüft die logische Richtigkeit der Datenbank-Kommunikation. Eine ausgefeilte Diagnostik stellt sicher, daß Kommunikationsfehler mit der Datenbank vor dem eigentlichen Testbetrieb erkannt und korrigiert werden können.

Abb. 270

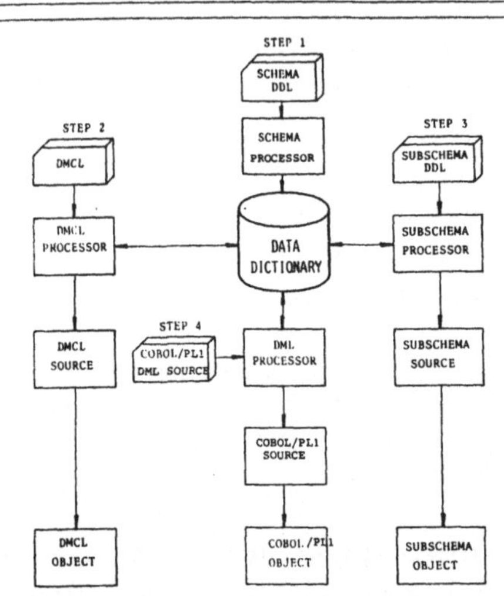

Standardmäßig stehen dem IDMS die folgenden Dienstprogramme zur
Verfügung:

- Database Initializer
- Security Dump (Print)
- Security Restore (Print)
- Journal Rollback (Print)
- Journal Rollforward (Print)
- Page Alteration
- Journal Close
- Calc Routine
- Fast Load
- Restructuring Utility

IDMS ist in der Lage, sowohl im DOS wie im OS mit einem DB-Modul
alle Anwender zu bedienen. Abb. 280 zeigt IDMS im Central Mode.
Es wurde eine eigene Partition zur Bedienung von zwei Batch-Programmen und zwei Online-Transaktionen gewählt.

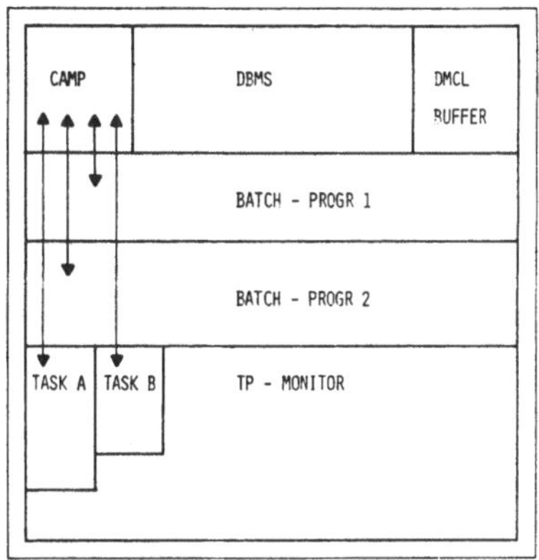

Abb. 290 zeigt die Arbeitsweise des IDMS in der TP-Partition.
Auch hier ist es wiederum nicht notwendig, für die Batch-Programme ein geträumtes DB-Modul zu nutzen.
Für DOS-Benutzer kann IDMS ebenfalls in der Power-Partition installiert werden.

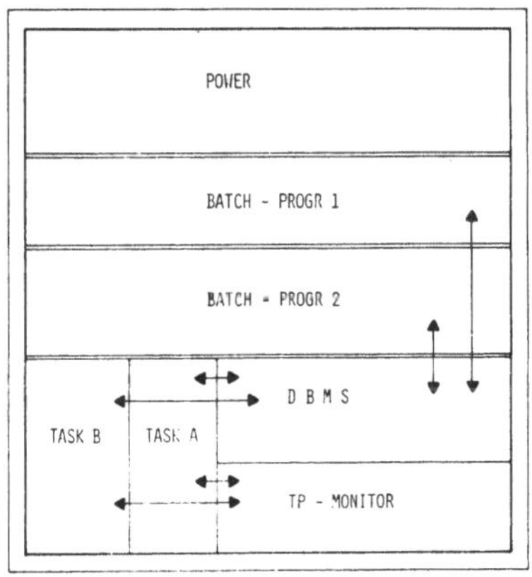

Zur Ausführungszeit benötigt IDMS einen virtuellen Kernspeicher-
bedarf von ca. 60 K.

IDMS wird weltweit von ca. 300 Anwendern genutzt (Stand Juni 1977).
In Europa gibt es ca. 50 IDMS-Anwender (Stand Juni 1977).

System 2000

Drs. Jos Peters
CAP/Gemini Düsseldorf

1.   Einführung

SYSTEM 2000[1] ist eines der verbreitetsten und bekanntesten Datenbank-Verwaltungssysteme. Es ist weltweit etwa 200 mal installiert
und wird von etwa 600 Firmen benutzt. Der Unterschied ergibt sich
daraus, daß SYSTEM 2000 von mehr als zehn namhaften weltweit-ope-
rierenden Service-Rechenzentren eingesetzt wird, allen voran CDC-
CYBERNET.

SYSTEM 2000 wird in Europa von CAP/Gemini/SOGETI vertrieben. Zur
Zeit ist es 200 mal installiert, und es gibt dazu etwa ebensoviele
Anwender über Service-Rechenzentren. Im deutschsprachigen Raum gibt
es zur Zeit 3 Installationen und etwa 15 Anwender über CDC-CYBERNET.

Das System steht zur Verfügung auf IBM 360/370 (DOS, OS und OS/VS),
Univac 1100 (EXEC-8, CSTS), CDC 6000, CYBER 70 und 170 (SCOPE,
KRONOS, NOS) und AMDAHL 470.

Es wurde entwickelt von MRI SYSTEMS Corporation in Austin, Texas,
USA.

Es bestehen kleine Unterschiede zwischen den Systemversionen auf
den einzelnen Anlagen. Was in diesem Dokument beschrieben wird,
steht aber auf allen Anlagen zur Verfügung. Die Beschreibung der
internen Struktur bezieht sich, insoweit es Unterschiede gibt, auf
die IBM-Implementierung.

[1] SYSTEM 2000 ist ein eingetragenes Warenzeichen der Firma MRI
Systems Corporation in Austin, Texas, USA.

2.   Allgemeines: Geschichte und Theorie

2.1. Geschichte der Datenbankpraxis und Entwicklung von SYSTEM 2000

Aufgrund ihrer internen Struktur und Grundkonzeption lassen sich
Datenbanksysteme in Familien zusammenfassen, wie in Bild 1 dargestellt. Die gezeigten Verbindungen deuten nicht immer auf direkte
Weiterentwicklungen hin. Gemeint ist darzustellen, wie Gedankengut
aus einem System in einem anderen wiedergefunden wurde.

Die vier Gruppen sind

1.   "Report Generator"- und Dateiverwaltungssysteme

2.   "CODASYL"-Systeme

3.   "Invertierte Datei"-Systeme

4.   Adressketten- und hierarchische Systeme.

SYSTEM 2000 gehört zu der dritten Gruppe und ist sogar das erste
kommerziell-erfolgreiche "Invertierte Datei"-System der Welt. Es
ist der Nachfolger von RFMS und wurde 1969/1970 daraus entwickelt.
Anfangs war es ein sogenanntes voll-invertiertes System, das heißt,
daß es keine Datensätze und keinen Datenbereich mehr gibt. Später
wurde es in ein partiell-invertiertes System geändert, und es wurde
auch zusätzlich die Möglichkeit aufgenommen, zwischen Datengruppen
hierarchische Beziehungen über Adresstabellen zu definieren.

Seitdem wurde das System ständig weiterentwickelt. Es gibt durch-
schnittlich ein neues Release pro Jahr, wobei den Anwendern ohne zusätzliche Kosten neue Features zur Verfügung gestellt werden.

Die jüngste Version enthält zum Beispiel ein Text-Search-Feature und
die Möglichkeit, auch auf nicht invertierte Elemente abzufragen.

Dieser ständigen Weiterentwicklung wegen gehört SYSTEM 2000 noch
immer, wie auch damals, zu den führenden Datenbank-Verwaltungs-
Systemen der Welt.

Bild 1

Geschichte und Entwicklung von Datenbanksystemen
56
57
58
59
60
61
62
63
64
65
66
67
68
69
70
71
72
73
74
75
RG/MARKI
MARKII
SURGE
GPAC
GIRLS
RPG
MARK1
MARK2
MARK3
MARK4
IDS
IDS/COBOL
APL
DBTG
IDMS
DBTG
DMS1100
PHOLAS
UDS
ETF
ADAM
COLINGO
C 10
LUCID
TDMS
RFMS
S 2000
ADABAS
BOMP
GUAM
RATS
DL/1
ICS
ICS/DLI
IMS1
TOTAL
DBOMP
IMS2

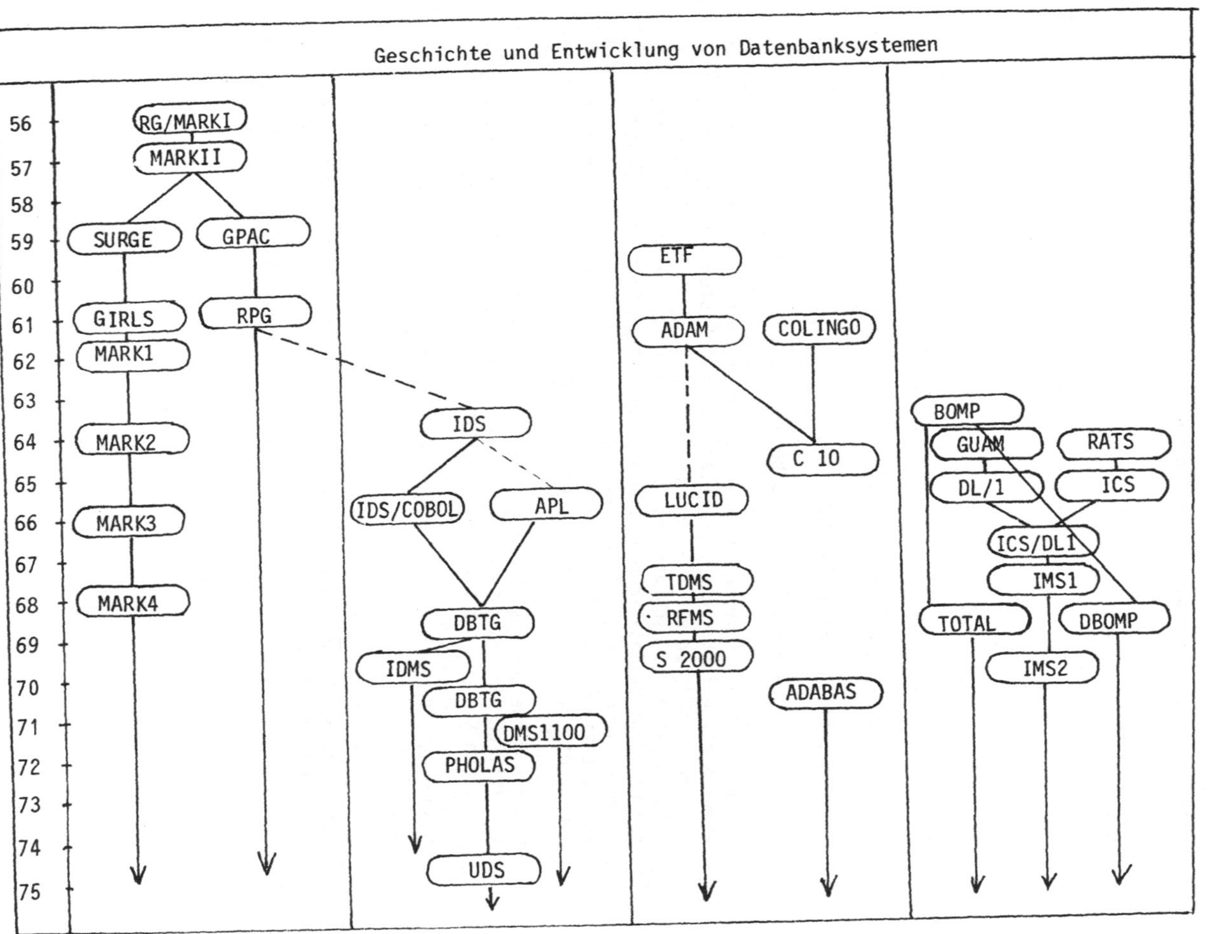

2.2   Zur Theorie

Die Theorie der Datenstrukturen ist in den letzten Jahren mit großem
Erfolg weiterentwickelt worden. Gleichzeitig sind auch eine ganze
Reihe von neuen Datenbanksystemen praktisch entwickelt und implemen-
tiert. Jedes dieser Systeme benutzt seine eigene Terminologie und
keines von diesen stimmt mit den in der Datenbanktheorie verwendeten
Terminologien überein. Eines der Ergebnisse ist mindestens eine große
Verwirrung, die vielleicht auch von manchen Herstellern gefördert
wird.

Wir möchten versuchen, diese Verwirrung zu verringern, indem wir ein
paar Grundgedanken noch einmal klar machen. Dabei werden wir vielleicht nicht die richtige wissenschaftliche Terminologie benutzen,
dafür aber damit rechnen, daß die Begriffe, die wir verwenden, bekannt
und geläufig sind.

Drei Arten der Struktur sollen klar voneinander getrennt werden, und
zwar:

Datenstruktur   - die Struktur, die in den Daten selbst vorhanden
                        ist. Diese Strukturen lassen sich mit den bekann-
                        ten Strukturmodellen abbilden

Datenbankstruktur - eine über EDV-Mittel definierte Struktur, in der
                      Praxis meistens eine Untermenge der Datenstruktur,
                      die über die physischen Entitäten der jeweiligen
                      Anlage hinaus geht, das heißt, die benutzten
                      Strukturelemente sind Konzepte, keine physischen
                      Größen. Begriffe wie Beziehung, Baum, Set, Wieder-
                      holungsgruppe usw. spielen eine Rolle
                      (Übrigens: hier tritt die Verwirrung auf).

Physische Struktur - die in physischen Größen festgelegte Speicher-
                      organisation. Mit physisch ist gemeint: nicht
                      über die Gegebenheiten des jeweiligen Betriebs-
                      systems hinausgehend. Benutzte Begriffe sind
                      Datei, Satz, Tabelle, Adresse usw.

Zusammengefaßt: eine Datenbankstruktur ist eine Abbildung einer
Datenstruktur, die mit Hilfe eines gewissen Betriebssystems realisiert wurde.

Wir möchten hier, wie gesagt, nicht auf die theoretisch begründeten
Datenmodelle eingehen, sondern nur feststellen, daß es folgende ge-
läufige Datenmodelle gibt:

a) Flache Struktur

    Datenelemente werden nur gruppiert, es werden zwischen den
    Gruppen keine Beziehungen definiert

b) <u>Einfache Hierarchie</u>

Zwischen Datengruppen werden hierarchische Beziehungen definiert,
wobei eine Gruppe auf jeder höheren Stufe jeweils höchstens eine
übergeordnete Gruppe hat

c) <u>CODASYL Hierarchie</u>

Zwischen Datengruppen werden hierarchische Beziehungen definiert,
wobei eine Gruppe (MEMBER) auf jeder höheren Stufe mehrere übergeordnete Gruppen (OWNER) haben kann

d) <u>Allgemeine Struktur</u>

Zwischen Datengruppen können alle Beziehungen definiert werden,
wobei von übergeordnet oder untergeordnet nicht gesprochen werden
kann.

Ein anderes Konzept, das mit Datenstrukturen nichts zu tun hat, ist
Datenzugriff. Dabei gibt es zwei Möglichkeiten:

1. <u>Zugriff über Inhalt:</u>   Access by Content
2. <u>Zugriff über Struktur:</u> Access by Relation

In der ersten Methode liest man eine Datengruppe aufgrund der Tatsache, daß man den Wert (Inhalt) eines Elementes kennt. Bei der
zweiten Methode kann man Gruppen lesen aufgrund der Tatsache, daß
eine Gruppe eine Stelle in einer Struktur hat.

Folgende <u>Strukturzugriffe</u> sind in den entsprechenden Datenstrukturen
beispielsweise möglich:

flach   - Gib mir die nächste Gruppe von diesem Typ

einfach hierarchisch   - Gib mir den Vater (oder auch Ahn)

                          Gib mir ein Kind (oder auch Nachkomme) von
                          diesem Typ

CODASYL hierarchisch   - Gib mir den OWNER

                          Gib mir ein MEMBER aus diesem SET

allgemein   - Gib mir eine Gruppe über diese Beziehung

Es gibt bei diesen Zugriffen sehr große Variationen, aber niemals
wird ein Element-Wert benutzt.

Bei <u>Zugriff über Inhalt</u> werden eines oder mehrere folgender Hilfsmittel meistens benutzt:

a) <u>Index -Sequentielle Dateien</u>

in denen z. B. der höchste Wert pro Datenblock und dessen Adresse
gespeichert werden

b) <u>Adress-Berechnung</u>

wobei eine Adresse aus einem Wert berechnet wird (VIA CALC)

c) <u>Invertierte Dateien</u>

in denen für gewisse (partielle Inversion) oder alle (vollständige Inversion) Elementwerte Listen erstellt werden, die pro Wert die Adressen der Gruppen enthalten, in denen dieser Wert vorkommt.

Bei <u>Zugriff über Struktur</u> werden folgende Hilfsmittel meistens benutzt:

a) Adressketten in Satz- oder Block-Praefixen

b) Adressketten in Adresstabellen

c) keine Hilfsmittel, das System verläßt sich auf die Reihenfolge der Sätze.

Ein kurzer Vergleich der benutzten Mittel:

Ketten in Satzpraefixen ergeben mit einem Zugriff weniger Glieder der Kette als Ketten über Adresstabellen.

Invertierte Dateien sind schneller bei Retrieval als die anderen Methoden, aber dafür aufwendiger bei Update der invertierten Elemente.

Zugriff über Inhalt kann nur erfolgen, wenn ein Inhalt vorhanden ist. Systeme, die keine Struktur haben, können Datenstrukturen nur dann abbilden, wenn ein Element mit dem gleichen Wert in beiden zu verknüpfenden Gruppen vorkommt, das heißt über redundante Werte.

Im nachfolgenden werden über Datenbankstruktur abgebildete Datenstrukturen als physisch, über redundante Werte als logisch bezeichnet.

Für die wichtigsten kommerziell verfügbaren Systeme wird diese Diskussion in Bild 2 zusammengefaßt, wobei gezeigt wird, daß SYSTEM 2000 Zugriff über Struktur mittels über Adresstabellen organisierte einfache Hierarchien erlaubt sowohl als auch Zugriff über Inhalt mittels invertierte Dateien.

Bild 2

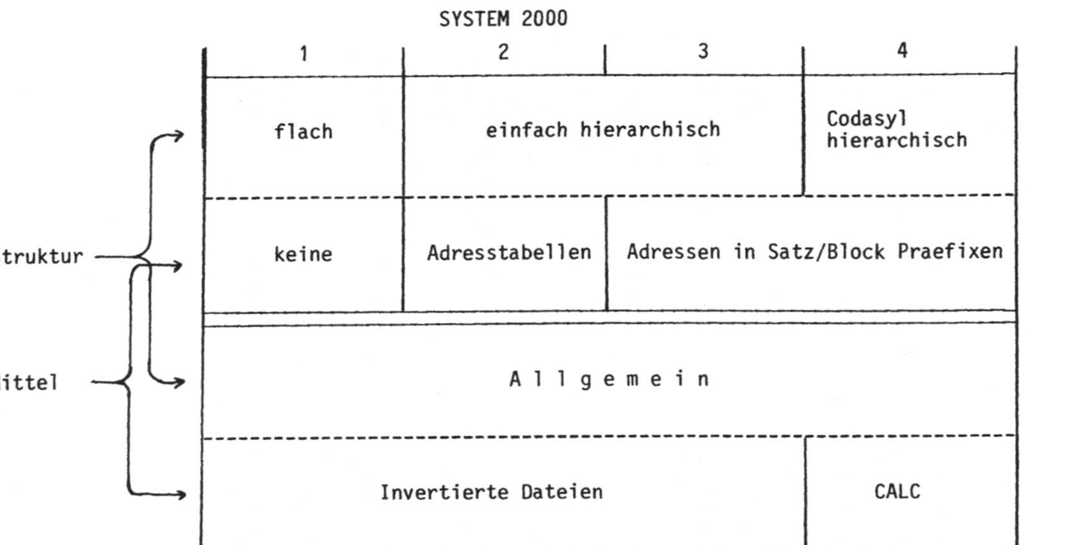

Die 4 wichtigsten allgemeinen Datenbank-Verwaltungssysteme für Groß-Datenbanken.

Eines dieser Systeme stammt von einem Hardware-Hersteller, die drei anderen nicht.

3.   Datenstrukturen in SYSTEM 2000

3.1.   Physische Strukturierung

Das kleinste Element in einer SYSTEM 2000-Datenbank heißt "Element".
Ein Element kann sein:

- NAME   d. h. ein Textfeld ohne überflüssige Leerstellen
- TEXT   d. h. ein Textfeld in beliebiger Form
- INTEGER   d. h. eine Ganzzahl
- DECIMAL   d. h. eine Zahl mit Nachkommastellen
- MONEY   d. h. ein Betrag
- DATE   d. h. ein Datum in beliebiger Form

In Elementen werden "Werte" gespeichert. Eine Gruppe von Elementen,
deren Werte zusammen vorkommen, heißt eine Wiederholungsgruppe
(Repeating Group). Wiederholungsgruppen bilden die Strukturelemente
einer Datenbankstruktur.

Jede Wiederholungsgruppe hat auf jeder höheren Stufe eine und höchstens eine übergeordnete Wiederholungsgruppe. Jede Wiederholungsgruppe kann beliebig viele untergeordnete Wiederholungsgruppen haben.

Als Datenbank werden definiert alle Werte, die mittels eines Definitionsbaumes gespeichert wurden. Ein Definitionsbaum besteht aus einer
höchsten Wiederholungsgruppe und allen direkt abhängigen Wiederholungsgruppen.

Zum Beispiel:

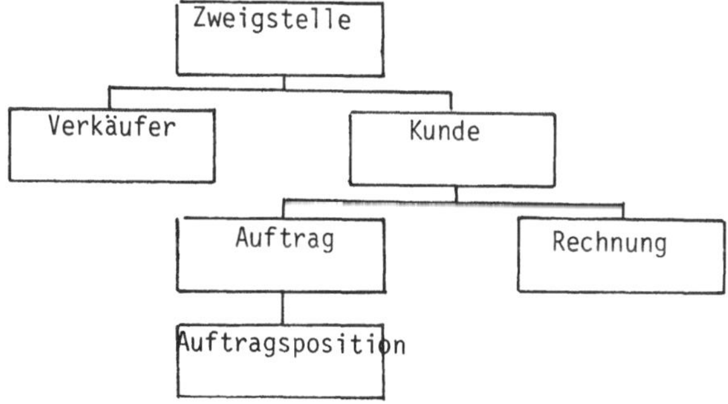

Pro Zweigstelle kann es beliebig viele Verkäufer und Kunden geben,
pro Kunde beliebig viele Aufträge und Rechnungen und pro Auftrag
beliebig viele Positionen. Eine Definition ist in der Tiefe auf 32
Stufen beschränkt, in der Breite überhaupt nicht. Die Zahl der Ausprägungen ist nur durch Plattenkapazität beschränkt.

Um für ein Element keine invertierte Liste zu erstellen, bezeichnet
man es in der Definition als NON-KEY. Für nicht derartig bezeichnete
Elemente oder als KEY bezeichnete Elemente wird SYSTEM 2000 eine invertierte Liste erstellen und warten.

In der SYSTEM 2000-Terminologie wird nicht von Eltern und Kindern gesprochen, sondern von Ahnen und Nachkommen, und zwar wegen der Tatsache, daß man in SYSTEM 2000, wenn man schon Zugriff über Struktur
benutzt, direkt auf die gewünschte Stufe zugreifen kann, ohne alle
zwischenliegenden hierarchischen Stufen zu durchgehen.

"Zweigstelle" ist also ein Ahn von "Verkäufer", "Kunde", "Auftrag",
"Rechnung" und "Auftragsposition", und "Auftragsposition" ist ein
Nachkomme von "Auftrag", "Kunde" und "Zweigstelle".

Weiter sind "Auftrag" und "Rechnung" Geschwister und "Verkäufer" und
"Kunde" auch.

3.2. Logische Strukturierung

Wie schon ausführlich erklärt, werden zur logischen Strukturierung
redundante Datenwerte benutzt. Zum Beispiel nehmen wir einmal an,
daß es außer der Vertriebsdatenbank, die in 3.1. gezeigt wurde, eine
Artikeldatenbank gibt, die wie folgt aussieht:

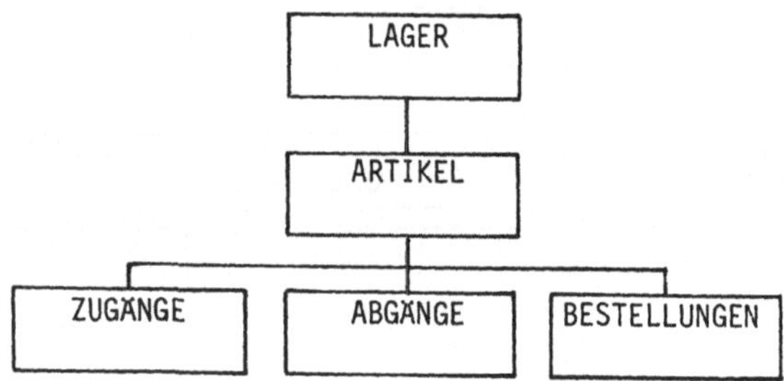

In der "ARTIKEL"-Wiederholungsgruppe wurde u. a. die Artikelbeschrei-
bung gespeichert. Wenn ein Programm nun zu den Auftragspositionen, die
ja eine Artikelnummer enthalten werden, die Beschreibungen braucht,
kann in diesem Programm (also völlig temporär) eine Verbingung zwischen
diesen beiden Datenbanken definiert werden, die dafür sorgt, daß zu
jedem Auftragspositionssatz, der gelesen wird, automatisch der entsprechende Artikelsatz dazu gelesen wird.

Für dieses Programm sieht das Ganze dann folgendermaßen aus:

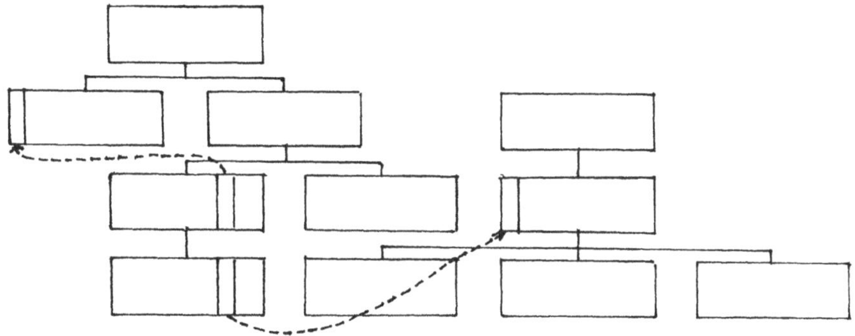

Diese Verbindung kann auch in eine Datenbank gelegt werden, wie hier
oben auch gezeigt wird an der Verbindung zwischen "Auftrag" und "Verkäufer". Man kann also hier die Aufträge lesen und bekommt immer die
entsprechenden Verkäufersätze dazu, ohne sich um die Hierarchie zu
kümmern.

Auf diese Art kann man also in SYSTEM 2000 Netzwerke abbilden. Vorteil
bleibt aber, daß man, wenn es eine Hierarchie gibt, diese auch physisch
abbilden kann mit den entsprechenden Einsparungen aufgrund verringerter
Datenredundanz.

4.   Datenbankerstellung

4.1. Datenbankdefinition

Wie schon erwähnt, gibt es in SYSTEM 2000 keine Utilities, sondern
dafür nur Befehle in selbständiger Sprache. Auch eine Datenbankdefinition wird also in selbständiger Sprache an SYSTEM 2000 mitgeteilt.
In Bild 3 ist die Definition der Vertriebsdatenbank gezeigt, die wir
bis jezt und auch weiterhin als Beispiel benutzen werden. Man könnte
sich an einen Bildschirm setzen und genau das eingeben, was hier gezeigt wird.

Die erste Zeile enthält den Standardsatz, mit dem jede Konversation anfängt, und zwar USER, password : Der Doppelpunkt beendet den Befehl.

Um eine neue Datenbank definieren zu können, sagt man NEW DATABASE IS Datenbankname :

Jetzt ist also für die neue Datenbank BRANCHS, BMGR das "Master-Password".

Was jetzt folgt, sind die Definitionen der einzelnen Komponenten (Elemente und Wiederholungsgruppen).

Diese bestehen für <u>Elemente</u> aus:

<komponent-nr> <Trennungszeichen><Name>

$$\left(\left\{{KEY \atop \underline{NON\text{-}KEY}}\right\} \langle TYP\rangle\ [\langle picture\rangle\ [(\langle länge\rangle)]\ )\right.$$
$$\left[IN\ \langle RG\text{-}nummer\rangle]\right]\ :$$

- Die Komponentnummer ist frei wählbar und braucht auch nicht aufsteigend zu sein

- Das Trennungszeichen ist wählbar. "Default" ist Stern

- Der Name ist wählbar und darf Leerstellen enthalten

- KEY ist "default". Für Key-Elemente werden invertierte Listen erstellt und gewartet

- TYP ist einer der in 3.1. erwähnten Datentypen

- PICTURE ist X oder 9

- Länge ist höchstens 250 für Picture X und höchstens 15 für Picture 9

  Picture "9"-Elemente müssen numerische Werte enthalten

- RG-Nummer erstellt die Hierarchie. Zu jedem Element sagt man, zu welcher Wiederholungsgruppe es gehört. Default ist "IN o", wobei o die Nummer der höchsten Wiederholungsgruppe ist.

Für <u>Wiederholungsgruppen</u> ist der Syntax

<komponent-nr><Trennungszeichen><Name> (RG [IN<RG-nr>]) :

Die Reihenfolge der Komponenten ist unerheblich, weil SYSTEM 2000 über das "IN" immer die richtige Struktur finden kann.

Das "MAP" am Ende verursacht, daß die Definition eingespielt und geprüft wird.

Bild 3

USER, BMGR:
NEW DATA BASE IS BRANCHS:
100* BRANCH-CODE   (KEY NAME XXX):
110* BRANCH-MGR   (NON-KEY NAME X(20)):
120* BRANCH-LOC   (NON-KEY NAME X(12)):
130* BR-OPEN-DATE   (NON-KEY DATE):
200* SALESMAN   (RG):
    210* S-MAN-NO   (KEY INT 9(5) IN 200):
    220* S-MAN-L-NAME   (KEY NAME X(10) IN 200):
    230* S-MAN-F-NAME   (NON-KEY NAME X(10) IN 200):
    240* S-QUOTA   (NON-KEY MONEY $9(7),99 IN 200):
    250* S-YTD   (NON-KEY MONEY $9(7),99 IN 200):
300* CUSTOMER   (RG):
    310* CUST-NAME   (NON-KEY NAME X(20) IN 300):
    320* CUST-ADDR   (NON-KEY NAME X(40) IN 300):
    330* CUST-NUM   (KEY INT 9(7) IN 300):
    340* CUST-CLASS   (KEY NAME X IN 300):
    350* CUST-CRED-LIM   (KEY-MONEY $9(5),99 IN 300):
    360* CUST-DISCOUNT   (NON-KEY DEC,999 IN 300):
    370* CUST-LAST-STMT   (NON-KEY DATE IN 300):
    400* ORDR   (RG IN 300):
        410* ORD-NUM   (KEY INT 9(7) IN 400):
        420* O-SALESMAN   (KEY INT 9(5) IN 400):
        430* ORD-DATE   (KEY DATE IN 400):
        440* ORD-AMT   (NON-KEY MONEY $9(5),99 IN 400):
        450* ORD-SHIPPED   (NON-KEY NAME X IN 400):
        460* ORD-COMMENT   (NON-KEY TEXT X(4) IN 400):
        500* DETAIL   (RG IN 400):
            510* PROD   (KEY INT 9(7) IN 500):
            520* QTY   (NON-KEY INT 9(7) IN 500):
            530* PKG   (KEY NAME X(6) IN 500):
        600* AR-STMT   (RG IN 300):
            610* STMT-DATE   (NON-KEY DATE IN 600):
            620* STMT-AMT   (NON-KEY MONEY $9(5),99 IN 600):

MAP.

4.2. Laden

Nachdem die Definition fehlerfrei eingespielt wurde, kann man die
Datenbank laden. Am einfachsten ist es, wenn man jetzt den Befehl:
LOAD: eingibt. Dabei müssen die Daten im Standard-Format ("Loader
String") in der Standard-Datendatei vorhanden sein. Diese Daten werden
dann diesem Befehl zu Folge in der Datenbank eingespielt.

Wenn die Daten nicht im Standardformat vorliegen, kann statt ein
Aufbereitungs-Programm zu erstellen auch ein Ladeprogramm geschrieben
werden, das über "INSERT"-Befehle die Datenbank füllt.

Dabei benutzt SYSTEM 2000 das "Optimised Load"-Feature und prüft,
ob die Daten der Definition entsprechen. Stufenweises Laden ist ebenfalls möglich.

4.3. Definitionsänderungen

Eine Definition wird wahrscheinlich öfter geändert als neu erstellt.
Definitionsänderung ist daher vielleicht mindestens so wichtig wie
Definition selbst.

Weil SYSTEM 2000 auf Element-Ebene funktioniert, ist Definitionsänderung in SYSTEM 2000 meistens ohne schwerwiegende Folgen möglich.

- Programme, die die geänderten Definitionselemente nicht ansprechen,
  brauchen nicht geändert und auch nicht neu compiliert zu werden.

- Programme sind unabhängig von der Element-Länge, d. h. wenn eine
  Änderung sich auf die Länge von Elementen beschränkt, brauchen
  sogar die Programme, die diese Elemente benutzen, nicht geändert
  oder neu compiliert zu werden.

- Wenn ein Element, das bis jetzt nicht invertiert war, zu Schlüssel-
  Feld geändert wird, braucht kein einziges Programm geändert oder
  neu compiliert zu werden. Auch braucht die Datenbank nicht neu
  geladen zu werden.

- Für das Ändern von Elementen, für die es noch keine Ausprägungen
  gab, braucht die Datenbank nicht neu geladen zu werden.

- Für das Hinzufügen neuer Wiederholungsgruppen braucht die Datenbank nicht neu geladen zu werden.

Für die Definitionsänderungen gibt es bestimmte Befehle, die eine
Änderung sehr einfach machen.

5.   Datenbankhandhabung

5.1. Wirtssprachen

SYSTEM 2000 hat Schnittstellen zu COBOL, FORTRAN, PL/1 und Assembler.

In ein Wirtssprachen-Programm schreibt man keine CALL-Befehle oder ausführlichen Daten-Syntax, sondern einfache Befehle und Daten-Beschreibungen, die von einem sogenannten Pre-Compiler zu syntaktisch richtigen Sprachkomponenten der jeweiligen Wirtssprache übersetzt werden.

Das hat außer Einschränkung der Schreibarbeit auch noch den Vorteil, daß Syntax-Fehler vor der Ausführung entdeckt werden, was bei Systemen ohne Pre-Compiler nicht der Fall sein kann, weil CALL-Befehle immer syntaktisch richtig sind.

In diesem Beispiel wird COBOL als Beispiel genommen.

Um in einem Wirtssprachen-Programm auf SYSTEM 2000-Datenbanken zugreifen zu können, braucht man:

- pro Datenbank einen sogenannten COMMBLOCK

- pro zu verwendende Wiederholungsgruppe ein sogenanntes SCHEMA

- in der Programmlogik aufgenommen: SYSTEM 2000 Befehle

5.1.1. COMMBLOCK

Der COMMBLOCK enthält Variablen, die von SYSTEM 2000 nach jedem Befehl bereit gestellt werden und die Auskunft geben über den Status der Datenbank, des Systems und den Erfolg des letzten Befehls. Das Ergebnis selbst steht nicht im COMMBLOCK. Die wichtigste Variable ist der "RETURN-CODE", der aussagt, ob der letzte Befehl funktioniert hat und wenn nicht, warum nicht.

Eine andere wichtige Variable ist das Password, das vom Programm bereit gestellt werden muß.

5.1.2. SCHEMAS

Pro Wiederholungsgruppe braucht man ein sogenanntes SCHEMA. Das "CODASYL"-SCHEMA ist zu vergleichen mit der SYSTEM 2000-"DEFINITION". Das CODASYL"-SUB-SCHEMA wäre zu vergleichen mit der Gesamtheit der SYSTEM 2000-SCHEMAS in einem bestimmten Programm.

Das SYSTEM 2000-SCHEMA funktioniert gleichzeitig als Ein-/Ausgabe-Bereich und als Maske über die Definition der Wiederholungsgruppe.

Für das COBOL-Beispielprogramm, das wir verwenden wollen, nehmen wir an, daß nur die in Bild 4 gezeigten Teile der Beispiel-Datenbank interessant sind, nämlich 4 Elemente aus der "Kunde"-Wiederholungsgruppe, 3 Elemente aus der "Auftrag"-Wiederholungsgruppe und die "Auftragszeile"-Wiederholungsgruppe vollständig. Die Gruppen "Zweigstelle", "Verkäufer" und "Rechnung" sind uninteressant.

Die notwendigen SCHEMAS sind in Bild 5 dokumentiert.

Folgendes fällt auf:

- Der "SCHEMANAME" ist frei wählbar.

  SYSTEM 2000 findet die Verbindung von SCHEMA zur Wiederholungsgruppe über die Element-Bezeichnungen.

- Die Element-Bezeichnungen können sein:

  ° Element-Name

  ° Element-Nummer mit C

  ° etwas anderes, dann allerdings mit EQ <Element-Name>

- Die Element-Länge darf von der Definition abweichen; SYSTEM 2000 erlaubt nämlich "Overflow" pro Element.

- Mit gewissen Einschränkungen darf auch das "PICTURE" unterschiedlich sein.

- Die Reihenfolge der Elemente darf unterschiedlich sein. .

Zusammenfassend: weil SYSTEM 2000 auf Element-Ebene arbeitet, ist fast vollständige Programm/Daten-Unabhängigkeit möglich. Das hat auch wichtige Folgen im Bereich Datenschutz.

<u>Bild 4</u>

SCHEMAS: WIE EINE DATENBANK FÜR EIN PROGRAMM AUSSIEHT

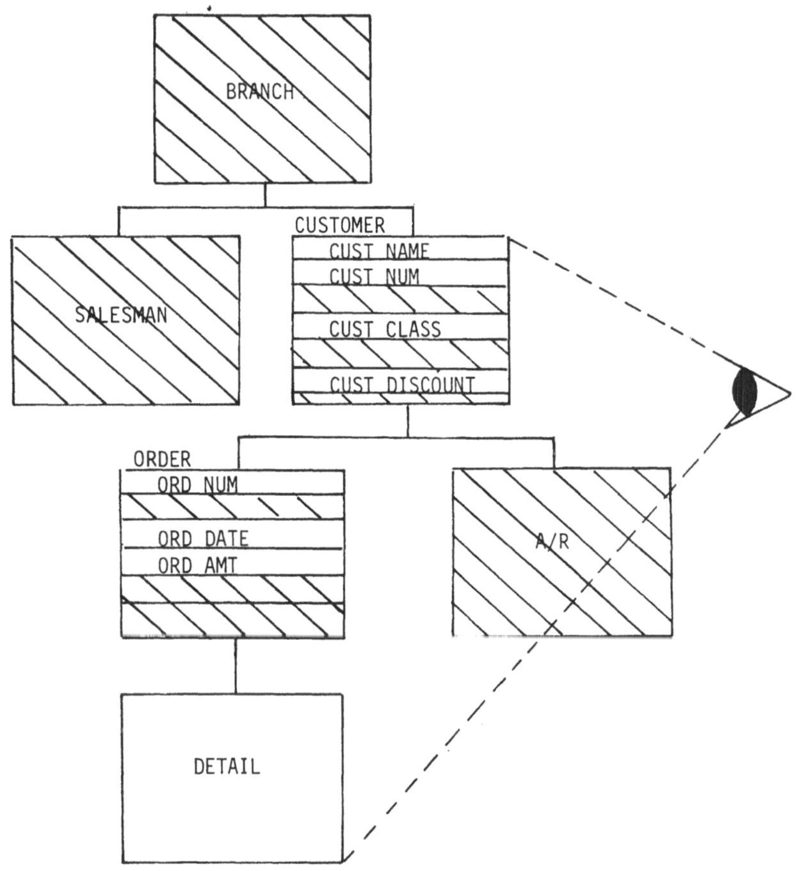

Bild 5

SCHEMAS

SCHEMA CUST02 OF BRANCHS.

```
01  CUST02.
    02  CLIENT                  PICTURE IS X(40).
        EQ CUST-NAME.
    02  CUST-NUM                PICTURE IS 9(7).
    02  C360                    PICTURE IS V999 COMP-3.
    02  CUST-CLASS              PICTURE ISX.
```

SCHEMA ORD02 OF BRANCHS.

```
01  ORD02.
    02  ORD-NUM                 PICTURE IS 9(5).
    02  C440                    PICTURE IS 9(5)V99 COMP-3.
    02  C430                    PICTURE IS 9(6).
```

SCHEMA DETAIL OF BRANCHS.

```
    02  PROD                    PICTURE IS 9(7).
    02  QTY                     PICTURE IS 9(7) COMP.
    02  PKG                     PICTURE IS X(20).
```

END SCHEMAS.

5.1.3. Retrieval-Befehle

a) <u>Direktes</u> Lesen: GET1 < SCHEMA > ......

Dieser Befehl stellt die gewünschte Wiederholungsgruppe im erwähnten SCHEMA bereit.

"Gewünscht" heißt:

FIRST	die erste in der DB
LAST	die letzte in der DB
NEXT	die nächste ab der jetzigen Position
S2KCOUNT	die Gruppe, die 'n' Stellen entfernt ist von der jetzigen Position, wobei 'n' der Wert ist, der in S2KCOUNT enthalten ist
WHERE < Bedingungen >	die erste Gruppe, die den Bedingungen entspricht

b) <u>Abhängiges</u> Lesen: GETA < SCHEMA > und
                                   GETD < SCHEMA > ······

GETA < Schema > liest eine Wiederholungsgruppe vom gewünschten Typ, die ein Ahn der jetzigen Position ist.

GETD < Schema > liest eine Wiederholungsgruppe vom gewünschten Typ, die ein Nachkomme von der jetzigen Position ist, und zwar

FIRST	die Erste
LAST	die Letzte
NEXT	die Nächste
S2KCOUNT	die 'n'-te

c) <u>Untermenge Lesen</u>:   LOCATE < SCHEMA > WHERE < Bedingungen >

Der LOCATE-Befehl erstellt eine Liste (in einer sogenannten LOCATE-Datei) von Adressen der Wiederholungsgruppen, die den Bedingungen im Bedingungssatz entsprechen. Diese Liste kann mit "ORDER BY" sortiert werden. Dieser Liste entsprechend kann man dann mit "GET" die

FIRST	erste	
LAST	letzte	
NEXT	nächste	Wiederholungsgruppe
S2KCOUNT	'n'-te	aus der Datenbank lesen
PRESENT	jetzige	
PREVIOUS	vorhergehende	

5.1.4. Update-Befehle

Die Update-Befehle in SYSTEM 2000 Wirtssprachen-Programmierung funktionieren alle in Abhängigkeit einer etablierten Position.

MODIFY < SCHEMA >< Elementen-Liste >

    ändert die Werte der aufgeführten Elemente oder, wenn
    Elementen-Liste leer ist, die ganze Wiederholungsgruppe

INSERT < SCHEMA > $\begin{bmatrix} \text{BEFORE} \\ \text{AFTER} \end{bmatrix}$

    erstellt eine neue Wiederholungsgruppe des genannten Typs
    unmittelbar vor oder nach der jetzigen Position

REMOVE TREE < SCHEMA >

    löscht eine Wiederholungsgruppe des genannten Typs im Pfad
    der jetzigen Position und, wenn vorhanden, alle deren Nach-
    kommen

Es gibt weitere Update-Befehle und Varianten von Update-Befehlen.
Eine Besprechung an dieser Stelle würde zu weit führen.

5.1.5. Mehrfach-Positionierung

Bis jetzt war mehrmals von "Position" die Rede. Eine Position ist
eine Stelle in der Datenbank, die man über einen erfolgreichen Lese-
Befehl etabliert.

SYSTEM 2000 erlaubt es, bis zu 16 Positionen gleichzeitig zu haben.
Man bezieht sich auf eine Position, indem man hinter den Befehl eine
Zahl 16 in Klammern schreibt.

Man kann auch mehrere Locate-files haben, nämlich maximal 10. Die
Positionen können in der gleichen Datenbank oder in unterschiedlichen
Datenbanken sein.

5.1.6. Netzwerk-Beziehungen

In SYSTEM 2000 Wirtssprachen-Programmierung kann man zwischen zwei
Wiederholungsgruppen in der gleichen Datenbank oder in unterschiedlichen Datenbanken einen sogenannten Link definieren. In einem Programm können bis zu zehn Links definiert werden. Diese Beziehungen
sind nur gültig für dieses Programm und für die Dauer eines Programm-
durchlaufes. Es werden hierfür keine Adress-Tabellen erstellt; die
Links sind völlig temporär. Um zum Beispiel folgende Beziehung zu erstellen,

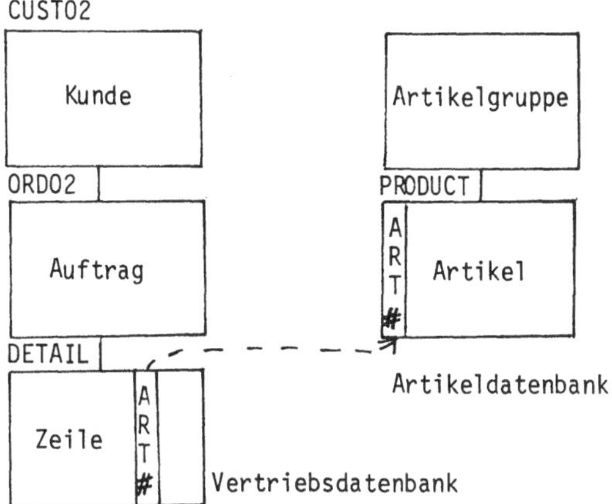

reicht es aus, in dem Programm, das die Beziehung braucht, folgenden
Befehl zu geben:

LINKØ DETAIL TO PRODUCT VIA PROD/PROD-CODE,

vorausgesetzt, daß in dem Programm auch für Artikel ein entsprechendes
SCHEMA aufgenommen war.

Das Ergebnis des Befehls ist, daß ab jetzt jeder erfolgreiche Retrieval
in das SCHEMA "DETAIL" einen automatischen Retrieval in das SCHEMA
"PRODUCT" zur Folge hat, und zwar die Artikel-Wiederholungsgruppe mit
der gleichen Artikelnummer wie die in der Auftragszeile. Man könnte also
sämtliche Auftragszeilen in einer Programmschleife lesen und hätte dann
jedesmal die entsprechenden Artikeldaten zur Verfügung, obwohl diese in
einer anderen völlig anders organisierten Datenbank stehen.

Ein Link kann auch innerhalb einer Datenbank definiert werden. Man
könnte dann in einer Datenbank die Hierarchie von unten her aufrollen.

5.1.7. Queue-Verarbeitungsweise

Einmalig ist in SYSTEM 2000 das Befehls-Trio:

QUEUE.

TERMINATE oder CANCEL QUEUE.

Wenn in einem Programm der QUEUE-Befehl vorkommt, geschieht folgendes:
ab jetzt werden die Update-Befehle nicht mehr in der Datenbank ausgeführt, sondern das Ergebnis des Updates wird in einer Zwischendatei
gespeichert. Beim TERMINATE werden die Updates in der DB ausgeführt,
und die Wartung der Pointer-Tabellen und invertierten Listen wird in
einem Durchgang der Datenbank stattfinden.

Wenn statt TERMINATE, CANCEL QUEUE durchlaufen wird, werden die Updates
nicht ausgeführt, und die Datenbank bleibt also in dem Zustand, in dem
sie war, als QUEUE ausgeführt wurde.

Diese Arbeitsweise ist optimal, weil in einem Update-intensiven Programm sehr viel I/O's gespart werden.

Dazu kommt, daß, wenn dieses Programm abnormal enden würde, ohne das
"TERMINATE" durchlaufen zu haben, die Datenbank nicht "DAMAGED" ist
und wiederhergestellt werden müßte, sondern eben noch in dem Zustand
ist, wie sie bei "QUEUE" war.

5.1.8. Fehlerbehandlung in Wirtssprachen

Nach jedem Befehl sollte man eigentlich die Return-Code im COMMBLOCK
prüfen.

SYSTEM 2000 hat dafür zwei Möglichkeiten:

a) Explizit

    IF RC = ...   THEN .....   nach jedem Befehl

b) Implizit

    FOR < DB-Name > RC 1-3, 5-99
       USE < paragraph-name >

                          einmal im Programm

    FOR < DB-Name > RC 4
       USE < paragraph-name >

Die zweite Möglichkeit spart nicht nur Schreibarbeit, sondern vermeidet auch den allzu gebräuchlichen Fehler, die Return-Code nicht
oder nicht richtig zu prüfen.

5.2   Report Writer

Zu SYSTEM 2000 gehört ein REPORT WRITER, der genau wie Selbständige
Sprache die eingegebenen Befehle interpretiert. Es werden also keine
Programme erzeugt, wie das bei vielen Berichtgeneratoren üblich ist.
Der SYSTEM 2000-Report Writer führt im allgemeinen alle Funktionen
aus, die man einem Report Writer zutraut, wie zum Beispiel:

- Formatisierung

        Seiten- und Spalten-Überschrift

        Zeilenbezeichnung

        Zeilen- und Seitenpositionierung

- Datenaufbereitung (Editing)

- Sortieren

- Arithmetische Funktionen

- Stufenwechsel

- Spalten-Summierung (Zwischen- und Endsummen)

- Zeilen-Summierung

- Zählen

- u. s. w.

Einzigartig für den SYSTEM 2000-Report Writer ist, daß die Ausführung
über einen Befehl verläuft, in dem der Bedingungssatz benutzt werden
kann:

        GENERATE < Bericht-Namen > WHERE .....

Bis zu 100 Berichte können mit einem GENERATE erzeugt werden.

5.3.   Selbständige Sprache

Die SYSTEM 2000-Sprache ist nicht ein zusätzliches Modul, wie bei
allen anderen Systemen. Sie gehört zu der Basis-Version von SYSTEM
2000 und war einmal die einzige Möglichkeit, mit dem System zu
kommunizieren.

Sie ist auch keine DDL oder DML. Sie ist die Systemsprache überhaupt,
mit der man sowohl

- das System steuern
- Datenbanken verwalten
- Daten definieren
- Daten aufsuchen

als auch

- Daten ändern

kann. Sie wird von Datenbankverwaltern, Operatoren, Programmierern, Organisatoren, Fachabteilungen und Managern gleichermaßen benutzt.

Die Befehle werden direkt ausgeführt, ohne daß kompiliert oder generiert wird. Sie hat einen einfachen und englisch-ähnlichen Syntax (daher auch "Natürliche Sprache") und ist schnell zu lernen. Oft gebrauchte Ergebnisse können als Funktionen gespeichert werden, und oft gebrauchte Befehlsreihen können als Strings definiert werden.

Sie besteht eigentlich aus zwei unwesentlich unterschiedlichen Formen: Immediate Access, in der alle Befehle unmittelbar nach der Eingabe verarbeitet werden, und Queued Access, in der mit der Ausführung gewartet wird, bis der TERMINATE-Befehl empfangen wird.

Es macht für SYSTEM 2000 nichts aus, ob die Befehle von einem Bildschirm oder vom zentralen Lochkartenleser empfangen werden. Die Zuordnung der Ein-/Ausgabe-Dateien (Terminal, Drucker, Bildschirm, Platte, Band) ist frei wählbar und kann während einer Konversation einfach über Befehle geändert werden.

Ganze on-line Systeme (wie z. B. Bibliotheks-Verwaltung) wurden in selbständiger Sprache, ohne je ein Programm zu schreiben, fertiggestellt.

Selbständige Sprache übernimmt alle Funktionen, die meistens von Utilities ausgeführt werden, und ist einer der wirksamsten und interessantesten Erzeugnisse der heutigen Software-Technik.

5.3.1. Retrieval

Der allgemeine Syntax ist:

```
⎡PRINT  ⎤
⎢LIST   ⎥   < Komponentenliste> ORDER BY < Komponentenliste >
⎣UNLOAD ⎦        WHERE < Bedingungssatz>:
```

PRINT   erzeugt eine Aufstellung, wobei je Variable eine Zeile
                 benutzt wird

LIST   erzeugt eine tabellarische Liste, wobei wirkungsvolle
                 Format-Steuerung zur Verfügung steht

UNLOAD   erzeugt eine sequentielle Datei

5.3.1.1. Der Bedingungssatz

Der Bedingungssatz wird sowohl in Wirtssprachenprogrammierung als
auch in selbständiger Sprache benutzt. Er enthält einfache Bedingungen, die über AND, OR oder NOT miteinander verbunden werden.
Eine einfache Bedingung enthält

- einwertige Operatoren (EXISTS, FAILS)

- zweiwertige Operatoren (EQ, NE, LE, GE, LT, GT)

- dreiwertige Operatoren (SPANS, NE).

Zu einer Bedingung kann man über AT<Stelle-Nummer> andeuten, daß
eine bestimmte Bedingung an einer bestimmten Stelle stimmen muß.
Die Klammer hat die gleiche Funktion wie in der Algebra, d. h. sie
erzwingt eine bestimmte Auswertungs-Reihenfolge.

Für TEXT oder NAME-Felder kann über CONTAINS auf Teilwerte oder
Teilwerte an gewissen Stellen abgefragt werden. Die Elemente, die
in einem Bedingungssatz benutzt werden, dürfen auf unterschiedlichen hierarchischen Ebenen vorkommen und brauchen keine invertierten Elemente zu sein. Man kann sogar im Bedingungssatz erzwin-
gen, daß die vorhandene invertierte Liste für ein gewisses Element
nicht benutzt wird, sondern statt dessen die Daten selber.

Einen einmal erstellten Bedingungssatz kann man weiterverwenden
(und die als Ergebnis erzeugte Liste der qualifizierten Wiederholungsgruppen auch), indem man beim nächsten Befehl "WHERE SAME"
eingibt.

5.3.1.2. Der Aktionssatz

Die Aktionen in einem Befehl in selbständiger Sprache können sich
außer auf Elemente auch auf Funktionen beziehen. Funktionen sind
entweder die System-Funktionen oder vom Anwender erstellte Funktionen.

System-Funktionen sind:

COUNT   die Zahl der Wiederholungsgruppen, die dem Bedingungssatz
         entsprechen

SUM   die Summe der Elemente

AVG   der Durchschnitt der Elemente

SIGMA   die Standard-Deviation der Elemente

MIN   der Kleinstwert

MAX   der Höchstwert

Das Objekt der Funktion ist das hinter dem Funktionsnamen erwähnte
Element. Der Bereich sind die über den Bedingungssatz qualifizierten Sätze. Über ein Adverb "BY", das soviel heißt wie "PRO", kann
man die Funktion auf Teilbereiche anwenden

PRINT COUNT AUFTRAG

> wird die Zahl der Aufträge anzeigen

PRINT COUNT AUFTRZEILE BY AUFTRAG:

> wird eine Liste erstellen, die die Zahl der Auftrags-
> zeilen pro Auftrag enthält.

Man kann auch selbst Funktionen codieren, und zwar "in-line" oder
vorher definiert.

PRINT KUNDENR, AUFTRNR, (BETRAG * (SKONTO/100)) WHERE SKONTO EXISTS:

> würde Kundennummer, Auftragsnummer und Skontobetrag,
> berechnet am Skontosatz und Auftragswert,ausdrucken.

Man könnte diese Funktion auch definieren:

705 * SKONTOBETR (DECIMAL FUNCTION (BETRAG * (SKONTO/100)):):

wobei 705 irgendeine freie Komponentnummer ist, und dann so verwenden:

PRINT KUNDENR, AUFTRNR, *SKONTOBETR* WH SAME:

Anwenderfunktionen können mit Systemfunktionen verbunden sein, und
Funktionen dürfen Funktionen enthalten.

Der nächste Befehl zeigt ein zusammenfassendes Beispiel für die
Möglichkeiten des Retrievas in selbständiger Sprache:

LIST MANR, COUNT GEHALT BY MA, SUM GEHALT BY MA, ((GEBDAT- * FTODAY*)
/365,25), NAME, ORDERED BY LOW PLZ WHERE (ABT EQ EDV OR ABT EQ EINK)
AND PLZ CONTAINS 000 FROM POSITION 2:

Dieser Befehl erzeugt eine tabellarische Liste, die folgendes enthält:

Mitarbeiternummer
Zahl der Gehälter pro Mitarbeiter
Summe der Gehälter eines jeweiligen Mitarbeiters
Das Alter des Mitarbeiters in Jahren
Der Name des Mitarbeiters

und zwar für die Mitarbeiter, die entweder in der EDV oder beim
Einkauf tätig sind und in einer der Hauptstädte der BRD wohnen.
Die Liste ist aufsteigend auf Postleitzahl sortiert. Das Beispiel
in Bild 6 zeigt die Formatisierungsmöglichkeiten des List-Befehls.

<u>Bild 6</u>

Formatisierung mit LIST

LIST/TITLE D(14) LISTING OF+CUSTOMERS IN + CLASS A,F(45)FOOTING AFTER
45 LINES, CUSTOMER+ NUMBER, ORDER+ NUMBER, DATE OF+ ORDER, ORDER+
AMOUNT/CUST-NUM, ORD-NUM, ORD-DATE, ORD-AMT, OB HIGH ORD-AMT,
ORD-DATE WH CUST-CLASS EQ A AND ORD-DATE GT 01/01/75:

```
                          LISTING OF        1
                          CUSTOMERS IN
                             CLASS A

CUSTOMER      ORDER              DATE OF         ORDER
NUMBER        NUMBER             ORDER           AMOUNT

2392603       3522008            09/13/1976      $ 1328,89
2012301       1614913            04/13/1975      $   301,16
2392603       3316815            05/15/1976      $   201,15
2392603       2511208            08/27/1975      $   186,22
2220218       2619907            09/21/1975      $   106,15
2392603       3020514            11/29/1975      $    16,30
   "             "                  "             "
   "             "                  "             "
   "             "                  "             "

FOOTING AFTER 45 LINES.
------------------------------------------------------------

                          LISTING OF        2
                          CUSTOMERS IN
                             CLASS A

CUSTOMER      ORDER              DATE OF         ORDER
NUMBER        NUMBER             ORDER           AMOUNT

   "             "                  "             "
   "             "                  "             "
   "             "                  "             "
```

5.3.2. Update

Beim Update in selbständiger Sprache funktioniert der Bedingungssatz genauso wie bei Retrieval. Der Aktionssatz enthält statt Retrieval-Befehle Update-Befehle, die für alle qualifizierten Sätze ausgeführt werden. Es gibt Befehle, die einzelne Werte ändern (CHANGE), hinzu-fügen (ADD) oder löschen (REMOVE), und Befehle, die ganze Wieder-holungsgruppen löschen (REMOVE TREE) oder erstellen (INSERT TREE).

CHANGE KREDIT-LIMIT EQ 100 000 WHERE KUNDENKLASSE EQ B:

    würde für alle Kunden der Klasse B den Kreditlimit auf
    100 000 DM ändern.

REMOVE TREE VERKAEUFER WHERE UMSATZ LT QUOTUM:

    löscht alle Verkäufer und deren Nachkommen, wo der Umsatz
    kleiner ist als das Quotum.

5.3.3. Strings

Strings sind Befehlsreihen, die unter einer Komponentnummer und einem Komponentnamen in der Datenbank gespeichert werden.

Zum Beispiel:

750 * MALISTE (STRING $ LIST MANR ....

....

......WHERE ABT EQ * 1 * AND EINTRITTSDATUM GE * 2 * : $) :

Was zwischen den beiden Dollarzeichen steht, sind die auszuführenden Befehle. Zwischen den Sternchen-Paaren stehen Zahlen, die die Stellen-nummer repräsentieren und beim späteren Aufruf durch positionelle Parameter ersetzt werden.

Wenn man an einen Bildschirm jetzt folgendes eingibt:

* MALISTE (EDV, 01/07/75):

wird die gewünschte Liste erstellt für die Mitarbeiter der EDV, die am oder nach dem 1.7.75 eingetreten sind.

* MALISTE (EINK, * FTODAY *):

würde die gleichen Daten ausdrucken für die Mitarbeiter des Einkaufs, die heute eingetreten sind oder später eintreten werden.

Innerhalb Strings kann man Strings verwenden, und alle Befehle sind für String-Verwendung zugelassen.

5.3.4. Queued Access

Genau wie bei der Wirtssprachenprogrammierung gibt es auch in selbständiger Sprache die Queued-Verarbeitungsweise, die aber teilweise anders funktioniert.

Die zwischen QUEUE und TERMINATE eingegebenen Befehle werden von SYSTEM 2000 alle in einem Arbeitsgang und mit einem Durchlauf der Datenbank verarbeitet. Bei der Eingabe jedes einzelnen Befehls wird nur der Syntax geprüft, und jeder Befehl bekommt eine Nummer. Die Ausgaben werden wieder den Befehlen zugeordnet und in der Eingabe-Reihenfolge ausgedruckt.

Es gibt geringe Syntax-Unterschiede und einige zusätzliche Features:

- Schwellenlogik

  PRINT TREE KUNDE WHERE <u>ANY 2 OF</u>

  (BETRAG LT 100 000, SKONTO GE 5, KUNDENKLASSE EQ X)

- Automatische Wiederholung von Befehlen

  REPEAT/PRINT ADRESSE WHERE KUNDENR EQ * DATA */:

  (für jede Kundennummer in der Datendatei wird die Adresse gedruckt)

6.   Datenbankverwaltung

Eines der wichtigsten Merkmale von SYSTEM 2000 ist, daß jede Datenbank eine physisch von anderen Datenbanken getrennte Entität ist. Als Datenbank ist definiert: alle Daten, die als Ausprägung <u>eines</u> Definitionsbaumes gespeichert wurden. Ein Definitionsbaum besteht aus Wiederholungsgruppen, die hierarchisch miteinander verknüpft sind. Eine durchschnittliche Anwendung hat drei oder vier Datenbanken. Das Verständnis einer Datenbank als "die Datenbank", die alles umfassende Kollektivität aller gespeicherten Daten, wie das bei vielen anderen Systemen der Fall ist, ist also bei SYSTEM 2000 nicht zutreffend.

Die physische Trennung hat sehr viele Vorteile, wie z. B.

- der eine Anwender beeinflußt den anderen nicht
- wenn eine Datenbank "damaged" ist, sind alle anderen noch anwendbar, und SYSTEM 2000 ist nicht "down"

  die Einschränkung der maximalen OS-Datei-Größe gilt nur für Teile einer Datenbank
- jede Datenbank kann einzeln optimiert werden
- Passwords usw. sind alle Datenbank- und daher Anwendungs-bezogen.

6.1. CONTROL 2000

CONTROL 2000 ist das Data Dictionary/Data Directory System, das als
Zusatzmodul zu SYSTEM 2000 lieferbar ist. Es verwaltet sämtliche in
der EDV vorhandene Entitäten (Programme, Elemente, Jobs, Datenbanken,
DD-Statements, Schemas usw.) und deren Verknüpfungen. Es erstellt auf
Grund der in einer SYSTEM 2000-Datenbank gespeicherten Information
Cross-Reference-Listen und bietet ein sehr brauchbares und gebrauch-
tes Hilfsmittel für den Datenbank-Verwalter.

6.2. Datenschutz

Wegen der schon erwähnten Tatsache, daß SYSTEM 2000 auf Elementebene
funktioniert, erlaubt SYSTEM 2000 auch Datenschutz auf Elementebene.
Derjenige, der eine Datenbank definiert, ist der "Master-Password-
Holder" für diese Datenbank. Nur er darf:

- die Definition ändern
- Datenbanken sichern oder reorganisieren
- andere Passwords bestimmen oder ändern.

Weitere Passwords können mit

R Retrieval

U Update

W Where-Clause Verwendung

N keine

Genehmigung zu jedem Komponent gegeben werden (in selbständiger
Sprache selbstverständlich):

VALID PASSWORD IS CLRK:

ASSIGN R,W TO C300 THRU C530 FOR CLRK:

ASSIGN U TO C400, C500 THRU C530, C460 FOR CLRK:

ASSIGN N TO C350 TO C370 FOR CLRK:

Über einfache Befehle kann der Master-Password-Holder die vergebenen
Passwords und Genehmigungen warten.

Eine weitere einmalige Datenschutz-Möglichkeit ist das sogenannte
"Security by Entry"-Feature.

Ein Password gibt eine Genehmigung für gewisse Elemente, unabhängig
von den jeweiligen Inhalten. Security-by-Entry bietet die Möglichkeit
eines inhaltsabhängigen Datenschutzes, indem man ein gewisses Element
als ENTRY KEY bezeichnet. Das hat zur Folge, daß jeder Anwender dann

den genauen Wert dieses Elementes kennen und im Bedingungssatz erwähnen
muß, um Zugriff zu den von diesem Element geschützten Daten zu bekommen.

Für Europa bieten wir zu SYSTEM 2000 auch ein Verschlüsselungsmodul an:
"CRYPTON 2000", mit dem Daten gemäß BDSG verschlüsselt und entschlüsselt
werden können.

6.3.   Datensicherung

In SYSTEM 2000 wurden vier Möglichkeiten der Datensicherung geschaffen:

A.   Ohne Update-Log

B.   Mit Update-Log (Roll-forward)

C.   Rollback - automatisch

D.   Rollback - mit FRAME Steuerung

A.   Die einfachste Art der Datensicherung ist das Erstellen einer Kopie
     der Datenbank. Wenn eine Datenbank dann "damaged" ist, bringt man
     sie wieder in den gewünschten Zustand, indem man die Kopie zur
     Wiedererstellung benutzt und eventuelle Updates neu fährt.

     SYSTEM 2000 bietet dazu die zwei Befehle:

     SAVE DATABASE ON $\begin{bmatrix} \text{VOL. SER. NO} \\ \text{DSNAME} \end{bmatrix}$

     und:

     RESTORE < Datenbankname> FROM $\begin{bmatrix} \text{VOL. SER. NO} \\ \text{DSNAME} \end{bmatrix}$

B.   Wenn man die Update-Programme nicht neu fahren will, kann man es
     SYSTEM 2000 überlassen, die geänderten Werte und deren Adressen zu
     speichern, damit sie bei Wiederanlauf automatisch wiederhergebracht
     werden können. Dazu gibt es folgende Befehle:

     SAVE DATABASE ON < Kopie-Datei>/<Log-Datei >

     RESTORE <Datenbankname> FROM < Kopie-Datei>

     APPLY $\begin{bmatrix} \text{ALL} \\ \text{THRU CYCLE} \langle \text{CYCLE} \# \rangle \end{bmatrix}$

C. Autorollback

Der Datenbankverwalter kann für eine Datenbank "Rollback" akti-
vieren, indem er eingibt

ENABLE ROLLBACK:

Ab dann werden <u>vor</u> jedem Update-Befehl die zu ändernden DB-Seiten
in einer "Rollback-Datei" geschrieben, und das "Damaged Database"-
Byte wird auf "1" gestellt. Wenn die Anlage "down" geht, bevor der
Befehl komplett verarbeitet ist, bleibt dieses Byte auf "1" stehen,
und der vorhergehende Zustand ist gespeichert.

Sobald ein Anwender diese Datenbank allociert, werden die gesicherten Seiten über die vielleicht fälschlich geänderten Seiten geschrieben und das Damage-Byte auf "o" gestellt. Damit ist die
Datenbank wieder zurückgerollt (Roll Back) zu dem Punkt wo sie war,
bevor der nicht kompletierte Update-Befehl stattfand.

Vor allem bei Multi-User on-line Verarbeitung kann dieses Feature
wichtig sein, weil es eine Verfügbarkeit der Datenbank garantiert.

D. Rollback mit Frame-Steuerung

Wenn eine Speicherung von DB-Seiten pro Update-Befehl zu aufwendig
erscheint, kann man die Zahl der zu speichernden DB-Seiten ein-
schränken, indem man über

FRAME:

END FRAME:

mehrere Update-Befehle zu einem sogenannten Frame zusammenfaßt.

Es ist dabei also wahrscheinlich, daß, wenn die Anlage "down" geht,
die in dieser Form gesicherten Datenbanken weiter zurückgerollt
werden als dies ohne FRAME der Fall gewesen wäre.

6.4. Statistik und Tuning

SYSTEM 2000 liefert eine ganze Reihe Hilfsmittel zur Optimierung des
Systemverhaltens hinsichtlich Laufzeit, Antwortzeit oder Speicherbedarf.

- Befehle bezüglich Speicherbedarf und Häufigkeitsanalyse, z. B.
  TALLY
  PRINT SIZE
  PRINT COUNT

- Befehle bezüglich CPU- und I/O-Zeiten, z. B.
  TIMING ON

- Befehle und Möglichkeiten zur Implementierung einer gewünschten
  Optimierung

REORGANISE	reorganisiert nur die invertierten Listen, nicht den Datenbereich selbst
UNLOAD/LOAD	erstellt eine vielleicht wünschenswerte Reihenfolge im Datenbereich
BUFFER POOL	Parameter beeinflussen das Datenbank-Paging
BLOCK SIZE	Parameter der einzelnen Dateien, über die eine Datenbank physisch organisiert ist

6.5. System-Aufbau

SYSTEM 2000 wird entweder als Single-User-System gefahren oder als
Multi-User-System. Der Unterschied liegt darin, daß in der Single-
User-Version ein Anwendungsprogramm in einem Bereich läuft, wobei
SYSTEM 2000 als Unterprogramm zu dem Anwendungsprogramm im gleichen
Bereich läuft. Wenn mehrere Anwendungsprogramme gleichzeitig SYSTEM
2000 brauchen, würde SYSTEM 2000 also mehrmals in der Anlage sein.
Die Multi-User-Version vermeidet das, indem SYSTEM 2000 als unabhän-
giges Programm in einem Bereich läuft und die Anwenderprogramme jeweils
in ihren eigenen Bereichen, wobei über das Betriebssystem mit SYSTEM
2000 kommuniziert wird und zu den Programmen nur ein sehr kleines
Modul (wenige Bytes) gelinkt sein muß. Die Datenbanken sind alle zu
SYSTEM 2000 allokiert.

In der Multi-User-Version verarbeitet SYSTEM 2000 die Anforderungen
der einzelnen Anwender-Programme der Reihe nach, wobei es bei hoher
Verkehrsdichte vorkommen kann, daß ein Programm auf die Antwort zu
einer Anforderung warten muß, weil SYSTEM 2000 noch mit einer Anforderung eines anderen Programms beschäftigt ist.

Dieses Queuing wird zu einem Höchstmaß vermieden, wenn das Multi-
Thread-Feature benutzt wird. In diesem Fall verwaltet SYSTEM 2000
intern kleine Arbeitsbereiche, wo die zu einzelnen Befehlen gehörenden
Zwischenergebnisse gespeichert werden. Das erlaubt es dem System, wenn
in der Verarbeitung eines Befehls ein Punkt auftritt, wo auf das
Betriebssystem gewartet werden müßte, mit dem nächsten Befehl weiter
zu arbeiten, bis auch da eine Anforderung an das Betriebssystem gemacht wird. Gleichzeitig können bis zu 10 "Threads" laufen.

7. Weitere Produkte

7.1. CONTROL 2000

Wie schon erwähnt wurde, gehört zu SYSTEM 2000 ein Data Dictionary/
Data Directory System, und zwar CONTROL 2000. Dieses System verwaltet
sämtliche in der EDV vorhandenen Entitäten über eine pre-definierte
SYSTEM 2000-Datenbank. Damit hat CONTROL 2000 die Fähigkeiten hinsichtlich der EDV-Daten, die ein Anwendungssystem hinsichtlich An-
wendungsdaten hat. Eine ganze Reihe von Funktionen sind vordefiniert,
wie das Erstellen von Cross-Reference-Listen, aber der Anwender kann
ohne weiteres seine eigenen Sonderwünsche befriedigen, z. B. über
Strings in selbständiger Sprache.

Genau wie SYSTEM 2000 wird CONTROL 2000 ständig weiterentwickelt. Das
Ziel ist, CONTROL 2000 zu einem kompletten EDV-Verwaltungssystem zu
machen, das nicht nur lebenswichtiges Werkzeug für den Datenbankverwalter bietet, sondern ein Hilfsmittel des gesamten EDV-Managements
ist.

7.2. TP 2000

Zu SYSTEM 2000 gehört der TP-Monitor TP 2000. Dieser TP-Monitor ermöglicht es, daß eine Vielzahl von Anwendern an eine Vielzahl von
vielleicht unterschiedlichen Terminals mit Programmen kommunizieren,
die Nachrichten, die von diesen Terminals geschickt werden, verarbeiten und beantworten. TP 2000 ist die Schnittstelle zwischen dem
Datenübertragungsnetz und den Anwendungsprogrammen. Es übernimmt u. a.
folgende Funktionen:

° Kode-Umwandlungen, Steuerzeichenbehandlung usw., damit ein Anwendungsprogramm absolut Terminal-unabhängig wird

° Ein- und Ausgabe-Warteschlangen

° Verwalten von Information bezüglich einer Konversation zwischen
  den Einzeltransaktionen

° ·Lösung von Zugriffskonflikten

° Formatisieren von 3270 Nachrichten

° Seitenbehandlung

° Accounting

Zu TP 2000 gehört ein Simulator-Programm, mit dem TP 2000 in Stapel-
verarbeitung getestet werden kann.

7.3. CRYPTON 2000

Speziell für Europa wird zu SYSTEM 2000 ein Modul geliefert, das die
Datenbank einschließlich der Steuerungstabellen usw. verschlüsselt
und Datenbankzugriff und Entschlüsselung überwacht.

Bericht über die Podiumsdiskussion

Ilse Nagler-Breitenbach
Helmut Schauer

Leiter: Prof.Dr.M.Brockhaus

Teilnehmer: Prof.Dr.R.Albrecht
               Prof.Dr.H.Kraus
               Prof.Dr.J.Mühlbacher
               Prof.Dr.G.Vinek

Die Teilnehmer an der Podiumsdiskussion, durchwegs Angehörige
österreichischer Universitäten, gaben ihrer Hoffnung Ausdruck,
daß dieses Symposium eine erste Annäherung zwischen Theorie
und Praxis einleiten möge.

Um dieses Ziel zu erreichen, ist es notwendig, daß die An-
wender versuchen, ihre Probleme hardwareunabhängiger zu lösen.
Dies kann zwar im Augenblick einen gewissen Verlust an
Effizienz bedeuten, ist jedoch auf längere Zeit gesehen auch
aus wirtschaftlicher Sicht sinnvoll. Auch auf dem Gebiet der
Programmiersprachen fand eine ähnliche Entwicklung statt.
"Heute wird zur Programmentwicklung bereits jenen Programmiersprachen der Vorzug gegeben, mit denen man die algorithmischen
Strukturen völlig unabhängig von Maschinenstrukturen formulieren kann" (Vinek). Dieses Ziel sollte auch bei der Dar-
stellung von Datenbeziehungen erreicht werden.

Selbst Fachleute sind von der Komplexität großer Datenbanksysteme überfordert. Dadurch entsteht dieselbe Gefahr, wie bei
der Einführung der EDV in Betrieben. Oft ist es schwer,
die Vorteile einer Datenbank gegenüber einer konventionellen
Datei zu erkennen.

Das in der Informatik anerkannte Schichtenmodell muß sich nun
auch auf dem Gebiet der Datenbanksysteme durchsetzen. Hierbei
werden zwischen Benutzer und Hardware mehrere Origanisations-
ebenen aufgebaut. Dabei wird nach dem Prinzip des information
hiding jedem Benutzer nur die Information über den System-
aufbau zugänglich gemacht, die er zur Lösung seiner Probleme
unbedingt benötigt. "Der Benutzer darf nicht die Möglichkeit
haben, an beliebiger Stelle in das Datenbanksystem einzu-
greifen". (Mühlbacher)

"Für den Benutzer einer Datenbank ist die innere Struktur der
Datenbank nicht relevant, für ihn ist nur wesentlich, daß sie
ihm zu einem bestimmten Zeitpunkt einen gewünschten Output
liefert" (Kraus).

Ideal ist jenes System, das die größte Entflechtung zwischen
Implementierung und Problemstellung ermöglicht.

Es ist notwendig, die Benutzerfreundlichkeit bei der Beurteilung
von Datenbanksystemen in stärkerem Maß als bisher zu berücksichtigen. "Oberstes Prinzip sollte eine bequeme Handhabung für
den Benutzer sein" (Albrecht).

Die Frage, ob das von Prof.Nijssen vorgestellte Übermodell anwendbar sei, wird von allen Diskussionsteilnehmern einhellig bejaht.
Die bisher entwickelten Datenbankmodelle können nun gleichbe-
rechtigt nebeneinander stehen. Der Streit zwischen Relationisten
und Hierarchisten gilt als beendet. Der Benützer soll das jeweils seinen Problemen am besten entsprechende Modell wählen
können, unabhängig von der physischen Realisation. Darüber
hinaus wird die Entwicklung weiterer den Erfordernissen der
einzelnen Benutzer besser entsprechender Modelle notwendig sein.

Es erhebt sich die Frage, ob die bisher entwickelten Datenbankmodelle aus der Sicht des Benutzers überhaupt berechtigt sind,

oder ob sie nicht nur den Forderungen der Informatik entsprechen
und die Bedürfnisse der Anwender außer´acht lassen.

Weiters wird angeregt, eine unabhängige Institution mit dem
Entwurf eines Katalogs von Entscheidungskriterien zur Auswahl
von Datenbanksystemen zu betrauen. Prof.Brockhaus schlägt vor,
den neu gegründeten Arbeitskreis "Datenbanksysteme" mit dieser
Aufgabe zu befassen.

Autorenliste

GARA Dr.Paul, Honeywell-Bull AG, Linke Wienzeile 236, A-115o Wien

GINDL, Österreichische Verbundgesellschaft, Am Hof 6A,
    A-1o1o Wien

GRABNER Dr.Helmut, Medizinisches Rechenzentrum, Allgemeines
    Krankenhaus, Garnisongasse 13, 8.Hof, A-1o97 Wien

KUDLICH Dipl.Ing.Hermann, Siemens Data Wien, Hollandstr.2,
    A-1o2o Wien

MITTHEISZ Dipl.Ing.Johann, Magistratsdirektion der Stadt Wien,
    Abt. Automatische Datenverarbeitung, Rathaus, A-1o1o Wien

NIJSSEN Dr.G.M., Control Data Europe, 111 Boulevard Leopold III,
    B-114o Bruxelles

PETERS Drs.Jos, CAP/Gemini, Grafenberger Allee 3o, D-4ooo
    Düsseldorf

PETRECZEK Ing.Karl, Burroughs Datenverarbeitung Ges.m.b.H.,
    Moerringgasse 1o, A-1151 Wien

PILAT Dr.Herbert, Österreichisches Statistisches Zentralamt,
    Neue Hofburg, Heldenplatz, A-1o1o Wien

RINGLHOFER Heinz, Control Data Ges.m.b.H., Martiellistr.2-4,
    A-1o4o Wien

SIMON Hans, IBM Wien, Obere Donaustr. 95, A-1o2o Wien

SCHOON J.P., ADV/ORGA, F.A.Mayer KG, Kurt Schuhmacherstr. 241,
    D-294o Wilhelmshaven

VORSTÄDT Dipl.Math.Norbert, Gesellschaft für Elektronische
    Informationsverarbeitung m.b.H., Albert-Einsteinstr.61,
    D-51oo Aachen

WANG Erich, Wirtschafts- und Sozialwissenschaftliches Rechen-
    zentrum Wien, Stumpergasse 56, A-1o6o Wien

WEDEKIND Prof.Dr.Hartmut, Technische Hochschule Darmstadt,
    Institut für Datenverwaltungssysteme, Hochschulstr.1,
    D-61 Darmstadt

Elektronische Datenverarbeitung

Berg, Claus C.
Programmieren mit FORTRAN
1972. IV, 128 Seiten. Broschiert
DM 16.–
ISBN 3 7908 0120 8

(= physica-paperback)

Brankamp, Klaus
Ein Terminplanungssystem für Unternehmen der Einzel- und Serienfertigung
Voraussetzungen, Gesamtkonzeption und Durchführung mit EDV
2., überarbeitete und erweiterte Auflage 1973. 163 Seiten. 1 Falttafel.
Leinen DM 46.–
ISBN 3 7908 0103 8

COMPSTAT 1974
Proceedings in Computational Statistics
Edited by G. Bruckmann, F. Ferschl, L. Schmetterer
1974. 539 pages. Paperbound DM 48.–
ISBN 3 7908 0148 8

COMPSTAT 1976
Proceedings in Computational Statistics
Edited by J. Gordesch, P. Naeve
1976. 496 pages. Paperbound DM 56.–
ISBN 3 7908 0172 0

COMPSTAT 1978
Proceedings in Computational Statistics
will appear summer 1978

Czap, Hans
Einführung in die EDV
1976. 115 Seiten. Broschiert DM 12.–
ISBN 3 7908 0169 0

Grafendorfer, Walter
Einführung in die Datenverarbeitung für Informatiker
1977. 194 Seiten. Broschiert DM 25.–
ISBN 3 7908 0176 3

Splettstößer, Dietrich
Grobprojektierung von Informationssystemen
Methodenanalyse und Grundkonzeption einer Dialog-Projektierung
1977. 152 Seiten. Broschiert DM 49.–
ISBN 3 7908 0187 9

(= Methoden der Planung und Lenkung von Informationssystemen, Band 3)

physica-verlag · würzburg–wien